THE
INTELLEC
RESISTA
IN EUROPE

James D. Wilkinson

Harvard University Press
Cambridge, Massachusetts
and London, England

Publication of this book has been aided by a grant from the
Andrew W. Mellon Foundation

Library of Congress Cataloging in Publication Data

Wilkinson, James D   1943–
    The intellectual resistance in Europe.

    Bibliography: p.
    Includes index.
    1. World War, 1939–1945 – Underground movements –
Europe.   2. Intellectuals – Europe.   3. Europe – Intellectual
life – 20th century.   I. Title.
D802.E9W54   940.53'4   80-24469
ISBN 0-674-45775-7 (cloth)
ISBN 0-674-45776-5 (paper)

The Intellectual Resistance in Europe

Thomas J. Wilson Prize

*The Board of Syndics of Harvard
University Press has awarded this book
the tenth annual Thomas J. Wilson
Prize, honoring the late director of the
Press.*

For my parents

Preface

Like the French Revolution of 1789 or the Russian Revolution of 1917, World War II offered European intellectuals an opportunity for translating ethical ideals into political reality. The values that had sustained men and women during the struggle against Fascism also influenced the course of reconstruction in the early postwar years. In this book I explore the cultural impact of World War II during the 1940s from the perspective of certain French, German, and Italian intellectuals who joined or were sympathetic to the anti-Fascist Resistance. More especially, I focus on the period between the liberation from Fascism and 1949, when these intellectuals found themselves engaged in a new resistance against the forces of restoration at work in Europe.

I begin by examining briefly the "spiritual crisis" of the prewar decade, a time when both Fascists and anti-Fascists directed their principal criticism against the beliefs and institutions of bourgeois Europe. Although I treat France, Germany, and Italy separately in the chapters that follow, I stress points of convergence rather than differences. All three countries suffered authoritarian rule, foreign occupation, and defeat; in all, the long ordeal of war fought on their territory was followed by divisive purges and the challenge of recovery. Intellectuals in France displayed the greatest interest in political engagement, while those in Germany faced the most trying conditions for implementing social change. Italy's situation lay somewhere between the two. There Resistance intellectuals headed the government immediately after the war, but were also the first to abandon their attempt to achieve the "revolution" that seemed so close in 1945.

The intellectuals I include within this comparative framework were roughly the same age and were of recognized prominence during the 1940s. Those men and women born too late to participate in World War I, for whom the turbulent decade of the 1930s provided a preliminary introduction to politics and the experience of World War II an opportunity for involvement, emerged as the chief spokesmen for change in 1945. With few exceptions, therefore, I confine myself to discussing intellectuals who were between the ages of twenty-five and forty at the war's end. The principal figures treated here— Mounier, Sartre, Beauvoir, Camus, and Merleau-Ponty in France; Eich, Kogon, Andersch, Richter, and Böll in Germany; Pavese, Vittorini, Levi, and Silone in Italy—perceived themselves as belonging to a sharply defined generation. In addition, they shared a loyalty to the non-Communist Left. Their attempt to delineate a via media between orthodox Marxism and traditional liberalism was one of the most significant characteristics of European political thought during the 1940s. They were by no means alone in supporting the goals of the Resistance or in contributing their energies to its cause; but it is their story that I tell here.

My principal sources are published works: articles, novels, plays, memoirs, and longer philosophical essays, supplemented by personal interviews. In addition, I rely heavily on the journalism of the Resistance and of the postwar period. Translations from all sources, unless indicated otherwise in the notes, are my own. Throughout this work, I attempt to integrate Resistance attitudes into the context of political events—a context that shaped these attitudes to an unusual degree. My chief concern, however, is the analysis of moral and social thought, especially the underlying assumptions and strategies that unified these intellectuals and defined their contribution to Europe's cultural history.

Among the pleasures of writing contemporary history is the chance for personal contact with the subjects of one's research. My understanding of the intellectual Resistance in Europe has been profoundly enriched by the opportunity to talk and correspond with many of the men and women who figure in this book, as well as with others who were eyewitness observers to the events recounted here. The generosity of all those who consented to be interviewed, and whose names appear in a separate section of the bibliography, merits special thanks. My greatest debt is to Gisela Andersch and the late Alfred Andersch, whose friendship, hospitality, and patience with endless questions have been a continuing gift since our first meeting in the summer of 1974. I am grateful as well to Walter and Marianne Dirks, the late Carlo Levi, Joseph Rovan, the late Jean-Paul Sartre, Wolfdietrich Schnurre, Altiero Spinelli, and Vercors, each of whom made unusual efforts to aid me in my quest for information.

The staffs of several libraries also greatly facilitated my research. I appreciate the help offered by the British Museum and the Institute for Historical Research in London, the Bayerische Staatsbibliothek and the Institut für Zeitgeschichte in Munich, the Centro Studi Piero Gobetti and the library of the Turin University Social Science Faculty in Turin, and the Bibliothèque Nationale in Paris. Brigadier General James L. Collins, Jr., chief of military history in the U.S. Department of the Army, helped me to locate material relating to re-education programs for German prisoners of war. Widener Library at Harvard gave invaluable aid closer to home.

I am deeply thankful for the financial assistance that made possible extended stays abroad. A Harvard Graduate Prize Fellowship enabled me to begin research in England and Germany during 1970-71; a first series of interviews were funded by a grant from Harvard's Center for European Studies in 1974. A Harvard Graduate Society grant and support from the American Council for Learned Societies permitted a return to Europe for more interviews and for further research and writing in 1976-77.

To H. Stuart Hughes I owe both the inspiration of example and the support of friendship. It was he who encouraged me to expand the scope of this project to include the Italian Resistance. Without his urging and his interest, I doubt I would have risked so ambitious a venture. Stanley Hoffmann, Charles Maier, and Gianfranco Pasquino all read the manuscript in its original form and offered valuable suggestions for improvement. John Clive, who encountered a later draft, gave me the benefit of his acute sense of style. To Masters Zeph Stewart and William Bossert of Lowell House, where this book took shape, I owe the pleasure of a quiet office and the intellectual companionship of a stimulating Senior Common Room. I have been extremely fortunate in my editors at the Harvard University Press. Aida Donald, Nancy Clemente, and Camille Smith shepherded the manuscript through its various revisions with enthusiasm, patience, and rigorous judgment.

Many friends aided this project in as many ways. I am grateful to them all. Dominique Moïsi and Diana Pinto deserve special thanks—Dominique for hospitality on the rue Lecourbe and for his theories about French intellectuals, Diana for her help in arranging for interviews in Italy and clearing permissions in France. Jane Burbank, with great good will and persuasive logic, diagnosed problems and suggested cures. Hillel Kieval listened to my unformulated thoughts on various themes and encouraged greater clarity. Laurie Burnham, Heather Dubrow, and Daphne Kempner kindly offered advice and assistance when they were most needed.

Jennifer, who shared in the book as it progressed, knows how much it benefited from her help at every stage, and how much I remain in her debt. My parents, too, have given support and understanding that I cannot adequately repay. To them the book is lovingly dedicated.

Contents

The Intellectual Resistance in Europe

Introduction: The Origins of the Intellectual Resistance

*There comes a time when force attempts
to subdue the mind . . . It is then that
the true humanist recognizes his role.
Refusing to give in, he opposes brute
strength with another, invincible power:
that of the spirit.*
André Gide, 1937

The Resistance spirit was a blend of defiance and idealism. The men and women who joined the underground movement against Fascism during World War II struggled to maintain self-respect in the face of humiliating authority, and to assert the claims of conscience against terror and coercion. For Europe's intellectuals, in particular, the Resistance experience gave to politics a moral dimension that led many to sacrifice their own safety and self-interest in an unequal combat. Their ideals inspired a common effort and forged a "united team, warm, fraternal, where rivalry, pettiness, intrigue were unknown."[1]

This sense of moral mission continued undiminished after the Liberation of 1945. Guided by their vision of a "spiritual revolution," Resistance intellectuals sought to initiate a process of renewal in which they themselves would play a leading role. Projects that had been conceived and elaborated in the underground were now discussed with growing confidence. The Resistance offered a model for the social order to be erected after the war—one in which individual freedom would coexist with social justice, human dignity would be accorded new respect, and the bonds formed in the underground would encourage trust and openness among citizens from all classes. These hopes were widely shared. The catastrophe that had engulfed the continent for six years seemed to assure a radical break with the past and to make a fresh start imperative.

The Resistance vision was not simply a response to World War II and Fascist tyranny, however. Both the affirmation of ideals and the desire for social change that emerged in 1945 provided an answer to the doubts and disorder of the 1920s and 1930s. Economic depression, international crises, and the erosion of faith in "bourgeois" values led many intellectuals to question the future of a declining Europe between the wars. Their mood, André Malraux wrote in 1927, was "nihilistic, destructive, fundamentally negative."[2] The longing for certainty and the search for spiritual commitment during these years shaped the origins of the intellectual Resistance. The questions raised in the interwar period are a prologue to the often contradictory, but powerfully appealing solutions found in the struggle that followed.

Intellectuals and Politics

Among the analyses of Europe's spiritual crisis published during the 1920s, none occasioned more debate than a slim work entitled *La Trahison des clercs* (*The Treason of the Intellectuals*). Its subject was the role of the intellectual in society, its author Julien Benda—a veteran of the Dreyfus Affair, a self-confessed partisan of "disinterested intellect," and a practiced critic of the French cultural scene. By 1927 Benda had come to believe that it was time to attack the "political passions" that were increasingly diverting his fellow intellectuals from the service of principle. His argument was summarized in the quotation from Charles Renouvier that prefaced his book: "The world is suffering from a lack of faith in a transcendent truth."[3]

With equal measures of lucidity and parti pris, Benda deplored the "fanaticism" infecting minds whose proper concern was dispassionate inquiry and the defense of Western rationalist tradition. He protested against the worship of utility, which had cast its spell on contemporary intellectuals. Nationalism, pragmatism, the pernicious influence of German thought (with Nietzsche as prime offender) all appeared to Benda to be corrupters of the soul, enemies of "the moral primacy accorded to spiritual matters and to the perception of universals." Under their corrosive influence, humanity seemed destined to revert to "a new Middle Ages—far more barbarous, however, than the first," with the acquiescence and complicity of the very intellectual caste that should have resolutely refuted these doctrines and barred their impending triumph.[4]

In an effort to counter the threat of "secular religion," Benda invoked the memory of that "uninterrupted procession of philosophers, religious figures, men of letters, artists, scholars . . . whose movement stands in formal opposition to the realism of the masses." Bacon, Galileo, Montaigne, Newton, Goethe were for him the exemplary custodians of human reason, models of a disciplined detachment from the petty, self-serving goals of the many who devoted their lives to personal gain. Their works embodied "a generality of feeling, an attachment to abstract views, a disdain for the immediate" that the modern intellectual should strive to emulate. Thus while Benda remained fiercely contemptuous of all forms of political authority, he revealed a solid respect for the authority of cultural tradition. In the conflict between what he termed the "real" and the "ideal"—narrow prejudice and the wisdom of the past—the "ideal" claimed his unquestioning loyalty.[5]

The dualism in Benda's thought has led a number of critics to conclude that *The Treason of the Intellectuals* should be interpreted as a total condemnation of political activity undertaken by intellectuals. A closer examination, however, reveals that Benda was primarily concerned with the *motives* of political behavior. "An intellectual," he noted, "seems to me to betray his function by descending into the public arena only if he does so . . . to secure the triumph of a realist passion of class, race, or nation."[6] As the champion of truth and justice, the intellectual possessed the right to intervene in temporal affairs for the good of mankind. But his political effectiveness, Benda observed, was by nature transitory, a response to crisis rather than a day-to-day contribution to government. The absolute nature of his ideals prohibited him from drawing too close to the world of half-truths and compromises in which the politician was enmeshed. His distance from the state ensured his impartiality.

By first defining the intellectuals as a separate group endowed with a special mission and then posing the question of how this mission might best be carried out, Benda touched upon a concern that was to become increasingly relevant during the 1930s. How could the primacy of moral issues be reestablished? And how could the intellectuals exert influence in the "public arena" without jeopardizing the ideals they sought to preserve? To many, Benda's conclusions proved disappointing. As one commentator wrote a year later: "Without doubt the most urgent task of the intellectual is to rescue the spirit. But he will not save it by retiring into the realm of abstract truth."[7]

Not all intellectuals between the wars accepted Benda's fundamentally pessimistic view of an irreconcilable tension between ethics and political institutions. While Benda stressed the intellectual's negative influence as judge and conscience of society, it was possible for some to conceive of a more positive alternative that emphasized the intellectual's contribution as artist and visionary, formulating new solutions to the problems of his time. This argument was advanced in 1929 by the German sociologist Karl Mannheim in his *Ideologie und Utopie* (*Ideology and Utopia*), a work predicated on the assumption that thought was "never an end in itself," but rather "a developing structure in whose compass the evolution of man takes place." Ideals, Mannheim maintained, could shape reality. He quoted approvingly the words of the French poet Lamartine: "Utopias are often merely premature truths." Mannheim rejected Benda's static vision of values forever denied adequate social expression, in favor of a dialectical process by which ideals "acted to transform the historical-social being" of men.[8]

What gave utopias this transforming power? Their capacity to inspire the "realities of tomorrow," Mannheim suggested, derived from their ability to transform human perception. Once men believed that reality could be changed, the present shape of society lost its illusion of permanence. Utopias thus provided a standard for judgment, like Benda's "ideal" concepts of justice and truth, but with the important difference that they succeeded in recasting historical reality. The belief that utopian thought had practical effects was crucial for Mannheim. It allowed him to respond to the objection that "transcending" the present imaginatively was simply an act of self-deception, an escape from conditions that could neither be faced nor mastered. It also served him as a useful norm by which to assess the results yielded by utopian thought in his own time. Here he found cause for deep concern. In contemporary Europe he observed a "gradual sinking of utopian intensity," a growing tendency to adjust hopes to conform with the narrow limits of things as they were.[9]

The diminished vitality of utopian thought, Mannheim asserted, was linked to its past successes. Having obtained the changes it had once sought, the utopian vision lost its dynamism and became a conservative creed. The "liberal-humanitarian" ideal of the Enlightenment, for example, had led to a broadened franchise, new rights for the individual, and increased productivity in the marketplace. Yet the once revolutionary aspirations of the cultivated middle class now yielded little further stimulus for change. The major aims had been met; the "liberal-humanitarian" future was one that merely preserved the present intact.[10]

At the same time, Mannheim was dismayed by the strategy that partisans of each utopia used in an attempt to discredit their rivals. The term "ideology" was applied to any opposing view that appeared conditioned and restricted by the interests of a single social group. Yet to dismiss utopias as mere "ideologies" because they failed to embrace a more general perspective, Mannheim felt, would be a tragic error. The solution lay elsewhere. In an age when tolerance and objectivity were increasingly threatened, men must strive to maintain a "constant readiness for synthesis." It was futile, however, to hope that such a synthesis would emerge from the current debate unaided. Who could halt the degeneration of the utopian impulse and make peace among the "mere struggling parties" who now held the field?[11]

Among contemporary advocates of a utopian ideal, Mannheim conceded, Socialists and Communists still affirmed a "unified alliance between utopia, scope, and action." But he placed his ultimate hopes for preserving the creative potential of utopian thought in another group: the "free-floating intelligentsia." Only the intellectuals (as Benda had also maintained) possessed the necessary distance from society to resist the temptation of conformity in the present and to recognize "productive thought" wherever it occurred. Because they were increasingly "recruited from all social strata and not only from among the privileged," the intellectuals were ideally suited to mediate among conflicting and partial views. Whereas the radical Left would one day achieve its program and abandon its revolutionary élan, the intellectuals would retain a spark of creative dissatisfaction, a critical spirit that would destine them to become the final guardians of the "fruitful tension" between ideals and reality.[12]

But while the intellectuals might preach the virtues of "synthesis," there existed no guarantee that they would be heard. Mannheim remained curiously vague about the means to promote their influence. He indulged in the doubtful logic of arguing that the "free-floating intelligentsia" served an educational function in society through the appeal to reason, while at the same time lamenting how little reason affected the current struggles among competing utopias. If, as Mannheim supposed, utopias reflected the influence of social milieu and class interests on the particular visions and aspirations that any group espoused, then intellectuals who had shed their ties with all such groups could not expect to appeal to them for support. By becoming "free-floating," they had forfeited their natural constituencies.

These contradictions, which Mannheim left unresolved, were addressed directly at the start of the 1930s by a third observer concerned with the intellectual's role. Antonio Gramsci, the Marxist theoretician and cofounder of Italy's Communist party, took exception to both Benda and Mannheim by insisting that the notion of an autonomous intellectual caste was based on a misunderstanding. For Gramsci, there existed no such thing as a nonintellectual, only greater or lesser degrees of an "intellectual activity that exists in each person at a certain stage of development." All men were intellectuals, not merely a self-selected elite. In their daily lives, all contributed "to maintain or to modify a conception of the world, that is, to engender new ways of thinking."[13]

Intellectual activity thus formed a bond among citizens who shared a common responsibility for safeguarding cultural and ethical values. Moreover, Gramsci argued, just as spiritual concerns informed daily life, so political considerations affected the spirit. No matter what their attitude toward politics, intellectuals could not escape the necessary connection between thought and action.[14] They might, of course, choose to defend the existing state of affairs. But if they sought to "engender new ways of thinking," as Gramsci hoped, then their thought would provide both a precondition and a determinant for political change.

Here Gramsci's views converged with those of Mannheim. Both drew upon a Hegelian view of history as a dialectical interaction between human consciousness and a reality perceived and modified by that consciousness. Where Gramsci parted ways with his German contemporary was in his insistence that the intellectuals should articulate the needs of the dispossessed and should seek to narrow the gulf that separated them from other social groups. Gramsci drew a distinction between "traditional" and "organic" intellectuals. The traditional intellectual believed, erroneously, that he owed allegiance only to his fellow intellectuals. Organic intellectuals, by contrast, expounded a utopian vision on behalf of a rising class. They were the spiritual innovators who challenged the entrenched political elite.[15]

Gramsci believed that political struggle was conditioned by a prior cultural confrontation. "One of the most prominent features of any group that progresses toward domination," he wrote in his prison notebooks, "is its struggle for the assimilation and 'ideological' conquest of the traditional intellectuals, an assimilation and conquest that is all the more rapid and efficient the more the given group simultaneously develops its own organic intellectuals." As editor of *L'Ordine Nuovo* in Turin from 1919 to 1922, Gramsci had devoted himself to educating and training "organic" intellectuals. These would try ultimately to impose their own cultural "hegemony" by introducing a new set of ideals to replace the outmoded values of those in power. Such a strategy was especially well suited to periods of political oppression, when ideas became the chief arm of resistance. As Gramsci discovered, the conquest of hegemony could begin from a prison cell.[16]

Thus Gramsci, no less than Benda and Mannheim, in the end assigned a role of spiritual leadership to one distinct group in society. All three men, concerned at the loss of purpose and coherence and at the absence of ideals and guidance in contemporary Europe, discerned the need for an elite whose vision transcended the present. Their feeling was shared by younger writers and thinkers, alarmed at the signs of crisis around them and determined to act before all hope of renewal had vanished.

The Assault on the Old Order

For the generation just reaching maturity before 1930, Europe's vitality seemed at an end. André Malraux, writing in 1926, compared Europe to a "vast cemetery"—lifeless, melancholy, haunted by the ghosts of "dead conquerors." He saw around him only the immobility of the status quo, a tired conformism that sapped both ideas and institutions. The young German journalist Hans Zehrer echoed this disenchantment. "Where is there movement in politics?" he asked in October 1929. "Where are new economic concepts being developed? Where is a new spiritual elite striving in mutual competition? Nowhere. We have a dull churchyard peace of deadening sterility."[17]

Contempt for a Europe incapable of self-renewal was an attitude that united intellectuals who would become bitter political enemies during the next decade. The negative consensus of the late 1920s that provided common ground for Right and Left, Fascists and anti-Fascists, is often lost from view, overshadowed by the future struggles of the Resistance. Initially, however, all sides agreed in condemning the failure of those whom they perceived as the cause and symbol of Europe's decay—the middle-class guardians of the old order. The French writer Robert Brasillach recalled that what had first appealed to him in fascism was "a nonconformist spirit above all, antibourgeois, in which irreverence played its part."[18] In examining the world around them, younger intellectuals defined their beliefs largely by what they rejected rather than by what they proposed.

The critique of the bourgeoisie voiced during the late 1920s was scarcely new. It drew heavily on themes that Georges Sorel, Maurice Barrès, Julius Langbehn, and other hostile observers of fin-de-siècle Europe had rendered commonplace well before World War I.[19] But antibourgeois rhetoric gained in virulence during the postwar decade as the prestige of the Western democracies declined. In the portrait of the bourgeois drawn by his intellectual detractors, it was difficult to recognize the descendant of the revolutionary ancestors who had challenged the aristocracy in 1789. The middle class had progressively abandoned its liberal heritage during the intervening century; rather than standing as the defender of liberty, equality, and fraternity, it now appeared the embodiment of conservatism, impotence, and hypocrisy. Its capacity to offer leadership and inspiration nad long since vanished.[20]

The political institution for which the intellectuals reserved their sharpest censure was parliamentary democracy. Parliaments in France and Germany were portrayed throughout the 1920s as venal and powerless, given to endless deliberations but commanding scant respect. The French Chamber of Deputies was "the house without windows"—an epithet inspired less by the architecture of the Palais Bourbon than by the behavior of its resident and isolated politicians. German critics such as the satirist Kurt Tucholsky found special reason to attack those Reichstag deputies of the Left who had abandoned their revolutionary principles for an accommodating docility: "Who will protect us? . . . The leaders of the moderate Left [are] without initiative, without a protest in their bones, without the slightest sense for movement, with beer in their veins. They doze on and perpetuate their kind, along with their laws and their injustice, like a chronic illness."[21] In Italy, where rival parties were suppressed by Mussolini's Fascist organization after 1925, few at first lamented their demise. The Fascists themselves, however, used party patronage and favoritism in much the same way as their predecessors, and thus soon provoked similar criticism.[22]

A more general failing associated with the old order was financial corruption. Money ruled the bourgeois world. And capitalism, in the judgment of many intellectuals, was the worst despot. Emmanuel Mounier, writing in the early 1930s, asserted that capitalism had subordinated human needs to the "primacy of production, cash, and profit."[23] The result was a class society that effectively thwarted the individual's capacity for self-expression and self-realization. Social relations obeyed the dictates of the marketplace, where men and women possessed no worth beyond their usefulness as cogs in the industrial machine. The rewards of capitalism went to the morally least deserving—those who were prepared to sacrifice the well-being of others to their own greed.

At the same time, the bourgeois invoked the principles of "order" and "measure" to justify his privileges. He took shelter behind pious homilies that bore no relation to his true behavior, and he connived at his own self-deception. "Rendered uncomfortable by the evidence at hand," Emmanuel Berl wrote in 1929, "the bourgeois struggles against it. He detests it. He continually tries to conceal and to distort it." For the intellectuals, such an attitude revealed the dangers of an abstract mode of thought that they scornfully dismissed. The term "abstract" figured repeatedly in their critique of the old order—a word whose pejorative connotations applied equally to timid evasiveness and empty grandiloquence. Instead, they preferred to lay bare the "evidence at hand." Recalling the rules of conduct adopted by his circle of friends in Turin during the 1920s, Norberto Bobbio observed: "Our first maxim demanded the practice of frankness, our second that of inner clarity. The observance of both implied an open war on every form of simulation and dissimulation, a ceaseless campaign against hypocrisy (toward others) and convenient excuses (for oneself)."[24]

The reality of middle-class existence, the intellectuals argued, was a materialism that corrupted all whom it touched. The bourgeois lavished such attention on his own affairs that he had little time to explore what lay beyond. He was a prisoner of his own well-ordered world of rights and possessions, suspended between avarice and fear. The immobility and lack of creative initiative that intellectuals such as Malraux and Zehrer attacked during the late 1920s could be directly attributed to the anxieties of ownership. As Mounier wrote: "In his soul, the bourgeois is a man who is afraid. Afraid of struggle, afraid of the unexpected day that will come to challenge his predictions, afraid of the changing faces of men, afraid of everything that he does not possess."[25] More than either the political or the economic sins of the middle class, it was its moral failings that caused the intellectuals to condemn and to reject the bourgeois world. The decay they discerned at the heart of the old order was a decay of the spirit.

The intellectuals' preoccupation with Europe's moral decadence, like their revulsion against its bourgeois institutions, had roots in the previous century. The writings of Nietzsche, which experienced renewed popularity during the 1920s, provided a brilliant though unsystematic exploration of this theme. World War I, in turn, aroused in many a deeper apprehension that the future would mean prolonged spiritual decline. The French poet Paul Valéry remarked that the war "merely aggravated and precipitated the movement toward decadence," which was by then already well advanced.[26]

It was Oswald Spengler who managed to provide a theoretical framework and a retrospective justification for these fears in his enormously successful work of historical speculation, *Der Untergang des Abendlandes* (*The Decline of the West*). Published on the eve of the German defeat in 1918, the book went through fourteen printings by 1920 and was read and reviewed throughout Western Europe. With his vision of history as a series of vast cycles, in which each individual culture experienced youth, maturity, and old age, Spengler had found an image that illuminated and articulated the contemporary European mood of crisis and decay. His biological metaphors seemed to explain the decline in Europe's fortunes. "We know that the tempo, character, and duration of the life of each organism . . . is determined by the attributes of the species to which it belongs," Spengler wrote in his introduction. Cultures, too, obeyed an inner rhythm of growth.

Through the comparative study of the lives of earlier cultures, one could discover that rhythm and then "chart the stages yet to be consummated" by the West.[27]

Spengler's assessment of current European prospects was bleak. The West, he argued, had now entered its ultimate phase of development, characterized by the tyranny of "Caesarism" and by growing conflict among rival dictators, much as in the days of the late Roman Empire. The springtime of cultural flowering was past. As he explained in 1921, "Hardness, Roman hardness is what is now beginning in the world. Soon there will be room for nothing else . . . We Germans will never again produce a Goethe, but instead a Caesar." Yet Spengler denied that his conclusions should lead to pessimism or resignation. Instead, he saw them as a bracing review of the possibilities still open to his age, which would permit "men with an eye for facts" (*Tatsachenmenschen*) to act in harmony with the demands of the time. Human beings could not modify these demands; they could, however, still decide their responses to them. "The unrestrained and headstrong 'it should be so,'" he wrote, "must give way to a cold, clear gaze that comprehends the possible, hence necessary, facts of the future and makes its choice accordingly."[28]

This counsel the younger generation of intellectuals refused to heed. While they shared Spengler's antipathy for the middle class and his conviction that its reign could not long continue, they believed in the power of the spirit to create a new reality. Their task was not to accede to an inevitable cultural decline, but to reverse it. They saw themselves as a new elite, possessing the energy, imagination, and moral integrity that the middle class had lost, free to challenge the determinist view of history if they chose. Yet as long as the middle class remained in power, neither the intellectuals' voluntarism nor their sense of mission could effect the transformation they sought. As an elite, they remained isolated; as visionaries, they lacked the means to give substance to their dreams.

This impasse was described by the German writer Erich Kästner in his novel *Fabian* (1931), subtitled "the story of a moralist." Jakob Fabian—young, honest, and penniless—struggles to make his way amid the temptations and cynicism of late Weimar Berlin. Fabian's ideals are tempered by a studied skepticism. He waits for the "triumph of decency . . . like an atheist waiting for a miracle," but the miracle does not occur. Instead, Fabian finds himself reduced to writing advertisements for a living, and loses his mistress to a rich film director and his best friend to suicide. His scruples have no place in a world where decency by itself is powerless to change men's lot. At the story's end, Fabian reflects: "He could not yet help or set to work, since where could he set to work, and with whom should he join? He wanted to vanish for a time into seclusion and listen to the age from a mountain top until he heard the starting gun that was meant for him, and for those like him."[29]

For many among the younger intellectuals, the sound of the "starting gun" became audible during the next half-decade. When the Depression struck Europe after 1929, they felt both vindicated and released. With the collapse of the "project of restoration" through which French Premier Raymond Poincaré had promised his country "complete recovery" from the effects of World War I, with the spreading unemployment and social polarization in Germany, with Mussolini's emergency intervention in the Italian economy, a new sense of fluidity and change entered European politics.[30] As the brief period of postwar stability ended, a radical reshaping of society once again seemed possible.

But Kästner's question—with whom should one join?—remained pertinent. The problem of overcoming their isolation and finding allies among other disaffected groups gained in urgency as the intellectuals' prospects for meaningful action increased. So, too, did the problem of defining what they hoped to achieve. Hence they were drawn to address another, no less urgent question: engagement for what cause, in the name of what truths? Where could they find a faith to replace the middle-class values they despised?

Action and Knowledge

During the 1930s the realm of action became the laboratory in which the intellectuals conducted their search for ideals. The testimony of direct experience constituted for them a privileged form of knowledge. Their distrust of the "abstract" led them to seek a more rigorous and more reliable source of insight than passive speculation, divorced from struggle and life. The term most often used for the dimension they aimed to recover was the "concrete." The concrete represented a tangible truth, encountered in the workplace, in the street, on a solitary journey, far from the plush drawing rooms of the bourgeoisie. Its acquisition was difficult but, once gained, secure.

The search for the concrete was paralleled by a shift in literary temper during the early 1930s. Unlike Proust and his contemporaries, who had explored the inner landscape of memory and the soul, the younger intellectuals yearned to escape this muted solipsism and deal with the world around them. "After 1930," as one critic later observed, "literature returns to face the times."[31] The changes wrought by direct contact with men and events are chronicled in a series of *Bildungsromane* and autobiographical accounts from the interwar period in which the heroes begin in a state of revolt, gradually pass from disappointment and mistaken faith to a growing certainty, and end with a new knowledge and sense of purpose gained from their experiences. These works simultaneously portray the individual's investigation of the outer world and point the way toward a fellowship of shared values, a new community of faith in which one is no longer alone.

Of particular interest as a forerunner of this genre is Joseph Goebbels's *Michael*, published in 1929. Indebted to Goethe's *Werther* in theme, to Nietzsche and the Expressionists in style, *Michael* charts the quest of a young German veteran of World War I as he seeks to find both himself and a cause to serve. Returning from the war, Michael begins life as a student in Heidelberg and there he falls in love with a fellow student, Herta Holk. Yet he remains dissatisfied. He eventually abandons his studies and his beloved and begins a period of wandering that takes him to the Bavarian Alps, where he decides to plunge into the "real" world of the proletariat. Michael works as a miner and gradually overcomes the mistrust occasioned by his middle-class origins. He is on the verge of achieving integration into a new community of comrades when he dies a martyr's death in a freak mine accident—a catastrophe that renders his courage and selflessness apparent to all.[32]

Michael's progress from uncertainty to fulfillment begins with a rejection of inherited values. At first he lacks a clear sense of self and is able to define his goals only by struggling against the settled, bourgeois world of Herta Holk. This negative identity is a prelude to his embrace of National Socialism, expressed in his decision to strike roots among Germany's workingmen. His new bonds with the miners confer a sense of worth through labor and define an alternative to the decadent middle-class order of "mating and business," as Goebbels described it in his diaries. The clear distinction between "us" and "them," between heroes at the mine and enemies in the stock exchange, creates a feeling of inclusion within an elite community that gives Michael both purpose and security. "Worker among workers— that I am, that I wish to remain. I am one of you; here I have won my right to citizenship."[33]

Michael does not elaborate an identity of his own, but rather immerses himself in an enterprise whose aims he willingly adopts. Despite Goebbels's emphasis on the difficulties of self-transcendence, his Nietzschean concern with the exceptional man who refuses to compromise with the "herd," the search he depicts ends with "the subordination of the I to the you, the sacrifice of the personality to the totality." At the same time, he reserves a special place for the intuitive and the irrational as guides to pragmatic action. Michael discovers his way at last in a moment of "revelation"; in Munich, he is "intoxicated" by a "prophet" (clearly Hitler) whose words are an "order."[34] His experience in the mines brings a mystical communion with the earth and his fellow men. Here one finds a hint of the reverence toward authority and the deep distrust of the intellect that were to characterize the Fascist approach to politics in the coming decade.

Two years after *Michael* appeared in Germany, a young French Communist published an account of his adolescence that paralleled Goebbels's *Bildungsroman* in a number of respects. With no less passion and considerably greater artistic skill, Paul Nizan reviewed his cloistered years as a student in Paris, his flight from the Ecole Normale Supérieure to the British colony of Aden, and his disillusioned return. Like Goebbels, Nizan directed his polemical fire chiefly at the institutions of a declining and decadent bourgeois society. Nizan, like Michael, gradually comes to recognize the roots of his own personal malaise within a middle-class order that he ultimately rejects. "Where was our discomfort? In what part of our lives? Here is what we knew: men do not live as men should. But we were still ignorant of the elements that compose this genuine life. Our thoughts were all negative."[35]

Aden, Arabie follows its narrator as he embarks on a search for illumination. Like Michael, Nizan flees the university; he seeks refuge as a tutor to an English family serving in a colonial outpost near the shores of the Red Sea. To his dismay, he discovers that the capitalist world he thought he had abandoned dominates Aden even more starkly than it does France. This radical simplifiction, however, enables Nizan to identify his oppressors in the British administrators, local merchants, and career soldiers who make up the elite of Aden society. "This is what had to be understood: Aden was a powerfully concentrated image of mother Europe . . . Several hundred Europeans piled together in a narrow space like a penal colony, five miles in length and three miles broad, reproduced with extraordinary precision the patterns that, on a larger scale, form the outlines and the interrelations of life in Western lands."[36]

Nizan recounts a painful process of self-liberation and self-discovery, leading finally to a new sense of identity based on unceasing opposition to all that Aden symbolizes. Like Goebbels's novel, *Aden, Arabie* is intended to provide a warning and example to its readers. But whereas Goebbels contrives to reintegrate his hero into an alternative "aristocracy of achievement," Nizan's concern is with knowledge rather than redemption. He shows how experience can lead the individual to revise his image of society and of himself. For Michael, solutions come through others; Nizan achieves independence through his own resources. There is no loving woman to bind him fast, no shadowy political figure to win his allegiance. Nizan's final message to his readers reflects this sense of isolation. It calls for vigilance and inner discipline, as if addressed to secret agents behind enemy lines: "You are alone . . . Be like spies. You will keep your anger warm, you will permit yourselves no rest. Will you ever pierce [your enemies'] secrets without hatred?"[37]

This emphasis on "piercing secrets" leads Nizan to view the intellectual's role very differently from either Goebbels or Benda. For Benda, reason opened the way to a perception of the eternal verities. For Goebbels, however, reason was a barrier to community, to shared values and enthusiasms, isolating the individual and paralyzing the will. Nizan rejects both idealism and irrationalism. His conception of the philosopher's task, as expressed in *Les Chiens de garde* (*The Watchdogs*), published in 1932, illustrates the new empiricism and distrust of abstract formulations that gained currency in the 1930s. He reverses Benda's definition of "treason" by arguing that idealist philosophy is in itself a political choice, and that it prevents its practitioners from coming to grips with reality. Nizan's revolt against idealism takes the form of confronting the philosopher's truth with the lessons of experience: "The perceptions which they have patiently taught must be subjected to revision . . . First [one must] destroy the system of illusions that philosophy constructs, and then open the way to true human experience and its problems."[38]

The appeal to "true human experience" meant in practice an appeal to knowledge gained under unusual, often extraordinary conditions. The routine of daily life, with its minor frustrations and modest successes, was not the school from which the intellectuals hoped to learn. Significantly, both Nizan and Goebbels's Michael began their search by fleeing a pattern of existence grown too comfortable and secure. The transition to an unfamiliar setting, the physical distance from their former homelands, emphasized the exceptional character of their experiences. But it was not merely distance that provided a new perspective; the danger encountered in the mines and the difficulties of adapting to Aden were also important. The depth of insight they gained and the extent of the personal transformation that followed depended directly on the magnitude of the challenge presented by the environment. Knowledge and action were thus linked in a way that favored tension, risk, the unforeseen and the unexpected. The more extreme the situation, the greater its power of revelation.

The advantages to be gained from confronting the extreme were reviewed in a work of German philosophy published in the same year as *The Watchdogs*. The second volume of Karl Jaspers's massive *Philosophie* presented a detailed discussion of what its author termed "limit situations" (*Grenzsituationen*), which included "death, suffering, conflict, guilt." Jaspers understood the word "limit" to signify both an extreme and a barrier. In confronting extremes, he maintained, the individual achieved a degree of self-illumination that was impossible under normal circumstances. One reason for this was that limit situations intensified awareness of what was specific and concrete in each person's existence. Suffering, for example, ceased to be an abstract concept for those it touched, and instead took on a private, highly personal character for each man or woman.[39]

Equally important was the knowledge conferred by events that contradicted the individual's assumptions or thwarted his desires. Paradoxically, such "resistance" served to confirm the individual's autonomy, just as the shape of an object might be said to emerge most sharply against a contrasting background. "The most relentless struggle against me awakens my certainty of my own existence . . . because it takes me seriously as a possibility of being." Finally, limit situations enhanced the individual's self-knowledge by forcing him to accept responsibility for confronting or avoiding them. "Each person must bear and deal with what befalls him. No one else can bear it for him."[40]

These themes of testing, discovery, and courage play a central role in the early novels of André Malraux, novels that typify his generation's search for values in an especially vivid and memorable fashion. Malraux's heroes, such as Garine in *Les Conquérants* (*The Conquerors*, 1928) or Perken in *La Voie royale* (*The Royal Way*, 1930), fit the pattern of the intellectual who abandons a decadent Europe to prove himself by pursuing adventure abroad. Equally important, they ponder the meaning of their revolt. Malraux's characters achieve a rare degree of self-consciousness in all they do. As a contemporary Italian critic noted, "More than novels, [these] are moral dialogues of a new sort, impassioned confessions of individuals who, while they act, wish to see clearly into their own actions."[41] The violence, eroticism, and political intrigue that engage their attention are ultimately transformed into knowledge gained through limit situations actively sought and freely accepted. They face the world as critical observers, determined to reach the understanding afforded a lucid mind, heroic in their desire to confront unpleasant truths without flinching.

Malraux's adventurers represented an ideal that could be abstracted from the exotic Asian settings in which they moved. The specific cause they served was relatively unimportant; it was their refusal to be content with the mediocre destiny of ordinary men that compelled admiration. Their lives symbolized defiance of a world that resisted their aims. Perken desires to leave "a scar on the map" of Indochina, and

Garine, as he directs a general strike in Shanghai, sums up his personal philosophy: "Command. Determine. Constrain. There is life." Yet these characters' actions, though they bring them both knowledge and a sense of accomplishment, also isolate them. In the final scene of *The Royal Way*, Perken realizes on his deathbed that "there is no death; there is only *myself who will die*."[42] This confession suggests the limits of the search for meaning through personal experience alone. The radically individual character of suffering, as Jaspers insisted, meant that it could not be shared. The attempt to escape from subjectivity into the realm of the concrete thus appeared to lead back to the private and the uncommunicable.

An answer to this dilemma emerged in Malraux's best known work of fiction, *La Condition humaine* (*Man's Fate*), published in 1933. Like *The Conquerors* and *The Royal Way*, it deals with political events in southeast Asia as the background for action and self-discovery, and concludes with an apparent defeat. Kyo Gisors, a young Communist leader in Shanghai, mounts a successful strike against the French colonial forces and is on the verge of consolidating his position by seizing power. But the French reach an agreement with Chinese forces on a national level, pledging them to demand Kyo's surrender. When he and his colleagues refuse to comply, they are captured and killed. Unlike Perken in *The Royal Way*, Kyo dies for a cause that transcends his own private fate. As he waits to be executed, he thinks: "Everywhere that men worked in suffering, in absurdity, in humiliation, they were thinking of condemned men like him . . . Out of all that this last night covered on earth, this place of death was doubtless the richest in virile love . . . He was dying, like each of these men lying here, for having given a meaning to his life."[43]

Malraux's response to the "nihilism" that he had observed among his contemporaries a half-decade earlier was to find meaning in man. His mature fiction defined the realm of the concrete as residing in human relations, and creativity as enhanced by contact with others. The vision of solidarity that he invoked in *Man's Fate* involved a common bond of understanding whose dimensions were not merely racial and national, as for Goebbels, but truly universal. All men, Malraux argued, were brothers in oppression, just as all were implicated in the struggle to win dignity for a few. The transition from heroic revolt to principled engagement that he depicted in this sequence of novels was one that other intellectuals were to discover in the course of the 1930s.

The Ideological Synthesis

The same desire to escape the rigid conventions of bourgeois society that produced a literature of action and exploration during the early

1930s was also evident in the realm of political thought. The intellectuals' impatience with the inflexible ideological systems inherited from the past led them to attempt syntheses in which elements from conservative and radical doctrines reappeared in new combinations, like stones wrenched from an old mosaic and placed in a fresh pattern. "Suddenly the old and meaningless concepts disappeared, the crazy categories of Left and Right," Hans Zehrer later recalled. "None of the ancient wisdoms that had been preached for years seemed to apply any more, and everything assumed a new meaning."[44]

Socialism, in multiple and often contradictory guises, served as a common denominator for this mood of experiment. Spengler's call for a "Prussian socialism," which had come as early as 1919, was echoed a decade later by Pierre Drieu la Rochelle's call for "socialist Fascism." From a different perspective, the anti-Fascist Carlo Rosselli, in exile from his native Italy, explored the outlines of a "liberal socialism" in Paris.[45] The appeal of socialism lay both in its celebration of community, of fraternal warmth and shared effort, and in its opposition to the values associated with the bourgeois order. The dignity of work, the break with self-centeredness, the critique of capitalism all found their way into fluid doctrines whose authors refused to be constrained by precise meanings or strictly defined goals. Socialism expressed the negative consensus that continued to unite Left and Right at the outset of the 1930s, as well as the common search for an allegiance that transcended the individual.

One man who typified this effort at synthesis was the French Catholic philosopher Emmanuel Mounier. Of lesser intellectual stature and originality than his older coreligionists Jacques Maritain and Gabriel Marcel, Mounier contributed to the social thought of the 1930s by reflecting and integrating the concerns of his rebellious contemporaries. What is more, his insistence on the need to act with others in response to these concerns articulated the demands for commitment that gained strength throughout the decade. Both the representative and the prophetic character of his criticism helped to ensure the survival of Mounier's journal, *Esprit*, in the years after World War II—one of the few French publications that would outlive the 1930s.[46]

The starting point of Mounier's program, as elaborated in successive issues of *Esprit*, was the rejection of that familiar trio of evils: parliamentary democracy, capitalism, and middle-class morals, collectively designated "the established disorder." All three together prevented the citizen from enjoying his personal freedom and political rights under a democratic regime. Mounier thus agreed with Marx that the political institutions of capitalist society benefited only those who controlled its economic system. He refused, however, to follow Marx in suggesting that the vices of capitalism could be overcome through a dictatorship of the oppressed. "The true disease of this century" he defined as "two ills . . . individualism and collective tyranny. Today they have reached their maximum virulence, and their effects reinforce each other, for they are but two phases of the same evil."[47]

Mounier found both choices unsatisfying because both transgressed against the individual they were intended to serve. Both took man, to paraphrase Kant, as a means rather than as an end in himself. The primacy of the individual was enshrined in Mounier's vision of a third alternative, "personalism": "a civilization whose structures and spirit are oriented toward the personal fulfillment of each of the individuals who compose it. Natural groups are recognized in it . . . They nevertheless have as their final end to enable each person to live like a person, that is, to be able to rise to a maximum of initiative, responsibility, and spiritual life." Mounier chose the rather ambiguous word "personalism" to avoid the negative connotations of "individualism," a term too easily perverted in capitalist society to mean the right of the individual to subordinate others to his economic needs. Instead, Mounier stressed that in order to realize his own potential the individual had to engage himself in care for others. An empty freedom remained an abstraction. "Man becomes concrete when he gives of himself."[48]

Mounier's insistence on the necessity for engagement grew directly from his Catholic faith. He interpreted the biblical injunction "he who loses his life shall find it" as a call for action in the secular realm, based on an ethic of mutual responsibility. No man, he believed, could become truly free, a whole person, while others were denied the same opportunity. His description of this moral imperative anticipates Sartre's definition of existentialist engagement by nearly a decade, using almost identical language.

> The first duty of any man, when men by the millions are thus excluded from the vocation of being a man, is not to save *his* person (he thinks far more of some delicate aspect of his individuality, if he holds himself aloof in this fashion), but rather to engage his person in any action, immediate or long-term, which might permit these outcasts to confront their vocation again with at least a bare minimum of material freedom. The life of a person, as we see, is not a separation, an evasion, an alienation. It is *presence* and *engagement*.

No longer was it sufficient to turn all one's energies toward self-liberation in the belief that others would follow this example. In Mounier's view, man was called to a "double vocation." "Each person

. . . grows vertically, toward his liberty, his personality, his self-mastery; but he is also drawn toward a horizontal exchange of self-sacrifice."[49]

Mounier considered himself a revolutionary of the spirit, and acknowledged a debt to the teachings of Charles Péguy. Although less fervent a nationalist and more staunchly socialist than his mentor, Mounier shared Péguy's belief that *mystique* was to be preferred over *politique* and that the aim of social change was to promote spiritual fulfillment rather than material abundance. In the first issue of *Esprit* in October 1932, he wrote: "A radical change in the body of all our values must precede their universal integration in the spirit. This is what it means to be revolutionary . . . People want the revolution to be a red flash with flames. No. Revolution is a more profound tumult . . . Change the depths of your heart." For Mounier, engagement took as its goal the enlightenment of one's fellow men. The teacher was superior to the politician. "It is not force that makes revolutions," he insisted, "it is light."[50]

Mounier devoted significantly less attention to the "objective" factors that might accelerate or retard the progress of revolution than to the patient work of education that would transform man's inner being. This emphasis reflected not only his own conviction that spiritual concerns were the primary stimulus for action but also a general belief that the Depression had brought the capitalist system to the verge of disintegration. "The decay of modern society," he contended, had reached such an advanced state by 1932 that it was possible to foresee "the collapse of its whole worm-eaten hulk." That same year, Thomas Mann observed to an audience in Vienna: "Today there is a great deal of talk about the decline and demise of democracy . . . If by democracy one means the middle-class, capitalist republic whose character is all too dominant in what was created in Weimar . . . then one must concede that the [future] history of this form of state and society no longer seems to warrant very extended trust."[51]

The year 1933 marked the end of the Weimar Republic and the advent of National Socialism. With the beginning of Hitler's Third Reich the focus of the intellectuals' concern began to shift from the "established disorder" of bourgeois mediocrity to the challenge posed by its Fascist successors. As long as Fascism had appeared to be a phenomenon of domestic Italian politics, nourished by factors unique to one nation's historical climate, the debate over its doctrine and consequences had been conducted, even by Italians themselves, in correspondingly narrow terms. Suddenly, Fascism was a movement of continental scope, and intellectuals used the label "Fascist" to refer to totalitarian parties throughout Europe. The Fascist claim to represent a "new religion" and the need to confront this claim became more insistent as the decade progressed.[52]

At the center of the intellectual clash between converts to Fascism and their adversaries lay the intersecting issues of freedom and authority. The opposing camps agreed that the individual must accept membership in a group whose purpose transcended his own narrow goals of personal comfort and well-being; freedom should not become a license for selfishness. But whereas writers such as Mounier argued in favor of a "double vocation" that accorded equal weight to private and communal loyalties, Fascists sought an absolute value in the state. In 1929 Mussolini noted proudly: "We are the first to have affirmed, in opposition to democratic-liberal individualism, that the individual exists only to the extent that he is within the state and subordinated to the needs of the state."[53] Fascism offered a vision of discipline, service, and unity that rescued the intellectual from isolation and endowed his life with new purpose. But it left no room for values not in harmony with its own.

The problem facing the anti-Fascist intellectuals was to chart a middle course that avoided the extremes of irresponsibility on the one hand and subservience on the other. They sought a different, more balanced conception of duty that would bind the individual to a larger cause while safeguarding his dignity as a person. The enterprise that first met these demands during the decade of the 1930s — in which they found the means to integrate moral concerns and political action — was the anti-Fascist cause itself. A number of international conferences devoted to the "defense of culture" and the elaboration of anti-Fascist principles were held in several European capitals, beginning with a small meeting in Amsterdam in 1932. The most notable occurred three years later in Paris. The list of delegates and speakers who assembled there during a hot June week in 1935 represented a remarkable breadth of views. André Malraux and Emmanuel Mounier were present, as well as Julien Benda and Paul Nizan. E. M. Forster shared the podium with Bertolt Brecht. There were delegates from the Soviet Union and from the German and Italian émigré communities, welcomed at the inaugural session by one of the French hosts, André Gide.[54]

Gide's opening remarks evoked the "peril" that had brought the congress into being. "All of us," he declared, "feel menaced to a greater or lesser degree." But it was a German delegate who stated the problem with greatest clarity. Klaus Mann, the son of Thomas Mann, began by asking why National Socialism exerted such a powerful appeal on Europe's younger generation: "Why could we not win [them] over? Why have we lost them? What force did we have to counter the shining and deceitful, the dynamic and infamously clever offerings of

Fascism?" The intellectuals' failure, Mann suggested, stemmed from their inability to distinguish between what was still positive and worth saving among the values of the middle class and what must be condemned. The assault on the old order had been conducted in too absolute a fashion. "We have defamed the original, indestructible, and noble desire of European peoples for *freedom*," he declared, "because in many cases liberalism has been degraded to a worthless phrase and an alibi for high profits."[55]

At the same time, the intellectuals should not abandon their socialist vision. It, too, could be preserved if they denounced its betrayal by the Fascists. What was needed was an ideal that restored the individual to honor while maintaining the importance of collective goals. This new synthesis Mann termed "socialist humanism." As he explained: "Fascism—however paradoxical this sounds—makes it easier for us to clarify and define the nature and appearance of what we want. Our vision will oppose, point for point, the practice of Fascism. What the latter destroys, socialist humanism will defend; what the latter defends, it will destroy."[56]

Mann's remarks proved prophetic. Once again, the intellectuals defined their goals through a negative response to regimes in power. Having rejected the bourgeois order and identified themselves with a series of opposing ideals, these same critics now rejected Fascism as an established regime and turned for inspiration to the threatened liberal tradition. Its humanist values might have seemed empty and meaningless when preached by middle-class moralists, but they retained a luster beneath the crust of long neglect. "Our final recourse against the bourgeois world," Mounier wrote in 1936, "is to tear from its grasp the one-sided use and interpretation of these values."[57] While they continued to battle against the patent corruption of the "established disorder," left-wing intellectuals borrowed arms from the liberal arsenal for the fight against the mounting power of Fascism. Liberty, the dignity of the individual, the rights of conscience—these gained in value as the threat to their survival became more apparent.

Yet the attempts to defend a "socialist humanism" during the latter half of the decade met with failure and disappointment. Nowhere was this disappointment more apparent than in the major confrontation between European Fascists and their opponents that became the Spanish Civil War. During three years of prolonged and savage combat, which pitted Franco's insurgent forces and their Italo-German allies against republican loyalists and an international band of volunteers, intellectuals viewed the events in Spain as a symbolic drama. Some joined the war themselves as combatants; many more identified their hopes with the survival of the republic and felt diminished when it fell. Albert Camus later compared this experience to a "nasty wound." In Spain, he wrote, "men discovered . . . that one can be right and still be beaten, that force can overcome spirit, that there are times when courage is not its own recompense."[58] Both the loss to Franco and the war's violence, with atrocities committed and suffered by both sides, mocked the ideals of humanism. More and more, "spirit" seemed powerless. The outcome of the Spanish conflict still weighed heavily on the intellectuals when they learned, with the rest of Europe, that Hitler's forces had invaded Poland on the night of September 1, 1939.

World War II began with the capitulation to Fascism and ended with a reassertion of values that had been close to perishing in 1939. The intellectual history of the war years is a history of this reassertion, shaped by the efforts of the Resistance. The Resistance experience exemplified what Jaspers had called a "limit situation" — one in which a person's true ideals and loyalties were revealed to himself and to others. The war gave these ideals a "concrete" validity through the test of personal experience. It justified the depth of conviction with which they were professed and the allegiance they continued to inspire among the intellectuals long after peace returned to greet the survivors in 1945.

EDITION SPÉCIALE

COMBAT

DE LA RÉSISTANCE A LA RÉVOLUTION

LUNDI 21 AOÛT 1944 — Le n° : 2 francs

4e Année - N° 59

L'insurrection fait triompher la République à Paris

LES TROUPES ALLIÉES SONT A SIX KILOMÈTRES DE LA CAPITALE

Le combat continue...

AUJOURD'HUI 21 Août, au moment où nous pensions, la libération de Paris s'achève. Après cinquante mois d'occupation, de luttes et de sacrifices, Paris renaît au sentiment de la liberté...

Après une fusillade, des blessés sont secourus rue du Château-d'Eau.

VON KLUGE CHERCHE UNE LIGNE DE REPLI

Mais les Américains le talonnent sans merci

HEURE PAR HEURE

deux jours de lutte dans la rue

SAMEDI

6 heures :

10 heures :

10 h. 30 :

11 heures :

12 heures :

14 heures :

(Suite en 2e page)

DE GAULLE A CHERBOURG

Une prochaine rencontre
Roosevelt-Churchill

De Gaulle acclamé

Les tickets-lettres de pain
pour août sont valides

COMBAT

PARAIT
TOUS LES MATINS
après quatre ans
de lutte
clandestine
contre l'ennemi

LE PEUPLE EN ARMES
Un combattant parisien attend l'ennemi au coin d'une rue, la mitraillette à la main

De la Résistance à la Révolution

Ce que nous savons

Ce que nous voulons

DERNIÈRE MINUTE :

LONDRES, 21 août.

LIRE NOS INFORMATIONS EN PAGE 2

1
The Lessons
of the Resistance
1939-1944

In addition to his patriotic feelings,
every writer aware of his calling finds a
political duty in his literary activity
itself: he must struggle to free his
country and his compatriots.

Jean-Paul Sartre, 1944

The war fought on French soil in 1940 was brief. Scarcely six weeks after German panzer divisions rolled out of the Ardennes in a surprise thrust past the Maginot Line, the French high command sued for peace. "It is with a heavy heart," Marshal Pétain announced to his countrymen on June 17, "that I tell you today that the combat must cease."[1] For the next four years, France experienced World War II not as a belligerent but as a captive. Its freedoms were restricted, its horizons limited, its daily life shaped by the pressure of constant surveillance. "All of France," wrote one observer in the fall of 1940, "all of Europe is in prison."[2]

It was an apt metaphor. The resources needed to resist the aggressor in Nazi-dominated Europe were no longer simply the soldier's courage and élan, but the prisoner's patience, reflection, and resourcefulness. Moral strength became as important for France's survival as the outcome of military campaigns beyond its borders. Throughout the underground struggle soon to be waged within France, recruits were roused by faith in an ideal, not by an order for mass conscription. Yet sustaining a measure of hope in the face of the overwhelming evidence of defeat was no simple task. "Above all," one Resistance leader recalled, "we needed to believe that the improbable was possible."[3] Who would provide the inspiration for continued resistance? Here was an opportunity for the intellectuals, through their clandestine writings and the force of personal example, to play a central role.

The Resistance did not spring to life overnight. It began slowly, almost imperceptibly, as French men and women were drawn to reflect on the causes of defeat. As Léon Blum wrote while incarcerated at Bourassol in 1941: "It is natural that after a great reverse a nation . . . should examine its own conscience, proceed to a rigorous scrutiny, try to see clearly within itself."[4] The conclusions drawn from this *examen de conscience* varied widely both among the intellectuals and in the country at large, and during the somber years 1940-1944, French attitudes toward the Occupation remained divided. Some intellectuals, like Mounier, rallied briefly to the Vichy government in the hope that it would carry out the "national revolution" promised by Pétain; some, like Drieu la Rochelle, cast their lot with the Nazis; still others, like Gide, withdrew altogether while events unfolded around them.[5]

Those who chose to resist were a minority, though their number grew as the Allied victory approached. In their struggle against the Nazis, Nazi sympathizers, and the officials of Pétain's nominally independent yet practically collaborationist Vichy regime, the *résistants* remained a small and isolated group. Their isolation magnified their sense of responsibility as a spiritual elite. When the collapse of Vichy and the retreat of the German occupying forces came at last, the Resistance could look with pride at its own prescience, and feel that it had won the right to guide the nation further on the road to reconstruction.

Among those who joined the ranks of the intellectual Resistance at the outset were a group of Parisian writers who had regarded political questions with either indifference or disdain before the war. The process of self-discovery and political apprenticeship initiated earlier by Nizan and Mounier had been slow to touch them. But with the defeat of 1940, they accepted the call to commitment. Their continuing sense of guilt for not having joined the struggle against Fascism during the 1930s helps to explain the enthusiasm with which they embraced the creed of engagement during and after the war.

The man who best typifies the change in outlook occasioned by the war and the Occupation is Jean-Paul Sartre. After the Liberation, Sartre became the most forceful European exponent of the ethic of engagement. As editor of the monthly journal *Les Temps Modernes* he explored, with his friends and associates Simone de Beauvoir and Maurice Merleau-Ponty, a number of issues raised by active intellectual participation in a program of social change. The manifesto he drafted for the inaugural issues in the fall of 1945 reveals the lessons he drew from their wartime experience:

The writer is implicated (*en situation*) in his era. Each word has repercussions; each silence also. I consider Flaubert and Goncourt responsible for the repression that followed the Commune because they did not write a single line to prevent it. One may say, it was none of their business. But was the trial of Calas any business of Voltaire? The condemnation of Dreyfus any business of Zola? The administration of the Congo any business of Gide? Each of these authors, at a particular moment in his life, measured his responsibility as a writer. The Occupation taught us ours.[6]

Sartre and the Age of Irresponsibility

Sartre has provided us with a detailed and severely critical account of his childhood in *Les Mots* (*The Words*), published in 1964. By his own testimony, he absorbed at an early and impressionable age the romantic doctrine idealizing the writer as a superior being apart from society. The only child in a family circle of adults, he discovered that conflicts arose between the role assigned to him and his own wishes, conflicts that were to lead in his maturity to a profound concern with the problems of choice and sincerity. "My truth, my character, and my name," Sartre recalled, "were in the hands of grownups. I had learned to see myself through their eyes." He became a captive of their expectations, a child who "lived beyond [his] age as one lives beyond one's means: with passion, with fatigue, at great cost, for the sake of show."[7]

After his father's death, the young Sartre was taken by his mother to live with her parents, an Alsatian couple residing in Paris. It was Sartre's maternal grandfather, Charles Schweizer, who first inspired the boy with a veneration for the written word. "I had found my religion," Sartre later wrote. "Nothing seemed more important to me than a book. For me, the library became a temple." The view of art as a secular faith and of the man of letters as its priest found a persuasive advocate in the elder Schweizer. Jean-Paul, it was assumed, would become a "guardian of culture" like his grandfather.[8] The atmosphere in which he spent his early years encouraged a mastery of the literary culture and an acquisition of the verbal facility demanded by the elite French institutions of higher learning. For a boy aspiring to a career in letters or philosophy, the summit of this system was the Ecole Normale Supérieure. Sartre entered the school in 1924. What he discovered there was to prove crucial for his values and attitudes in the years to come.

The Ecole Normale in the middle and late twenties was more conservative than it had been in the heroic period of the defense of Dreyfus, or than it would become during the heated ideological controversies of the 1930s. From the school's quiet courtyard, located on the rue d'Ulm in the heart of the Latin Quarter, students could lift their gaze to the busts of Descartes, Pascal, and other intellectual luminaries of the past — grave reminders of a frozen cultural tradition. Paul Nizan, Sartre's roommate and close friend at the Ecole Normale, painted a most unflattering picture of the school at this period:

> There one offers to adolescents worn out by years in the lycées
> . . . the example of illustrious predecessors . . . One promises
> them the Cross [of the Legion of Honor] as a matter of course
> and the French Institute for their old age . . . In 1924 there was
> still one man; that was Lucien Herr . . . But he died. All that re-
> mained was the Ecole Normale, comic and more often odious,
> presided over by a patriotic, hypocritical, and powerful little old
> man who respected the military.[9]

The loss of Lucien Herr's magnetic presence — uniting personal warmth, moral rigor, and socialist convictions — may help to explain the political quietism of so many of the school's graduates during the late 1920s. There was no one at hand to stimulate a change in their political outlook.[10] Herr's death left the school under the uncontested guidance of Gustave Lanson, Nizan's "little old man," a literary historian devoted to the French classics. "For many of our contemporaries," Lanson had written in the introduction to his history of French literature, "religion has vanished and science is distant. Literature alone invites them to break away from narrow egoism or a stultifying profession."[11] These were the views of Charles Schweizer, familiar to Sartre since childhood. For him they confirmed an established creed.

What little political orientation Sartre's group of *camarades* did receive had come from the Radical philosopher Alain (Emile-Auguste Chartier) as they prepared for admission to the Ecole Normale. Alain imparted a Cartesian rationalism and a cynical distrust of the Third Republic's parliamentry regime to those who passed through his classes at the Lycée Henri IV in Paris. "I would prefer," he wrote in 1923, "that the citizen remain inflexible for his part, inflexible in spirit, armed with mistrust, perpetually suspicious of the plans and reasoning of his leaders." Alain's faith in the power of judgment to unmask political self-interest and his emphasis on the critic's role in curbing the abuses of power anticipated Benda's message in *The Treason of the Intellectuals*. The themes of individual choice and principled resistance to the political order stressed by Alain were to gain a new relevance for Sartre under the German Occupation. But for the moment, Alain's views were not calculated to encourage active participation in the nation's affairs or to engender sympathy for the complexities of government. "Our politics," he admonished his readers, "consists principally in defending ourselves against the politicians."[12]

Lacking direction from without, Sartre and his friends formed a tightly integrated and self-consciously superior group—a *bande à part*. Simone de Beauvoir, who first came to know Sartre during his residence at the Ecole Normale, recalled: "They associated with no one; they attended only a few selected courses and sat well apart from the others. Strongly opposed to the Catholic students, they belonged to a group composed for the most part of former pupils of Alain and known for its brutality. Its members threw water bombs on those distinguished *normaliens* who returned at night in evening dress."[13] Such adolescent attacks on pompous convention from within its own citadel represented the extent of Sartre's protest against the rigidity of the educational system. Sartre and Nizan demonstrated their irreverence toward the set curriculum by drawing caricatures of Leibnitz and Spinoza,[14] but they took examinations seriously: when Sartre failed the written part of the *agrégation* he refused to be discouraged, tried again, and was rewarded the following year with first place.

The academic subjects Sartre found most interesting were philosophy and psychology. But he rejected the doctrine of "critical idealism" that dominated the philosophy taught in Paris during the 1920s. Its principal exponent, Léon Brunschvicg, approached the works of the great Western philosophers as a record of the "methodical contemplation of the spirit concerning itself," treating truth and the progressive "development of spiritual being" through the ages as one and the same. Sartre did not agree. "In vain," he recalled, "the simple and uncultivated among us [students] looked for something solid, something, in the end, which was not spirit. Everywhere we found nothing but a formless though decorous haze—ourselves."[15]

Psychology offered an antidote to Brunschvicg's idealism. It attracted Sartre and others in his circle by its promise of concreteness, the possibilities it seemed to hold for defending the solidity of the external world against the "digestive philosophy" of their teachers. Psychology, as Sartre conceived it, went beyond the analysis of "abstract" mental processes to include the study of objects that enter consciousness as independent phenomena, distinct from the responses they elicit. While Brunschvicg focused on the ideas and the generalizations that were the result of reflection, younger investigators concerned themselves with the experience that preceded it. In *Vers le concret* (*Toward the Concrete*), published in 1932, the philosopher Jean Wahl contrasted the idealist and the realist interpretations of the "shock" produced by sensory data. "If one takes this simply as the point of departure for reflection, then one is an idealist." The realist, on the other hand, "asks himself whether this shock, this event are not realities and whether . . . they do not combine with other shocks and other events to constitute a description of the palpable world."[16] Wahl's sympathies clearly lay with the second approach, as did Sartre's.

When Sartre settled on a topic for his *diplôme d'études supérieures* (the equivalent of a master's thesis) at the Ecole Normale in 1926, he chose a problem that centered on the relationship between perception and the "palpable world." In revised form ten years later, this study became one of his first published philosophical works. What intrigued Sartre was the process by which the mind distinguished between the immediate perception of reality and the store of mental images that remained from objects perceived in the past. A strict idealist, he argued, would be forced to conclude that the two were identical occurrences, separated only by the passage of time. But experience showed this conclusion to be false. "If," Sartre explained, "I examine myself dispassionately, I will notice that I spontaneously discriminate between existence as a thing and existence as an image . . . At the very instant they appear, [images] have another quality than that of objects present to view. I never mistake one for the other."[17] For Sartre, the difference in "quality" was crucial. It indicated that reality could not be reduced to a series of subjective images, indistinguishable from the original act of awareness, because the mind itself confirmed the existence of objects outside consciousness through a direct, intuitive perception of their distinctive character.

Sartre's early views were to prove significant for his later work in several ways. His concern with describing the manner in which human consciousness encountered external reality led to his increasing interest in the German phenomenological school of Edmund Husserl during the 1930s, and to the distinction between *en-soi* and *pour-soi* that underlay the epistemology of *L'Etre et le néant* (*Being and Nothingness*), published in 1943. Equally important, Sartre adopted a highly introspective, self-analytic mode of investigation as his starting point in philosophy. In both his choice of subject and his reliance on lucid introspection as a method, he returned to the Cartesian tradition that informed Husserl's work. Like Descartes, he maintained that what we know with greatest certainty is our inner self. We can verify the fact of our own existence through reflecting on the mind as it meditates, a process for which Sartre adopted Descartes's familiar term *cogito*. But objects and persons beyond ourselves, Sartre held, elude our perfect understanding; they retain an "opaqueness" that we perceive but cannot penetrate.[18]

Sartre departed from orthodox Cartesian principles, however, when he insisted that such limited perceptions nevertheless provide a direct and unmediated link with reality. If the observer cannot know all aspects of the world around him, he can at least trust the partial evidence provided by his senses. Sartre offered a theoretical foundation for this view in an essay published in 1936, asserting that the same mode of perception governs our investigations of the inner world and our explorations of what lies outside. "The world has not created the *me*," he wrote, and "the *me* has not created the world." Both exist as independent and coequal objects of consciousness, known in an identical manner, though not in a similar wealth of detail. Because we can rely on consciousness to provide an accurate image of who we are, Sartre argued, we must extend the same degree of trust to its revelations concerning the world of things. This insight had the practical consequence of reinforcing Sartre's tendency to regard his own perspective on affairs as the most reliable. Even when friends were able to demonstrate logical fallacies in his arguments, he remained unshaken. For him the understanding achieved through experience and introspection had a greater claim to objectivity than the abstract reasoning of his critics.[19]

During the 1930s, Sartre continued to prefer a self-contained, self-absorbed mode of personal existence that differed little from his routine as a student. Socially, he perpetuated with Beauvoir and their friends the small-group ethos of the old *bande à part*, a circle that satisfied its members' emotional needs while allowing them to remain independent of other sources of contact and support such as family or political ties. Academically, he was well launched on the traditional path that led scholars from the Ecole Normale to a lycée post in the provinces, back to Paris and the Sorbonne, and finally to the pinnacle of prestige at the Collège de France or the French Institute. Financially, both he and Beauvoir were cushioned from the full effects of the Depression by their status as government employees in their respective lycées; in addition, Sartre had received a small inheritance.[20] As writers and teachers, they belonged simultaneously to two of the most privileged groups in French society—the intellectuals and the civil servants—and thus enjoyed a comfortable measure of both status and security.

Beauvoir characterized Sartre's political outlook during this period as *anarcho-métaphysicien*—that of a philosopher "prompt to detect the mystifications of the social order." Both adopted the stance of independent critics with good conscience and no sense of inconsistency. "The bourgeoisie as a class was inimical to us and we wished its liquidation," wrote Beauvoir. Sartre's repellent portraits of self-satisfied bourgeois in his short stories of the late 1930s, such as "The Room" or "Boyhood of a Chief," bear out this contention. At the same time, their situation was profoundly ambiguous. They were indeed against the bourgeois order, but they were supported by the very order they opposed. Sartre was thoroughly integrated, both economically and professionally, into the bourgeois Third Republic. Like his rebellious gestures during his stay at the rue d'Ulm, his anarchism was a symbolic protest against a situation that in practice he accepted, and accepted in part precisely because it allowed this minimal opportunity for protest.[21]

Freed in their own minds from the necessity of redefining their basic relations with society, Sartre and Beauvoir were able to mistake the congruence between their expectations and their situation for proof of their liberty. "Nothing limited us, nothing defined us, nothing restricted us; it was we who created our ties with the world. Liberty was our very substance."[22] During these years, man's freedom remained a fundamental tenet of Sartre's philosophy, a general principle derived both from his theory of the autonomous consciousness and from his own experience.

Yet such freedom as Sartre and Beauvoir enjoyed could not in itself provide an adequate source of meaning for their lives. They found themselves as divorced from temporal concerns as Benda's ideal philosopher, without sharing Benda's dogmatic certainty about the intellectual's proper goals. The autonomy they prized so highly was also an invitation to narcissism. Did their existence, which permitted them to shape their activities in whatever pattern they chose, serve any purpose beyond simple self-gratification? If not, what was the sense of their liberty?

These questions became the metaphysical center of Sartre's major work of the 1930s, the novel La Nausée (Nausea), published in 1938. His answer was consistent with the philosophical views he had adopted while at the Ecole Normale. Because meaning and value fell outside the limits of observation, Sartre concluded, they must be presumed to be absent altogether. Both the human and the physical world, he argued, were "contingent"; they obeyed no inner logic, stemmed from no higher design. His novel portrayed the narrator, Roquentin, as progressively overcome by the sheer materiality and senseless profusion of nature. At length, he begins to perceive even his own hand as inert matter. Human beings, he realizes, exist with no more justification for their presence than a stone or a tree. "Everything is gratuitous, this garden, this city, and myself. When one realizes this, it turns one's stomach and everything begins to waver . . .

That is 'nausea.'" Only a few bars of jazz heard in a café seem to escape from the "sin of existence," and inspire Roquentin with the faint hope that he, too, might create a redeeming work of art, "beautiful and hard as steel."[23]

Though Roquentin strips the daily world of its surface in an effort to discover a bedrock of reality and "salvation," the inhabitants of his adopted city, Bouville, make no such attempt to examine the raison d'être of their lives and habits. Sartre's description of Sunday in Bouville seen through the eyes of Roquentin reduces the town's inhabitants to marionettes, prisoners of their own "ready-made solutions," mechanical and purposeless. Roquentin's one claim to superiority is that he perceives the hollowness of these lives, including his own, while they do not. This insight provides a clue to Sartre's own placid situation in 1938. His negative verdict on the values of the interwar period was itself a justification for his privileged position. As he later admitted, "I succeeded at age thirty in . . . writing in *Nausea*—very sincerely, believe me—of the unjustified and brackish existence of members of my own class and in putting mine beyond discussion. I *was* Roquentin, I showed in his character, without complaisance, the pattern of my life. At the same time I was *myself*, the elect, the annalist of hell."[24]

The 1930s were thus a time of irresponsibility for Sartre and many of his friends, a prolongation of the mocking airs and games of their adolescence. The only one who succeeded in breaking away from the magic circle, unable to tolerate its contradictions, was Paul Nizan. His scruples were greeted with incomprehension. "At the Ecole he suffered, and I reproached him for suffering," wrote Sartre. "We were going to write, we would create beautiful books which would justify our existence. What could he complain about, since I complained not at all?"[25] When Nizan joined the Communist party soon after leaving the rue d'Ulm, Sartre felt that his friend had abandoned his liberty for a very dubious form of political engagement. He did not take Nizan's criticism seriously even when Nizan portrayed him obliquely as the weak, self-satisfied lycée teacher Lange in *Le Cheval de Troie* (*The Trojan Horse*, 1935).[26] Sartre's position as critic of the bourgeois world absolved him from the faults he condemned; his sense of election justified his detachment.

War and Commitment

The outbreak of World War II dramatized for Sartre the precarious nature of his liberty. He was mobilized into the Seventieth Division at

Nancy as a private on September 2, 1939, and was soon transferred to Brumath in Alsace. Mobilization destroyed his illusion of independence; but it did not reduce him to an attitude of passivity or of fatalism. He refused to become merely "a plaything of circumstances," with an "obligation to fulfill an 'engagement' that others have signed for you." Instead, he became engaged by his own choice.[27] This resolve, prompted by anger and defiance as much as by patriotism, triggered a burst of intense creativity during the fall and winter of the "phony war." Sartre started work on *Being and Nothingness*, kept a detailed diary of day-to-day happenings, and began a critique of his former life in the autobiographical novel *L'Age de raison* (*The Age of Reason*). Doubts concerning his role as a writer and intellectual, which had remained latent in *Nausea*, suddenly surfaced, and he began to deal with them openly.

Beauvoir noticed a great change in Sartre when he returned to Paris for a week's leave in February 1940: he "was firmly resolved not to remain aloof from political life. His new moral attitude, based on the notion of authenticity, and which he was attempting to put into practice, demanded that man 'assume' his situation. The only way to do so was to pass beyond [the situation] by engaging in action; any other attitude was a flight, a vain pretension, a masquerade based on bad faith."[28] Sartre thus sought to temper the complacency and hermetic self-interest of his earlier life with a new ethic of responsibility. In hindsight, he felt that he and those around him had been unable to see themselves as they truly were—a failure that contrasted ironically with their success in detailing the faults of middle-class Frenchmen—and had willingly acquiesced in their own self-deception.

Such faith in convenient falsehoods (*mauvaise foi*) could be overcome by a process of self-liberation through which one accepted one's responsibility toward others. Sartre had already adopted this view in the most general terms during the 1930s. His insistence that man discovers himself "on the road, in the city, in the midst of a crowd, a thing among things, a man among men" awaited only the final identification of himself with his fellows, of Sartre the author with his characters, in order to bridge "the gap . . . between literary myth and historical reality." As it was, he managed to describe in *Nausea* a psychological process that though attributed to Roquentin, foreshadowed his own transformation. "A series of little changes occurs in me," Roquentin remarks, "without my being aware of it, and then, one fine day, a veritable revolution takes place."[29]

In May 1940 the German offensive brought the first stage of Sartre's own reorientation to an end. It dispersed his group of friends as well. Nizan was killed at Dunkirk; Raymond Aron escaped to England;

Sartre was captured on June 21 in Lorraine. In August he was transferred from the internment center in Nancy to Stalag XII D at Trier, where he was to experience the first practical consequences of his ethic of responsibility and to glimpse a new sort of fraternity very different from the *bande à part* at the Ecole Normale.

The eight months he spent in German captivity completed Sartre's conversion to activism by placing him for the first time in a situation where group solidarity derived from a common misfortune rather than from a common privileged status. He was no longer merely an observer of society, but a prisoner united with other prisoners in a community of suffering and hope. "Little by little there, this kind of human mass gave me my first connection with men . . . The passage toward fellowship was very easy, was even obligatory, when one was in a prisoner of war camp . . . Private life, if you wish, no longer existed."[30] Although conditions in the German POW camps of 1940 were far less savage than those in the concentration camps at Buchenwald or Auschwitz, cooperation among the prisoners was nevertheless essential to ensure the welfare of all. Food had to be fairly distributed, and a basic regimen of personal hygiene had to be maintained to prevent the spread of disease. Prisoner morale similarly became a common concern. The courage of some, the defeatism of others influenced the outlook of the camp inmates in general. The individual no longer acted anonymously or in isolation; his decisions were felt and registered by the group whose fortunes he shared.[31]

During his captivity Sartre wrote his first piece of *littérature engagée*, a Christmas play entitled *Bariona ou le fils du tonnerre* (*Bariona, or the Son of Thunder*). The play was both a gesture of solidarity with fellow prisoners and a literary rendering of his recent insights into his past. The dramatic form permitted him to oppose differing points of view and to embody his own internal struggle in the different characters. As a result of this conflict, his protagonist experiences a "conversion" not unlike Sartre's own. For the first time also, Sartre was able to witness the immediate and powerful effects of literature on an audience: "As I addressed my comrades across the footlights, speaking to them of their state as prisoners, when I suddenly saw them so remarkably silent and attentive, I realized what theater ought to be—a great collective, religious phenomenon."[32]

Sartre's play was ostensibly a dramatization of the Nativity. In fact, by portraying the Romans as masters of Judea and the Jews as a conquered people, he suggested the situation of contemporary France in a manner clear to the prisoners yet shielded from German censorship. His hero, Bariona, has resigned himself to the continued suffering of the village he governs under Roman exactions of tribute. But

Balthazar, a wise man from the East (portrayed in the prison camp by
Sartre himself), persuades him to accept his obligation to act against
the Romans. The final scene interweaves Bariona's revolt with the
story of the Massacre of the Innocents, as he and his men set forth to
delay Herod's soldiers long enough to permit the escape of the Holy
Family. The play's message is one of hope through commitment, of
resignation overcome by fresh resolve. Having made his decision,
Bariona cries, "I am free, I hold my future in my hands," then turns to
address the prisoners, declaring: "I believe that for you as well, on this
day of Christmas—and all other days—joy will come!"[33]

At the end of March 1941 Sartre gained his release from Stalag XII
D by producing false papers, exaggerating his partial blindness, and
claiming that he had been given a medical discharge from the French
army. As a "civilian," he was permitted to return to Paris. Upon arrival there his first reaction, unexpectedly, was one of regret for the
human warmth and community he had left behind. Entering the café
Les Deux Magots, as he later recalled, "I had the strange impression
that people were isolated from one another. It was simply that they
were not touching each other, whereas in the prisoner-of-war camp we
touched each other all the time . . . This sort of contact was, as it were,
the superficial expression of a much more profound contact . . . which
I first experienced there."[34] Despite the anonymity of occupied Paris,
Sartre was determined to remain true to his new feeling of solidarity
with others and his new ethics. Beauvoir now found him "imbued with
principles" that took the form of "universal maxims" of conduct.
Whereas he had rejected any "abstract notion of duty" before the war,
fearing that it would compromise his freedom, Sartre now recognized
an obligation to resist the Germans at all costs.[35]

It was as a member of this new moral elite, a more responsible elite
than the old band of school friends, relying for its justification on a
sense of social commitment, that Sartre now saw his chance to play a
role in occupied France. He was not alone. Raymond Aron, writing
from London in June 1941, observed: "Philosophers, poets, novelists,
all feel the tragedy of the fatherland, all discover, with a sort of
naiveté when brought face to face with the event, the eternal truth that
the writer, even he who professes solitude and distance, lives in a national community and participates in its fate."[36]

The Birth of the French Resistance

Throughout the first two years of the war, France was a country
divided into occupied and "free" zones—the former under direct German control, the latter nominally ruled by Marshal Pétain from the

health resort of Vichy. This division isolated Frenchmen from friends and family in the other zone and from the world beyond "fortress Europe." The speed of the German advance, the collapse of the familiar if vilified Third Republic, and a sudden feeling of isolation all help to explain why the nation turned with relief toward a father figure like Pétain. In defeat, the quarrels of the 1930s were temporarily submerged by a wave of sorrow, shock, and helplessness. As Sartre later wrote, "We felt our fate escape us."[37]

Trauma and disorientation also underlay the general passivity displayed by the French population toward the Germans during the first phase of the Occupation, from late summer 1940 until the winter of 1940-41. The immediate question for those in the northern zone, as it had been for Sartre in his stalag, was what attitude to adopt toward the occupier. To this there seemed two possible answers: collaboration or reserve. The Germans tried to make harmonious cooperation appear natural and palatable; their behavior during the first six months of the Occupation was scrupulously correct, even chivalrous. Posters appeared showing a smiling soldier dispensing bread to children, inviting the "abandoned population" to "have confidence" in their captors. Hitler's ambassador to Paris, Otto Abetz, seemed cultivated, accommodating, and sincerely eager to promote cordial understanding between the two nations.[38]

Few French observers in the autumn of 1940 doubted that Germany would soon become absolute master of Europe. England alone still remained at war with the Reich, and British capitulation to superior Nazi forces appeared certain. French apologists for collaboration therefore presented their choice as conforming to the dictates of "realism." They argued, plausibly enough, that their country should seize the offer of friendship extended by Berlin rather than further antagonize so powerful a neighbor. Peace, not continued defiance, would best serve France's interests. Only by acceding to the victor's wishes, they maintained, could the nation secure Nazi consent to begin rebuilding a shattered homeland.[39]

Attempts to win support for this view at a time when cooperation with the invader still appeared possible found their most striking expression in Jacques Benoist-Méchin's book *La Moisson de quarante* (*The Harvest of '40*). Published in early 1941, it detailed the author's increasingly cordial relations with the Nazi New Order during his recent internment as a prisoner of war. Interspersed with graphic descriptions of camp life and outbursts of indignation offered as proof of Benoist-Méchin's patriotism, the reader discovered a romanticized vision of sturdy French peasants and friendly German soldiers working together to gather in the harvest. Divided by war, they were still bound by the values of the land. Germany, Benoist-Méchin suggested, would gladly aid in the task of reconstruction once the French abandoned their suspicion and hostility. As he remarked: "We have been constantly *face to face*. Now we must take our stand *side by side*."[40]

An opposing point of view was presented in the justly celebrated short novel by Vercors (Jean Bruller), *Le Silence de la mer* (*The Silence of the Sea*). Against the lure of collaboration, he held up the ideal of stoic self-respect, expressed in stubborn silence. Vercors felt that Pétain's call for "sincere collaboration," symbolized by his handshake with Hitler at Montoire, was nothing but a seductive trap. Alarmed by the weakening resolve among his fellow countrymen, and anxious to fortify the will of the "many hesitant intellectuals more or less tempted to collaborate with the occupier," Vercors tried to show that even the best German was powerless to redeem the perverted and dehumanizing aims of the Occupation.[41] The heroine of *The Silence of the Sea*, who fights against her love for a young, idealistic German officer, typified for Vercors the sole attitude consistent with honor in defeated France.

Vercors delivered his message indirectly through a series of monologues in which the officer, Werner von Ebrennac, seeks to conquer the mute resistance of his French hosts. Ebrennac cherishes France's cultural tradition and believes that Germany has much to learn from its foe. The "marvelous union of our two peoples," he predicts, will purge the Reich of its barbarism and permit the French to educate their captors. Yet in the end, he comes to understand the reasons for the strategy of silence that he had vowed to overcome. He is forced to recognize that his dream is an illusion and that he has blinded himself to the reality of the Occupation. As he takes his leave, he recounts a conversation in which his brother officers in Paris revealed their true objectives. "They said, 'Haven't you realized that we're duping them?' That's what they said. Exactly. '*Wir prellen sie.*' They said, 'You don't suppose we will foolishly allow France to recover on our very borders, do you?'"[42]

In the spring of 1941, when Sartre returned from captivity, the pressure for choice was growing. France now entered an intermediate phase of the Occupation that would last until the Allied invasion of North Africa and Hitler's occupation of the semiautonomous Vichy zone late in 1942. The French population had begun to polarize into two groups, collaborators and resisters, although a large majority still hesitated between these two positions, fearing to take a stand while the outcome of the war remained undecided. At the same time, the Germans were beginning to act with fewer scruples. In May 1941 more than one thousand foreign Jews residing in Paris were arrested and deported. Bilingual posters appeared announcing the execution of hostages in reprisal for anti-Nazi acts. The Gestapo set up its Paris headquarters on the rue des Saussaies—an address that soon became synonymous with dawn arrests and brutal torture.[43]

This was the period when the first cautious attempts were made to organize the French Resistance. Sartre gathered a group of like-minded friends, including Merleau-Ponty and Beauvoir, into a circle that he baptized Socialisme et Liberté. His was one of many groups forming in the Paris area, all characterized, as Beauvoir observed, by "their tiny membership and their lack of prudence." Most, like Sartre's, concerned themselves initially with establishing contacts with possible adherents and with elaborating a political program for the future.[44]

Planning for the future was partly an attempt to combat the pervasive feeling of helplessness by an act of faith in the Allies' victory. But it also focused the intellectuals' attention on the role they might be able to play in creating a new France once that victory had been achieved. Participation in these groups was thus for many intellectuals an initiation into political concerns. Such initiation, despite its dangers, offered the experience of activism in the service of high moral purpose and among friends—a radical departure from the petty, impersonal party politics these same intellectuals had viewed with disgust during the 1930s. Merleau-Ponty, Sartre's chief assistant in Socialisme et Liberté, later recalled that "it was easy to unite within the Resistance, because its relations were almost always those of one individual with another."[45]

The intellectuals were among the first active *résistants* during the early months of indecision and inertia, when the French Communist party was still paralyzed by the Hitler-Stalin Pact and the mass of French citizens refused to commit themselves. The outlook for Sartre's personal venture was jeopardized, however, both by the political inexperience of its members and by the strong attraction exerted on all groups of the Left by the Communist Resistance, which quickly formed after Hitler's attack on the Soviet Union in the summer of 1941. The Communist tactics of direct action differed dramatically from the passive, educational aims of organizations like Socialisme et Liberté. The Communists' boldness eclipsed the initiatives of their rivals and won new converts to their cause.

By the end of October Sartre had realized that he was exposing his friends to the risk of arrest and Gestapo interrogation through activities connected with Socialisme et Liberté. Contacts and money eluded him, since the Communists spread the rumor that his release from captivity had been secured by his willingness to spy for the Germans. In the face of mounting obstacles, he reconciled himself to a less dramatic role than that of a political activist. As Beauvoir recalled, "It was a bitter blow for Sartre to renounce . . . this project, which he had long meditated in the stalag. He abandoned it nonetheless, much against his will. He then stubbornly set himself to writing the play he had begun; it represented the only form of resistance open to him."[46] Yet this decision cannot be explained solely by the pressure of events. Though Sartre was probably wise to dissolve his own group, since he was "little accustomed to this sort of work" and thus exposed his friends to unnecessary risks, it would not have been impossible for him to participate in another underground organization. Even an intellectual with as little political experience as the historian Marc Bloch took on planning and liaison duties as a member of the Resistance group Franc-Tireur, activities for which he was arrested and shot by the enemy in June 1944. Sartre's decision to return to literature must therefore be seen as a deliberate rejection of more militant engagement rather than as a forced choice. Writing was the arm of combat he preferred.[47]

Sartre's play *Les Mouches* (*The Flies*), which for financial reasons was not staged until the spring of 1943, had taken shape as he and Beauvoir bicycled through southern France during the summer of 1941 in search of adherents to Socialisme et Liberté. His earlier success with *Bariona* encouraged Sartre to write a new work on the same theme, the necessity for revolt. Once again he portrayed a central character beset by doubts concerning the wisdom of resistance, then showed these doubts resolved in favor of action against an oppressor. But whereas *Bariona* progresses swiftly toward its resolution, a large part of *The Flies* deals with the hesitation and passivity that precede commitment.

This shift in emphasis reflected the prevailing mood of guilt and uncertainty in occupied France. Marshal Pétain had declared on the first anniversary of the armistice with Hitler that "we have not yet finished expiating all our faults." A belief that the German victory was a merited punishment for France's sins, Sartre realized, would gravely cripple the nation's will to resist the invader. As he recalled in 1948: "I wanted, as best I could, to contribute in a small way toward rooting out this disease of penitence, this acceptance of repentance and shame. It was essential to strengthen the French people and to give them courage."[48] Rather than dwelling on the mistakes of the past, they should turn their attention toward a future that they were still free to shape. The idea that a historically predetermined course of events held the French prisoner was, Sartre thought, a dangerous fallacy. The true barriers to action, he believed, were imposed not from without by the Germans but from within by a nation that acquiesced in its own captivity.

One vivid illustration of the penchant for self-accusation that Sartre hoped to discourage among the French was the wide success of Lucien

Rebatet's *Les Décombres* (*The Ruins*), published in July 1942. These bitter memoirs of a French Fascist, seething with contempt for the Third Republic and hatred for the Jews, were introduced by their author as a "chronicle of the long downward slide and successive collapses" of the nation, culminating in its recent defeat. The fears that lay beneath Rebatet's outrage and sarcasm struck a responsive chord among his readers. So, too, did the simplicity of his analysis. French decadence, already much deplored in the 1930s, was contrasted with the virility and vision of the new Reich. *The Ruins* identified those who had betrayed France—politicians, capitalists, inept army officers, "foreign" races—as well as the victors, who were worthy of emulation. For Rebatet, the war was a retribution and a warning whose meaning must be understood. "This war," he noted at the moment of Nazi triumph, "has followed its logical course. The apocalypse is illuminating. But imbeciles and false prophets cannot read, and my fatherland is still imbecilic."[49]

The Ruins, like Benoist-Méchin's *The Harvest of '40*, offered a first-person account of the recent past. Its persuasive power derived from this claim to authenticity. *The Flies*, by contrast, resorted to classical allegory to convey its political message. Sartre had to camouflage his real intent if he wanted the play to be performed openly in occupied Paris; and he judged, correctly, that the Greek myth he had chosen would be interpreted in contemporary terms. The story of Orestes returning to Argos to avenge his father's death was an elegant parallel to the political situation of France under German rule. Aegisthus and Clytemnestra suggested Hitler and Pétain; the curse of Agamemnon's death, the legacy of French defeat; Orestes' murder of the king and queen, political revolt against Berlin and Vichy.[50]

Orestes, like Bariona, discovers his freedom in a gesture of defiance against the established order. His act reveals the power of human freedom over superstitious fear and tradition, and by implication encourages others to imitate his revolt. As Zeus admits to Aegisthus, "The painful secret of gods and kings is that men are free. They are free, Aegisthus. You know it, but they do not." Merleau-Ponty, reviewing the play in the fall of 1943, was thus justified in calling it "a drama of liberty."[51] Yet Orestes' murder of Aegisthus and Clytemnestra remains an individual and not a collective act. In the final scene the citizens of Argos remain passive spectators only, as Orestes takes with him the swarms of flies that have plagued the city since Agamemnon's death. The people are saved, but they have taken no hand in their salvation.

In *Bariona* the hero teaches others by his own example; he unites a group of armed villagers against the Romans. One may ask why a similar act of solidarity does not occur in *The Flies*. Orestes' self-conscious isolation seems to suggest a projection of Sartre's position after the dissolution of Socialisme et Liberté and, more generally, his understanding of the writer's role in occupied France. The writer was one who acted alone to secure the liberation of others by exorcising their fears, inhibitions, and self-deceptions. He would do for his readers what they could not do for themselves. In the absence of free expression, the writer assumed a tutelary role. He watched over the mass of his fellow citizens, interpreted their needs, spoke in their name.

This aristocratic conception of the writer was shared by others in the French intellectual community. The Parisian author Edith Thomas wrote: "We thought . . . that the trade of the writer carried with it a greater responsibility than that of the other professions." Gabriel Péri, one of the Communist party's most prominent Resistance martyrs, declared some months before his death, "I have held my profession to be a kind of religion, of which the drafting of my daily article was the sacrament." The authorities in Paris and Vichy further increased the writers' sense of importance by censoring their works; the "Otto List" of forbidden books held to have "systematically poisoned French public opinion," including writings by Julien Benda and André Malraux, signified that the Nazis viewed literature as a threat. Jean Guéhenno noted with mingled irony and pride in 1940: "They do us a great deal of honor. A tyrannical power, by attributing such importance to our thoughts, forces us to admit their singularity and scandal for ourselves. We did not dare believe ourselves to be so interesting."[52]

The New Moral Elite

The summer of 1942 marked the beginning of the last and most brutal phase of the Occupation. While material life in France continued to deteriorate, repression and resistance alike reached new levels of intensity. Paul Eluard's poem "Courage," published in *Les Lettres Françaises*, describes Paris in the winter of 1942-43:

> Paris is cold Paris is hungry
> Paris no longer eats chestnuts in the street
> Paris has put on an old woman's rags
> Paris sleeps standing in the fetid subway air
> Still greater misfortune afflicts the poor.

The search for food during that winter became an obsession. Neighborhood black market enterprises flourished, supplied by cousins in the country with rabbits or a few eggs. Coal for heating was almost unobtainable, and at night, with a curfew and blackout in effect, Paris seemed to Beauvoir "a vast prisoner-of-war camp."[53]

Such want and hunger were caused by the Germans' increasing exploitation of the physical and human resources of France. Far from fulfilling the dreams of fruitful cooperation depicted in *The Harvest of '40*, the Nazis stripped their conquered provinces to replace heavy material losses in the war.[54] The French Resistance struck back with partisan raids and widespread sabotage. Thousands of young men, faced with the prospect of forced labor in Germany, disappeared into the *maquis,* swelling the ranks of the underground. The gradual unification of the Resistance under the leadership of Jean Moulin and his successor as head of the Conseil National de la Résistance, Georges Bidault, further increased the movement's scope and effectiveness. Despite disagreements and internal jealousies, danger promoted solidarity in the face of the enemy.

The appearance of *Les Lettres Françaises* in September 1942 marked a new level of self-confidence and activity among the Resistance intellectuals as well. The original idea for a clandestine publication in Paris, treating both literary and political topics from a Resistance perspective, had come from Jacques Decour, a Communist writer, in late 1941. Decour's arrest and execution by the Gestapo just as the first edition was due delayed its appearance for months. His chief assistant, Claude Morgan, eventually felt it safe to establish contact with the paper's contributors, who included Edith Thomas, Jean Guéhenno, and Jean Paulhan. Their little group gradually grew to more than a score during the last two years of the Occupation, as Paul Eluard, François Mauriac, Sartre, and, for one issue, Albert Camus joined the enterprise. Sartre remembered the atmosphere of their editorial meetings as "très, très agréable."[55] By the fall of 1943 the paper's circulation reached 12,000, a figure well below its total readership, since it was passed from hand to hand. At first only four mimeographed pages long, it was later printed professionally and eventually doubled in size. It appeared regularly each month, thanks to the ingenuity of a devoted technical staff, until well after the Liberation.

Like other underground papers such as *Combat* and *L'Humanité*, *Les Lettres Françaises* countered the powerful propaganda machines of Berlin and Vichy by giving its readers news suppressed by government censors. Its mission, Edith Thomas proclaimed in the second issue, was to "cry out the truth." In an effort to lift morale and to encourage the faint-hearted, it reported the successes of the Allies in

Russia and North Africa, as well as the many acts of Resistance sabotage at home, relying on French-language broadcasts from the BBC and contacts in the underground for news. Editorials stressed the need for unity in the continuing struggle against the invader, celebrated past French victories, and eulogized such victims of German brutality as Decour, Péri, and the poet Max Jacob. An editorial that Decour composed before his death declared: *"Les Lettres Françaises* will be our arm of combat. By its publication we intend to integrate ourselves, in our role as writers, in the struggle to the death begun by the French nation to free itself from its oppressors."[56]

In addition to informing and exhorting its readers, the paper waged a bitter campaign against authors who accepted positions and honors, at a price, from the new regime. From the start of the Occupation, Paris had become the chosen refuge for the most pro-Nazi among the intellectual collaborators. This "shameful little troop," as François Mauriac later called them, exercised a cultural monopoly in the "official" world of German-approved publications.[57] Their dissident colleagues challenged both the motives and the talents of these turncoats in the columns of *Les Lettres Françaises*, and mounted a counterattack against those who wished to place French letters in the service of the enemy.

Chief among the accused was the Nazi sympathizer Pierre Drieu la Rochelle, whose evident sincerity and position as the new director of the prestigious *Nouvelle Revue Française* made him an especially dangerous spokesman for those who saw in Fascism "the sole means to check and to reduce this decadence" in France. Sartre's first contribution to *Les Lettres Françaises* was a condemnation of Drieu as the weak-willed nihilist who hoped "that a bloody catastrophe would come to fill the emptiness in himself which he had been unable to subdue." Drieu's subsequent resignation from the *Nouvelle Revue Française*, complaining of his isolation, occasioned general satisfaction among his critics. Rebatet, Benoist-Méchin, and other collaborators were treated no less severely. The Comité National des Ecrivains, speaking for the intellectual underground, proclaimed its intention to initiate formal proceedings following the Liberation against both writers and editors guilty of commerce with the enemy.[58]

While chastising collaborationist writers, *Les Lettres Françaises* bestowed warm praise on works of Resistance literature. Sartre's *The Flies*, for example, was greeted as "the most powerful [play] seen in France for many years." Special enthusiasm was reserved for the publications of Les Editions de Minuit, hailed as "an affirmation of the tenacity and the will to live of the French spirit." During the years 1943-1944, Les Editions, founded by Vercors and Pierre de Lescure, became the most important publisher of clandestine literature in

France. Its first offering and its greatest success was *The Silence of the Sea*, which the reviewer for *Les Lettres Françaises* found "compelling in its simplicity."[59] By the time of the Liberation it had issued thirty-five works of fiction, poetry, and essays. Some took the form of short stories set in occupied France, such as Edith Thomas's *Contes d'Auxois* (*Stories of Auxois*), others pages of a private journal, such as Jean Guéhenno's *Dans la prison* (*In Prison*). A translation of John Steinbeck's *The Moon Is Down* brought a "voice from the other world," demonstrating the sympathy the European Resistance evoked abroad. All these works were a protest against the insipid, morally anesthetized literature through which the authorities, as Edith Thomas wrote, wished to create "a world of dreams, of fairyland, of irresponsibility, of puerility, of childhood."[60]

Les Editions de Minuit also represented a conscious effort to reassert the value of literature as reflection, commenting on events without succumbing to "political passions." "Our domain is not that of propaganda," read the declaration of intent introducing *The Silence of the Sea*. "What is at stake is the spiritual purity of man." "The real question," Vercors noted after the war, "was to show to world opinion that France, in the midst of misfortune and violence, could remain faithful to its most noble claim: that of thinking clearly." Other literary magazines served a similar end. In the southern zone, where censorship was less strict, the review *Confluences* managed even as an open publication to accord a generous place to fiction that challenged Vichy's cultural conformism.[61]

Above all, the *écrivains résistants* believed that their task was to formulate moral ideals opposed to Fascism. They recognized that the German victory of 1940 was not due to military might alone. Pierre Dunoyer de Segonzac, a young French officer who had witnessed the blitzkrieg at its height, concluded: "We had thrown ourselves against an army inspired by an ideal, a mysticism or a faith . . . I had the feeling that we had no similar élan with which to oppose it." Like Ernest Renan after the Prussian victory of 1871, men like Segonzac emerged from the shock of France's defeat with a conviction that the nation was ripe for "intellectual and moral reform." Vichy at first sought to turn this desire for change to its own advantage and to impose a conservative vision of a rural, hierarchical France devoted to work, family, and fatherland. But by 1943 the "national revolution" proclaimed with such pious ceremony by Pétain had faltered, weakened by its inner contradictions and the harsh realities of German rule. Its failure increased the likelihood that the populace would welcome an alternative Resistance program.[62]

The ideals to which the Resistance intellectuals rallied were traditional ones: freedom of expression, freedom of conscience, the defense of human dignity, all as set forth in the *Declaration of the Rights of Man and Citizen* of 1789. These values were associated with the pre-eminence of French culture. Their support involved not only a universalistic humanitarian concern but also a strong cultural nationalism. "We will defend the values that have created the glory of our civilization," wrote the editorialist of *Les Lettres Françaises.* "The regime that is forced upon us, where all liberty of thought and expression is suppressed, prefigures the fate of our culture at the hands of the 'New Order.'"[63]

The practical problems of life in occupied France gave rise to the further ideal of individual responsibility for action. The Occupation presented a "limit situation" of the type so often described in the literature of the 1930s, forcing each Frenchman to test his basic loyalties in the face of fear and danger. The plausible argument that such behavior under stress, far from revealing a person's true character, would on the contrary distort it, was an objection that the Resistance intellectuals refused to consider. In a moral sense, a man was only as good as his acts. This belief prompted a new respect for heroism and a search for heroes both past and present. Charles Péguy, the champion of Dreyfus whose patriotic *mystique* had carried him to a martyr's death in 1914 at the Battle of the Marne, became a sort of patron saint of the Resistance, for he typified the very faith transformed into action that they sought to recapture for themselves and for the nation.[64]

During the Occupation Sartre's philosophic interests shifted from the phenomenology of perception to the problems of freedom and choice. As early as 1939, in his *Esquisse d'une théorie des émotions* (*Sketch for a Theory of the Emotions*), he had rejected Freud's view that we may become victims of subliminal forces over which we exercise no conscious control. Sartre argued instead that the individual consciousness sought refuge from a threatening situation in fear or anger, and freely consented to the "magic" of an emotional state in order to avoid dealing with a problem in rational terms.[65] Choice was therefore both revelation and commitment—through it man both defined and engaged himself. There was no escaping responsibility for one's actions, for man was defined (in Sartre's paradoxical view) as a being whose being was undefined, and whose freedom rendered him wholly responsible for his choices.

Sartre developed this argument in a work that was to win him his reputation as a serious philosopher, the brilliant though idiosyncratic treatise *Being and Nothingness*. Published (almost unnoticed) in 1943, it had absorbed a major part of his time and provided an outlet for his abundant energies after the collapse of Socialisme et Liberté. In it he wrote: "I am engaged in a world for which I carry the entire responsibility, without being able, whatever I do, to escape this responsibility even for a moment. For I am responsible even for my desire to flee my responsibility. To render myself passive in the world, to refuse to act upon objects and upon others, is still to choose the person I am." The phenomenological categories of *pour-soi* and *en-soi* elaborated in the first two sections of *Being and Nothingness* reflect a preoccupation with choice. The *en-soi,* or being deprived of consciousness, is all that is not freedom. Hence it determines the character of the "situation" against which the voluntaristic *pour-soi* strives to assert its liberty in a never ceasing duel between stasis and movement, matter and will.[66]

Sartre's theory contains a number of important if insufficiently elaborated ethical corollaries for individual conduct. For the lack of a fixed definition of man creates a void, which the individual can fill with definitions borrowed from his own surroundings. Thus, in a famous description, Sartre depicts the café waiter who "plays" at being a café waiter, whose gestures are "a bit too precise, a bit too rapid," and who betrays in this slightly mechanical behavior the effort he is making to be something he is not.[67] This is the start of bad faith. An established social role—and here Sartre thinks pre-eminently of the bourgeois—is an invitation to insincerity. It frees us from the necessity of inventing our being at each moment, and allows us to believe (erroneously) that our condition is natural and inevitable, like that of an object. Hence Roquentin's mordant critique of the bourgeois of Bouville, who adopt a mode of existence inherited from their forebears and as a result appear to be without a will or personality of their own.

"There is no difference," Sartre wrote in *Being and Nothingness,* "between existing and choosing oneself." But not all choices are of equal importance; underlying each individual's conduct is a "fundamental choice" that is the individual's particular way of coming to terms with the possibilities offered by his environment. He can either settle for a "ready-made" solution or accept the challenge of self-definition.[68] From this it follows that other people are a threat to the authenticity of the self, for they suggest modes of behavior not properly our own. Then again, in a world in which each pour-soi is isolated from every other, change can occur only on the level of the individual. Each person must be led to make an authentic "fundamental choice," but that choice cannot be commanded from above. Finally, the crucial role of self-awareness in making this choice grants a high value to psychology in determining a proper path of conduct and assigns a similarly high value to the imagination in "inventing" oneself. Sartre's discussion of authentic conduct is couched in terms appropriate to the artist: creation, invention, discovery. It is, at bottom, an aesthetic view of the world.[69]

Sartre's conviction that man lucidly chooses his own being harmonized with the moral elitism of the Resistance, their belief that the war and the Occupation were gradually creating a new class of moral leaders who could legitimately claim the right to supersede the old elites at the war's end. At the same time, the pressures for collaboration appeared to Sartre as yet another instance of the temptation to adopt ready-made solutions and to indulge in bad faith. The question of why some chose to betray fascinated him. He made several detailed psychological studies of collaborators, including his analysis of Drieu la Rochelle, his essay "What Is a Collaborator?" (1945), and the character of Daniel Lalique in his trilogy *Les Chemins de la liberté* (*Roads to Freedom*), the first two volumes of which he completed during the Occupation. In these works he portrayed the collaborator as a person in search of the security conferred by obedience to values imposed by others. Drieu, Rebatet, and their fellows, Sartre maintained, so feared their freedom that they sought to abandon it while refusing to admit their true motives for doing so. "If the collaborators drew from the German victory the conclusion that they must submit to the authority of the Reich," he wrote, "this was due to a fundamental and antecedent decision that constituted the basis of their personality: a decision to defer to the status quo, whatever it might be."[70]

Sartre found such passivity contemptible. It proceeded, in his opinion, from a belief that "everything that exists is good," which left room neither for creating personal values nor for revolt against present conditions. Moreover, he argued, to abjure one's own liberty placed the freedom of all in jeopardy. As long as others remained free, the collaborator was forced to confront the fact that he might have chosen differently. In his desire to justify his own cowardice, he attempted to reduce those around him to the servile status he had adopted for himself, and was thus led to aid his captors in their work of repression.

Sartre's account of the French collaborationist mentality—incorporating a "rejection of what is universal," a "desire for rigid constraints," and a "hatred of man"—once again demonstrated his skill at revealing unavowed motives and dissecting comfortable alibis. At the same time, however, there existed a contradiction between Sartre's absolute judgment that collaboration was an inauthentic choice and his belief in each person's freedom to create himself. Might not a collaborator choose to side with the Germans lucidly and sincerely rather than in a spirit of bad faith? Sartre's failure to raise this question reflected a serious weakness in his analysis. Because his categories of judgment applied exclusively to the manner of selecting a goal rather than to the goal itself, he could not argue that collaboration was always wrong. Instead, he was forced to reason backward and to disqualify the collaborator's choice as invariably insincere. Despite the logical difficulties that such a strategy entailed, this was the only ground on which collaboration could be condemned. For to exclude the possibility that a decision to collaborate could ever satisfy Sartre's criteria for an authentic choice meant to restrict another's freedom in an a priori fashion. And if there was but one path that led to an "authentic existence," could man still be considered totally free?[71]

Sartre's answer was that liberty, correctly understood, entailed an obligation to respect the liberty of others. Yet in adopting this position, he endowed the concept of liberty with a new meaning. Rather than defining freedom as a natural condition, he now considered it a moral value threatened by the Occupation. It ceased for him to be an ontological category and became instead an ethical norm, an "ideal" to be defended, much as it had been for Benda. Sartre thus ultimately accepted an immutable and universal standard of conduct, prescribing the ends as well as the manner of authentic choice. His philosophy could furnish no formal justification for such a standard, yet he and other Resistance intellectuals upheld it nonetheless.

This contradiction was masked for the time being by the clear and immediate ethical imperatives of the war. The men and women of the Resistance lived in a Manichaean world; rarely had such a broad moral gulf existed between opposing sides as between the Fascist and anti-Fascist forces in World War II. In this situation the Resistance fostered a sense of social mission that was to prove central to its members' political outlook after the Liberation. Good and evil were self-evident, plainly perceived realities in the life of the underground, unquestioned bases of judgment and action. In the face of combat, philosophical niceties of proof and logic receded into insignificance.

The Resistance also gave the intellectuals a sense of community. Through their individual efforts, they found themselves united in spirit with a broader group that brought together elements of every social class in a common enterprise. Emmanuel d'Astier de la Vigerie, interviewed in Marcel Ophuls's documentary film *The Sorrow and the Pity,* summed up this aspect of the Resistance experience: "What did I get out of the Resistance? The most important thing, besides a certain dignity, was . . . that it is the only period of my life when I lived in a truly classless society." The Resistance mystique of solidarity and camaraderie, based on common danger and the reconcilation in action of widely differing ideological tendencies, contrasted in the minds of many with the fragmented France of the 1930s and with the remoteness of its leaders from the masses. As Sartre wrote in 1945: "The Resistance was a true democracy. For the soldier as for his leader, the same danger, the same responsibility, the same absolute liberty within the bounds of discipline. Thus, in shadow and in blood, the strongest of republics was formed."[72]

The Resistance in effect substituted one social hierarchy for another. Its heroic ideal, by offering the possibility of an elite based not on wealth or education but on moral worth, allowed the intellectuals to maintain a place of distinction in French society while no longer feeling isolated or superfluous. Their aspirations were well illustrated in Beauvoir's political novel *Le Sang des autres* (*The Blood of Others*, 1945), completed during the Occupation. It tells the story of a young intellectual, Hélène Bertrand, who passes through the successive stages of irresponsibility, guilt, and commitment that Beauvoir herself had experienced. Bertrand's search for identity ends with the revelation of Resistance solidarity; she dies knowing that she has found her true vocation in service to her fellow men. In one of the novel's closing scenes she sets out on her first Resistance mission: "Now she was no longer alone, no longer useless and lost under the empty sky . . . The shell had been broken; she existed for something, for someone. The whole earth was a fraternal presence."[73]

Yet when the Liberation came in August 1944, such certainties became blurred in a complex pattern of conflicting rights and interests that threatened to shatter the solidarity of the Resistance and its intellectual adherents. The moral energy accumulated during the previous four years began to dissipate as summary judgments of guilt or innocence yielded to a sort of weary tolerance. The profound disappointment felt by many French intellectuals explains why even today they retain a sense of nostalgia for the Resistance, for the purity of its inspiration and the nobility of its sacrifices. Vercors wrote at the end of his memoirs of the Occupation: "Now I was forced to recognize, already, with a sort of poignant nostalgia, how happy we had been . . . The sorrows, the misery, the anger, the tears, the anguish felt for friends, and yet happiness . . . The reward for what we did was that happiness. And I knew that from then on, any other would seem pale."[74]

2
Liberation
1944-1946

*We have won the means to carry out the
profound revolution that we desired.
It still remains for us to make it a
reality.*
Albert Camus, 1944

Hope, resolve, and elation dominated the first weeks of
Liberation. The psychological release that followed four years of war
and occupation brought with it a wave of optimism. For men and
women grown accustomed to the constraints of a long captivity, the
perspectives that now opened seemed unlimited. The immediate past
of hardship and humiliation was forgotten; one could start again.
Beauvoir later remembered, "I kept telling myself: it's over, it's over.
It's over, and everything is beginning."[1]

During the next eighteen months, as France embarked on the massive task of recovery, the intellectuals attempted to carry the Resistance to a successful conclusion. Their efforts were not yet at an end;
victory against the invader was merely the first step in a broader program of renewal. As Sartre wrote in August 1944, it was "not simply a
matter of ridding France of the Germans, but of beginning a more difficult and more patient struggle to win a new order." The intellectuals'
hopes of the 1930s for a radical restructuring of society revived, but
with a greater measure of confidence that they were accepted and
shared by the nation as a whole. A return to old habits and prejudices
seemed impossible after the upheavals of the war. "One cannot imagine," wrote Albert Camus on the eve of the Liberation, "that men
who have fought for four years in silence and for days on end in the
tumult . . . of gunfire will agree to the return of resignation and injustice under any form."[2]

The term most often used to describe the aims of the Liberation period was "revolution." But what did revolution mean in the context of liberated France? In a negative sense, it signified an end to the abuses of the Third Republic and the repressive measures of Vichy. More positively, it conveyed a promise of social justice and a new political style. Above all, for Resistance intellectuals, it carried hopes for a profound change in behavior and attitudes. The new France was to be neither rigidly hierarchical (as under Vichy) nor fiercely self-centered (as under the Third Republic), but humane and generous, modeled after the Resistance itself. Citizens would become less fearful and selfish, less petty and materialistic, more concerned for one another and more willing to achieve *égalité* and *fraternité*, if necessary at the cost of their own comfort. The journal *Combat*, speaking for the largest and most prestigious Resistance group within the non-Communist Left, had declared as early as 1942: "The revolution that we carry within us is more than a material revolution; it is the revolution of the spirit, that of youth and the people. The bourgeois [Third] Republic was the embodiment of egoism, narrowness, and fear . . . The men of the Resistance, steeled by their daily ordeal, will instill in France a spirit of generosity, grandeur, and audacity."[3]

These ideals, though inherited in large part from the 1930s, underwent a shift of emphasis as a result of the experience of Vichy and the Occupation. For the *résistants* were not alone in censuring parliamentary corruption, capitalism, and individualism. Pétain and Hitler opposed them as well—in word if not in deed. The Vichy and Nazi regimes both claimed to serve a "national revolution" directed against the liberal order. As the Liberation neared, the problem of sharing vocabulary with their enemies led the Resistance intellectuals to redefine their aims. One elementary step toward this redefinition was simply to deny any similarity between the Resistance revolution and Vichy's "ridiculous parody"; another was to emphasize the inability of Fascism to translate its propaganda into meaningful action. But on a deeper level, the war brought a new respect for individual rights and for genuine democracy. *Le Franc-Tireur* noted in March 1944 that the adjective "democratic" no longer aroused the same scorn as it had before 1940: "Perhaps no other word was more devalued, more subject to ridicule. In the recent past it still evoked the speeches of petty politicians and parliamentary impotence. And now it is more radiant and fraught with future significance than in the days of . . . the barricades of [18]48 and the Commune of Paris."[4]

Memories of Pétain's authoritarian rule and German oppression rendered Resistance members double suspicious of any political power unchecked and unresponsive to demands from below. Hence their insistence on balancing socialism with personal freedom. Hence also their dilemma when faced with the question of how the Resistance should carry out its own revolution. For if the Occupation had put the intellectuals on guard against abstract concepts and empty slogans and induced them to place even greater value on "concrete" gains than before, it simultaneously had increased their distrust of the administrative tools needed to implement social change. Was it possible to realize the goals of the Resistance without infringing on the rights of the individual? If government action was necessary to achieve these goals, what new institutions could be devised that would prevent the abuse of power by those entrusted with the welfare of the nation?

Sartre, for one, saw in the Liberation a promise that this dilemma could be resolved. The Liberation, he later wrote, had triggered an "explosion of liberty, the bursting of the established order and the creation of an order [that is] efficient and spontaneous." For a brief moment the Resistance and the nation seemed as one. If all desired the same revolutionary changes, then their ideals could be given institutional expression without the risk of coercion or dissent. Some observers, however, feared that the revolutionary ardor kindled in armed struggle might dissipate in the hour of peace. Léon Blum, who had witnessed similar hopes and their disappointment after World War I, observed in 1941 that the essential task of the Resistance would be "to seize this possibility of enthusiasm, to maintain it and forge with it a creative spark during what may be a rather short period open to useful action, before it exhausts itself in wearying struggles and before it recedes into daily routine."[5]

The Resistance Confronts de Gaulle

The care the Resistance devoted to preparing for the future can be measured in the scores of programmatic tracts published by the clandestine press as early as 1940. Devoted to a multitude of topics ranging from French constitutional law to principles of educational reform, these first projects dealt for the most part with what Henri Frenay later termed "broad, distant, and in some cases perhaps unattainable objectives."[6] As the end of the Occupation drew within sight, however, the planners' focus narrowed in an effort to frame concrete goals to which all could subscribe. In March 1944 a plenary session of the Conseil National de la Résistance (CNR) drafted a program that superseded previous statements of purpose and secured wide assent. This body, composed of representatives of all major clandestine groups as well as delegates from six political parties, spoke with con-

siderable authority. Thus its program offers both a guide to
Resistance expectations on the eve of the Liberation and a yardstick
against which to measure the achievements of the months ahead.

The document that emerged from the March meeting was intended
to orient the transition from combat to reconstruction. An initial,
detailed section dealt with the "plan of immediate action" that all
Resistance groups were directed to implement in order to "hasten the
Liberation, reduce the sufferings of our people, and secure the future
of France." Its central provision called for a network of local committees, placed under the supervision of Comités Départementaux de
Libération, whose paramount task was to "mobilize and train the
French" for the coming struggle. Through this means the CNR sought
to create a parallel, clandestine government within the territory still
under German control. The spirit of cooperation and common sacrifice engendered by these committees, the CNR hoped, would be a decisive asset following the Liberation, and would permit the Resistance
to communicate its ideals more effectively to the populace. "Thus in
combat," the program's authors concluded, "a purer, stronger France
will be forged, capable of undertaking . . . the greater task of
rebuilding and renewing the fatherland."[7]

The second half of the CNR charter dealt with this "greater task" in
a series of ambitious proposals. Taken as a whole, they offered a synthesis of individual freedoms in the tradition of 1789 with guarantees
of a basic right to economic well-being derived from the Popular
Front and Vichy's "national revolution." The purely political recommendations were the least specific, perhaps because (as later events
were to show) they were the most difficult on which to achieve agreement. Support for de Gaulle, a republican form of government, and
universal suffrage constituted the fundamentals of the Resistance platform. Greater attention was devoted to the need for punishing collaborators and for confiscating "the profits made at the expense of the
people and the nation" during the Occupation. Most important, however, was a general declaration of civic rights, including free speech,
"the liberty of the press, its honor and independence," freedom of
assembly, equality before the law, and "respect for the human
person." The Resistance thus acknowledged the need to restate and to
reaffirm the fundamental freedoms whose vulnerability had been
demonstrated during the Occupation.[8]

In the economic and social fields, the CNR called for a comprehensive series of nationalizations, "returning to the nation all the major
means of production, fruits of common effort, energy sources, underground wealth, insurance companies, and large banks." Its aim was a
mixed economy administered jointly by the state and private interests,
as proposed by Léon Blum and the Socialists at the time of the 1936

Popular Front. But it went well beyond prewar proposals in demanding the creation of a national plan for economic growth and a
guaranteed annual wage "that assures each worker and his family
security, dignity, and the possibility of a full human existence."⁹ The
CNR's definition of freedom was very broad indeed. In addition to including formal rights, it recognized an obligation to liberate Frenchmen from poverty and want, and thus proposed to integrate spiritual
and material freedom such that each buttressed and complemented the
other.

How would these goals be implemented? On this question the CNR
charter observed a prudent silence. Although their recommendations
implied a far greater role for the state than it had possessed before the
war, the authors of the CNR program remained mute concerning the
structures intended to accomplish their objectives. Machinery for
punishing collaborators, confiscating illicit profits, arriving at national economic goals, or administering a guaranteed income would
presumably be created in due course. But in contrast with the detailed
attention given to the "liberation committees," the problems of
postwar government were largely ignored.¹⁰ This imbalance is instructive. The institutions with which the Resistance leaders felt the greatest
affinity were those of the clandestine struggle—groups of comrades
united by personal loyalty and mutual respect, overseen by committees whose decisions were reached in a collegial fashion. Just as the
Occupation led them to place liberty above order in the scale of civic
virtues, so it rendered them more concerned with the abuse of power
than with its exercise, more inclined to dilute executive authority than
to reinforce it.

Such attitudes contrasted sharply with those embodied by the man
who was to prove the key figure in French domestic politics during the
first year of the Liberation—Charles de Gaulle. Though his wartime
speeches embraced many of the CNR's objectives, and though the Resistance was unanimous in acclaiming him its leader, de Gaulle was a
man for whom the state and the exercise of power through traditional
channels were of prime importance. He returned to France in August
of 1944 determined to place administration in the hands of legally constituted authorities as soon as possible. The values of military
discipline and clearly defined hierarchy that shaped the General's
political outlook reinforced his distaste for the improvised, independent, and unpredictable methods of the domestic Resistance. At the
same time that he attacked Vichy for betraying the republic, he voiced
his alarm at "the slow decadence of public authority" and his hope
that "the powers invested by [the people] with the control of the state
may have the means to do this with force and continuity."¹¹

De Gaulle's relations with the French Resistance movements during

his four years of exile in London and Algiers had been subject to
numerous strains. At first he appeared quite unaware that any opposition groups existed besides his own Free French. His radio appeal
from London of June 18, 1940, was a call for resistance based abroad
rather than within France itself. When emissaries of the various
movements succeeded in contacting the General early in 1941, he was
surprised to learn that a Resistance had grown up spontaneously on
French soil. At the same time he worried that its recruits might prove
difficult allies, and tried to restrict their role to espionage alone.[12]

As de Gaulle's objectives shifted in the course of the war from
bringing the resources of the Empire into play against the Germans to
"building a strong French state in exile which could be exported to
France," the prospects for major disagreement with the domestic
Resistance leaders increased.[13] The General feared the growing influence of the Communists in the French underground. Moreover, he
disliked the prospect of another elite of whatever ideological persuasion coming between himself and the French people, who, as he saw it,
were the ultimate source of his legitimacy. In fact de Gaulle and
Resistance leaders in France defined their mandate in similar terms.
Both viewed themselves as guardians of the nation's moral and civic
integrity who stood above party politics. And both could claim, in the
absence of electoral evidence to the contrary, that their views enjoyed
significant popular support. The Resistance accepted the General as
its titular head—the symbol and embodiment of its defiance of the
enemy—but it expected de Gaulle to reciprocate by according it a major share of power until free elections could once again be held.

These expectations were not fulfilled. Whereas the Resistance remained committed to substituting "new men" for prewar leaders at all
levels of the provisional government, de Gaulle was more concerned
with French unity than with revolutionary justice. He accepted the
need for continuity in the civil service, while he tried to protect his
own independence as interim head of state by drawing his subordinates from a variety of milieus. "In the nation tomorrow, as in the
Resistance today," he proclaimed in January 1944, "there will be a
place for all the children of France." It was therefore scarcely surprising that de Gaulle bypassed the metropolitan Resistance in many ap-
pointments to administrative posts after the Liberation, showing
equal preference for his own Free French companions from London
and Algiers, industrial figures prominent before the war, and all-too-
familiar faces from among Third Republic politicians. The men and
women of the domestic Resistance found themselves to be merely one
possible elite among many—and not the most favored—rather than
the logical and unrivaled successors to the ruling groups of Vichy and
the Third Republic.[14]

Yet de Gaulle's determination to rebuild a strong state with which to support his quest for *grandeur* did not blind him to the dangers of ignoring a widespread "desire for social renovation." He contemplated lending his patronage to "vast reforms . . . removing the menace of upheaval that weighed upon the nation." De Gaulle preferred to initiate change himself in order to retain some control over its pace and extent. He therefore accepted a number of the CNR's proposals on political rather than moral grounds, reasoning that the Communists would be hampered by a move to preempt some aspects of their program.[15] This pragmatic attitude made possible a certain degree of cooperation between de Gaulle and the CNR; but their motives and priorities remained as divergent as ever.

The liberation of Paris triggered the initial confrontation between de Gaulle and the Resistance. In late August 1944, as the Allies continued their advance eastward from Normandy, the Parisian underground rebelled against the German Occupation forces. Strikes by railwaymen, postal workers, and the police preceded fighting against the 20,000 enemy troops quartered in the capital and assaults on convoys retreating from the front. The combat spread from quarter to quarter as armed insurgents threw up roadblocks, ambushed German patrols, occupied public buildings, and traded fire with motorized infantry from windows and rooftops. Throughout the liberated sectors of the city, French flags suddenly appeared in profusion. Fighting on a limited scale and with improvised means, the Forces Françaises de l'Intérieur confronted the foe whose humilating yoke they had borne throughout four long years.

Courageous as such actions were, the primary significance of the Paris insurrection lay in its psychological effect on the French rather than in its military consequences for the enemy. Von Choltitz, the German commander, had neither the forces nor the desire to engage in full-scale hostilities with the *insurgés*, and wished only to evacuate the city in good order. For the Parisians, however, engaging in street combat helped to renew a sense of national pride and honor. The insurrection became a symbol of French rebirth. Among the combatants, one of them later recalled, there existed a "feeling that all of France would be judged according to what happened in Paris."[16]

Resistance leaders were well aware of the insurrection's value as a lesson in civic responsibility, a confirmation of the CNR's hope that a "purer, stronger France" would emerge from a show of strength against the invader. Accordingly, a general call to arms was issued to the city's population by the Comité Parisien de la Libération, exhorting the French to "fell trees, dig antitank trenches, erect barricades." The city would not passively await its liberation, the committee proclaimed: "A victorious people will receive the Allies."[17] As the combat continued, it seemed as if the legends of Paris's revolutionary past—the people in arms, liberty, equality, and fraternity won with courage against great odds—had come to life again. A sense of reliving a glorious history colored the highly emotional accounts of the battle that appeared in the Resistance press, now openly distributed for the first time since 1940. *Combat*'s edition of August 24 evoked the old revolutionary *journées* in lyric tones. "Barricades of liberty have arisen once again," wrote Camus. "Once again, justice must be bought with the blood of men."

Sartre was commissioned by *Combat* to observe and report on the popular reactions to the street fighting. He, too, noted that "the street . . . has once again, as in '89, as in '48, become the theater of the great popular movements of social life." In a series of articles he depicted the transformation of the people of Paris from passive onlookers to committed participants. His account centered on an incident in which a crowd of bystanders turned against a Latin Quarter concierge who had refused shelter to a wounded Resistance fighter: "The crowd has finally decided to takes it fate into its own hands. Toward eleven o'clock, one sees the first barricades appear. The path leading from . . . docility to insurrection has been traversed at last." For Sartre, this chain of events dramatized the true meaning of the Paris uprising. Men and women, acting freely and spontaneously out of shared emotion, had put aside their private fears and "cozy little dreams" and instead embraced the "spirit of revolt."[18] Now there could be no turning back. The populace had at last made its "fundamental choice" in favor of revolution.

The euphoria kindled by the liberation of Paris reached its height when General Leclerc's Second Armored Division entered the city of the morning of August 25. The entire populace turned out to dance in streets still littered with broken glass and to fraternize with the Free French infantry. De Gaulle's arrival that same afternoon, however, produced a certain chill among the leaders of the Resistance. Rather than proceeding directly to the Hôtel de Ville where the CNR executive awaited him, de Gaulle honored with his initial visits the forces of order and continuity—the army and the police. He was clearly not disposed to treat the domestic Resistance with more than polite condescension. Three days later the decisive interview between the General and the CNR took place. De Gaulle categorically refused to allow another "autonomous authority" to function alongside his own or to have the CNR program "constantly waved in the face of the executive." The Conseil National de la Résistance would duly enter "the glorious history of the Liberation," but henceforth it no longer "had reason to exist as an active agency."[19]

What political role remained for the Resistance? Some of the CNR's leaders, including Georges Bidault, accepted ministerial posts in de Gaulle's provisional government. Others took their seats in the enlarged consultative assembly that was to advise the government during the first months of transition. But the CNR's basic stance was ambiguous. While it continued to hope that de Gaulle might become an ally in instituting change from above, it also intended to pressure the General into compliance with its own scheme of priorities by appealing directly to the nation. Poised between elitist and popular alternatives, it hoped to retain a measure of influence through the force of its moral prestige. "The men of the Resistance have thought it their duty to continue through words and action what they began in silence," Camus wrote in October 1944, "because they possess a clear perception of their role as teachers . . . The Resistance does not wish to dominate; it demands only to be given a hearing."[20]

Camus and the Rhetoric of Humanism

On the night of August 20, 1944, while the insurrection was gathering strength in Paris, men from the clandestine Resistance papers occupied offices and press facilities recently abandoned by their collaborationist rivals. Within a few hours, the first issues of *Combat, L'Humanité, Résistance,* and *Le Parisien Libéré* appeared openly on the streets. It was a swift and bloodless coup that augured well. When de Gaulle proved hostile to CNR hopes for a major voice in government, the intellectuals' attention thus shifted to the press. As Emmanuel d'Astier noted, this was a "fief" that was theirs by right of conquest.[21]

Camus portrayed the intellectuals' sense of mission in the August 31 issue of *Combat*: "Since the means for expressing ourselves are now in our hands, our responsibility vis-à-vis ourselves and the country is total . . . If our voice can remain one of energy rather than hate, of proud objectivity rather than mediocrity, then . . . we will not have failed our trust." The role of the Liberation press, Camus believed, was to "awaken [the reader's] critical faculties rather than appealing to his spirit of complacency." Journalists would not dictate opinion, but would enlist the public's active cooperation in judging the reliability of news reports and in drawing the appropriate lessons from contemporary events. Above all, the press would serve as an example of open-mindedness, reflection, and the respect for truth, thus encouraging readers to rise "to the level of what is best in them."[22]

The desire for principled journalism was prompted not only by the positive example of the Resistance papers but also by a determination to avoid a return to practices that had haunted the profession in the past. The French press of the 1930s had been an open scandal: venal, biased, faction-ridden, consciously exploiting the prejudices of its readers. The war had brought worse. Pétain, though sworn to combat "the lies that have done us so much harm," tried to create a docile press in the Vichy zone, while in Paris the apostles of the Nazi order preached the gospel of hate and revenge. When the CNR program called for liberty of the press "with respect to the state, monied interests, and foreign influences," it was because the French journalistic establishment had yielded to all three before and after 1940.[23]

The central figure in promoting the ideal of a renewed and more responsible French press was Camus himself. Though Camus's reputation now rests on his stature as a moralist and moral philosopher, during the decade 1938-1947 a major portion of his energy was devoted to journalism. Throughout the latter part of the Occupation, he worked on the underground paper of the Resistance group Combat. He had joined the movement in 1943 through the mediation of Pascal Pia, with whom he had edited *Alger Républicain* and its successor *Soir Républicain* in Algiers in 1938-1940. As arrests and reassignments within the underground progessively depleted the staff of *Combat*, Camus rose rapidly to a position of major responsibility. By the time the Liberation came, he had attained wide respect as an intellectual spokesman for the Resistance. Sartre later credited him with having "summed up . . . the conflicts of the period" and having come "close to being an exemplar."[24]

Camus was raised in Belcourt, a lower-class European quarter of Algiers. He never knew his father, who died from wounds received at the Battle of the Marne in 1914; his widowed mother, silent and withdrawn, earned a meager living as a charwoman during the ensuing years. In the Mediterranean world of his youth, human misery presented a sobering contrast with surroundings of great natural beauty. Yet despite its darker side, Camus's childhood later inspired him with a sense of privilege and gratitude. Whereas Sartre looked back on his early years in Paris with a mixture of guilt and loathing and saw his family circle as a prison of false values from which he had longed to escape, Camus remained nostalgic for the "world of poverty and light" of Algiers. "A person's work," he later wrote, "is nothing other than the long voyage to rediscover by the detours of art the two or three simple and lofty images that first gained access to his heart."[25] These "images," drawn from the North African landscape, provided

Camus with the self-evident truths in which his philosphy was grounded. They were the starting point for his early essays in *L'Envers et l'endroit* (*The Wrong Side and the Right Side,* 1937) and *Noces* (*Nuptials,* 1939), which linked poetic insights to moral generalizations: the grandeur and indifference of nature, man's comparative insignificance, and the dignity man achieved in his long and difficult struggle for happiness.

The philosophical views espoused by Sartre and Camus on the eve of World War II, despite their different backgrounds, showed certain similarities. Both refused to acknowledge a higher meaning for human existence; both were "anti-idealists" in that they rejected transcendent values not founded in daily experience. Sartre's theory of "contingency," developed in *Nausea*, was paralleled by Camus's vision of the "absurd," a capricious and unfathomable dimension to human existence that defied explanation. The narrator in his novel *L'Etranger* (*The Stranger*), published in 1942, appeared as alienated from his surroundings as did Sartre's Roquentin. In an admiring review, Sartre characterized the work as depicting a "world . . . from which causality has carefully been removed." Yet Camus's dissatisfaction with this purely negative view of man's relations with his surroundings was evident as early as 1938, when he wrote in response to *Nausea*: "To declare the absurdity of life cannot be an end, but only a beginning."[26]

The war and the Occupation, though they did not cause him to break with his past as radically as had Sartre, nevertheless marked the onset of a new phase in Camus's intellectual development. They stimulated him to adopt a more nuanced attitude toward the "absurd" and to accord man's stubborn search for values the respect due to an act of defiance. "For a long time," Camus explained to an imagined German interlocutor in his *Lettres à un ami allemand* (*Letters to a German Friend,* 1943-1945), the most important of his Resistance writings, "we both believed that this world had no ultimate purpose . . . [Yet] as you can see, we have drawn different morals from this same principle." The Nazis, Camus maintained, presumed that "everything was equivalent and that good and evil could be defined however one wished." They had concluded that "in the absence of any human or divine ethic, the only values were those that governed the animal world, that is to say, violence and ruse." For Camus, by contrast, Germany's enslavement of Europe demonstrated the danger of pursuing nihilism to its logical conclusion. "I persist in my belief that this world has no ultimate meaning. But I know that something in it has meaning, and that is man, because he alone insists on having one. This world has at least the truth of man, and our task is to provide its justification."[27]

The Resistance, Camus later noted, encouraged his own "transition from an attitude of solitary revolt to the recognition of a community whose struggle one must share." This new feeling of solidarity was reinforced and prolonged after the Liberation by the cohesiveness of the *Combat* staff, a tightly knit group that for Camus was the equivalent of Sartre's *bande à part*. The collective support and teamwork exemplified by *Combat* provided him with a model for human relations in the new France. *Combat* also served in the first months after the Liberation as a focal point for the Parisian intellectual community. Its list of contributors was long and impressive, including André Malraux, Sartre, Raymond Aron, and Emmanuel Mounier. Beauvoir recalled that "on opening the paper each morning, it seemed to us almost as if we were opening our private mail."[28]

Combat was devoted above all to shaping French postwar politics in accordance with the ethical precepts of the Resistance. In an editorial that appeared in October 1944, Camus stated: "We think that political revolution cannot do without a moral revolution that parallels it and gives it its true dimension." Social justice, he wrote a month later, required chiefly that one recognize "a few truths of common sense," for "human affairs are complicated in their details, but simple in their principles."[29] These reflections conformed to the vogue for programmatic generalities that characterized much of the journalistic comment of the early Liberation period: prescriptive rather than analytic, morally impeccable, exultant and militant in turn.

Behind this rhetoric lay a desire to classify contemporary events according to the same moral and conceptual categories that had guided patriots during the war. Despite Camus's professed respect for "proud objectivity," his terms of reference served not to describe but to judge a world divided into the noble and the reprehensible. His style derived much of its persuasive force from a skillful use of repetition and contrast. Grandeur and mediocrity, truth and duplicity, struggle and compromise were arrayed against one another in constant tension, creating an impression of clarity, of politics reduced to elemental choices for and against. What some observers viewed as Camus's excessive rigor in delivering these judgments stemmed less from a sense of moral infallibility, however, than from a conviction that his ideals could be attained only through strenuous self-discipline. Determined to spur the French toward reaching "the level of what is best in them," he sought to make his readers aware of the dangers of complacency. His exhortations betrayed a fear that the dreams of the Resistance would be lost through lack of courage.[30]

Intellectuals like Camus thus gravitated toward an opposition stance dictated by their fidelity to the goals of the underground. *Combat*'s major function—besides soliciting support for a "spiritual revolution"—was to provide a forum for criticism of de Gaulle's provisional government. Despite accusations of disloyalty to France's new leaders, the paper's staff felt it essential to disassociate the Resistance from the policies of the regime. As Camus wrote in February 1945:

> It appears that *Combat* has changed its orientation and has been seized with a regrettable penchant for opposition. It is true that a great many things and individuals have changed since the Liberation . . . I personally find opposition regrettable, and hope it can be avoided. But we will choose it tomorrow without hesitation if the program of domestic policy . . . does not prove that the government has remained faithful to what it promised. For we, too, have our promises to keep.

Among the pledges that Camus intended to honor was an earlier vow to "remain vigilant" and to defend the Resistance legacy with "obstinacy and intransigence."[31]

Opposition reflected the popular mood. The end of the Occupation had brought disappointingly little change in the material situation of most Frenchmen. Rationing became more severe during 1944-1945; the black market continued to flourish, fed by the chocolate, coffee, and cigarettes brought from across the Atlantic by American GIs. Despite a rise in salaries of almost 50 percent, the real purchasing power of the franc remained low because of rapid inflation. Few of the major changes sought by the CNR were initiated during the first year of the Liberation, save in the areas of press reform and nationalizations. Coal mines, the Renault auto works, electric utilities, insurance companies, and a number of major banks passed from private to public ownership. But these developments were not enough to sustain hope in an otherwise gloomy period when, as *Combat* noted, the nation was rapidly "taking leave of its euphoria." Public confidence in the government declined. "In 1944 the French were unhappy," de Gaulle observed a year later. "Now they are angry."[32]

During the fall and winter of 1944 *Combat* expressed a growing exasperation over the failure of financial reforms, government indifference toward the CNR charter, and the halting progress of the "revolution." "There is no doubt," the paper remarked in early 1945, "that the government of General de Gaulle has been curiously inhibited, even paralyzed, in its efforts toward renewal since the Liberation." But where the government showed signs of greater vigor, as in the program of nationalizations, its activities were greeted with more alarm than satisfaction. The intellectuals, in accord with the CNR charter, expected that nationalized concerns would enjoy a significant degree of self-management. Instead, they were administered by a state bureaucracy in which the intellectuals had little confidence. The end of private ownership, it now appeared, did not automatically mean a new era of industrial democracy. The state might simply inherit the powers once exercised by the former owners, leaving employees and the public with no more rights than before.[33]

These misgivings forced Resistance intellectuals to deal with the problem of institutional reform previously skirted by the CNR. Mounier, writing in *Combat* in January 1945, presented the issue in the form of a premise and its logical corollaries: "In order to remake France, we need a tool. The administrative tool will become increasingly more powerful as collective measures are taken. No reconstruction [is possible] without administrative reform." What was essential for accomplishing the "revolution," the paper argued in another editorial, was not administrative skill or technical expertise but honesty, selflessness, and the qualities of character that had sustained the French underground. The time had come to "replace those whose interests are exclusively private with those who possess the will to serve the common interest."[34] Mounier's call for administrative reform was thus interpreted as an invitation to the moral elite of the Resistance to assume managerial duties on a large scale. This proposal, which placed greater value on moral integrity than on administrative efficiency and dealt with individuals rather than with institutions, reflected the limits of the Resistance vision. Even when the intellectuals attempted to suggest alternatives to the "administrative tools" at hand, their hopes remained tied to a revolution directed by the pure and the just.

Yet these same intellectuals were well aware that the Resistance might soon lose its power to influence the course of reconstruction. Its record was not encouraging. As *Combat* was compelled to acknowledge in January 1945: "For the last four months, the Resistance has vacillated between obsequious inaction and an anarchic activism . . . What could we have expected from it after the Liberation? That it infuse new blood into politics, that it permit the renewal of personnel and ideas that France so badly needs. None of this has really been accomplished, or even attempted with the desirable rigor."[35] If the Resistance vision could not be translated into a positive renewal of personnel, however, it might still serve to inspire a salutary purge of the old. As the government prepared to bring accused traitors to trial, the intellectuals looked on with renewed hope. The French Minister of Justice, François de Menthon, was a man whose Resistance record inspired their respect and confidence. The settling of accounts in the forthcoming *épuration*, they believed, would show whether the Resistance spirit had survived the Liberation.

The Postwar Trials

Political trials have long held a peculiar fascination for intellectuals. More dramatically than normal criminal proceedings, such trials test the conflicting claims of individual conscience and public order, encourage the spectator to reflect on his own values, and conclude with a verdict that illuminates the foundations of authority on which a society rests. The character of the accused—whether a genius like Socrates or Galileo, a deposed monarch like Louis XVI or Charles I, or such relatively modest individuals as Dreyfus or Sacco and Vanzetti—is thus overshadowed by more general issues. The beliefs of the accused are as much on trial as his deeds. Whatever the judgment rendered, those for whom beliefs matter have a stake in the outcome.

The twentieth century has seen political trials increasingly employed as a means for repression and propaganda. The cynical manipulation of legal machinery to intimidate onlookers attained new scope and effectiveness in Europe during the 1930s with the so-called show trial, whose main purpose, as Goebbels frankly declared, was to rid the state of internal dissent. In 1944 the French retained vivid memories of the rigged courts and summary executions witnessed during the Occupation, when magistrates had tried Resistance "terrorists" and pronounced capital sentences with scant regard for judicial procedure or proof. Through these experiences, Resistance intellectuals came to see respect for the formal apparatus of courtroom practice as a symbolic affirmation of individual rights. They reacted with distaste to the outburst of vigilante actions against suspected traitors that followed the Liberation, and they looked forward to a return to legal norms that would be just as well as rigorous, healing the breach between right and law.[36]

The French *épuration* can thus be viewed as both a moral drama and a repudiation of the misuse of the courts under the previous regime. The CNR charter had devoted two of its first three demands to the necessity for legal and economic sanctions against collaborators. A sense of obligation to the Resistance dead demanded that those responsible for their arrest and deportation should now be called to account. In an article entitled "A Time for Justice," published while fighting continued in the streets of Paris, Camus wrote: "These men who have rationed everything save shame, who blessed with one hand while they killed with the other, who added hypocrisy to terror . . . can expect of France neither pardon nor indulgence."[37] A sign that collaborators would find little sympathy in the courts had come already in March 1944, when Pierre Pucheu, former Vichy

Minister of the Interior, was judged and executed in Algiers. The severity shown in his case, widely approved in the underground press, was expected to set a precedent for those to follow.[38]

Yet when the long-anticipated trials became a reality, they provoked open disagreement within the Resistance. Although in theory all groups represented by the CNR agreed on the desirability of rapid and rigorous justice, in practice they differed on how far the trials should go. The most implacable supporters of a far-reaching purge were the Communists. Throughout the first year of the Liberation, the Communist party daily, *L'Humanité*, demanded that all collaborators be stripped of their rights as citizens, imprisoned, or shot. The party's motives were political as well as moral; the greater the number of former officials removed from office, the greater the number of Communist sympathizers who might replace them. Major opposition to this intransigence came from Georges Bidault, François Mauriac, and other Catholic intellectuals, motivated by Christian compassion and a fear of Communism akin to General de Gaulle's. Between the two extremes, calling for both justice and understanding, were *Combat* and Camus.

The fall and winter of 1944 witnessed a polemical duel between Camus and Mauriac in the columns of *Combat* and the conservative daily *Le Figaro*. Mauriac—christened "Saint Francis of the Assizes" by his opponents for what they considered an excessive tolerance—initiated the exchange in mid-October by suggesting that a spirit of charity would more become the Resistance in its hour of triumph than the strict pursuit of justice. In an article entitled "Honorable Errors," he argued that it was as important to consider sympathetically men's motives as to pass judgment on their actions. He urged that Frenchmen whose sense of loyalty had led them to side with Pétain not be placed in the same category as those who had knowingly betrayed France. "All things considered," he wrote, "my heart takes the side of the man who is misled, mistaken, and duped by his virtues."[39]

Though he did not deny the collaborationists' guilt, Mauriac stressed the need for pardon in the interests of national unity. This reasoning ran counter to that of Sartre and the editors of *Les Lettres Françaises*, who maintained that a person's acts provided the sole basis for moral judgment, irrespective of his motives. In making such broad allowance for human weakness, Mauriac seemed intent on undermining the ideal of strict moral accountability by which the Resistance justified its rejection of "extenuating circumstances" as a defense for collaborationist activities. His Christian faith led him to assume as given men's inability to resist evil; his intellectual opponents were less pessimistic, hence more exigent.

Mauriac's desire for "appeasement at any price," Camus insisted, could only lead to diminished respect for the humanist values in whose name the Resistance had sacrificed so much. Some Frenchmen had dared to oppose the invader and Pétain's puppet government; their resolute stand demonstrated for Camus that such courage could have been expected from all. The automatic, unexamined obedience with which men like Pucheu had carried out Vichy policies he found inexcusable. As early as May 1944, soon after Pucheu's execution, Camus had written in *Les Lettres Françaises* that neither Pucheu nor his fellow Vichy ministers grasped the human consequences of the laws they enacted. They did not possess "enough imagination *really* to see that [such laws] would be transformed into early mornings of agony for innocent Frenchmen led off to die." Insensitive to what Camus termed a "physical notion of justice," they could not measure the blood and suffering caused by the "abstract administrative system" they served so well. Lack of feeling was their major crime. Far from excusing them, it should ensure their condemnation. For "all France must know," Camus concluded, "that the time of abstraction is at an end."[40]

Camus realized that this course imposed painful choices. The "terrible law" of the Liberation period, he stated in *Combat*, "forces us to destroy a still living part of this country in order to save its soul." But were humanist values such as the worth of the individual compatible with the grim means that Camus proposed? To condemn a collaborator to death, it could be argued, was to display the same barbarity as the Vichy *milice* or the German Gestapo. In an article entitled "A Response to *Combat*," Mauriac demanded that Camus define the "terrible law" that justified such extremes. "Either I have misunderstood," he wrote, "or what I do understand is repellent."[41]

Camus answered that the general principle of justice was "proportion." Although far from defending all the actions taken to punish traitors, and while insisting that "we do not think it necessary to shoot our fellow citizens on street corners," he argued that "one cannot ignore the fact that there have been errors of clemency as well as of excess. Our duty is to denounce both simultaneously and to show the middle road that unites revolutionary force with the light of justice. M. Mauriac speaks only of the excesses of this revolution."[42] In effect, both Camus and Mauriac acknowledged the need for a "middle road" between disproportionate severity and undue leniency. Each, in his own way, upheld the principle of proportion. Yet each saw this principle threatened from a different quarter. Whereas Mauriac focused on holding popular vengeance within bounds, Camus threw his weight on the side of the avengers for fear that the guilty might otherwise go free.

Late in October the first trials in Paris began. Eight prominent journalists were among those heard and sentenced during the next three months. Of these cases, the one that aroused the most interest among the Parisian intellectuals was that of Robert Brasillach. During the 1930s, after graduating from the Ecole Normale, Brasillach had been one of the young intellectuals on the Right whose alarm at French decadence and desire for national renewal led them to embrace the "virtues of action" in the Fascist camp. As director of the collaborationist weekly *Je Suis Partout* from 1937 to 1943, he had proclaimed the need for France to make the Fascist spirit its own, and had attempted to purge the enemies of this "path toward France's redemption" through an especially odious campaign of denunciations. His defamatory articles attacked Jews, Socialists, Communists, republicans, and *résistants*. Hitler he admired. In 1944 he was brought before the court accused of "commerce with the enemy" — a capital crime.[43]

At his trial Brasillach never denied the acts alleged by the prosecution; he denied only that they had been wrong. Yet in his role as a defendant, stripped of his former influence and risking death by his outspokenness, Brasillach won a grudging admiration from the spectators. Beauvoir recalled that "the dignity with which he bore himself in this extreme situation demanded our respect at the moment when we would have most preferred to despise him. We desired the death of the editor of *Je Suis Partout*, not of this man steeling himself to die well." The account of the trial published in *Combat* similarly paid tribute to Brasillach's personal courage, a quality that held special meaning for the Resistance: "He did not tremble, he did not attempt to sway the jury with platitudes or with tears. He stated outright that he stood by what he had done."[44]

The contradictions between the character and the actions of the accused were difficult to reconcile. Which should have more weight? A letter from Mauriac was read in court by the defense, describing Brasillach as "one of the most brilliant minds of his generation." The prosecution, making indirect reference to Benda's *The Treason of the Intellectuals*, argued that Brasillach had misused his gifts in repeated acts of "intellectual betrayal." "How many young, unstable people did your articles goad into taking up arms against the Resistance?" asked the prosecuting lawyer.[45] The verdict of the court was seen as a dramatic test case, illuminating both the issues raised by the *épuration* and the special responsibilities of the intellectuals in time of war.

Brasillach's trial lasted one day. Late on the afternoon of January 19, 1945, he was judged guilty and sentenced to death. Unmoved, he declared that it was "an honor" to be condemned. The Communist editors of *L'Humanité* voiced their satisfaction. Just as predictably,

Mauriac made a personal plea for clemency to de Gaulle, who as head of the provisional government could exercise the right of pardon. But the reaction of the moderates was unexpected. Those who had called for "justice without vengeance" split over the severity of the verdict. Camus signed a petition for clemency, while Sartre, Beauvoir, and the aging André Gide refused to protest the sentence. As Beauvoir later wrote, her ties of loyalty to those who had perished in the Resistance outweighed all else: "It was to these friends, dead or dying, that I was bound. If I had lifted a finger in favor of Brasillach, I would have deserved that they spit in my face."[46]

Why was Camus willing to extend pardon? One reason can be found in his commitment to "proportion." In the context of other verdicts handed down during the same period, Brasillach's sentence was indeed difficult to justify. The journalist Henri Béraud received an identical sentence in December 1944 for offenses far less severe, while some collaborationists whose guilt exceeded Brasillach's escaped trial altogether. In an editorial written in early January 1945, Camus indicated a growing disillusionment with the possibility of achieving uniform justice in France:

> Now it is too late . . . But we do not say that without bitterness and sorrow. A country that does not succeed in its purge is on the way toward failing in its renovation. Nations have the face of their justice. Ours should have something else to show the world than this look of confusion. But clarity, severe and humane rectitude, cannot be learned. Without them, we are going to have mock consolations. One sees clearly that M. Mauriac is right. We are going to need charity.[47]

The spectacle of false denunciations motivated by private quarrels, the seeming caprice of condemnations and acquittals, and the impossibility of attaining verdicts acceptable to all led Camus reluctantly to distance himself from the *épuration*. His faith in his moral principles remained unshaken. But he began to doubt whether the "terrible law," which claimed Brasillach's life when the petition for clemency was refused, could bring those principles closer to fulfillment.

Camus also believed that the "physical notion of justice" was being compromised by the *épuration*. Magistrates and juries in the Liberation courts often appeared as unable to comprehend the conditions under which prisoners awaited trial or the privations suffered by their families as had collaborationists such as Pucheu. The Vélodrôme d'Hiver in Paris and the camp of Drancy on the city's outskirts, detention centers that had housed Jewish deportees during the war, now received a new population of suspected collaborators, who were exposed to the same cold and filth as their earlier victims. Benoist-Méchin and Rebatet, along with other members of the pro-German literary intelligentsia, remained in custody for nearly two years before being tried. Their books, together with Brasillach's, were blacklisted by the Conseil National des Ecrivains in the fall of 1944, just as the works of authors on the "Otto List" had been withheld from public sale during the Occupation. The Liberation authorities were not above imitating the methods of their predecessors. They pursued vengeance, not justice, and thus contributed to the inhumanity the Resistance had sworn to oppose.[48]

When Pétain and his former prime minister, Pierre Laval, were finally brought to trial a year after the Liberation, the proceedings seemed to justify Camus's worst fears. What should have been the climax of many months of expectation satisfied no one. Pétain was condemned to death by a thin majority of jurors, outraging those in Mauriac's camp, then had his sentence commuted to life imprisonment, outraging the Communists. Laval's trial was a disaster—hurried, vindictive, poorly supervised by Justice Mongibeaux, and dominated by the bitter wit and intelligence of the accused. Laval reminded the court and the prosecuting attorneys that they had supported Vichy with a fervor equal to his own; when he was convicted nonetheless, the verdict appeared dictated by malice rather than by reason. Defiant to the end, Laval attempted suicide a few hours before his scheduled execution, giving his death before the firing squad an aura of needless cruelty. The cathartic sense of good triumphant over evil that had marked the first weeks of the Liberation now lay far in the past.[49]

The judicial machinery upon which the Resistance had relied for a reassertion of due process and a decisive rejection of the "show trial" was increasingly an object of suspicion and disrespect. It was not just that the trials divided the Resistance itself or failed to demonstrate the guilt of collaborators. More troubling, Camus noted in August 1945, was that the purge undermined an "elementary concern for clarity and [moral] distinctions." In order to safeguard the values in which they believed, Resistance intellectuals found themselves obliged to censure the courts. "Perhaps," Camus admitted, "the one sure course at present is to do whatever is necessary to prevent . . . flagrant inequities from poisoning still further an atmosphere in which Frenchmen already find it hard to breathe." Those who remembered his early editorials calling for an exemplary show of justice could measure the bitter disappointment that dictated his words. "Our defeat," he concluded, "has been absolute."[50]

Beauvoir and the Ethics of Ambiguity

The demands of the Resistance for justice, democracy, economic reforms, and a responsible press could all be reduced to a single overwhelming desire: to bring French government and society closer to human needs. They aspired to the politics on a "human scale" of which Léon Blum had written during the war. When the first months of the Liberation brought one disappointment after another, the intellectuals responded by reasserting the primacy of those moral goals now in danger of being lost from sight. Camus wrote of the fundamental principle that gave meaning to the struggle waged since the early days of the Resistance: "If this period belongs to politics, politics is motivated by this simple and ardent wish, felt by the working majority of this nation: to see man restored to his place. We do not want politics without an ethic, because we know that this ethic alone justifies politics."[51]

At the core of the conviction that morality and politics were compatible lay a belief in human dignity, denied by Fascism and passionately reasserted by the Resistance. But in the course of 1945, this belief was challenged as survivors of German concentration camps, liberated by the advancing Allies, returned to France with tales of brutality so extreme that few at first would believe them. The systematic, organized sadism of the camps had been a terrible test of its victims' ability to preserve even a shred of *dignité humaine*. The Nazis had created the most severe "limit situation" of all.

One of the most vivid and compelling of the accounts of camp life that appeared after the war was David Rousset's *L'Univers concentrationnaire* (*The World of the Concentration Camps*), published in 1946. Rousset drew on his experience as a prisoner at Buchenwald to offer a "coherent picture and general interpretation" of what he had witnessed there. The camp life he described appeared at first to present the exact opposite of the generous, supportive moral order envisioned by the *résistants*. In this "universe" it was the prisoners themselves who regularly beat and tortured one another, gave and withheld extra rations under the watchful eyes of the SS. Solidarity among the inmates proved a hollow ideal when confronted with the petty intrigues, revenge, and hatred born of suffering and desperation. The camp was further splintered into national, political, and occupational groups of Byzantine complexity. This situation, Rousset noted, destroyed any common basis from which resistance might have emerged. "The existence of an aristocracy among the prisoners, enjoying powers and privileges, exercising authority, renders impossible any unified discontent or the formation of a homogeneous opposition. It is in essence . . . a marvelous instrument of corruption."[52]

Yet Rousset's final message was one of hope. Despite years of almost inconceivable moral and physical degradation, a few individuals held fast to their self-respect. These exceptional cases, the slim margin by which the Germans failed to gain total victory over their prisoners, sufficed to confirm Rousset's basic belief in man's capacity for courage and selflessness. Rousset elaborated these positive conclusions in the final scene of his mammoth novel *Les Jours de notre mort* (*The Days of Our Death*, 1947). He described the reactions of prisoners liberated by American troops and the significance of their triumphant survival: "Just as we were, so miserable and hideous, we nevertheless achieved a victory reaching beyond us for the whole community of mankind. We never gave up the struggle, we never renounced, we never blasphemed against life . . . We never believed in the final disaster of humanity."[53]

Human dignity and hope had thus been preserved under conditions far more brutal than those experienced by Sartre as a prisoner of war, conditions that call to mind instead the account offered by Solzhenitsyn three decades later in *The Gulag Archipelago*. The irreducible value in this perverted universe was not the political system that created it but the victims it sought to destroy. From the determination of at least some of those victims to survive in spirit as well as in body it was possible to derive an ethic based on man's nobility and on the primacy of the individual's needs over the demands of the state.

Sartre's contributions to defining this ethic, despite the importance moral questions assumed for him during the war, remained largely indirect and, as noted earlier, inconsistent. The first two volumes of *Roads to Freedom*, published in the fall of 1945, far from celebrating the nobler side of man's nature, seemed to one contemporary critic to reveal Sartre's fascination with "the abjectness of existence." His defense of the humanist values of existentialism in *L'Existentialisme est un humanisme* (*Existentialism and Humanism*, 1946) was too brief and sketchy a rebuttal to deal adequately with these suspicions, while his study of Baudelaire, published in the same year, was an individual portrait of "bad faith" that skirted more general issues by focusing on one man's "original choice."[54]

It was Sartre's companion, Beauvoir, who attempted to define more precisely an ethic of humanism, above all in *Pour une morale de l'ambiguïté* (*The Ethics of Ambiguity*), begun a year after the Liberation and published in installments in *Les Temps Modernes*. In this treatise she sought to reconcile firm ethical standards with the freedom of choice proposed by Sartre's existentialist doctrine, and at the same time to avoid the moral uncertainty that had characterized the recent *épuration*. She stated the problem in the opening pages: "But if man is free to define by himself the conditions of a valid life as he sees it, can he not choose anything, and act in any way? Dostoevsky affirmed: 'If God does not exist, all is permitted.'"[55]

This dilemma Beauvoir proposed to resolve through a "coherent humanism." She was determined to avoid an ethic that sought guidance and sanctions in an authority beyond the moral agent himself. Such an attempt to discover an alternative to Christian morality had been undertaken in the early years of the Third Republic by Emile Durkheim, who had assigned to society the transcendent role as repository of moral values hitherto assigned to God and the priesthood. "Society alone," Durkheim argued, "can serve as the end of moral activity."[56] The Third Republic did its best to buttress this view with a Rousseau-like appeal to a "state religion" with nationalistic overtones. But by the 1930s both the state and society had ceased to command respect. The Occupation further discredited the notion that citizens should be compelled into submission by a secular authority. Refusal to obey despotic power was the first duty of every *résistant*. Yet at the same time, a purely solipsistic view of the individual as an end in himself was rejected by the Resistance in the interests of group solidarity. How were the notions of liberty and morality to be reconciled?

Beauvoir proceeded by indirection. She devoted the first half of her work to negative definitions of moral conduct. By presenting two examples of the misuse of liberty, drawn from her reading of Hegel, she was able to indicate what her conception of humanist morality was *not*. The first example was the "adventurer"; the other she termed the "passionate man." The adventurer, reminiscent of the isolated heroes in Malraux's early fiction, "loves action for the sake of action; he finds his delight in displaying to the world a liberty that is oblivious to the ends it serves."[57] Like Perken in *The Royal Way*, he accepted risks for the sport of overcoming them rather than for the sake of the goal to which his exertions might lead. The passionate man was, like the Marquis de Sade, a prisoner of his own desires, isolated in an inner world of pure subjectivity. Both types of conduct corrupted liberty into selfishness by encouraging every person to place supreme value on his individual fate. Both failed to recognize the claim of other men to the same freedom the individual demanded for himself.

Seen in proper perspective, one man's freedom depended on the freedom of all. "To wish freedom for oneself," Beauvoir maintained, "is also to wish for others to be free." A reciprocal duty to respect others as they must respect you supplanted the notion of a common obeisance to secular or religious authority. Such a view, though rooted in the experiences of the recent struggle against Fascism, bore a striking similarity to Kant's teachings in *Foundations of the Metaphysics of Morals* (1785). For both Kant and Beauvoir, the autonomy of the individual as *selbstgesetzgebend*—the author of his own morality—was balanced by the universal implications of each moral act. Each individual was, as Kant had said, an end, not a means.[58] Such a moral system, which refused to sacrifice the individual for the sake of abstract values not grounded in his welfare, was now revealed by Beauvoir to be the "coherent humanism" she had promised.

Beauvoir saw her ethical stance as a restatement of individualism, insofar as "it accords an absolute value to the individual and grants the power of justifying his existence to him alone." Like Sartre, she argued that liberty both resided in each human being and set limits to his actions. "Man is free," she wrote in conclusion to *The Ethics of Ambiguity*, "but he finds his rule of conduct in his freedom itself." Where Sartre in his formal philosophy had left the interpretation of this "rule of conduct" open and unresolved, however, Beauvoir offered a further qualification: "We can take as our starting point that the welfare of an individual or of a group of individuals deserves to be considered the absolute goal of our action; but we are not empowered to decide a priori in what this welfare consists." The "ambiguity" of her ethic resulted from the need constantly to reassess the appropriateness of the means chosen for pursuing this "absolute goal." Consistent with the distrust of abstract values displayed by so many of her generation, Beauvoir insisted that no moral system could offer the certainty that one type of conduct was invariably right or wrong. She rejected a formalist approach to ethics in which fixed rules freed the individual from the responsibility of choice. Should a friend, she asked, intervene to prevent the suicide of another? It was impossible to give a general answer. Only the context in which the aid was extended could determine whether it advanced or hindered the welfare of the individual concerned. "The first point is always to consider what true human interests invest the abstract form that one proposes as the goal of action. The politician always places ideas in the foreground: Nation, Empire, Union, the Economy, and so on. But none of these has a value in itself. It has one only to the extent that it deals with concrete individuals."[59]

This argument reflected a general tendency among Resistance intellectuals to reduce political questions to the level of personal conduct. In an effort to avoid abstract concepts such as "party" or "national interest," both Beauvoir and Camus clung to a vision of politics that spoke to the concerns of the governed. As Camus had written to a young admirer during the war, "It seems to me that no truth is valid which is not reached through human beings." From this perspective, the distinction between public and private spheres of action became blurred. Moral principles appropriate to relations among individuals—honesty, sincerity, respect for differing needs and wishes—came to be seen as applicable to decisions and behavior at all levels of government. "Man is one, the world he inhabits is one," Beauvoir asserted. "To reconcile morality and politics is thus to reconcile man with himself."[60]

The Resistance groups that had sprung up under the Occupation had embodied this ideal. They provided a focus for common action while at the same time respecting the freedom of their members. They were small, flexible, decentralized, and in direct contact with the populace. Above all, their scale and purpose remained bounded by the wishes of those they served. As political associations, such groups possessed neither the coercive power nor the bureaucratic conservatism of the traditional state. They created "spaces of freedom," in Hannah Arendt's phrase, which withstood the assaults of an oppressive regime and sheltered the individual without imposing a tyranny of their own.[61]

The results of the repeated efforts to apply this style of politics to the problems of postwar France revealed its fragility and limitations. The CNR's conflict with de Gaulle, the shortcomings of the nationalization program, and the failure of the *épuration* all demonstrated that an ethic of human ends was an inadequate guide for assessing the role of governmental institutions in peacetime. The power of the Resistance, never absolute in any case, now was delegated to authorities who thought in terms of priorities and constraints for which the intellectuals had little respect or understanding. Yet intellectuals like Beauvoir continued to argue as if the link between morality and politics were still direct, not mediated through a bureaucracy or the courts. To relegate these collective institutions to the realm of the "abstract," as Beauvoir appeared to do, denied their reality at a time when France's centralized administration affected the lives of all. To neglect the context in which individualist values must be applied meant adopting a view as abstract as those she and Camus had condemned.

A curious event in the summer of 1945 underscored the difficulty of finding an appropriate political vehicle for Resistance ideals. The Etats Généraux de la Renaissance Française, composed of more than two thousand delegates from the local liberation committees created by the CNR, met in Paris to consider both the "sum total of French desires" in matters of national policy and the "distrust, if not hostility" of the government toward the Resistance. The name chosen for the assembly, the use of *cahiers de la Résistance* to express the grievances under review, and the timing of the final session to coincide with

Bastille Day were all intended to evoke the potent tradition of 1789. The Resistance was attempting, earnestly though somewhat artificially, to restore its fading prestige by laying claim to the symbols of the French Revolution.[62]

The need to inject new hope and purpose into national life was the central message of the meeting's president, Louis Saillant: "We seek to create first the moral climate, then the elements of renewal that will permit France to surpass itself, leaving behind its apathy, indolence, and indifference." But as various motions were presented and debated, it became clear that the delegates were far from united on the question of how this could best be done. Communists clashed with non-Communists, each group accusing the other of wishing to turn the meeting to its own advantage. The convocation represented a gesture toward the principle of direct democracy, but at the same time demonstrated that the true locus of power within the Resistance had shifted to the political parties. The session's final resolutions did little to justify Saillant's trust in the moral leadership of the Resistance. In mid-July the Etats Généraux disbanded; they were not reconvened.[63]

In September 1945 Camus withdrew from active participation on the staff of *Combat*. His decision symbolized the impasse reached by the Resistance intellectuals. A year had passed since the liberation of Paris, and the moral fervor of those first days of freedom had largely spent itself. Vercors expressed apprehension on overhearing Frenchmen "no longer talking as they had of their revolt and their hopes, but already and exclusively of their little problems and their little maneuvers and their little malices." Camus's own faith that the "revolution" could be won through a continuing struggle had been deeply shaken. With the clear recognition that his vision of a generous humanism was not shared by all came a decision to devote himself to the defense of the individual in a modest way and without hope of permanent victory. It was fully in keeping with this new spirit of resignation that the character whom Camus designated as the "real hero" of the novel to which he now returned—*La Peste* (*The Plague*)—was a minor functionary who "asked only to make himself useful in small tasks."[64]

This shift in the public mood, as well as the growing power of the parties he himself had done so much to revive, also contributed to General de Gaulle's departure from the public scene. On January 21, 1946, he resigned from the government over which he had presided since the Liberation, having resolved to "leave the helm in silence, without laying blame on anyone, publicly or privately, without accepting any post, reward, or pension, and without announcing what I would do next."[65] His successor, the Socialist Félix Gouin, was a veteran politician of the Third Republic, a symbol of continuity rather than of change. The old French state—distant, ponderous, lacking in both empathy and imagination—was gathering strength even before the new republic was officially proclaimed.

Thus the Resistance and de Gaulle, wartime allies and postwar rivals, found themselves in the political wilderness a scant eighteen months after the Liberation. The reforms that both had pledged to introduce were in doubt; the belief that they reflected the popular will could no longer be sustained. Neither moral principles nor the appeal to the "Resistance spirit" sufficed to make the "revolution" a reality. Jean Bloch-Michel, a contributing editor of *Combat*, later recalled the illusory nature of the intellectuals' hopes:

> Following the war, many of us believed that new social forms would be born. Something had to emerge from such an upheaval. It seemed to us that we had acquired a certain wisdom that could favorably replace the systems and doctrines we felt had failed . . . In truth, we had believed that the conduct of public affairs required more good faith than experience, more imagination than systematic thinking, and more common sense than ruse. We were childish.[66]

3
The Limits
of Choice
1946-1949

*The future is only a likelihood; but it
is not like an empty space in which we
can construct whatever we please. It
takes shape before our eyes like the end
of a day already begun, and this shape
is our own.*
Maurice Merleau-Ponty, 1947

      The late 1940s were a time of indecision and discord among the French. De Gaulle's departure, though greeted with relief in some quarters, made it painfully apparent that no leader of comparable authority was available to replace him. Instead the Fourth Republic came increasingly to resemble the Third, presided over by a National Assembly that drifted while its members debated who should take the helm. "Something new has died and something old has taken its place—for how long?" wrote Jean-Marie Domenach somberly in *Esprit*.[1] France's future remained in doubt. The fragile unity of the Resistance, already severely strained during the Liberation period, disintegrated further amid mutual accusations of opportunism and betrayal.

As party strife and labor unrest grew at home, France found itself caught up in the international tensions of the Cold War. Rivalry between Washington and Moscow exacerbated the rifts in French domestic politics and provoked speculation that an armed clash between West and East might transform Europe into a battlefield once again. Camus noted in November 1946 that a "widespread fear of war" gripped his countrymen. It was a fear nourished by heightened awareness of France's vulnerability, by memories of the recent Occupation, and by visions of an atomic armageddon more dreadful than Hiroshima or Nagasaki. But though pervasive, it remained curiously diffuse. "We are living through a very strange era," Vercors observed in 1947. "It is difficult, disquieting . . . We are neither at war nor at peace."[2]

Beset by shifting and shadowy perils, many Frenchmen retreated into fatalism. How could they act if their country was both deeply divided and powerless to influence the Soviet and American decisions on which its security depended? The intellectuals, while no less apprehensive, preferred to stress the need for moral courage and renewed will in a time of adversity. The Resistance had drawn its strength in large part from such a stubborn capacity for hope. It had set faith against the realities of defeat and refused the counsels of prudence or compromise. Yet the setbacks experienced since the Resistance victory in the autumn of 1944 suggested that certain compromises, however distasteful, could no longer be avoided. As Emmanuel Mounier observed: "If every act plunges us into a world of given facts . . . there can be no purity of action. All situations are impure, mixed, ambiguous, and hence divisive. To wish [both] to act and to abandon none of one's principles is a contradiction in terms."[3]

It remained to be seen whether a criterion could be found for deciding which compromise to adopt. How could one choose among imperfect alternatives? "We are not dreamers," Vercors wrote in 1946. "We know very well that politics is not a business for saints and poets . . . The question that remains is the following: *where is the limit to what we can tolerate?*"[4]

One answer, it seemed, lay in establishing the true limits of choice, in distinguishing between imaginary and actual dangers. Truth and sincerity need not be sacrificed while evaluating the present. Maurice Merleau-Ponty insisted: "French intellectuals are not obligated to feed an atmosphere of sanctimony and terror . . . but should instead take stock of this century and the ambiguities that it offers us. If these ambiguities . . . can be understood thanks to information and facts, then perhaps our public life will cease to be haunted by these phantoms, perhaps it will regain some reality."[5] Thus the problem of choice was construed as a problem of perception. Given accurate and dispassionate analysis, Frenchmen might still reassert control over issues that touched their lives. Yet such control, as Merleau-Ponty acknowledged, remained tenuous at best: "All things considered, nothing is sure . . . Never have men more fully appreciated the fact that the course of events is a tortuous one."[6]

These uncertainties and contradictions suffused the intellectuals' debate during the final years of the decade. The conflict between ends and means, not surprisingly, became the subject of extended commentary.[7] The need to justify their political choices, both to themselves and to others, led the intellectuals to address a further problem: that

of history and the shape of things to come. The discussions of the late
1940s abounded in references to "history" (often capitalized),
understood both as a set of constraints inherited from the past and as
a pattern of events projected into the future. History, in this double
sense, justified a great deal. It accounted for what was intractable and
impervious to change in Mounier's "world of given facts," providing
grounds for a refusal to intervene in certain situations. At the same
time, it permitted some to argue that what might appear mistaken or
wrong in the present would prove wise and desirable when viewed in a
longer perspective. The concept of action was redefined to accom-
modate deferred expectations and tactical retreats. To act in the present was no longer to take a moral stand for its own sake, but also to
wager on the unknown and the unforeseen.

The intellectuals' fundamental goal remained to preserve what
could be salvaged from the aims of the Resistance. The test that lay
before them, however, was to prove in many ways more challenging
than the trials undergone during the recent Occupation. As they en-
deavored to adjust their strategy to the postwar political climate, the
résistants were forced to re-examine many of the beliefs inherited from
the underground. Their faith in the power of spirit to reshape society
became increasingly difficult to sustain. Even Sartre felt obliged to
acknowledge the limits to his freedom. "To be free," he observed in
1946, "is not to do what one wants, but to want to do what one can."[8]

The "Existentialist Offensive"

The autumn and winter of 1945 marked the birth of existentialism
as a major intellectual phenomenon in France. Within the space of a
few months, what had been a philosophy largely unknown to the public, associated in university circles with prewar German thought,
achieved broad notoriety and a specifically French connotation. The
person most responsible for both these developments was Jean-Paul
Sartre. For it was primarily as an existentialist that Sartre became
known in France and throughout Europe during the late 1940s—the
object of controversy and adulation that together gained him sudden
prominence as the leading intellectual figure of his generation. The
"existentialist offensive," Simone de Beauvoir recalled, brought Sartre
an "idiotic glory," and made him "famous and scandalous at the same
time."[9]

Sartre did not coin the term "existentialism," nor did he willingly
adopt it. "The word has acquired such broad implications these days,"

he complained in the fall of 1945, "that it no longer means anything at all." To clarify his basic message and hasten its understanding, he published a stream of plays, novels, essays, articles, and interviews whose diversity was as remarkable as their sheer abundance.[10] Sartre's decision to treat philosophical and moral themes through the medium of literature reflected his conviction that existentialism sought its truth in the "concrete." Defending his philosophy before a packed audience at the Club Maintenant in October 1945, he explained that existentialism "defines man through action." For "man is nothing other than what he makes of himself—that is the first principle." The central role that Sartre assigned to action in revealing man's character and values made the theater an especially appropriate vehicle for his exploration of existentialist themes. There the audience was confronted with men and women whose conflicts and decisions could be immediately grasped and directly shared. Between the years 1944 and 1948, Sartre wrote four plays and two movie scripts, each dealing with some aspect of the problem of moral choice. As he observed: "What the theater can show in the most compelling fashion is a character in the process of creating itself, the moment of choice, the free decision that engages an ethic and a whole life . . . For the decision to be profoundly human, for it to bring the whole of a man into play, one must show 'limit situations' on stage, that is to say, those whose alternatives include death."[11]

With its emphasis on freedom and responsibility, humanism and choice, postwar existentialism drew directly on the moral teachings of the intellectual Resistance. Sartre's works embodied this element of continuity. In fact the two novels whose publication signaled the start of the "existentialist offensive" of 1945 — *The Age of Reason* and *Le Sursis* (*The Reprieve*)—were both composed during the Occupation. The delay in their publication meant that what appeared to constitute the opening salvo of a new movement was in reality a final message from the intellectual underground. During the late 1940s, then, existentialism provided the doctrine through which the Resistance legacy exercised its strongest influence in France.[12]

It was also in October 1945 that the first issue of *Les Temps Modernes* appeared, with Sartre its editor in chief. His growing reputation and the high quality of the journal's articles soon made it a reference point for the Parisian intellectual community, much like *Les Lettres Françaises* during the Occupation and *Combat* during the first months of the Liberation. The original conception of the review provided another link with the war years; plans for *Les Temps Modernes* had taken shape amid the hopes and projects of the Resistance period, when, as Beauvoir recalled: "We listened to the BBC, we passed on news to one another, we discussed events. Together we were elated,

uneasy, we became indignant, we hated, we hoped . . . We would furnish an ideology for the postwar period . . . Camus, Merleau-Ponty,
Sartre, myself would issue a group manifesto. Sartre had decided to
found a review which we would all direct together." The manifesto
that introduced *Les Temps Modernes* to the reading public in 1945,
however, indirectly reflected the setbacks of the months following the
Liberation. There Sartre disclaimed any intention to "furnish an
ideology," insisting that "we have no political or social program." Instead he modestly characterized the review as an "organ of research"
dedicated to "the study of concrete problems of our time."[13]

This aim answered the need for analysis during a period of uncertainty and doubt. Yet on a more fundamental level, Sartre's basic objective remained intact, its realization merely deferred. "It is not just a
question of preparing an advance in the field of pure knowledge," he
continued. "The long-range goal we have set ourselves is a *liberation*."
For the staff of *Les Temps Modernes*, the prospects for "liberation"
were closely linked to the individual's understanding of himself and
the world around him. The purpose of analysis was to reveal unsus-
pected opportunities for action, to overcome the inner barriers of ig-
norance rather than the external barriers of political or economic constraint. The French sense of being trapped by postwar events seemed
to Sartre largely self-induced, just as the feelings of guilt exploited by
Vichy during the war had needlessly crippled the nation's will to resist.
What Sartre had stated in *The Flies* remained true; men were free, if
only they knew it. "We must *release* this free man," he argued, "by
widening his possibilities of choice." The cumulative effect of such informed decisions would be a transformation in the outer world as
well. As Sartre declared: "We take our stand on the side of those who
wish to change both the social condition of man and the conception he
has of himself."[14]

To fulfill this program, *Les Temps Modernes* cast its nets very wide
indeed. Politics, philosophy, literature, social commentary were for
its editors complementary modes of investigation, and were accorded
equal status. Each issue carried a half-dozen major articles or book
excerpts, in addition to shorter documentary pieces under the rubrics
"Lives," "Testimonies," and "Exposés." By integrating disparate views
of contemporary life, Sartre hoped that the review could furnish a
"synthetic anthropology" that would enable the reader to choose and
to act with full knowledge of his surroundings. The actual "synthesis"
of this material was left largely to the reader himself. Yet despite its
diverse content, the review managed to preserve a general coherence
of outlook that stemmed in large part from a reservoir of shared experience and close group feeling among the editors. Sartre, Beauvoir,

and Merleau-Ponty were joined by Raymond Aron, Michel Leiris, Albert Ollivier, and other friends who gathered informally and irregularly to offer criticism and support.[15]

Les Temps Modernes was controversial from the start. Some of the most spirited discussion it aroused during its first months of publication concerned the concept of "engagement." Literature, Sartre argued, could be justified only insofar as it performed a "social function."[16] But how could the writer's depiction of the contemporary world alter the conduct of his readers? If knowledge was gained by personal experience, as the intellectuals believed, then how could literature be assimilated into experience with a revelatory impact equal to that of the "concrete"? The problem in defining the writer's influence—a problem to which Sartre returned on several occasions in the pages of *Les Temps Modernes*—was that it remained necessarily indirect. Literature could affect consciousness; consciousness, in turn, affected action. The primary aim of *littérature engagée* was to initiate the first of these two steps. But in Sartre's view, that was enough to produce far-reaching consequences.

In *Being and Nothingness* Sartre had explored the way our perception of ourselves is modified by the way others see us. A man committing a reprehensible act—the example Sartre gives is a voyeur peering through a keyhole—suddenly experiences shame if he is discovered. Another person's perception reveals a new aspect of the voyeur's identity and causes him to respond in a different way than if his behavior had gone unobserved. This insight into what Sartre termed *l'être-pour-autrui* ("being-for-others") differs from the "inauthentic" definition of self exemplified by the café waiter in *Being and Nothingness*, who tries to conform to a pattern of behavior he has seen at his place of work. The voyeur is not the prisoner of a pre-existing model; he is forced to reinterpret the meaning of his action only *after* it occurs. "Being-for-others" thus discloses a truth not previously suspected. Rather than an invitation to inauthentic existence, it constitutes, in Sartre's words, "a constant element in my reality as a person."[17]

The concept of revelation through others was the basis for Sartre's interpretation of the role of literature after the war. The effect produced by a glance, he maintained, was strictly analogous to that produced by the written word. Words conveyed an image of the world as seen by others, and hence altered the reader's view of his surroundings and of himself. The term that Sartre chose to describe this process—*dévoilement* ("unveiling")—was a visual metaphor, suggesting the close relationship between the two modes of perception. Literature both forced the individual to confront bad faith within himself, making it possible for him to choose a more "authentic" existence, and revealed aspects of his environment of which he had been ignorant, permitting him to make choices with greater knowledge of his "situation."[18]

Sartre's exploration of the role of literature during the late 1940s culminated in his long essay "What Is Literature?," published serially in *Les Temps Modernes* in 1946-1947. There he discussed the writer's motivation, the nature of his audience, and the mechanism of *dévoilement*. "Anything that one calls by name is no longer completely the same; it has lost its innocence. If you give a name to the conduct of an individual, you reveal it to him. He sees himself. And since you simultaneously name it for everyone else, he knows that he is *seen* at the moment he *sees* himself . . . After that, how do you expect him to act as he did before?" This was why Sartre had been able to assert with such confidence that *Les Temps Modernes* aspired to "change both the social condition of man and the conception he has of himself." But though he firmly believed that "the written word can be an essential condition for action," Sartre was careful to insist that the link was neither direct nor automatic. "It is not true that the author *acts* on his readers," he noted. "He merely appeals to their freedom, and for his works to have some effect, the public must deal with them on its own."[19]

For Sartre, author and public were equals. *Littérature engagée* held up a mirror to its readers; it was for them to decide how they would respond to what they saw. But though Sartre professed to see the relationship of writer and reader as a "magnanimous pact," in which "each trusts the other, each counts on the other," his extended defense of these views suggested that a number of barriers hindered this cooperative enterprise.[20] He found himself in the uncomfortable position of defending in theory the public's right to construe a text freely, while suffering in practice the consequences of misconception. It was ironic that a literature dedicated to "unveiling" the world should evoke a response that illuminated the prejudices of its public instead. For many readers existentialism appeared not as a call to freedom but as a philosophy of gloom and despair, detailing the abject and noisome side of human life with a realism that was both fascinating and indecent. Sartre's play *Huis clos* (*No Exit*) was remembered for a single phrase: "Hell is other people." When he described a character in *The Age of Reason* as having "a faint odor of vomit on her lips," this breach of decorum provoked general censure. To conservatives, Sartre's theory of *littérature engagée* seemed an affront to the dignity of art. They believed, as had Charles Schweitzer (and the young Sartre), that the writer should worship at the shrine of beauty alone. "Those who want to understand you will understand," Sartre observed with resignation. "Those who do not will not."[21]

But though Sartre's antibourgeois sentiments led him to expect a certain degree of antagonism on the Right, he was totally unprepared for the hostility that met him from the Left. *Les Lettres Françaises* was especially harsh in its criticism. Under the new editorship of Louis Aragon, the most prominent French Communist writer, the review began a series of attacks in the fall of 1945 that spared neither Sartre's ideas nor his person. Existentialism was vilified as a "phenomenon of decay," Sartre dismissed as a "false prophet." Roger Garaudy inveighed against Sartre's failure to recognize the necessity of choosing sides in the class struggle and made light of his call for engagement: "Sartre and his followers have never felt themselves part of the masses, united with men and their history . . . It is up to Marxism to teach our intellectuals that there are better things to do than . . . to allow their desire for incarnation to evaporate in the smoke of metaphysics."[22] Jean Kanapa, a former student of Sartre's who had contributed to the inaugural issue of *Les Temps Modernes*, unleashed a tirade against existentialism that bordered on hysteria. For Kanapa, Sartre and his friends were "ideologues of the reactionary bourgeoisie," and hence could be dismissed as belonging to "the anguished, the torn, the abandoned . . . liars, enemies of the people, ENEMIES OF MAN."[23]

Sartre's increasing reputation among the young undoubtedly prompted some of the Communists' hostility. Three decades later he argued that the party's attitude had been "very simple—I had a following, and they wanted to recapture it." Yet at the time, a working alliance between the Parti Communiste Français (PCF) and the French intellectual Left appeared to him both possible and desirable. Each would benefit from the other's support; why should their common project not go forward in an atmosphere of warmth and mutual trust? The choice lay with the party. "After all," he wrote to the Communist readership of the review *Action*, "you are free as well. You, who are fighting for the revolution, just as we believe we are, can decide as well as we whether it will take place in good or bad faith."[24]

The intellectuals' relations with the Communist party were the subject of much analysis and self-scrutiny during the years after the Liberation. "The temptation of communism," Mounier wrote in an issue of *Esprit* devoted specifically to this problem, "has become our familiar spirit." With its impressive Resistance record, its revolutionary doctrine, and its claim to speak for the least privileged sectors of society, the PCF enjoyed more prestige than other political groups on the Left. It had emerged from the war as the embodiment of idealism united with efficient organization, a party whose vigor and discipline justified the Communist boast of being "different from the rest." No real political change, it seemed, could be accomplished without its help

and support. Intellectuals in the PCF, Edgar Morin recalled, belonged
to a party that "inspired respect, timidity, and deference" among their
non-Communist colleagues.[25] Those outside its ranks felt obliged to
explain their reluctance to join forces with so powerful an ally.

Sartre's eventual reply to the Communists' attacks showed that he
was eager for a substantive debate and that he, too, acknowledged the
party's potential as a revolutionary force in France. In June 1946 he
published the first of two articles in *Les Temps Modernes* entitled
"Materialism and Revolution," outlining at some length his basic ob-
jections to dialectical materialism in a tone of candor and moderation
that suggested an earnest desire to prove his good faith as a sympathetic unbeliever. Like Georges Sorel before him, he paid tribute to
the inspirational power of an idea whose philosophic premises remained open to question: "Materialism is undoubtedly *the sole myth*
that is suitable for revolutionary needs. The politician looks no further; the myth is useful, he adopts it. But, if his enterprise is to be a
long-term one, it is not a myth he needs but *truth*. It is the business of
the philosopher to bring together the truths inherent in materialism
and to construct bit by bit a philosophy that meets revolutionary needs
just as well as the myth."[26]

The burden of Sartre's critique was that the French Communist
party remained a prisoner of an outmoded conception of materialism.
The PCF had emerged from the Resistance as a political force of impressive vitality, but its Marxism was intellectually dated. In the late
1940s the party clung to the mechanistic view of history advanced by
Engels in his later years and adopted with more zeal than understanding by French Communists after World War I. This conception of a
world governed by the "objective" laws of matter, progressing inevitably from lower to higher forms of creation in nature and society,
Sartre now condemned as "vague and contradictory." "By what
miracle," he asked, "can the materialist, who reproaches the idealists
with creating a metaphysics when they reduce matter to spirit, escape
the same reproach when he reduces spirit to matter?"[27]

For Sartre, both materialism and idealism were flawed and unacceptable views. But materialism was especially distasteful to him
because it appeared to elevate the *en-soi* to the status of a moving
agent in human affairs, displacing and subordinating the *pour-soi*
altogether. If the materialists were right, man possessed not the
slightest claim to freedom. He was an object like any other. Yet this
belief possessed one powerful advantage when applied to the realm of
politics. By interpreting the dialectical movement of history in so
mechanical a fashion, French Communists eliminated any reason to
doubt the eventual success of the revolution. By disguising the true
nature of human freedom and the uncertainties of any common enter-

prise, they could mobilize the working class for action with impressive results. These tactics posed a direct challenge to Sartre's strategy of *dévoilement*. Was it possible that insight and choice might actually inhibit social change?

In the second part of his essay Sartre attempted to outline a "philosophy of the revolution" that would reconcile the conflicting demands of truth and political effectiveness: "What we need is a philosophical theory that shows that the reality of man is action, and that action in the world is identical with understanding the world as it is—in other words that action is an unveiling of reality and a modification of this reality at the same time." To illustrate his point, Sartre offered the example of a worker in a factory. The worker, he argued, grasped the concept of liberty through "the control of objects" used as tools on the job. This concrete experience formed the basis for the realization that he was at liberty to enlarge his tiny sphere of freedom, to "rise above a situation (*décoller d'une situation*)" in order to choose and pursue his own goals rather than those imposed by his employer.[28]

But here the defect in Sartre's argument became apparent. Why should an individual's isolated discovery lead to a common project? What guarantee was there that all workers would choose to exercise their freedom in the same way? By confining his analysis to the level of the individual's private motives, Sartre constructed a plausible model for the "unveiling" of freedom even under the most adverse circumstances, yet he was unable to show how it could be given organized political expression. His chief concern still lay with deriving values rather than with applying them.

For this reason Sartre viewed the act of joining the PCF with grave mistrust. The process by which men achieved new insight into their freedom, he believed, could not occur within a political party that locked its adherents into a rigid hierarchy and that preached a materialism expressly denying the importance of personal choice. Garaudy had reproached Sartre for remaining aloof from the masses; Sartre now accused Garaudy of seeking a mindless security in the ranks of the Communists. The party member, Sartre asserted, entered a world where there were "no risks, no worries, everything is sure, the results are guaranteed." This charge recalled Sartre's earlier attack on Drieu la Rochelle and other collaborationists. He was convinced that, like Drieu, the Communist intellectuals desired a refuge from responsibility and preferred the party's discipline to the dangers of achieving liberty unaided.[29]

The true revolutionary, Sartre maintained, "in no way demands that his path be traced in advance; on the contrary, he wants to mark it out himself." Here again, as in his discussion of authentic conduct in

Being and Nothingness, Sartre's sympathies lay with the creative individual, the explorer who refused to be content with existing maps of knowledge. When Sartre argued that "the reality of man is action," he saw this action as simple, private, and direct, reflecting the desires of the actor rather than the dictates of a group. His was still the heroic ideal of the Resistance, which invested men and women with the power to invent their future. Each person, he believed, would contribute to the discovery of a "concrete truth, desired, created, maintained, conquered in the midst of social struggles by those working for the liberation of man."[30]

Merleau-Ponty and Marxist Humanism

Others within the circle of *Les Temps Modernes* questioned Sartre's wisdom in equating revolution with the liberation of the individual. Sartre's friend and fellow editor Merleau-Ponty chided him for treating liberty "outside of any compromise with things." A defense of individual freedom that ignored the social and historical context in which it must be achieved appeared to Merleau-Ponty both evasive and simplistic. Like Sartre, Merleau-Ponty was anxious to restore to Marxism its genuine power of analysis by rescuing it from the neo-positivistic confines of Communist orthodoxy. At the same time, he understood and respected the party's tactical concerns. As the polemics exchanged between the PCF and the non-Communist Left grew more heated during the mid-1940s, it fell to Merleau-Ponty, who by Sartre's own admission was "better oriented in the ambiguous world of politics," to guide *Les Temps Modernes* through the reefs and shallows of French ideological debate and to propose a more pragmatic response to revolutionary practice.[31]

It was Merleau-Ponty's concern with history that most clearly distinguished his thought from Sartre's—a somber view of forces too great to ignore, too complex to control. In the article he contributed to the first issue of *Les Temps Modernes* he described the French loss of innocence that accompanied World War II as a sudden awakening to the power and brutality of historical change. Prior to 1939, he observed, "we had secretly resolved not to recognize violence and misfortune as elements of history." But with the war and the Occupation, it became evident that "we are in the world, enmeshed with it, compromised with it." Individuals were compelled to recognize how vulnerable their plans and desires remained to disruption by events, how easily their acts assumed a different meaning in defeat. "In short," Merleau-Ponty wrote, "we have made the acquaintance of history."[32]

Though he agreed with Sartre on the necessity for engagement in the present, Merleau-Ponty also insisted that the mode of action must evolve with the times. Nothing could be more dangerous than to believe in permanent solutions patterned after a successful response to past events. For this reason, the Resistance, despite the importance of the values for which it stood, possessed little enduring value as a political experiment. At the conclusion of his article, Merleau-Ponty argued that the style of initiative to which the intellectuals had become accustomed in the wartime underground was no longer appropriate to the postwar era. "We have returned to the time of *institutions*," he noted, "when the distance between laws and those to whom they apply reappears." Whereas the Resistance had offered the "rare phenomenon of a historical action that does not cease to be personal," the present allowed far less scope for the politics of conscience.[33]

The conviction that men and women must continually take new bearings on the world around them and adjust to changing norms was implicit in Merleau-Ponty's previous work as an academic philosopher. The two major studies that he completed during the war years— *La Structure du comportement* (*The Structure of Behavior*, 1942) and *La Phénoménologie de la perception* (*Phenomenology of Perception*, 1945)—focused on how the individual experienced and made sense of his environment. As students at the Ecole Normale, both he and Sartre had been fascinated by human perception. This problem oriented their research over the next two decades, though in different directions. Sartre's *Being and Nothingness* presented a vision of the world sharply divided between *en-soi* and *pour-soi*, between impenetrable objects and a sovereign, self-creating consciousness. Merleau-Ponty refused to acknowledge such a gulf. Observer and observed, rather than relating to one another from a distance, were for him mutually and closely bound. The distinction between Sartre's approach and Merleau-Ponty's, one might say, was analogous to that between an observer looking into a fishbowl from the outside, and an observer who found himself in the fishbowl with the fish. Criticizing Sartre's philosophy for being "too antithetical," Merleau-Ponty declined to divorce the individual from the "knot of relationships" in which human values were defined and expressed.[34]

Such a perspective might seem to deny man's freedom to choose, and instead to encourage the determinism against which Sartre had so often warned. Yet for Merleau-Ponty the interplay between actor and environment was in no way predetermined. The present was characterized by the "meeting and reciprocal action" of an infinite number of elements, no one of which could be isolated as dominant or decisive.

"Every enterprise," Merleau-Ponty insisted, "possesses some element of adventure, never being guaranteed by some *absolutely* rational structure of existence." Far earlier than Sartre, he realized that "every engagement is ambiguous, because it means the affirmation and restriction of liberty at the same time."[35]

Hence it was not surprising that Merleau-Ponty sought a philosophical doctrine that would illuminate the tension between the given and the unknown, that would link freedom and constraint within a single framework. His search led him to Marx. The Marxist synthesis, "midway between idealism and metaphysical materialism," appeared to him to incorporate the existentialists' concern with liberty and choice, while correcting their tendency to view the individual in isolation.[36] Merleau-Ponty's first encounter with Marxism occurred during the 1930s, at a time when the recent discovery and publication of Marx's *Paris Manuscripts* from 1844 encouraged a fresh evaluation of his work. Rather than accepting the official Communist view, which stressed the "scientific" nature of Marxist doctrine reduced to impersonal economic laws, it was now possible to show that a more complex and less dogmatic outlook pervaded his early writings. There Marx outlined a "practical humanism" that laid principal stress on man's struggle for fulfillment—the "true recovery of human nature through and for mankind."[37]

The war and the Occupation created a climate in which Marxist thought could be sympathetically reappraised and assimilated. The moral concerns that guided the French underground in its fight against the invader also dictated the perspective from which Resistance intellectuals interpreted Marx's message. It was not the economic but the ethical implications of Marxism that absorbed their attention—not his theory of knowledge, but his promise, stated in *Toward a Critique of Hegel's Philosophy of Right* (1844), to oppose "all those conditions in which man is an abased, enslaved, abandoned, contemptible being."[38] Under the peculiar circumstances of this "limit situation," the humanism of the Resistance and the social philosophy of Marx converged.

When the CNR program encountered serious and unforeseen opposition after the early months of the Liberation, it appeared in retrospect that the Resistance had been far too willing to ignore the uses of power and the machinery of the state, and far too inclined to entrust its hopes to spontaneous good will. Marx had not made the same mistake. His writings revealed a thoroughly unsentimental appreciation of interest politics in the modern world. Could the Resistance intellectuals learn from his example? Some argued that Marx might offer a solution to the conflict between ends and means that was both politically effective and ethically acceptable. His approach typified the virtues of the "concrete." As Merleau-Ponty observed: "The central idea of Marxism . . . is to replace the morality of platitudes with an effective morality . . . to destroy morality as a dream outside of things by giving it shape in the actual relations among men."[39]

Just as the French postwar press began to address Marxist theory, a political novel appeared that gave sharp focus to the issue of revolutionary ethics. Arthur Koestler's *Darkness at Noon,* published in France in late 1945, directly challenged the premise that Marxism offered an "effective morality." Written during the late 1930s under the impact of the Moscow Purge Trials, Koestler's novel attempted to explain why old Bolsheviks whose revolutionary sympathies were beyond doubt had agreed to plead guilty to charges of treason against the Soviet state. Koestler, a former Communist familiar with what he termed the "rules of the game," numbered several purge victims among his friends and acquaintances. Both the emotional drama of *Darkness at Noon* and its exploration of the clash between humanist ideals and revolutionary practice stirred a heated exchange within the French intellectual community. "Even if it does not address it as one should," Merleau-Ponty conceded, "the book raises the problem of our times."[40]

Darkness at Noon is the fictional biography of an old Bolshevik, N. S. Rubashov, on trial for his life after being falsely accused of treason by his party superiors. Exhausted by a long and brutal interrogation, Rubashov admits in court that he "acted as an agent of the counter-revolution," though he knows full well that the charge is baseless and his confession a lie. The logic that has led him to sacrifice others for the sake of the revolutionary cause now claims Rubashov himself as its victim. But during the final hours before his death Rubashov begins to question this logic. He realizes that his belief in "the precept that the end justifies the means" has made him the accomplice of the suffering and inhumanity that he had hoped to diminish by joining the revolution. "Was such an operation justified?" he asks himself. "Obviously it was, if one spoke in the abstract of 'mankind'; but, applied to 'man' in the singular . . . the real human being of bone and flesh and blood and skin, the principle led to absurdity."[41]

Darkness at Noon ended with an indictment of the Communist party's willingness to sacrifice individual rights for the sake of revolutionary ends. Those ends, in Koestler's view, remained "abstract"; "man in the singular" deserved higher respect. Though Merleau-Ponty acknowledged the power of Koestler's novel, he took issue with its political conclusions. In a series of articles in *Les Temps Modernes* during the fall and winter of 1946, later published together as *Humanisme et terreur: Essai sur le problème communiste* (*Humanism*

and Terror: An Essay on the Communist Problem), he presented a
lengthy critique of what he termed the book's "mediocre Marxism"
and went on to offer his own reading of Marxist thought. Where
Koestler had been content to restrict his focus to contemporary Communist practice, Merleau-Ponty insisted that this practice could be
judged only from the broad perspective provided by a true understanding of Marx and Lenin. Where *Darkness at Noon* had shown the
revolution in ruins, he tried to discover grounds for continued hope.[42]

Merleau-Ponty began by observing that all political regimes used
force. "Communism does not invent violence," he wrote. "It finds it
[already] established." To condemn the Communists for their recourse
to terror was a misdirected attack that merely obscured more fundamental issues of the debate: "The question for the moment is not to
decide whether one accepts or refuses violence, but whether the
violence with which one is involved is 'progressive' and tends toward
its own abolition, or whether it tends to perpetuate itself." Marxism,
Merleau-Ponty asserted, revealed a superior respect for ethics by
openly espousing force. Such a statement appeared paradoxical, if not
disingenuous. Yet, he argued, what was admitted could be abolished;
the violence of bourgeois society, by contrast, was camouflaged by appeals to "order" or to the economic laws of free enterprise. Liberals
could not alter a situation they refused to recognize. "In hiding
violence, one becomes accustomed to it and institutionalizes it. On the
other hand, if one calls it by name . . . there remains a chance that it
can be eliminated from history."[43]

Not only did Marxism display a commendable honesty in its choice
of political means; its ultimate aim, Merleau-Ponty wrote, was to
"seek a violence that is transcended in the direction of a humane
future." But this orientation toward the future made it difficult to pass
judgment on Marxist action in the present. The dilemma that confronted the revolutionary was not that of deciding between the claims
of conscience and the will of the party, as Koestler suggested, but of
accepting the ambiguity inherent in all human initiatives. The liberal
was blind to this dilemma, which had no place in his ethical system.
For him, violence (unless exercised by the state according to legal
norms) was condemned a priori. To be sure, there existed no guarantee that Marxist violence would prove justified and be "transcended"
in the long run. Without a readiness to act despite this uncertainty,
however, the aims of the revolution could never be fulfilled.[44]

The interplay between ends and means emerged with greater clarity
in Merleau-Ponty's discussion of the Moscow Trials. These were not
ordinary proceedings in a sense familiar to the West, he argued, but
revolutionary judgments. The real issue was not the intentions of the
accused but the "objective results" of their acts in delaying or

furthering the revolution. Strictly speaking, a purge victim like Nikolai Bukharin was not *yet* a traitor; still, the Soviet judges deemed that his opposition would eventually weaken the unity essential to the revolution, and convicted him on these grounds. Because Bukharin accepted their premise, he agreed to admit his guilt. Merleau-Ponty insisted that his behavior derived naturally from a revolutionary's view of history, since his activities in the present could be justified only in terms of their future outcome. "To be [a] revolutionary," he noted, "is to judge that which exists from the perspective of that which is not yet in existence, considering [the latter] more real than the real."[45]

Merleau-Ponty shrewdly reminded his readers that a similar reasoning underlay the purge trials in France. The defeat of 1940 had forced Frenchmen to weigh the probable course of history when deciding whether to support Pétain or de Gaulle. The postwar *épuration*, like the Moscow Trials, held individuals responsible for the decisions they made, regardless of their motives. Many had sided with Vichy out of patriotism. "And yet," he insisted, "we refuse to absolve them as if they had simply made a mistake." Here Merleau-Ponty returned to the question of the motives for collaboration that had so interested Sartre three years before. But instead of declaring the act of collaboration to be an inauthentic choice, prompted by a fear of liberty, he characteristically stressed the way its meaning was determined by the historical context. "Good or evil, honest or venal, courageous or cowardly," he wrote, "the collaborator is a traitor for the *résistant*, and thus a traitor historically or objectively, the day the Resistance becomes victorious."[46]

The Moscow Trials, however, differed from the French *épuration* in one major respect: they occurred before the verdict of history was apparent. Yet the Soviet judges condemned Bukharin and rejected his activities as harmful to the cause. Their authority for doing so, Merleau-Ponty asserted, derived from their responsibility toward the proletariat, whose needs and interests they were pledged to serve. It was the proletariat that provided a "limit and justification" for the violence exercised in its name. Without a belief in the special mission of the proletariat, destined to emancipate all mankind in the course of its own progress toward freedom, neither the verdicts in Moscow nor the policies of the PCF could be defended. Merleau-Ponty continued: "If the proletariat is the force on which revolutionary society rests, and if the proletariat is that 'universal class' that we have described in accordance with Marx, then the interests of this class carry human values in history, and the power of the proletariat is the power of mankind." As long as the Communist party remained faithful to its role as guide and spokesman of the working class, the actions it undertook were sanctioned by the logic of a grand historical plan: "The party and its leaders draw the masses toward their true liberation, which is to come, by sacrificing formal liberty when the occasion demands."[47]

But in bringing his argument back to the familiar terrain of ideals and their realization in practice, Merleau-Ponty ran the danger of applying a less rigorous standard to Marxist humanism than to its liberal counterpart. Why should Marxism benefit from suspended judgment when liberalism was condemned solely on the basis of present faults? Were Marxist promises to "transcend violence" in the direction of humanism—constantly repeated though as yet unredeemed—an adequate substitute for values incorporated into existing social relations? The ultimate test for Marxism, as for liberalism, must come in daily experience. This much Merleau-Ponty acknowledged. "One cannot defer indefinitely the moment when one must decide whether or not the proletarian philosophy of history is accepted by history itself," he wrote. "The time has come to fix a term for the historical test of Marxism."[48]

Merleau-Ponty declined to specify when that term should fall due. "The world in which we live," he noted, "is ambiguous in this respect." But his almost ritualistic invocations of history's ambiguity masked growing doubts. Toward the end of *Humanism and Terror* came a noticeable change in tone; in shifting from a critique of Koestler to an analysis of contemporary Communist practice, Merleau-Ponty became more somber and more tentative. Determined to state his disagreements with the Communists while situating his discussion within a Marxist framework, he could not avoid a certain equivocation. He protested the French Communists' reluctance to admit past errors yet urged that they remain true to their original goals. He conceded that "the Soviet Union is not the crowning chapter in the history of the proletariat as Marx defined it," and refused to accept Stalinism as the inevitable outcome of a Marxist movement. He demonstrated that Marxism had so far failed to achieve a "concrete" synthesis of values and action superior to those of its rivals, but he insisted that no better alternative was in sight. His strongest defense of Marxism was in fact a negative one: "As a critique of the world as it is and of other humanisms, [Marxism] remains valid . . . Even if it should prove incapable of shaping world history, it remains powerful enough to discredit other solutions."[49]

The concluding message of *Humanism and Terror* was a counsel of prudence. Merleau-Ponty urged that the intellectuals resist hasty condemnations of the Communist position and instead engage in a holding operation, defending a middle ground against both the traditional liberals and the orthodox Left: "Our role is perhaps not very important. But we cannot abandon it. Effective or not, it consists in clarifying the ideological situation, . . . calling Marxists back to their humanist inspiration, impressing on the democracies their fundamental hypocrisy, and maintaining intact the possibilities that history may still possess."[50] To argue that all was shrouded in ambiguity for the moment meant that the prospects for transforming terror into a humanist reality had not yet been foreclosed. Thus, ironically, the historical perspective that Merleau-Ponty had earlier championed as an advance toward understanding the "concrete" now proved a means for evading the difficulties of the present.

The Limits of Violence

Humanism and Terror appeared at a time when the open dialogue with Communists and liberals concerning contemporary politics was becoming hard to maintain. "Perhaps," Merleau-Ponty admitted, "this essay is already an anachronism." The events of 1947 confirmed this fear. The argument that one could still support the Communists without fully subscribing to their program—in particular that one could criticize the Soviet Union or the tenets of dialectical materialism without being an enemy of the PCF—lost its plausibility. As the Cold War intensified, Resistance intellectuals found themselves under increasing pressure to declare for one side or the other on the domestic front. "It appears that we must choose," Camus observed in April 1947. "Those who urge us on believe that nothing is more important. It has become an *idée fixe*."[51]

Despite the attempts made to enroll them as partisan fighters in the Cold War, many intellectuals preferred the risk of isolation to that of servility. They retreated toward a stance of principled nonalignment that signaled a new phase in the intellectual Resistance. Relations with the French Communist party reflected this change; where they had once been accommodating, the intellectuals now inclined toward mistrust. Even Merleau-Ponty, whose apologia for the use of terror had appeared to endorse Communist *Realpolitik*, revised his position and reasserted the need for critical independence during the "terrible year" of 1947.[52]

Merleau-Ponty's change of heart was precipitated by a change in the Communist party's political strategy. To be sure, there had been shifts in the party line since the Liberation. But on balance, the Communists had downplayed their revolutionary aspirations during this period, emphasizing instead the need for harmony and national reconstruction. Party chief Maurice Thorez had done his utmost to maintain peace on the labor front, and had advised workers that "one must know how to end a strike." The *parti des fusillés*, with members now serving as Vice Premier and Minister of Labor, had become a *parti du gouvernement* that took pride in its contributions to stable recovery. There seemed more to be gained from participation in the government than from opposition, especially since before 1947 the Soviets strongly supported moves toward accommodation with the West.[53]

But disillusion and unrest had been building up in France since the autumn of 1944. As inflation continued unchecked and worker discontent grew, the party found it difficult to stem demands for mass action. In April 1947 a strike at the recently nationalized Renault auto plant near Paris finally induced the PCF to change course. Unable to halt the strike, and fearful of being outflanked on the Left, the Communist ministers announced that they could no longer support the economic policies of the government. They reasoned that Paul Ramadier, the Socialist premier, would be unable to carry on in the face of Communist opposition and would therefore have to accept the strikers' demands or resign. In either case, the PCF could reaffirm its power and regain the allegiance of the Left. Much to their surprise, Ramadier ordered the offending ministers expelled instead. For the first time since the Liberation, the PCF found itself outside the governing coalition. Thorez optimistically predicted that "we will very soon rejoin the government in still greater numbers."[54] But the exclusion was to last far longer than he foresaw.

The wave of strikes that had begun the previous spring reached its height in November. Millions joined walkouts throughout France, clashing with police, troops, and nonstriking workers in a series of bloody skirmishes that continued for several weeks. Though the strikers' motives were primarily economic, the PCF seemed determined to use the strikes as a revolutionary challenge to the Fourth Republic. Merleau-Ponty was taken aback by this abrupt shift in tactics, which suggested that the party might be capable of sacrificing the interests of the proletariat for its own political ends. In an anonymous editorial in the December issue of *Les Temps Modernes*, he delivered a new warning: "Give the order for a general strike when one knows (having repeated it for three years) that an attempted revolution would be crushed, if need be through foreign intervention, and one exhausts the working class instead of defending it. Say 'we will be masters or nothing' when one is losing ground, and one has chosen the destruction of the working class as well as of the Communist party."[55] A cornerstone of the analysis that Merleau-Ponty had presented in *Humanism and Terror* was that the interests of the proletariat justified the party's exercise of terror on its behalf. If the interests of the workers and the party ceased to coincide, then, in Merleau-Ponty's eyes, the PCF forfeited all claim to support.

But militant anti-Communism carried dangers of its own. The crisis atmosphere of 1947 catalyzed a mass movement on the Right, led by the familiar figure of Charles de Gaulle. The General emerged from retirement to announce that he had decided to form a Rassemblement Populaire Français as an alternative to "separatists who exploit distress and arouse anger so that . . . they can establish their dictatorship." Gaullism exercised a considerable attraction for intellectuals who were more worried by the Communists' intentions than by the General's. André Malraux was its most prominent convert; Raymond Aron and Albert Ollivier also found Gaullism congenial and deserted the editorial board of *Les Temps Modernes* as a consequence. "In less than two years," Beauvoir observed, "the words 'Right' and 'Left' had taken on meaning again, and the Right was gaining ground."[56] An anti-Communist crusade, drawing its strength from fears of foreign domination and its recruits from among the former supporters of Vichy, seemed to the Left to be flirting with totalitarianism. *Esprit* noted that Gaullism raised "a very serious risk, if not of Fascism in the strict sense, then at least of a slide toward Fascism."[57]

It is against this increasing ideological polarization that one should view Camus's *The Plague*, published in June 1947. He had abandoned active work at *Combat* more than a year earlier, largely in order to finish this novel, which took final shape during the conflicts of the intervening months. The perfection of its taut, restrained style, the drama of its story of a Mediterranean city fighting an epidemic, the heroism of its central figure, Doctor Rieux, added to Camus's reputation as the literary conscience of postwar France. Many readers interpreted *The Plague* as an allegory of the Resistance. The author's prefatory quotation from Defoe—"it is as reasonable to depict one kind of imprisonment by means of another as to depict anything that really exists by means of something that does not"—suggested meanings beyond those of a simple adventure story. Some of the novel's major themes, such as the psychological effects of the quarantine imposed on the city, were drawn from Camus's own wartime experience as an exile far from his Algerian homeland. The wearying struggle to contain the epidemic could be seen as an expression of the long fight against Nazi tyranny. "The plague," Camus noted early in 1944, "will give a picture of those who, during this war, have had as their share reflection, silence, and moral suffering."[58]

Some critics, however, noted a shift in viewpoint as the narrative progressed. At the outset, Camus depicted the civilian population and the city government of Oran as far too passive when faced with the first signs of the plague. Their failure to recognize the danger until too late could be understood as a criticism of French appeasement of Hitler, an indictment of the selfish indifference to the fate of the nation that Marc Bloch had singled out as a major cause of the French defeat in 1940. Yet by the story's close Camus seemed to be arguing for the innocence of the very citizens he had previously condemned. The narrator, Doctor Rieux, describes his account as intended "to bear witness in favor of these victims of the plague, to leave at least a memory of the injustice and the violence they had suffered, and simply to tell what one learns in the midst of epidemics—that there are in human beings more things to admire than to despise."[59]

Nor was the symbol of the plague itself free from ambiguity. The Occupation had been the work of men, not of a mysterious, virulent bacillus. Opposing this human enemy raised ethical problems that were absent from a struggle against disease. The painful decisions to kill, to expose one's family to reprisals, to risk betrayal and torture—all these were suppressed in Camus's description of Oran gripped by the plague. Jean Pouillon, in a review published in *Les Temps Modernes*, protested that Camus had presented an idealized view of the Resistance, one that pitted "a virtuous and oppressed minority against an anonymous and depersonalized aggressor." Camus's choice of image made the suffering of the war years seem groundless and inexplicable, part of the human condition yet without human cause.[60]

One clue toward resolving these contradictory interpretations lies in the book's prolonged gestation. Camus began noting ideas for *The Plague* as early as 1939; his first draft was completed four years later, on the eve of his engagement in the Resistance. At that time the question of responsible action in the face of the Nazi threat lay uppermost in his mind. But when he finished his final revisions in 1947, Camus's attention had turned to the need to protest against totalitarianism in the postwar world. Viewed from this perspective, the citizens of Oran were the victims of an ideological struggle in which their own desires played little part. The widespread death caused by the plague could be equated with the mass murder committed by totalitarian regimes of all kinds. The very "anonymous and depersonalized" character of the plague, which Pouillon criticized as inadequate to convey the atmosphere of the Resistance, assumed a special relevance when applied to the faceless bureaucracy of the state.[61]

Commenting in 1948 on his adaptation of the novel for the stage, *L'Etat de siège* (*State of Siege*), Camus made his intentions explicit: "I wished to make a direct attack on the type of political society that has been organized, or is being organized, on the Right and on the Left, according to the authoritarian model. No spectator of good faith can doubt that this play takes the side of the individual . . . against the abstractions and the terror of the totalitarian state." Camus thus rejected both the need for France to join sides in the Cold War and the justification of inhuman means by revolutionary ends projected into the distant future. But in "taking the side of the individual," he did not mean to suggest that permanent victory was possible over the political afflictions of this world. At the conclusion of *The Plague* he depicted the survivors' feeling of triumph as naive; they had merely won a stay of execution. Doctor Rieux, he wrote, "knew what this joyful crowd did not . . . that the bacillus of the plague never dies or disappears." It would some day return, to be opposed as best men could in a continual cycle of struggle and remission. The most that could be done, Camus suggested, was to "take the side of the victims in order to limit the damage."[62]

Camus accepted the claim that men must practice as well as suffer violence; what he could not accept were attempts at justifying it. Although the Resistance had shown him that armed revolt was sometimes the sole recourse for victims of oppression, he nonetheless insisted that "one must limit violence, restrict it to certain sectors when it is inevitable, brake its terrifying effects." The principle according to which this could be done, he believed, was personal responsibility for the exercise of terror. As he wrote to Emmanuel d'Astier, "I will cease to despise those who call for murder when [they at last] hold the guns of the firing squad themselves."[63]

Camus's play *Les Justes* (*The Just*, 1949) dealt specifically with the limits of violence to which men might justifiably resort in their revolt against tyranny. There a group of Russian revolutionaries is shown preparing to assassinate the Grand Duke Sergei Alexandrovitch. The central character, Yanek Kaliayev, refuses to throw the bomb when he discovers that the Grand Duke is accompanied by his two children. He justifies this refusal by invoking the distinction between a *justicier* and an *assassin*, between a man who kills when he must and one who kills indiscriminately. When Kaliayev is apprehended and executed for a second, successful attempt on the Duke's life, his willingness to die for the act he has committed renders the assassination "just." "If I did not die," he observes while awaiting sentence, "then I would be a murderer."[64]

Willing to accept the same fate he meted out to the Grand Duke, and unwilling to inflict violence on the innocent, Kaliayev met Camus's conditions for responsible revolutionary practice. After sparing the Grand Duke's children, he declares: "It is for [the living] that I struggle and consent to die. For a distant goal of which I am uncertain, I will not strike the face of my brothers. I will not add to living injustice for the sake of a dead justice." Kaliayev, the "scrupulous killer," exemplified Camus's attempt to derive the limits of violence from man's own limits and imperfections. If man was, as Camus believed, the sole irreducible value in an amoral universe, then ethical conduct should be guided by rules that accorded with human nature. To reject measure and restraint in the hope of achieving a perfect society by force meant to abandon the natural sphere and to demand the inhuman. "Every revolution," Camus wrote four years before *The Just*, "should take account of the limited character of human experience, allow discussion, accept the approximate . . . The only revolution of human proportions should consist in a conversion to the relative."[65]

Camus's ethics of revolution were an attempt to generalize the Resistance experience as a continuing and permanent condition. He no longer saw this continuity in the fulfillment of ideals of justice or freedom, as he had at the Liberation, but in struggle itself. Revolution as a "conversion to the relative" was to be transformed into the concept of "revolt" that underlay Camus's long philosophical essay *L'Homme révolté* (*The Rebel*, 1951), in which Kaliayev again appears as a hero who "triumphs over nihilism" and at the same time "refuses to be God." A revolt that respected freedom and the conditional character of any human enterprise, that refused to lose sight of the means employed to gain uncertain ends, was for Camus the only political course that remained faithful to those it claimed to serve.[66]

In the bitter exchange over *The Rebel* that terminated their "difficult friendship" in 1952, Sartre reproached Camus with having "rejected history." It would be more accurate to say that Camus deeply distrusted the role that *l'Histoire* played for the French intellectual Left. Both he and Merleau-Ponty acknowledged that the present was ambiguous and offered few guides to conduct. But whereas Merleau-Ponty felt that this ambiguity encouraged risk, Camus insisted that it should enforce caution. The complex calculations of the revolutionary, who proposed to purchase a distant salvation at the price of blood shed in the present, appeared to Camus the most dangerous of all "abstractions." History possessed no inner logic upon which such calculations could be grounded; it was neither rational nor just.[67]

Rather than viewing history as leading to a slow but perceptible amelioration of man's condition, Camus adopted a static conception of history as a perpetual struggle against further erosion of man's tenuous claim to happiness. In diminishing the hopes that could be vested in history, however, Camus made it possible for each person to judge his own actions. If history was dethroned, then man bore a moral responsibility for the events in this world, and a new dignity as well.

The Resistance Disbands

The late 1940s saw a final attempt by some Resistance intellectuals to recapture the spirit of the war years and to form a political alliance with other groups in society. One of the key figures in this initiative was Sartre, whose optimism concerning the possibility of "creative" solutions to contemporary problems remained undiminished. His analysis of French politics following the 1947 strikes hinged on the belief that many citizens felt disenchanted with both the sectarian PCF and the conservative parliamentary majority. If the ideological forces in France were pulling toward both extremes of the political spectrum, the center Left remained vacant and invited capture. As Beauvoir noted: "Sartre thought that between a Communist party that took its cues from the USSR and a Socialist party that was *embourgeoisé*, there was a role to play."[68]

In February 1948 Sartre found a way to give his ideas practical shape. David Rousset, Gérard Rosenthal, and a small band of intellectual colleagues approached him with the proposal to join the Rassemblement Démocratique et Révolutionnaire (RDR). Sartre accepted. As with his previous foray into political activism, the wartime group Socialisme et Liberté, this movement's name suggested the ideological synthesis it was intended to achieve. Sartre's fondness for trying to conciliate opposite concepts would clearly receive support there. In some notes written for his personal use, he outlined the significance of the Rassemblement for his own thinking: "The RDR for me: (1) Middle classes and proletariat (I do not understand why the non-Communist proletariat should choose the bourgeois [parties]. It has another structure). (2) Europe. Neither America nor the USSR, but the intermediary between the two (thus a bit of both). (3) Democratic liberties and material liberties. Basically, I would like to resolve the conflict without going beyond (*dépasser*) my situation."[69]

It was not just the growing tensions of the Cold War, but also a new willingness to participate in mass politics, that prompted Sartre to join the RDR steering committee. After the collapse of Socialisme et Liberté in 1941, he had turned to literature as a means of encouraging social change. By the beginning of 1948, however, the intellectuals' attempts to influence events through literature seemed to him a failure. His works had been misinterpreted and attacked by some, ignored by others. *Littérature engagée* alone was an inadequate response to the need for education and political leadership. Merleau-Ponty entered the RDR as well, though Sartre later suspected that his motive was personal loyalty to Sartre rather than any real hope of success.[70] Camus contributed articles to the movement's newspaper, *La Gauche*, and lent the prestige of his presence to several mass meetings but did not formally become part of the organization.

The RDR manifesto was published in *Combat* on February 27, 1948, signed by Rousset, Sartre, and other members of the steering committee. "We believe," the authors announced, "that an association of free men who support revolutionary democracy is capable of giving new life to the principles of liberty and human dignity, by linking them to the struggle for a social revolution." Noting the menace of war and the need for Europe to remain a neutral buffer between the two blocs, the manifesto offered the RDR as a haven for all those who refused to choose sides in the Cold War yet who could not resign themselves to helpless passivity. "Nothing is lost," it insisted, "but everything must be begun anew."[71]

The RDR may be seen as an attempt to revive the type of political group that had flourished in France during the last two years of the Occupation. It was a new Comité National des Ecrivains, with aspirations toward mass membership. This continuity became apparent in the discussions among its leaders that were published in *Les Temps Modernes* in late 1948. Entitled "Conversations on Politics," they were the transcriptions of actual talks among Sartre, Rousset, and Rosenthal, attempts to define the methods and goals of the movement. All emphasized that the RDR was deliberately conceived as something other than a political party. It was intended to cut across traditional party boundaries, as did de Gaulle's RPF, uniting both those already enrolled in other political groups and those who belonged to none. The liberty and spontaneity that had marked the Resistance were expected to emerge again from this "flexible organization." "The Rassemblement," Rousset noted in the first issue of *La Gauche*, "takes up the tradition of a community of struggle experienced under the Occupation."[72]

Familiar Resistance attitudes also emerged in the discussion of the movement's role in forming and directing the convictions of those who could not speak for themselves. Once again, the leaders of the RDR asserted that they represented the true interests of those in France who were committed to social change. Only the absence of an attractive alternative had allowed the PCF to win the trust of the proletariat and to exploit the workers' allegiance for its own ends. Rousset commented:

> If the Communists play the preponderant role that they do today among the working class, this is because there are no other currents [of social change] that take charge of the workers' interests in an authentic way. We ourselves know that the Communists make use of the workers' misfortunes to sustain a political line foreign to the workers' interests. We ourselves further know that the end result of that political line is a regime hateful to the workers. But the workers do not.[73]

Thus the RDR strongly implied that it should assume the task of guiding the proletariat, since the Communists had proven unworthy stewards and betrayed those they were pledged to protect.

The attitude of Sartre and his colleagues toward the proletariat was not merely one of intellectual paternalism, however. They believed that of all groups in French society, the workers retained the greatest sympathy for the Resistance program and had remained least affected by the nation's shift to the Right. They further argued that their program demonstrated a greater respect for the proletariat than that of the PCF. The RDR would contribute to the liberation of the French working class, not through a mass organization held in check by a tightly controlled bureaucracy, but by giving the workers an opportunity to experiment with genuine self-government. As a first step, Sartre proposed a network of "neighborhood committees, village committees, [and] factory committees," each of which would compose a list of "concrete demands." This suggestion, combining features of the *cahiers de la Résistance* presented to the Etats Généraux de la Renaissance Française and of Sartre's call for independent initiatives in "Materialism and Revolution," grew out of his conviction that established political institutions ignored the people's will. "The party apparatus, bureaucratic apparatus," he noted scornfully, "can only issue slogans."[74]

The conflict between this program and the RDR's claim that it presented no threat to the Communist party was obvious. The Communist press lost no time in attacking the RDR's pretensions to speak for the workers and demanded that the RDR, if truly concerned with advancing the cause of the proletariat, join ranks with the Communists. Sartre's wish to create a *rassemblement* that transcended party loyalties, insofar as it needed mass support to survive, could be realized only by an unambiguous attempt to win workers away from the Communist ranks. But this would only further divide and weaken the Left at a time when the Right was showing progressively greater strength. The second "Conversation on Politics" of late November was therefore distinctly defensive in tone. The participants attempted to refute the Communists' critique while at the same time professing devotion to the proletarian cause. Sartre continued to argue for the good faith of the RDR, as he had argued earlier for his own good faith in the face of Communist mistrust: "They [the PCF] see very well that where they think 'utilization of the masses' we think 'liberation of the proletariat.' Where they think 'bureaucracy,' we think 'concrete liberties,' and . . . yet they reproach us with being traitors to the working class."[75]

The problem of maintaining freedom for maneuver and individual initiatives in competition with the Communists was one that Sartre had already explored in a play published in the March and April 1948 issues of *Les Temps Modernes*—*Les Mains sales* (*Dirty Hands*). Sartre later recalled that the play "was inspired by the difficulties that some of my students, well-meaning and middle-class, experienced with the Communist party." The plot was suggested by the assassination of Trotsky.[76] The familiar themes of choice and responsibility recur once again, but with a significant difference in emphasis that sheds light on Sartre's political outlook during the intial phase of the RDR.

Dirty Hands, like Camus's *The Just*, deals with political murder and its justification. Hoederer, a Communist party leader in the East European country of Illyria, pursues a policy of accommodation with the conservative forces that his own party condemns. A young bourgeois intellectual, Hugo, is dispatched with his wife to serve as Hoederer's secretary, with secret instructions to kill him. But Hoederer gradually wins Hugo's admiration; far from wishing to sabotage the policy of his party, he shows a superior political instinct, recognizing that temporary compromise with the two other parties is a more promising road to future victory. Hugo eventually commits the murder, not out of obedience to the party line, but in a jealous rage when he discovers his wife in Hoederer's arms. Hoederer is vindicated shortly after his death when the party abruptly adopts his tactics. His one crime is to have been right too soon.

Just as Sartre had conveyed his understanding of the intellectuals' Resistance role through the character of Orestes in *The Flies*, so the vacillation and doubt that overcome Hugo in *Dirty Hands* reflect the difficulties of action in the more uncertain political world of the late 1940s. The contrast between the two plays emerges clearly in the final scene of *Dirty Hands*, when Hugo learns that the party has rehabilitated Hoederer's reputation. Like Orestes, Hugo has believed that by killing a man he can both define himself and free others. Yet the party now demands that he conceal the political goal of his original mission and admit that he acted purely out of jealousy. In accordance with the logic described by Merleau-Ponty, it reserves the right to determine the real meaning of Hugo's crime. Hugo must now struggle to give his act the significance *he* intends. He therefore refuses to accept the party's judgment. "Someone like Hoederer," he insists, "does not die by chance. He dies for his ideas, for his politics." Hugo chooses to die himself at the end as a *non-récupérable*—a man useless for party work—in order to restore Hoederer's honor and his own.[77]

Also in 1948 Sartre finally abandoned work on the fourth novel that was to have completed the series *Roads to Freedom*. The question on which he foundered again concerned the problem of relations with the Communists. In the only excerpts Sartre published, appearing in *Les Temps Modernes* the following autumn, the Communist Brunet loses faith in his party and elects to escape from a German prison camp with a fellow prisoner expelled from the PCF two years earlier. The bonds of friendship that unite him with this *non-récupérable* become more important to him than party discipline. But the attempt to reach liberty, to evade both the Germans and the party, fails. A Communist prisoner warns the Germans of the escape attempt; Brunet's companion is killed and Brunet is recaptured. The confidence with which Sartre had begun this series during the war was gone. All that remained was a stubborn insistence that the search for freedom be pursued for its own sake, even if it should lead to imprisonment or death.

Late in December 1948 the RDR held its most ambitious gathering to date in the Paris Salle Pleyel. Four thousand participants came to hear speeches delivered by Sartre, Camus, and a group of foreign guests including the German Theodor Plievier and the Italian Carlo Levi. The theme was the writer's role in postwar Europe. The speakers left no doubt that they viewed this role as primarily defensive, a response to external pressures rather than an assertion of the will for change. At the same time, their diminished expectations made it possible to reject both violence and compromise more firmly than in the recent past. As long as it had seemed realistic to hope that parts of the Resistance vision might be achieved, other parts could be jettisoned and the results still be justified. Now such flexibility was a fault. "Faced with contemporary political society," Camus insisted, "the sole coherent stance of the artist . . . is resistance without concessions." Sartre reiterated the call for opposition, but cautioned that the intellectuals should not expect their influence to be widely felt. "We cannot do very much," he concluded, "save to denounce oppression every time and in whatever form it occurs."[78] The Pleyel meeting, which marked yet another stage in the intellectuals' retreat from hopes of positive intervention in postwar politics, also was the final display of unity mustered by the non-Communist Left. As Rousset later recalled, "This was the moment when, for the last time in France, a certain number of people found themselves united who, thereafter, divided and dispersed."[79]

Dissension soon appeared within the leadership of the RDR. The same forces of ideological polarization that had created a role for the movement between Left and Right now threatened its further existence. Rousset and Rosenthal appeared to Sartre to be moving toward an open espousal of the American cause, abandoning the concept of European neutrality in favor of a more resolutely anti-Communist posture. Their trip to the United States in search of funds to support the financially ailing RDR did nothing to allay Sartre's fears. On the eve of a second giant meeting at the Vélodrome d'Hiver on April 30, 1949, Sartre and Merleau-Ponty wrote a letter stating that they had no sympathy with the new orientation of the RDR and would not attend. An extraordinary session of the directors called by Sartre in June was unable to heal the division. The break became formal in

October when Sartre officially resigned his post on the directing committee. In his private notes, he wrote an epitaph for the movement: "The breakdown of the RDR—a bitter blow. New and definitive lesson in realism. One cannot create a movement."[80]

For a short period Sartre had believed that the intellectuals could again rally the country around an uplifting vision, that they could appeal to the working class over the heads of its leaders and to Frenchmen from all backgrounds over the din of Cold War propaganda. But the Resistance style of politics, as Merleau-Ponty had warned shortly after the war, no longer answered the demands of the times. Reflecting on these changes a decade later, Sartre himself acknowledged: "Choice [during the Resistance] was easy, even if a great deal of energy and courage were required to adhere to it. One was for or against the Germans. It was black or white. Today—and since 1945—the situation has grown more complex. One needs less courage to choose, perhaps, but the choices are far more difficult."[81]

It is possible to argue, as H. Stuart Hughes does in *The Obstructed Path*, that the isolation of France's intellectuals after the Resistance conforms to a pattern that is typical of France alone. If compared with the experiences of the German and Italian intellectual émigrés, the problems of the French indeed seem unique.[82] But if the fate of the French is compared instead with the experiences of the intellectuals who remained in Germany and Italy during the war, a number of parallels emerge. A search for community through political commitment, an elitist sense of mission, a desire to redefine moral standards, and a concern for understanding history were shared by intellectuals in all three countries. Though they emphasized different aspects of these themes, the war that touched them all created a community of outlook that led to an exchange of views and solutions at its end. In Germany, especially, where the French established a military presence in their zone of occupation after 1945, this dialogue enabled intellectuals who had spent twelve years under Nazi rule to learn from the French Resistance experience. Whatever their limitations in France, the postwar "existentialist offensive," the concept of engaged literature, and the intellectuals' claim to moral leadership all took on a new resonance east of the Rhine.

DER RUF
UNABHÄNGIGE BLÄTTER
DER JUNGEN GENERATION

NR. 1   1. JAHRG.   PREIS 90 PF.   MÜNCHEN, 15 AUGUST 1946

Das junge Europa formt sein Gesicht

(DR) — In dem zerstörten Ameisenberg Europa, mitten im ziellosen Gewimmel der Millionen, sammeln sich bereits kleine menschliche Gemeinschaften zu neuer Arbeit. Allen pessimistischen Voraussagen zum Trotz bilden sich neue Kräfte- und Willenszentren. Neue Gedanken breiten sich über Europa aus. Der auf die äußerste Spitze getriebenen Verneinung entspricht, wie einst dem Haupt des Jupiter die Athene, ein neuer, jugendfrischer, jungfräulich-athenischer Geist. Die Bedrohung, die hinter uns liegt und diejenige, die unserer wartet, hat nicht zur lähmenden Furcht geführt, sondern nur unser Bewußtsein dafür geschärft, daß wir uns im Prozeß einer Weltwende befinden.

Die Träger dieses europäischen Wiedererwachens sind zumeist junge, unbekannte Menschen. Sie kommen nicht aus der Stille von Studierzimmern — dazu hatten sie keine Zeit —, sondern unmittelbar aus dem bewaffneten Kampf um Europa, aus der Aktion. Ihr Geist ist der Geist der Aktion. In Frankreich scharen sie sich um die Gruppe der „Existentialisten" und deren Mentor Jean Paul Sartre, dem sich Albert Camus und Simone de Beauvoir gesellen, oder sie bilden Experimentierzellen in den bestehenden Parteien, so etwa Emanuel Mounier mit dem „Esprit" in der jungen Partei Bidaults oder Aragon bei den Kommunisten. Ihr Leben in den letzten Jahren war gleichbedeutend mit dem Leben der französischen „résistance".

Kristallisationspunkte des jungen Italiens sind der aus der Emigration zurückgekehrte Dichter Ignazio Silone, der eine Synthese von Sozialismus und religiösem Denken versucht, oder Ferruccio Parri, der Leiter der Aktionspartei. Der Sieg der Labour Party in England ist nicht denkbar ohne die innere Erneuerung der Arbeiterbewegung durch ihre jungen Kräfte. Skandinavien gab seine besten Geister in diesem Krieg: den dänischen Pfarrer Kaj Munk und den jungen norwegischen Dichter Nordahl Grieg, der über Berlin abstürzte. Diese Namen sind nur die äußerlichen Zeichen einer Bewegung, in der sich, wenn auch noch zögernd und unklar, so doch schon in großer Tiefe und Breite, die europäische Jugend manifestiert.

Das Gesetz, unter dem sie antritt, ist die Forderung nach europäischer Einheit. Das Werkzeug, welches sie zu diesem Zweck anzusetzen gewillt ist, ist ein neuer, von aller Tradition abweichender Humanismus, ein vom Menschen fordernder und an den Menschen glaubender Glaube, ein sozialistischer Humanismus.

Sozialistisch — das meint in diesem Fall, daß Europas Jugend „links" steht, wenn es sich um die soziale Forderung handelt. Sie vertritt wirtschaftliche Gerechtigkeit und weiß, daß diese sich nur im Sozialismus verwirklichen läßt. Sozialismus, nicht in „sozialen Reformen". Der Menschengeist hat eine Stufe erreicht, in dem ihm der private Besitz von Produktionsmitteln ebenso absurd erscheint wie vor 2000 Jahren die Sklaverei. Die sozialistische Forderung schließt die Forderung nach einer geplanten Wirtschaft und eine — trotz allem — Bejahung der Technik ein. „Links" steht dieser Geist ferner in seiner kulturellen Aufgeschlossenheit, seiner Ablehnung nationaler und rassischer Vorurteile, seiner Verhöhnung des provinziellen Konservativismus.

Humanistisch aber ist Europas Jugend in ihrem unerschöpflichen Hunger nach Freiheit. Humanismus bedeutet ihr Anerkennung der Würde und Freiheit des Menschen — nicht mehr und nicht weniger. Sie wäre bereit, das Lager des Sozialismus zu verlassen, wenn sie darin die Freiheit des Menschen aufgegeben sähe zugunsten jenes alten orthodoxen Marxismus, der die Determiniertheit des Menschen von seiner Wirtschaft postuliert und die menschliche Willensfreiheit leugnet. Fanatismus für das Recht des Menschen auf seine Freiheit ist kein Widerspruch in sich selbst, sondern die große Lehre, welche die Jugend Europas aus der Erfahrung der Diktatur zieht. Sie wird den Kampf gegen alle Feinde der Freiheit fanatisch führen.

Eine starke Wurzel dieses doppelten Suchens nach Freiheit und sozialer Gerechtigkeit liegt in dem religiösen Erlebnis, das die junge Generation aus dem Kriege mitbringt. Echte religiös ist nicht möglich, wo der Mensch Bluts- oder Klassengesetzen unterstellt wird, die er angeblich nicht durchbrechen kann. Nichts beweist die Freiheit des Menschen mehr als seine freie Entscheidung für oder gegen Gott.

Der Inhalt des jungen Denkens bedingt die Haltung seiner Träger. Sie fordern nicht nur richtiges Denken, sie fordern auch das dazugehörige Leben. Sie haben in sich erfahren, weil sie sich für ihre Grundsätze eingesetzt haben, weil viele von ihnen dafür ihr Leben hingegeben haben. Besonders Sartre und die jungen Kämpfer aus der „résistance" fordern diese Übereinstimmung von Tat und Gedanken, die bruchlose Existenz.

Von hier aus spannt sich ein dünnes, sehr gewagtes

Bedingungslose Uebergabe: „Wir haben in Jalta erklärt — und ich wiederhole es jetzt —, daß bedingungslose Waffenniederlegung nicht die Vernichtung oder Versklavung des deutschen Volkes bedeutet. Das deutsche Volk wie der deutsche Soldat müssen einsehen, daß sie nur durch bedingungslose Kapitulation beginnen können, wieder ein Volk zu werden, das von der Welt respektiert und als Nachbar akzeptiert werden kann — Ich würde meinen tiefsten religiösen und politischen Überzeugungen untreu werden, wenn ich die Hoffnung, in den Glauben aufgäbe, daß in allen Völkern, ohne Ausnahme, ein Sinn für die Wahrheit, ein Streben nach Gerechtigkeit und eine Sehnsucht nach Frieden lebt — wenn auch dies alles im Falle Deutschlands von einem brutalen Regime unterdrückt sein mag — Wir klagen nicht das deutsche Volk als solches an, denn wir können nicht glauben, daß Gott irgendein Volk auf ewige Zeiten verdammt habe. Wir wissen aus unserem eigenen Lande, wie viele gute Männer und Frauen deutscher Herkunft sich als loyale, freiheitsliebende und friedliebende Bürger bewährt haben. Das deutsche Volk wird nicht versklavt werden; die Vereinten Nationen betreiben keinen Sklavenhandel."

(Präsident Roosevelt)

4
The Dilemmas
of Opposition
1933-1945

*To think and act for the sake of the
coming generation, yet to be ready to
die any day without fear or anxiety—
that is the attitude which we are forced
to adopt in practice.*
Dietrich Bonhoeffer, 1943

It was in Nazi Germany that intellectuals were forced most dramatically to re-evaluate the beliefs and aspirations that had guided their critique of European society during the late 1920s. Engagement, community, the appeal to a spiritual dimension missing in the "materialistic" Weimar decade—these familiar ideals found their way into the official Nazi canon, imbued with a new and sinister meaning. The socialism with religious and ethical overtones portrayed in Goebbels's *Michael* became a gospel of dictatorship. "Here the intellectual stands next to the worker; a whole people has risen up!" These words might have introduced an article in *Esprit* or concluded one of Malraux's novels. Instead they were spoken by Goebbels at a public book-burning in 1933.[1]

Hitler's skillful adaptation of the rhetoric of revolution for his own ends created uncertainty and confusion among German intellectuals. Would the Nazis initiate a positive break from Weimar, or did they pose an even greater danger than the hypocrisy and corruption of the old regime? Some observers allowed their hopes for radical change to silence their doubts about the true motives of National Socialism. Others, despite a wish for renewal, saw far more reason to fear than to welcome these self-proclaimed saviors of the nation. The former Expressionist writer Gottfried Benn, a member of the Prussian Academy of Poetry, hailed the "shift from an economic to a mythic collective" and urged his colleagues to accept the "yoke and law" of the Nazi state. Thomas Mann, by contrast, warned in March 1933 that the Nationalsozialistische Deutsche Arbeiterpartei (NSDAP) threatened to plunge Germany "with deadly certainty into physical and moral ruin if one does not oppose them."[2] He and his brother Heinrich resigned from the Prussian Academy in protest and soon left Germany for exile abroad.

The Manns' departure from their homeland suggests one aspect of the German experience under Hitler that contrasted sharply with that of the French intellectuals under the Occupation. A "great migration" took hundreds of writers, philosophers, and scientists to Zurich, New York, London, or Moscow in 1933. Whereas some Frenchmen such as Georges Bernanos, Claude Lévi-Strauss, and Raymond Aron sought refuge beyond the borders of France after 1940, they were the exceptions. The forced exodus of German intellectuals was a massive loss of talent, and it dramatically thinned the potential ranks of the Resistance. Thousands of German Jews found themselves initially deprived of the right to work and later threatened by deportation to the death camps. Communists and Socialists also became targets of political persecution. Those who had most reason to oppose National Socialism were thus under greatest pressure to leave Germany altogether; they could not risk a struggle on home ground.[3]

German émigrés contributed to a wide range of anti-Fascist activities abroad — founding journals, addressing meetings, volunteering for service in the Spanish Civil War. Thomas Mann regularly spoke to his countrymen over Allied radio during World War II, just as Communist intellectuals offered words of hope and encouragement to the German Left via Radio Moscow after 1941. But these efforts had only a limited impact within the Third Reich. Some Germans accused the émigrés of deserting the fatherland at a critical hour in its history and of enjoying a pampered existence far from the rigors of Nazi rule — judgments that Goebbels's propaganda was only too happy to reinforce. The émigrés gradually lost touch with the evolving situation in Germany, and their broadcast remarks, though motivated by the highest patriotism, frequently appeared condescending or ill-informed to their hearers.[4]

A number of intellectuals did choose to remain in Germany, either because of family ties or with the conviction, as one expressed it, that "a spiritual influence on a country subjected to a dictatorship is scarcely possible from the outside." Yet the twelve years of Nazi terror created far more difficult conditions for resistance than those faced by the French. Dawn arrests, interrogations in the cellars of the Gestapo, and the ever-present danger of denunciation by one's neighbor or colleague all forced the German Resistance to move with extreme caution. "The desire to fight against this apparatus," a dissident recalled, "seemed madness to many, as if one wished to stand alone against a landslide or a deluge." Keeping any spark of opposition alive seemed a significant achievement. Hence the tendency of many anti-Nazi Germans to judge their efforts not against a standard of rapid and visible success but rather within a much longer perspective. They would sow, and others would reap the harvest. "The ultimate question for a responsible man," Dietrich Bonhoeffer wrote, "is . . . how the coming generation will live. Only from this question, with its responsibility toward history, can fruitful—though for the time being exceedingly modest—solutions arise."[5]

Weakened in force and numbers by inner uncertainty, emigration, and police terror, those who opposed Hitler were never able to unite into a coherent Resistance movement. Their efforts—anonymous and often unrecorded—were a patchwork of individual initiatives directed against a more powerful foe. Though Benn and other early converts to the National Socialist mystique shed their illusions in due course, the intellectuals remained divided over the means through which resistance should be pursued. Many adopted an attitude of "inner emigration," as it was later, and somewhat defensively, described.[6] Disdaining the New Order but unable to combat it openly, they retreated into self-imposed spiritual seclusion during all or part of the Hitler regime, venturing only indirect criticism in their writings. The momentum that carried the French Resistance into the Liberation period with a confident sense of mission and a new-found solidarity thus had no true German parallel. When the end finally came in 1945, the "other Germany" neither spoke with a common voice nor looked back to a common past.

Yet, as in France, the German experience of opposition shaped the outlines of postwar cultural renewal. The many dissidents who shared Bonhoeffer's belief in "responsibility toward history" viewed the coming of peace as a critical test for the choices and sacrifices they had made under Hitler. A resistance whose activities had been largely confined to the realm of thought and discussion could best justify this course (and allay its guilt at not adopting another) by now fulfilling the larger goals that had been deferred until victory was at hand. At the same time, the failure to mount a decisive challenge to the Third Reich from within, however comprehensible, weakened the dissidents' claim to moral leadership, especially in the eyes of the Allies who assumed control of Germany in 1945. The legacy of the German Resistance was thus negative as well as positive, both a target of criticism and a source of inspiration. What it had saved had been purchased at great price; what it had not accomplished limited its prestige and lessened its influence on the course of German reconstruction.

National Community and Inner Emigration

National Socialism shared with the social critics of the 1920s a desire to transform the individual. "The nature of revolution is that it changes a people inwardly," Goebbels noted soon after the Nazis seized power. "New virtues are springing up everywhere, signs of the revolutionary upheaval from which they issue: magnanimity, heroism, masculinity, readiness for sacrifice, discipline." But the peculiarly military rather than broadly political nature of these virtues suggests the gulf that separated the Nazi "spiritual revolution" from the vision of men like Emmanuel Mounier. Goebbels stressed obedience rather than judgment, self-denial rather than self-fulfillment. The responsibilities that Mounier saw divided equally between the individual and the claims of others in a "double vocation" were here to be directed exclusively toward what Goebbels termed the "national cause."[7]

This cause was embodied in the concept of national or racial community—the *Volksgemeinschaft*—which superseded the more restricted loyalties of class, region, or profession. Hitler's proclamation that "the individual must subordinate himself to the whole, to a higher common interest" did not merely imply that the citizen owed loyalty and obedience to the state.[8] It also meant that the state ceased to be simply a vehicle for politics and became instead the focus and expression of all values and expectations. The Germans supported their new leaders with a fervor accorded to no politican during the Weimar Republic, in large measure because the New Order appeared to bridge the gap between morals and institutions, between spirit and power. It offered everything, and demanded everything in return.

The "mythic collective" that held such fascination for Benn, though ultimately relying on force to impose its will, was able to inspire a voluntary sacrifice of individual autonomy through orchestrated acts of participation. Even skeptical foreigners who observed the German scene during the 1930s were impressed by the "pageantry and color and mysticism" that suffused public life. Parades and rallies not only gave tangible expression to the *Volksgemeinschaft* but enhanced its capacity for emotional coercion. Hitler described this process in *Mein Kampf* (1924):

When [the individual] enters a mass rally for the first time and now has thousands and thousands of similarly disposed men around him; when in his groping he is swept along by the powerful effect of the suggestive intoxication and the enthusiasm of three to four thousand others; when the evident success and approval of thousands confirm the truth of the new teaching for him, then he himself submits to the magical influence . . . The man who entered such a meeting wavering and in doubt leaves it inwardly strengthened. He has become a member of a new community.[9]

The values of the collectivity were substantiated by the loyalty they evoked; their truth was not debated, but affirmed. In accepting the standards of the group as his own, the individual experienced a "spiritual revolution" that diminished his capacity for dissent. In Sartre's terminology, he took on a "ready-made" identity.

The Nazi regime required that artists and intellectuals who were not racially or politically suspect be integrated into the national community. This demand was couched in terms that spoke to the intellectuals' long-standing disquiet over their isolated position in society. "The worst offense of artistically creative men from the previous period," Goebbels argued in 1933, "[was] that they no longer maintained a vital [contact with] the roots that offered them daily sustenance." The writer was therefore enjoined to address themes taken from "active life," and to resist the temptation of "artistic snobbery."[10] Goebbels's Ministry of Enlightenment and Propaganda, through the various sub-agencies of the Reich Chamber of Culture, assumed direct patronage of the arts with the intent of "assigning them a political task in the broadest sense." As the party functionary and author Werner Beumelburg explained, this task was "to purify and shape the German destiny, to give expression to the new type of German man, to embody the concept of individual sacrifice and uncompromising duty toward the community." Beumelburg's remarks make clear that a literature drawn from "active life" was not to mirror reality, but rather should transcend and transfigure it. What Goebbels demanded was an idealized portrait of the *Volk*, a contribution to the "color and mysticism" that characterized Nazi propaganda as a whole.[11]

What was the "new type of German man"? He assumed several guises. Dietrich Strothmann, in his study of National Socialist literary policy, has argued that there existed three distinct phases of taste during the Third Reich. At first, what might be termed "party literature" predominated, celebrating the political struggles against the Weimar Republic, glorifying brutality and violence in the service of the NSDAP. From 1935 until the outbreak of World War II, Nazi writers turned to regional literature of a heavily romantic cast, portraying the timeless virtues of the German peasantry and the organic union of "blood and soil." After 1939, military and heroic themes again came into fashion, obviously intended to stimulate wartime morale. These contrasting genres suggest both the heterogeneity of the Nazi cultural platform and the rivalries within the movement that pitted traditionalists such as Alfred Rosenberg against revolutionaries such as Goebbels. But underlying the changing image of the National Socialist hero was a basic continuity in values. The fighting *Sturmabteilung* (SA) man, the peasant clinging tenaciously to his native soil, and the steadfast *Wehrmacht* soldier appealed to communal solidarity. "We no longer want to make money above all else," declares a character in Hanns Johst's drama *Schlageter* (1934), "but to *serve*. The individual [exists] as a corpuscle in the bloodstream of his people."[12]

For the *innere Emigranten*, holding oneself aloof from this national community was a gesture of spiritual self-preservation. The greater the pressures to conform, the greater was the need to distance oneself from the "magical influence" of mass consent. Intellectual opposition to the regime therefore commonly took the form of studied indifference. The journalist Ursula von Kardorff noted that anti-Nazi Germans would systematically "avoid party meetings and processions" and "turn off the radio when a Hitler speech begins." As in France during the first months of the German Occupation, the progressive regimentation of daily life, the "total engagement of all energies" demanded by Goebbels, gave new meaning to silence and reserve after 1933.[13]

Although withdrawal might seem a purely negative act, it was based on something more than a rejection of Nazi ideals. It involved an implicit recognition of individual obligations transcending the demands of the national community. "To be a person," in the words of Rudolf Pechel, "signified a higher order than to be a German." Intellectuals felt particular responsibility to resist the Nazi definition of engagement. Ernst Wiechert spoke for many inner émigrés when he argued that the writer's calling was to preserve and defend values threatened by political expediency, to act as one who "in a noisy world is the last and quiet guardian of permanent things." Wiechert's address to students at the University of Munich in April 1935, usually accounted one of the few calls to opposition in the early Hitler years, was in fact a plea for principled disengagement and an apologia for "the poet [who stands] beyond time." "Beneath all the loud words and songs of the day," Wiechert told his audience, "he seeks the calm and the everlasting, nourishment for the hungry that will satisfy them when all the songs and words have died away."[14]

The appeal to "permanent things" cherished in solitude suggests one of the major sources of inspiration for the inner émigrés. For men like Wiechert and Pechel, an aesthetic ideal, with its moral corollaries, provided an alternative to the Nazi "spiritual revolution." Beauty, harmony, awe before nature, renunciation of worldly success all possessed a more universal and less transient validity than exalted nationalism. Moreover, they were values well suited to a state of spiritual exile, since they did not demand collective action for their attainment. Direct contact with "the everlasting" offered security and guidance independent of society or the state. Introspection and deference to inherited standards, rather than conformity to the judgment of others, pointed the way to "a goal not of our time."[15]

This outlook, which met the intellectuals' needs under the Third Reich so readily, had deep roots in the German Idealist tradition. A belief that the individual should be concerned with enriching his inner life and cultivating his own special gifts—"the highest and most proportionate development of one's resources into one whole," as Wilhelm von Humboldt expressed it—had gained wide currency among educated middle-class Germans during the nineteenth century. Their model was Goethe, whose serene creativity and overwhelming poetic achievement exemplified the ability of the individual to find fulfillment within himself. The key to this fulfillment was culture, which mediated between the absolute and those trained to recognize its embodiment in art and literature. "A visual representation," Goethe wrote in *Wilhelm Meister's Apprenticeship* (1795-96), "should also say something to me, should teach, touch, improve me."[16]

Aesthetic education (*Bildung*) was not only a source of inner enrichment, however. It was a possession, enshrined in the finely bound volumes of one's personal library, to be treasured and passed on. For the German academic elite, maintaining the standards of *Bildung* became an acceptable alternative to full political participation in Bismarck's empire after 1870. Goethe's admonition "to live resolutely in the whole, the good, the beautiful" could be interpreted as a call to act as guardians of the nation's cultural heritage. By 1933 such a custodial role was more than mere compensation for lost political prerogatives; it became a defense against the leveling influence of Nazi taste and the myth of the *Volk*. Friedrich von Reck-Malleczewen, for example, complained bitterly of the "resentment against academics" and "the masses' infernal hatred of everything spiritual" encouraged by Germany's new rulers.[17] His remarks demonstrate the degree to which a concern for status and an allegiance to "the whole, the good, the beautiful" reinforced each other in the minds of the *innere Emigranten*. Warding off the encroachments of brown-shirted philistines in the field of art meant preserving a distinction between high and popular culture, and with it a distinction between moral rigor and expediency.

While the tradition of *Bildung* appealed primarily to an elite, there is evidence that many middle-class Germans remained open to the ideal of withdrawal proposed by the inner émigrés. If they did not seek solace in Goethe or Schiller, they at least read Ernst Wiechert, whose novels achieved tremendous popularity during the Third Reich precisely because they offered, as Wiechert himself noted, a "dream-land" in which the strains of daily life could be forgotten. They begin with a flight from chaos and end in a safe haven of order and content-ment. *Das einfache Leben* (*The Simple Life,* 1939), which sold more than a quarter of a million copies despite the official NSDAP hostility toward it, is one of many variations on Wiechert's basic romantic theme. The former navy captain Thomas von Orla, oppressed by the meaninglessness of his life in middle age, leaves his family and the city to "begin afresh." At length he finds peace and illumination amid the lakes and forests of East Prussia. Laboring as a fisherman, Orla enters into the rhythm of the seasons, of "long days full of work and clear nights with many stars." The plot does not build toward a resolution of tensions, but resolves them at the outset with a gesture of renuncia-tion. In this contemplative, almost monastic existence, Orla desires nothing more than a "happy heart." "No adventures, no heroic role, no shining brow. Casting the nets and drawing them in again, keeping his house and island in order, reading a few pages and sitting at the water's edge in the evening, gazing at the stars."[18]

The Simple Life offers not the slightest hint that its author had recently returned from internment at Buchenwald, where he had been imprisoned during 1938 for his moral opposition to the Third Reich. Wiechert later described his experiences as a captive and his vow to "forget nothing" in *Der Totenwald* (*The Forest of the Dead*, 1945). But in recounting the life of Orla, his intention was to create an "asylum, inviolable, sacrosanct, to which one could flee from the world of loudspeakers, forced marches, barbed wire." Wiechert's col-league Werner Bergengruen argued that such escape literature "set up a contrary image by which this era could be measured."[19] Yet Wiechert's "contrary image" was not conducive to critical judgment. It was too far removed from the truth of the Nazi regime to illuminate a tragic present, and, ironically, too close to Hitler's professed ideals to reveal their lack of substance. The National Socialist movement represented, in part, a reaction against the dislocations of modernity and the "rootlessness" of urban living, and Wiechert's conservative vi-sion failed to challenge the myths exploited by his opponents. In this unintended complicity with Nazi literature lay a major weakness of the inner emigration. By encouraging Germans to shut their eyes to what was happening around them, it assisted Goebbels in drawing a veil over the distasteful realities of power.

Not all inner émigrés acquiesced in this evasion of reality; some voiced a sharper protest. Anonymous political jokes abounded—"the small change of hostility," as one observer termed them—and some writers and journalists strengthened morale among anti-Nazis by resorting to "camouflaged" criticism. Their message, Bergengruen recalled, was "you are not alone, not abandoned, there are many who share your convictions and who stand beside you. Do not let your courage fail; this winter, too, will one day be past." At a time when so many topics were forbidden, the art of allusion reached new heights.[20] The principal forum for such indirect censure was the dwindling number of "bourgeois" reviews and newspapers that had survived the Weimar era. The venerable *Deutsche Rundschau*, the Catholic monthly *Hochland*, and daily papers such as the *Frankfurter Zeitung* and the *Deutsche Allgemeine Zeitung* kept up a game of political hide-and-seek with Goebbels's censors. Rudolf Pechel, editor of the *Deutsche Rundschau*, explained: "One criticized despots and crimes committed in all periods of history, illustrated with figures such as the tyrants of antiquity, Roman caesars of the late Empire, Ghenghis Khan, Tamerlane, Napoleon, and others, and left the reader to draw the proper conclusions."[21]

Such stratagems were made necessary by the absence of a true underground press in Germany. Yet the form of intellectual discipline that this journalism encouraged was not analysis but identification. It depended on a pre-existing set of associations and values that could merely be confirmed, not explored. Editors like Pechel were preaching to the converted; unable to state their premises openly, they were prevented from guiding their readers toward new insights and could only hope that their public would remain loyal to its old beliefs.

Relations between dissident journals and the Nazi regime were tense and ambivalent. Though Goebbels complained that he was forced "continually to warn and continually to exhort" a captious bourgeois press, he was still able to turn it to his own uses. Its editors made concessions to the Propaganda Ministry's guidelines regarding news management and performed obligatory exercises such as congratulating the Führer on his birthday. More important, the continued existence of these journals reassured liberal opinion abroad by creating the illusion of diversity and tolerance in the Nazi cultural sphere. Walter Dirks, a veteran contributor to the *Frankfurter Zeitung*, remembered that he and his colleagues debated whether their limited freedom was not purchased at too great a cost:

> Naturally we asked ourselves time and again, can we justify this? To the extent that Herr Ribbentropp and Herr Goebbels can say to the world that a free press exists in Germany, we prop up the regime . . . If the Nazis win in the end, we have helped them. We are the fig leaf, the alibi. Then we said to ourselves, if, on the other hand, *we* survive, then we will have preserved something. Thanks to the Allies, we survived.[22]

Here again the difference between the French and the German intellectuals' attitudes toward resistance becomes clear. For the French, "preserving something" demanded absolute moral integrity. Collaboration, for whatever motives, was tantamount to capitulation. The Germans, whose struggle had begun a half-decade earlier and was pursued at greater odds, believed compromise to be a necessity. What mattered was to bolster the inner reserves and the spiritual autonomy, no matter how restricted in the present, on which one could some day build anew.

A view of the intellectual as guardian of the spirit, with its accompanying overtones of both elitism and resignation, is the central theme of the single most important work of "camouflaged" criticism to appear under the Nazis—Ernst Jünger's novel *Auf den Marmorklippen* (*On the Marble Cliffs*), published in 1939. Jünger had earlier been a fierce champion of spiritual renewal through action. As a young lieutenant in World War I, he had sought his ideal in a warrior aristocracy that displayed "cool joy in danger, the chivalrous longing to stand the test of battle." By 1932 he had transferred his allegiance to a different elite, one of "sharing and service" within a community of work whose spirit seemed to conform to the aims of National Socialism. For Weimar and its fragmented, materialistic society he felt only contempt. Yet when confronted with the realities of Hitler's regime, Jünger turned away from his earlier support for the heroic activism of soldier or worker. Instead he defended the moral and aesthetic values that the Third Reich placed in jeopardy, taking his stand alongside those who preserved a spiritual superiority in the "battles between idols and the mind."[23]

The setting of *On the Marble Cliffs*—a mythic landscape whose features recall the Alpine lakes of northern Italy—gives this battle a timeless, allegorical dimension. The narrator and his brother live in harmony with nature, patiently gathering and classifying botanical specimens in their hermitage beneath the marble cliffs. They have withdrawn from a life of adventure—as had Jünger—to devote themselves to scholarship and contemplation. But their peaceful labors are disrupted by the Chief Ranger, lord of a dark and savage forest country beyond the cliffs, whose forces invade and at length subdue the lands in which the brothers have found refuge. Rather than promising asylum, as Wiechert did in *The Simple Life*, Jünger concentrates on the violence that destroys this promise. His images are prophetic in their horror. "Streets littered with ruined walls and broken beams," and a "torture house" filled with severed heads anticipate the air raids and extermination camps of World War II. As the brothers' hermitage is laid waste by fire, they abandon the harvest of many years' work and, like so many Europeans during the coming decade, depart into exile.[24]

In one sense Jünger underscores the futility of resistance. His novel poses in stark terms the question of what constitutes meaningful action when men cannot alter their fate. Yet though he shared Spengler's sense of determinism, Jünger continued to hope that spiritual values would survive the cataclysm that he saw menacing Europe in 1939. The faith these values inspired would prove stronger and more lasting than armed conquest. Not even death could extinguish the moral authority of those whose allegiance transcended the temporal rewards of wealth and power. Jünger expressed this conviction in a scene that many German readers perceived as a key to the novel's message. At the height of the final battle between the Chief Ranger and his foes, the narrator enters the Köppelsbleek "torture house," and there discovers the mutilated body of a young prince slain opposing the Ranger: "Now I became certain of a thing I had often doubted: there were still noble souls among us, in whose hearts the knowledge of a greater order lived and was confirmed. And as a lofty example induces us to follow its teaching, I swore to myself . . . in all times to come that I would prefer to fall alone among the free, rather than to march in triumph with the slaves.[25]

The Spirit of Martyrdom

Wiechert and Jünger, writing on the eve of World War II, chronicled the search for a secular ethic that would permit the individual to defy the community. Their heroes are exceptional men whose efforts are directed toward promoting their own spiritual development, who seek a mystical union with nature in preference to the bonds of society, and who endure reverses with stoic reserve. These visions typify the response of the inner émigrés to Hitler during the first six years of the Reich. But by the late 1930s a sense of accelerating crisis led a number of intellectuals to ask whether this retreat into a "metaphysically oriented, apolitical individualism" could be justified. Observing the new brutality of anti-Jewish measures at home and the Nazis' aggressive and predatory actions abroad, they felt implicated by their own inaction. "Only at the price of self-deception," Bonhoeffer was to write in 1940, "can [the individual] preserve his private blamelessness . . . In all his undertakings, what he fails to do will give him no rest."[26]

The outbreak of war in 1939, which lent new urgency to this examination of conscience, made concerted action against the regime both more difficult and more dangerous. Himmler's SS police tightened their hold over the country in the interests of "state security," with instructions to eliminate those who attempted to "undermine the determination and will to fight of the German people."[27] More important, the war further isolated the opposition from the nation. French and Italian *résistants* could appeal to patriotic sentiments among their fellow countrymen; the German dissidents could not. Many anti-Nazis found it difficult to accept a choice between betraying their principles or their homeland. "The situation is truly tragic," one of them wrote. Sympathizers with the Resistance "love their country. They think patriotically as well as socially. They cannot wish for victory, even less for a severe defeat." Torn by this conflict of loyalties, the German could salve his conscience by arguing that he was serving the fatherland, not Hitler, and by condemning resistance as a form of treason. The Weisse Rose dissidents at the University of Munich found themselves obliged to state emphatically that they were not in the pay of a foreign power merely because they urged all to join the "determined struggle against Hitler."[28]

And yet German underground activities did spread, as shown by the appearance of groups such as the Weisse Rose, the Kreisau Circle organized by Count Helmuth von Moltke, and the military conspiracy linked with the Army Intelligence Service (*Abwehr*). The dissident Fabian von Schlabrendorff, returning to Berlin in 1938 after a half-decade's absence, was struck by a "changed picture." In contrast to the "loose mosaic" of individual opponents characteristic of the preceding period, there had sprung up a "multiplicity of circles that intersected one another." These groups originated primarily within corporate bodies such as the universities, the churches, the civil service, and the army, where daily contacts were facilitated and where a traditional autonomy encouraged resistance to Nazi pressure for political conformity (*Gleichschaltung*). But even at the peak of this development during the years 1942-1944, the resisters were few, their range of contacts limited. There was no central coordinating body for the German Resistance analogous to the French CNR that might have linked groups drawn from differing milieus. Isolation both within Germany and within occupied Europe produced notable gaps in the opposition's assessment of other Resistance efforts, as when Moltke argued in 1942 that in France "as far as we can find out, there is no really effective opposition on a fundamental basis, but only on the basis of casual activity."[29]

To overcome the liabilities of numerical weakness and uncertain communication, the German groups invested much of their time in identifying potential allies and "gathering reliable reports." Like Sartre's Socialisme et Liberté, they attempted to make up with scrupulous planning and detailed intelligence what they lacked in force. "Now we must find our way back to one another, enlighten one another," the Weisse Rose proclaimed. The Nazi treatment of conquered territories in the East, the shifting fortunes of war, and the shape of the new regime to come after Hitler's defeat were staple topics of discussion. Yet there was a danger that these activities could become ends in themselves. From the diaries and documents that have survived, one receives an impression of endless visits, conversations, proposals, and counterproposals that generated a sense of brisk enterprise while in fact doing little to advance the cause. A diary entry from February 1942 by Ulrich von Hassell, a former diplomat engaged in the Resistance, gives the flavor of many others: "Oster and Dohnanyi visited me, somewhat disconcerted by the news that the Gestapo was watching them closely. They are also interested in Popitz and myself . . . I spoke with Goerdeler and Jessen. It seems that at the moment nothing can be done about Hitler."[30]

The isolation of the Resistance groups in Germany helps to explain their ambivalent attitude toward pursuing more vigorous measures against the regime. Not only did many of their members, like Sartre, feel themselves unfit for acts of sabotage or political murder; even if such acts succeeded in overthrowing Hitler, the opposition doubted whether the German populace would support them. Whereas the inner émigrés struggled to maintain their independence from the national community, the Resistance needed to establish bonds of trust with the populace. Yet each step toward challenging the regime only divided them more deeply from the *Volksgemeinschaft*. In the end, they judged that a coup conducted by an elite without followers might prove a greater liability to the anti-Nazi cause than total German defeat. For Germany to learn from the war, they argued, it was imperative that no stab-in-the-back legend arise to cloud the responsibility of the Nazi leadership. When the final attempt on Hitler's life was made in July 1944, news of its failure stirred mixed emotions. As Ursula von Kardorff, bound by ties of family and friendship to many of those involved, observed sadly: "If one looks at the matter dispassionately, it may be good that Hitler now has to bear the blame for our bitter fate (*muss die bittre Suppe auslöffeln*). Had the assassination succeeded, the conspirators would have been obliged to end the war immediately, and take all the consequences of the lost war on themselves."[31]

The dilemma posed by the attempted assassination formed part of a broader debate within the German Resistance during the war years. Could violence of any kind be justified in the struggle against National Socialism? It seemed to some that the dissidents would corrupt their ideals by adopting the Nazis' methods of force. French intellectuals, confronting this problem, had tried to define the limits of violence without justifying it in an absolute sense, as in Camus's distinction between a *justicier* and an *assassin*. Violence was permissible when its end was clear and immediate, though the burden of guilt and responsibility it imposed could not be evaded. Beauvoir's novel *The Blood of Others*, for example, had emphasized the responsibility of the Resistance for the death of innocent victims. Beauvoir argued that to act with a clear conscience was impossible. "After years of pacifism" the novel's hero "accepted violence. He organized assassinations, despite the reprisals [that followed]. This decision did not bring him inner peace, but he no longer sought it; he resigned himself to live in anguish."[32]

It was far more difficult for the German dissidents than for the French to regard results as justification for the use of violent means since their chances of victory were slight. The German Resistance therefore came to reject violence with the same moral intransigence with which the French rejected the possibility of collaboration. At the same time, virtually all German dissidents accepted the prospect of death for themselves. Their stand against National Socialism was a form of private witness, exemplary rather than practically effective, invested with a value that transformed political failure into the triumph of martyrdom. The Resistance became, as Bonhoeffer noted, an "act of contrition" whose spiritual force would redeem its political impotence. Only from this perspective is it possible to understand the mixture of relief and pride with which Moltke asserted that the Kreisau Circle had not even "drawn up a leaflet. There are only thoughts, without even the intention of force." As he wrote to his wife shortly before his execution on charges of treason, his trial had demonstrated that "not plans, not preparation [for a coup], but the spirit as such is to be persecuted."[33]

The willingness to bear the consequences of such persecution, to accept suffering as a path toward redemption for oneself and others, points to the Christian inspiration that underlay much of the German Resistance. Traditionally, neither Lutheran Protestantism nor Roman Catholicism had encouraged rebellion against the temporal order. Yet as Hitler began to move against the churches in the late 1930s, abandoning his earlier attitude of calculated tolerance in religious matters, Christian belief assumed a more definite oppositional character. It also provided a bond among isolated dissidents. Both the Kreisau Circle and the Weisse Rose movement found a basis in Christian teachings. "We see in Christianity," read the report of the first Kreisau conference in 1942, "the most valuable source of strength for the religious-ethical renewal of the nation." That same year Moltke wrote to his British friend Lionel Curtis: "The most important [development] is the spiritual awakening which is starting up, coupled as it is with the preparedness to be killed, if need be. The backbone of this movement is to be found in both the Christian confessions, Protestant as well as Catholic . . . We are trying to build on this foundation."[34]

Religious faith, like the aesthetic idealism of the inner émigrés, provided an alternative to the worship of the national community and reasserted traditional values in the face of the Nazi "spiritual revolution." It also carried a conception of personal responsibility that led many members of the Resistance to view their faith not only as a source of consolation but also as a command to help others. "Passive waiting and apathetic contemplation are not Christian attitudes," Bonhoeffer argued. "Personal experience is not the primary focus for the Christian, but the experiences of his brothers for whom Christ suffered."[35]

It was Bonhoeffer, cofounder and leading member of the anti-Nazi Bekennende Kirche, who attempted most tenaciously and systematically to define the relations between Christian teachings and Resistance practice during the war. In his brief essay "After Ten Years" (1942), and above all in the more discursive *Ethik* (*Ethics*, 1939-1943), on which he labored up to the moment of his arrest, Bonhoeffer sought to explore the Christian's moral duty "in the hour of danger." "The structure of a responsible life," he maintained, was "determined in two ways: through the linking of [that] life to man and God, and through the freedom of one's own life." This dual accountability restored the individual autonomy suppressed by the *Volksgemeinschaft*, while maintaining the claim of men upon each other. For Bonhoeffer, as for Mounier, responsibility toward oneself implied responsibility toward others, "grounded in the responsibility of Jesus Christ for man."[36]

Bonhoeffer and Mounier further agreed that this obligation was exercised pre-eminently in the "world of things." Bonhoeffer's decision to return to Germany from the United States in 1939, "in total clarity and with the best conscience," exemplified his belief that the responsible individual could not remain aloof from the life of his compatriots. When he was arrested by the Gestapo four years later, one of the notes that he left behind on his desk read, "Be there for the world." Yet while Mounier sought to direct the spiritual energies of his readers toward social change, Bonhoeffer's Resistance activities led him instead to emphasize a mediating, "representative" *(stellvertretend)* role for the man of good conscience, who assumed burdens that others were unable to bear. The "readiness to take on guilt" for their actions, as Christ had done, was the duty that "no responsible man can escape."[37]

It was in this sense that Bonhoeffer referred to the Resistance as an "act of contrition." The problem that confronted the German opposition was how to balance the dictates of "responsibility" with the belief that action against the regime would prove ineffectual or even harmful to Resistance aims. This dilemma could be resolved only by removing action from the political realm altogether and elevating it to the level of a moral statement undertaken by the few in the name of the many. By stressing the "representative" character of the Resistance, Bonhoeffer freed it from dependence on uncertain allies, and offered the hope that it might cleanse Germany of shame through its own sacrifices. The decision to "take on guilt" in this way rested with the individual, who could determine not how, but for what he died. "We still love life," Bonhoeffer wrote, "but I believe that death can no longer surprise us much . . . We ourselves will be the ones to make of our death what it can be—a death of voluntary acceptance."[38]

Both the aesthetic ideals of the inner emigration and the religious inspiration of the German Resistance coalesced in the clandestine verse that circulated during the war. Walter Dirks recalled that such poetry offered "encouragement, spiritual inspiration for [the cause of] freedom, and so forth. We devoured it, typed it up, and secretly passed it on." The best-known war poets, the Catholics Werner Bergengruen and Reinhold Schneider, both displayed a concern for Christian values, a recognition of German guilt for the war, and a preference for tight, traditional poetic structures, especially the sonnet. Their attempts to uphold a standard of moral order in the midst of chaos attained symbolic expression in the formal, metrical order of their verse. The sonnet's paired stanzas facilitated contrasts between lies and truth, despair and hope, present misery and future grace, while its traditional diction affirmed cultural continuity in a barbaric age. The need to maintain old standards, to outlast the forces of disorder, was a recurrent theme in these poems. As Bergengruen declared:

> He who endures to the end
> Is crowned most truly.
> No breath of constancy is lost.[39]

Unlike French and Italian Resistance literature, which sought to express a collective experience of revolt, German underground poetry of the same period depicted the nation as a prisoner awaiting a freedom that could be earned only through suffering. These poems convey an atmosphere of fatalism; men wait and hope, but cannot influence their destiny. This passive attitude emerges clearly in a poem that Schneider composed in the last days of the war:

>At the battlefield's edge, helpless, hour by hour
>I hear the growing power of the thunder
>Blow upon blow, echoing in the heart.

The destruction of Germany is seen as a merited punishment. An acceptance of guilt and of the need for atonement (as Bonhoeffer had argued) remains the one contribution the poet can offer toward the goal of achieving liberation from Nazi rule. Schneider writes that "Hate and death's night/Are broken only by guilt that awakes as guilt." In sacrifice lies the way to renewal.

>Where is hope, if not in the martyrdom
>Of the pure, who with holy courage
>Passed into the fatal night of our sins.[40]

It is difficult to judge this poetry, or the "camouflaged" criticism of writers like Jünger, in a manner that does justice either to the extraordinarily difficult conditions under which it was produced or to its limited effects. Opposition in Germany was a lonely and dangerous task. To dismiss the inner emigration as mere aesthetic escapism overlooks the degree to which it was motivated by a concern for "preserving the image of man undefiled" as a source of "courage and solace" for the present and as an ideal for future generations.[41] The question of why this ideal had proven powerless to prevent Hitler's rise was seldom asked. Abstracted from its social setting, it possessed a self-evident superiority to National Socialism. This was sufficient to justify the fight for its survival.

Yet ultimately these writers failed to provide a model for postwar thought. The traditional German culture that they tried to preserve was rejected by its designated heirs among the younger generation. For the latter, Bergengruen's "image of man" was both too narrow and too abstract, a humanism that stressed the vertical bonds of the individual with the absolute rather than the horizontal bonds that united him with other men in active, daily life. The features of the *Bildungsideal* that gave it such persuasive force during the Third Reich—its promise of spiritual election and inner freedom to meet the challenge of the authoritarian state—offered little guidance for the task of social reconstruction that commenced in 1945. Even Bonhoeffer, though he strove to give moral duties toward others a dominant value in his *Ethics*, confined them largely to the realm of conscience. Nor did the Resistance provide the sense of release and self-discovery that it brought to so many in France. On the contrary, it sapped the inner reserves of those it touched. "Are we still of any use?" Bonhoeffer asked in 1942. "Experience has made us suspicious toward others and kept us from being truthful and open to them; intolerable conflicts have worn us down and even made us cynical."[42]

The dissident writers, like the conspirators of July 20, 1944, bore witness to the "other Germany" that refused to capitulate to Hitler. But their moral legacy proved difficult to adapt to the demands of peacetime. Their contribution to postwar culture and politics remained symbolic and indirect, that of martyrs, not prophets. Their work marked not a beginning, but an end.

Poetry and Truth

Among those who showed least sympathy for the aims of the inner émigrés was a group destined to play a major role in the reorientation of German culture after 1945. These were the young intellectuals, conscripted into the *Wehrmacht*, who had spent the war in uniform. Whereas their contemporaries in France and Italy provided the partisan movements with the bulk of their recruits, German youth who rejected Nazism were nonetheless forced to fight in its defense. The moral conflicts arising from the experience were severe and inescapable. They could not share what Camus termed the "overwhelming certainty" issuing from "four years of terrible struggle." Instead they were burdened with guilt, cynicism, and doubt. For them, the war's end precipitated a break with the past that threw all values into question. "We were unbelievers," one of them later recalled. "Where could we pick up again, since everything around us lay in pieces?" In their search for an answer, they had no resources at first but their own.[43]

In 1945 younger German intellectuals directed their energies toward a quest for first principles on which to rebuild their faith and self-respect. After twelve years of being lied to, misled, and manipulated by Germany's leaders, these veterans sought to determine at first hand what could be known with certainty. "The compulsion for truth," noted Günter Eich, "that is the writer's situation." Only by freeing themselves from all preconceptions and by rejecting any "embellishment of what exists" could the postwar generation re-establish contact with reality. Hence their suspicions and their ruthless skepticism, which often shaded off into self-pity. "We live without God, without shelter, without promises, without certainty," wrote Wolfgang Borchert shortly after the war. "All we can do is add, reckon the total, draw a balance, note things down."[44]

Men like Eich and Borchert hoped to take a first step toward the certainty of precision by translating personal experience into an appropriate literary form. But they felt little confidence that the German writer possessed the tools needed for such a task. They worried about the inadequacies of language—a concern that had been voiced by others well before the war. The Viennese critic Karl Kraus, for example, whose review *Die Fackel* waged a long campaign against declining literary standards, wondered in 1933 whether the realities of Hitler's New Order could be expressed in rational discourse at all. "There is so much to be amazed at [in the Nazi movement]," he stated, "that it is not easy to find words. In order to say what happened, speech can only haltingly mimic events." By the war's end, the challenge facing younger writers seemed even more difficult. Not only did the chaos of the present defy description, but the written language that might encompass it had been further corrupted during the Third Reich. Nazi rhetoric had flattened the linguistic contours of German prose, erasing old distinctions and reducing complex ideas to a few simple slogans. As Hitler argued in *Mein Kampf*, effective propaganda "must restrict itself to very little, and repeat this endlessly."[45]

Language was thus subordinated to the party's needs and became an instrument of control devoid of all formal integrity. The term *Wehrmacht*, for example, suggested a simple defensive force, whereas its mission had been to subjugate a continent. Even more striking was the change undergone by adjectives such as "fanatical," which Goebbels and Hitler employed in a fully positive sense. Moltke noted in 1941: "Words have lost their unequivocal meaning, symbols no longer evoke a uniform concept, works of art have been robbed of their true significance and—like all cultural values—have become functional. They serve the state . . . and have become relativized." Opposition writers, forced to take refuge in double meanings and allusions, offered little more than what one postwar critic, Gustav René Hocke, called "a curious stylistic exoticism." Neither camouflaged prose nor naked propaganda could serve as a model for postwar writing. "Clarity of form and immediacy of expression" were needed now, Hocke argued. "For what can spiritual freedom ultimately be except pure harmony between assertion and truth?"[46]

How would it be possible to restore such harmony and to anchor language once more in concrete experience? One answer was to prune literature to its bare essentials. Flights of rhetoric and stylistic embellishment invited ambiguity and harbored lies. Truth was simple. Borchert expressed this distrust of artistic refinement when he wrote: "We don't need poets with good grammar. We lack patience with good grammar. We need those . . . who call a tree a tree and a woman a woman, who say yes and say no. Loud and clear and simply and with

no subjunctives."[47] Like Camus, Borchert equated linguistic clarity
with ethical integrity. The written word was an appeal to reason, while
the abuse of the implicit compact between author and reader for
aesthetic effect or political ends was an offense against human dignity.
A restoration of simplicity and honesty to literature would not only
provide a new coherence to a shattered world but also establish a basis
of communication among Germans long separated by war and lies.

The problem of language became a central issue for those young intellectuals who felt alienated both from traditional German culture
and from its perversion under the Nazis. The renewal of language
symbolized hopes for a more basic renewal of the nation's ethical and
intellectual foundations. But in order to move from the zone of
"relative" meaning to that of absolutes, it was essential to begin by
describing physical objects rather than emotions or values. The narrower the field of vision, the smaller the risk of subjective distortion.
Where the Resistance had discovered certainty in a transcendent moral
order, the first postwar writers sought it in a rejection of transcendence. They would describe only what they could perceive directly and
name unambiguously; they would record rather than interpret.[48]

This concern for precision within a restricted sphere of experience
was especially appropriate for the many young Germans who made
the transition from war to peace as prisoners of the Allies. During the
months of waiting for release from prisoner-of-war camps in Western
Europe, the United States, and the Soviet Union, countless soldiers attempted to fix their thoughts in verse. The first authentic genre of
postwar German writing was the lyric poetry of these captives. It was
the work of amateurs, predictably uneven in quality and often
derivative in technique. A comparison of the styles represented in
prison-camp newspapers or in anthologies such as *Deine Söhne,
Europa* (*Your Sons, Europe,* 1947) reveals the degree to which it was
also a literature of transition. As one former prisoner wrote in 1946:

> Just as a spiritual and artistic vitality could emerge among
> French POWs in Germany, one whose special qualities enriched
> the cultural renewal of France, so there arose in the German
> POW camps . . . a new cultural life that may bear similar fruit
> for us . . . Lyric poetry flourished in almost unimaginable quan-
> tity [in the camps]. There it derived from two different
> sources—from images of the past, reproduced ever anew from
> memory, and from the real spiritual experience of captivity.[49]

This poetry was by no means exclusively innovative or anti-Nazi. Its
forms were as varied as its inspiration. Nature poems of nostalgia and
delight in a sunlit world, where "An ancient folk tune / Sings softly of

bright garlands" contrasted with poems that focused on the sights and sounds of camp life. While the former offered escape from the present, the latter at times displayed something that approached "pure harmony between assertion and truth." What unity the two types possessed stemmed from a common emotional situation. Their authors, writing for themselves alone, poured out their feelings with little attempt at self-censorship or restraint. Few acknowledged guilt, still fewer repentance. What predominated instead, among both Nazi sympathizers and opponents of the Third Reich, was a sense of estrangement and isolation. Men separated from their families by war and captivity, men who had lost close friends in combat and felt betrayed by the regime that ordered them into battle, sought the meaning of these sacrifices and found none.[50]

Of the thousands of poems to emerge from the experience of captivity, the best known is Eich's "Inventory," composed in 1945 when its author was interned at an American camp on the Rhine:

> This is my cap,
> This is my coat,
> Here my shaving kit
> In the linen bag.
>
> Tin cans:
> My plate, my cup,
> I have scratched my name
> In the tin.
>
> Scratched here with this
> Precious nail,
> Which I hide from
> Covetous eyes.
>
> In the haversack are
> A pair of woolen socks
> And a few things that I
> Reveal to no one.
>
> Thus it serves as a pillow
> For my head at night.
> The cardboard lies here
> Beneath me and the earth.
>
> The pencil lead
> I love most of all:

> It writes verses for me by day
> That I devise at night.
>
> This is my notebook.
> This is my tent,
> This is my towel,
> This is my twine.[51]

The stark simplicity of these lines brings to mind Borchert's plea for
poetry that "calls a tree a tree and a woman a woman." The author's
vision is restricted to the things he can call his own—objects for the
most part not described, but simply named. The final stanza resumes
the enumeration begun in the first, as if this survey were the poet's
most pressing task. Even these few belongings are threatened by the
desires of others; the poet must hide even a single nail from "covetous
eyes." "Inventory" shows his attempt to reassert possession and to impose meaning on his surroundings through the resources of language.
"I write poems in order to orient myself in the real world," Eich
observed a decade after the war's end. "I look on them as trigono-
metric points or buoys, which mark out a course in an unknown
area."[52]

Eich's camp poetry marks a break with much of his earlier work and
illustrates the desire—felt by many in the postwar generation—to
shake off the models and the influence of the past. After passing his
childhood in the small Prussian town of Lebus-an-der-Oder, Eich
moved with his family to Berlin in 1918, where he succumbed to the
spell of the Expressionists just as their influence on German letters
was beginning to ebb. His early work, published in *Die Kolonne* and
other avant-garde literary reviews during the last years of the Weimar
Republic, was romantic and self-absorbed, offering predictable variations on the themes of longing, nature, and death. He rejected any
suggestion that poetry should convey a political or social message. "A
lyric poet," he declared in 1932, "commits himself to no cause; he is interested purely in himself."[53]

During the Nazi years, Eich's stance remained apolitical. He wrote
radio plays and adaptations of the German classics for broadcast in
the Third Reich; the fragments of these works that have survived
display no great literary merit.[54] More significant is the fact that Eich
wrote no poetry between the mid-1930s and the war's end. He seems to
have offered neither support for nor opposition to the New Order, except for the passive resistance implied by his refusal to join the National Socialist party. His military service from 1939 to 1945 was
uneventful; a friend secured him a post as a supply officer far from
the front. Yet immediately after being captured by the Allies in the

spring of 1945, Eich resumed writing with a new poetic maturity attained during his decade of silence.

The changed perspective embodied in Eich's camp poems shows in his treatment of themes previously explored by the inner émigrés — above all the relationship between man and nature. Wiechert and Jünger, as noted earlier, believed that the natural order of "ancient laws, which creation obeys" could provide a haven from the disorder of society or serve as a beacon of certainty in troubled times. Jünger observed in his diary late in 1944: "The life of plants and their cycle safeguard the reality that threatens to disintegrate under demonic forces. The adversaries of the Chief Ranger are gardeners and botanists."[55] Eich himself had evoked a pantheistic vision of union with the natural world in his prewar poems. "Your Days," published in 1927, suggests a common understanding among living things: "Once you had the feet of a tree / And you were anchored in the harbor of the earth." But this mystical unity was shattered by the Nazi years and the war. Just as men were now strangers to one another, suspicious and afraid, so, in Eich's camp poetry, they were estranged from nature as well.[56]

The one landscape that is not foreign to Eich is a square of hard earth ringed with barbed wire. Here nature shows a hostile face; rain, cold, and vermin assail the prisoners, while "the green of spring on the paths will be crushed to mud." Eich's attempt to portray camp life without sentimentality can be seen as a repudiation both of the inner émigrés and of the traditional German *Naturlyrik* of Heinrich Heine, Joseph von Eichendorff, and Eduard Möricke, with their nineteenth-century vision of pastoral idyll. A poet who "sees through Eichendorff's eyes," Eich later noted, "deceives himself and others, as if there still existed oases of beauty and a calendar of the soul." Poems such as "Latrine" or Eich's ode to a louse are intended as affronts to romantic canons of taste. His denial that the classics of the past could be relevant to a tortured present becomes explicit in "Spring along the Golden Mile":

> At home clothing and shoes were in flames,
> *Niebelungen* and *Faust*.
> I gaze at the flight of mosquitoes
> With feverish eyes, apathetic and lousy (*verlaust*).

The juxtaposition of *Faust* and *verlaust* confronts the world of artistic convention with the distasteful but insistent reality of physical needs. Again, in "To the Lark," Eich cautions against a poetry of sweet lies:

> Oh sing us no false comforting lullaby,
> Be a prophet for us and sing the cold future.[57]

A similar attempt to break with the romantic tradition characterizes the short stories of another war veteran, Wolfgang Borchert. Of all the voices that emerged in Germany during the early postwar years, Borchert's was perhaps the most urgent and most arresting. His premature death in 1947 from a liver disease contracted while a Nazi prisoner left an aura of martyrdom about his work. As Heinrich Böll wrote, he had just time "to say what the war dead, to whom he belongs, could no longer say."[58] For Borchert, as for Eich, the end of hostilities marked the beginning of a new artistic maturity. During his adolescence in Hamburg he had written mannered, imitative poetry, strongly influenced by Rilke. Following his induction into the *Wehrmacht* at age twenty in 1941, he began to compose short prose pieces that reflected his later themes, but his style remained sentimental and vague. The earliest of these, entitled "The Flower," begins with an apocalyptic vision: "I was dreaming. On all sides were destruction and death. Life sank senselessly into nothingness, with no hope of resurrection. Where is the meaning of the world, I asked creation. Is there no meaning? Despairing and powerless I wandered from epoch to epoch, but in all of them was war." Borchert's dream ends with the discovery of a flower (reminiscent of the *blaue Blume* dear to Novalis, Tieck, and other German romantics) that restores his belief in a meaningful universe. "Oh endlessness of being in you, flower of God. In you I find the meaning and the life I had lost."[59]

The bathos, strained rhetoric, and pretentious use of abstractions of this literary effort are characteristic of Borchert's wartime writing as a whole. He struggled to convey his emotions with a language whose hysteria undercut their force. After the war, however, he abruptly found a solution to these stylistic problems in a short story whose theme and title make it a sequel to his earlier failure: "The Dandelion," written in his hospital bed in 1946. The opening lines immediately reveal a new simplicity and directness: "The door closed behind me. It often happens that a door is closed behind you; you can imagine it being locked as well . . . And now the door was pushed closed behind me, yes, pushed closed, since it is a surprisingly thick door that cannot be slammed shut. A hideous door with the number 432."[60] Instead of being dissipated in appeals to universal abstracts, the reader's attention is directed to a single concrete object. As Borchert gradually refines his description, adding detail upon detail, he associates his audience with the effort to map an unfamiliar environment. Before the author has made it explicit, they grasp that he is describing a Nazi prison.

Objects acquire a new vividness and importance in these bleak surroundings, much as they did for Eich in the POW camp. More important, however, imprisonment brings Borchert face to face with himself: "And I have been alone with the one being, no, not simply left alone with but locked up together with the one being whom I fear most—myself. Do you know what it is like to be given over to your own care . . . to have nothing at all but yourself?"[61] This confrontation—"one of the most amazing adventures we can have in this world"—is the starting point of Borchert's postwar writing. Deprived of all external sources of value and authority, the individual discovers their ultimate source within his own person. He emerges from his isolation, not through the "magical influence" of mass conformity, or by submitting to nature's "ancient laws," but as a result of his own efforts to shape and give meaning to his life.

"The Dandelion" illustrates this lesson under the most adverse conditions. The narrator at first succumbs to a sense of helplessness and awaits his fate without hope. One day he picks a small flower that grows in the prison exercise yard, a dandelion that "soon assumed the value of a person, of a secret loved one for me." This modest act of rebellion liberates him from his fear and impotence and makes it possible for him to renew his ties with other living things. Taking possession of the flower, "he put aside and shook off everything that weighed upon him: imprisonment, loneliness, hunger for love, weakness."[62] The dandelion becomes a symbol of self-assertion, of the ability to introduce change into a static and oppressive environment through a creative impulse like that of the writer or artist.

Borchert's other writings of this period do not all conform to the realist canon. Like the poetry of the camps, his work hesitates between stylistic innovation and reliance on inherited forms and models such as Expressionism. The veterans' belief that one could create without drawing on earlier traditions thus proved naive. "Even in 1945," the critic Urs Widmer has observed, "no one was working in a vacuum. It was impossible to close one's eyes completely to a literary and linguistic past."[63] But Borchert's periodic recourse to the romantic, emotionally charged vocabulary of the 1920s is more than a mere failure of inspiration. The message he sought to convey strained the limits of the stylistic asceticism he attempted to impose on his work. It is this tension between style and content that gives his prose its true character and impact.

For Borchert is ultimately less concerned with a neutral description of reality, with "drawing a balance, noting things down," than with probing his characters' response to their surroundings. At first they are bewildered and lost in an unfamiliar environment—a prison, the Russian front, or the bombed-out cities of their homeland. But whereas their first reaction is simply to identify the physical outlines of objects such as the "surprisingly thick door that cannot be slammed shut," these objects soon take on a deeper symbolic significance. The flower in "The Dandelion" becomes a "beloved one," just as factory chimneys in the story "Billbrook" become "bones of a giant skeleton, . . . fingers of the dead." The truth of words comes to signify the truth of personal emotions, an attempt to reorder the world from the standpoint of the subjective individual. "And behind everything? Behind what you call God, river, star, night, mirror or cosmos, Hilde or Evelyn—behind everything can always be found yourself. Icily alone. Pitiable. Great. Your laughter. Your need. Your question. Your answer."[64]

Thus, within a year of the German defeat, writers such as Borchert were moving toward the positions defended by the French intellectual Resistance. The individual was seen as a touchstone and final arbiter of values. "Are we without an answer?" Borchert asked, and replied with a second question: "Are we ourselves this answer?"[65] Stripped of the false comfort provided by the national community, the individual was at liberty to innovate, to create a new future of his own. Both their renunciation of transcendence and their emphasis on innovation set the postwar writers apart from the inner émigrés, who wished to restore man to a place within an unchanging, hierarchical order of nature. For the younger intellectuals, neither God nor nature interposed their presence between man's questions and the answers he must learn to seek from himself.

The Antifascist Experiment

German soldiers who had spent the end of the war as captives abroad returned to a homeland they scarcely recognized. The defeated Reich lay exhausted and impoverished. "I must have had no conception of the Germany I came back to," wrote Alfred Andersch, "or else I would have filled my duffel bag with food instead of books . . . What I encountered was a Germany of darkness, of catastrophe, of chaos." The massive destruction wrought by Allied bombing in the final months of the war had reduced most major cities to a landscape "like the cratered surface of the moon," as one British officer reported, "unrecognizable save as a mass of chaotic rubble."[66] Many bridges, rail lines, and munitions factories had been dynamited by the Nazis to prevent them from falling into Allied hands. One of the Führer's final orders to his officers in the field was to "activate the struggle against the approaching enemy in the most fanatical way. No respect for the population," he added, "can be shown at this time."[67]

Worse than the destruction was the lack of planning for its sequel. Hitler's entourage could not discuss preparations for defeat without arousing suspicion of high treason. Only a few Nazi leaders like Albert Speer, the armaments minister, faced the problem of what was to follow with any degree of realism. And even Speer was more concerned with "rescuing industrial installations" through blocking attempts at sabotage than with any positive steps toward assuring a minimum of food and shelter for the population at large.[68] Abdication of responsibility at the apex of a governmental structure geared to the Führer's "leadership principle" brought confusion and paralysis at all levels.

By the time of the German surrender in May 1945, the state had ceased to exist in all but name. The mass exodus of civilians from the battle zone, the suspension of mail and telephone service throughout Germany, and the lack of supplies and transport facilities fragmented society into progressively smaller units. Personal accounts of this period stress the feeling of unreality created by a sudden narrowing of horizons. The writer Erich Kästner, who fled Berlin in the last days of the war for a small town in the Bavarian countryside, wrote in his diary on June 19, 1945: "Towns and cities are islands that know nothing of one another. They are living points, and between them is a void. The lines between the points are lacking. If radio did not exist, one would think one was living on the moon. Individual localities are monads, and only radio broadcasts provide a faint reminder of former and future relations together."[69] For those who had grown accustomed to the constant presence of a police state and the forced solidarity of the *Volksgemeinschaft*, the transition was disorienting.

From March to August of 1945, during the "interregnum" between Germany's military collapse and the formal adoption of Allied occupation policy, an attempt was made to fill this political vacuum at the local level. Groups of anti-Fascist Germans set to work almost immediately to clear debris, restore essential public services, and collect and distribute food and fuel. The speed and decisiveness with which these local groups—"Antifas," as they came to be known—assumed the immediate burdens of reconstruction suggested that Hitler's fall had liberated energies and hopes long repressed under Nazi terror, forces that could now be mobilized for the tasks that lay ahead. A leaflet circulated by one such group in Bremen proclaimed: "For the first time after twelve years without rights, we can breathe freely again. We may again feel ourselves to be human beings and need not tremble before the bloody despotism of murderous criminals . . . If we wish to go on living, the ruins must be removed and rebuilding must begin." The Antifas' membership, though drawn largely from the Left, included representatives of diverse political currents. The Bremen group advertised itself as a "union of all anti-Fascists, regardless of their former party affiliation, devoted to the common struggle against Fascism."[70] Since the most pressing problems were practical ones, requiring technical rather than political skills, harmonious cooperation was not difficult to secure in the early stages of the Antifas' work.

Both the pattern of participation and the internal structure of the Antifas recalled the French underground. Only now, when the immediate danger of denunciations and reprisals was past, could German dissidents risk the expansion and diversification of activities that had characterized French movements such as Combat during the war. The Antifas were independent, necessarily decentralized undertakings that operated without rigid lines of command or formal statutes. Their most common method of organization divided responsibility for specialized tasks among a network of committees, under the supervision of a coordinating chairman. One such group, in Berlin's Charlottenburg district, included units assigned to repairing streets, restoring gas and electric service, even assembling an archive on the July 20 conspiracy. "The whole thing," a visitor noted with some surprise, "gives the impression of a very well-functioning administration."[71]

Meeting immediate needs was only the first step in a more ambitious program. Both through public proclamations and through the force of their example, the Antifas aspired to "penetrate the country with a new attitude and anti-Nazi principles." With their emphasis on close cooperation and spontaneous initiative for the good of the community, they embodied an alternative to the interest politics of Weimar and the regimentation of National Socialist rule. Like the French Resistance, the Antifas combined elitist and populist tendencies, speaking for the Germans in matters of civic interest while seeking to avoid a return to the rigid bureaucratic structures that had marked local administration in the past. They actively engaged in direct democracy, and they believed that they might win the support of the population for their vision of political reform. Change from below was their goal. As one member told an American political intelligence officer, "To me and my colleagues, this is the beginning of a new revolution for Germany."[72]

The term "revolution" must be understood in the rather loose sense associated with its use during the same period in France. The aims of the Antifa movement, set forth in mimeographed tracts and manifestos (of which regrettably few survive), have a familiar ring: the punishment of Nazis, the restoration of civil rights, the reconstruction of trade unions, and the creation of workers' committees in the factories. In addition to this basic platform, the Antifas proposed the adoption of a truly socialist economy to replace the "false" socialism of the NSDAP. A manifesto in Hamburg, for example, declared that anti-Fascists should strive for "nationalization of key economic sectors, especially mines, steelworks, . . . transportation, civil service, banks, and insurance companies." Like the CNR charter, the Antifa manifestos sought a synthesis between freedom and social justice. And as in France, the prospect of rebuilding was seen as a new start, not simply a return to old institutions and habits. "The construction of a new order must not be a 'restoration,'" declared the Bremen committee, "no restoration of a past which the harsh hand of history has swept away! For it is not simply the Hitler regime that has been carried to the grave. The pernicious spirit of Prussia, the spirit of obedience and limited understanding . . . were the roots from which the Third Reich grew and which must be destroyed along with it."[73]

The Antifas initiated a general purge of former Nazis and Nazi sympathizers from positions of power. Although many prominent local party functionaries had slipped away during the last days of the war, a large number of their subordinates were still conspicuously at liberty. Nazi businessmen and members of the liberal professions also continued to practice their trades, evidently believing that the Allies would not take action against men whose skills were an asset for reconstruction. The Antifas assigned "political committees" the task of tracking down the worst offenders. In some areas of Stuttgart, the local committee even assumed police powers to arrest those under suspicion until they could be given over to the Allies for trial. Through interrogation and the promise of more lenient treatment for suspects who cooperated fully, it was frequently possible to assemble a detailed and incriminating picture of a past many preferred to conceal. "The Nazis denounced one another very energetically," the Stuttgart group reported with satisfaction. "They even revealed some filthy dealings that were as yet unknown to the anti-Nazis."[74] For the "average" offender, typical punishment was forced labor under the supervision of the Antifas. Thus the purge indirectly aided reconstruction efforts.

Though the duties and goals of the Antifas resembled those of the French Resistance, the major inspiration for their movement came from surviving elements of the left-wing opposition that Hitler had effectively crippled during the first years of the Third Reich. Their socialist economic principles, their strong ties to what remained of the trade union movement, their rejection of both Weimar and Fascism all had counterparts in opposition goals of the early 1930s. What appeared to be new, however, was the widespread desire for unity on the Left. The bitter feuding between Socialists and Communists that had helped to open the way for Hitler's rise to power now yielded to declarations of mutual support against a common enemy. One former member of the Munich Antifa recalled that the "solid core of the organization lay in the so-called active community of Socialists and Communists."[75]

Yet signs of the old rivalry soon began to appear. Once the immediate needs for social services had been met, the political aspects of their program sparked internal disagreements. It proved easier to reach consensus on repairing bridges and power plants than to frame a consistent policy of denazification or to reorganize trade unions. The return of Communist and Socialist officials from foreign exile and Nazi prisons provided the Antifas with needed personnel, but diluted the influence of the early recruits for whom party allegiance was a secondary concern. Moreover, as the political parties began to regroup during the summer of 1945, the question of allegiance became increasingly difficult to ignore. Should the Antifa members devote a part of their energies to rebuilding the old party organizations? Although both the Communists and the Socialists were initially committed to "the banner of unity," their continued existence as separate parties created two rival centers of attraction outside the Antifas, heightening the tensions within.[76]

An equally important source of weakness was the Antifas' failure to mobilize broad popular support for their goals. In a sense, they became the prisoners of the same conditions of anarchy and social fragmentation that had favored their initial creation. Their isolation from the populace shielded them for a time against outside interference, but it also blocked attempts to expand their influence. Because they had neither press facilities nor an adequate distribution network, the leaflets they circulated and the calls they issued reached only a few. The Bremen group, whose journal, *Aufbau*, was a significant exception to the general lack of publicity given Antifa aims, complained that many Germans remained indifferent to the movement. "The events of the past twelve years," *Aufbau* noted in June 1945, "have created a situation in which a large number of Germans wish to 'hear and see nothing more' of politics."[77] An elite without followers, the Antifas possessed neither the time nor the resources to educate the population they aspired to serve.

A final threat to the Antifas lay in the attitude of the Allies. The occupation forces viewed any independent political initiatives by the Germans as a threat to military security. Because lax enforcement of the Treaty of Versailles was presumed to have aided the Nazis' rise during the 1920s, proponents of a "hard peace" argued for an opposite approach after Potsdam. The American military governor, General Lucius Clay, was accordingly instructed that "no political activities of any kind shall be countenanced unless authorized by you." The so-called nonfraternization directive in force in the Western zones, discouraging cooperation with anti-Nazi Germans, "was intended to impress on the Germans the prestige and superiority of the Allies—to show them that they had earned the distrust of other peoples and that they had been completely defeated."[78]

Just as de Gaulle distrusted a Resistance movement that he did not directly command, the Allies proved reluctant to share power with any group that was outside their control. No matter how successful the Antifas might be in matters of refugee resettlement or local administration, their very existence contravened the occupation statutes. Within a few weeks after Germany's unconditional surrender in May, they were stripped of their self-assigned duties, forbidden to engage in political organizing, and often forcibly dissolved. In the American zone, their Communist sympathies aroused suspicion, while in the Soviet zone they found themselves accused of harboring Nazi sympathizers. Some groups were allowed to function on a consultative basis, providing lists of suspected war criminals or of technical experts who would be useful in the work of reconstruction, but they were treated as subordinates, not as equals. By August 1945 the role of the anti-Fascist committees as an experiment in German self-government was at an end.[79]

The disbanding of the Antifas had the one advantage of sparing them from charges of complicity with the occupying powers. The mistakes made in the early postwar period could not be laid to their account. Yet with their disappearance, a great deal of goodwill and honest desire for a new beginning was irretrievably lost. Willy Brandt, returning to Germany from Norwegian exile in August of 1945, found a sense of wasted opportunity: "The prohibition of 'fraternizing' was politically short-sighted and practically unworkable; the prohibition of any political activity was directed against the very forces whose active cooperation in rebuilding a new Germany was essential. Almost everywhere that opposition groups sought to prepare the ground for a new democratic order in the days of the breakdown [of the Nazi regime], they were blocked from doing so by the Allied authorities."[80] The fate of the Antifas can be seen as the final chapter in the dilemmas of opposition to National Socialism. German adversaries of the Third Reich were forced to bear the stigma of a regime that they repudiated, but could not defeat alone.

5
A Foundation for Change
1945-1946

Now that the flood waters of propaganda have subsided at last, we have come to the conclusion that many people in this country desire analysis and orientation. And so we have taken up the task.
Eugen Kogon, 1946

Autumn 1945 brought a temporary halt to the German intellectuals' political initiatives. With the end of the Antifa experiment came the realization that hopes for revolutionary change in Germany had been misguided, or at least premature. Hitler's intellectual opponents could not expect to dictate policy to the Allies. "As former anti-Fascists," Hans Werner Richter recalled, "we could do more than others, but only within the limits prescribed by the occupying powers." These constraints prompted them to focus on the more modest goal of guiding public opinion toward honest self-appraisal and moral insight. As Rudolf Pechel wrote in September 1945: "Our people can be aided only if they achieve a clear view, truthfully and without compromise, of their own condition, their mistakes as well as their merits . . . The more seriously we set off on the path of recognizing the true, inner causes of our debacle, the more readily and gladly we will lay the foundations for reconstruction."[1]

Focusing on inner change was a logical consequence of the intellectuals' enforced political passivity. But an equally compelling motive for adopting the course was the belief that Germany could transform itself socially and politically only by first transforming traditional values and attitudes. French intellectuals concerned with creating a society that conformed to humanist ideals set to work in 1945 with a confidence that these ideals were understood and accepted by the nation. Their German counterparts had still to prepare the ground. Before rebuilding for the future, Germany needed to confront the past. "Our task today," wrote the Hamburg weekly *Die Zeit*, "must be to clear away not just the ruins from the streets of our bombed-out cities, but also the spiritual debris of a ravaged era."[2]

Would Germans be able to learn from their recent history? The war and the collapse of the Third Reich were rich in lessons for those with the courage to face them directly. But they offered material for reflection rather than the training in applied civic virtues provided by the French Resistance. The resurgence of German nationalism after the defeat of 1918 was a sobering reminder that a lost war might nourish resentment and self-pity rather than insight into the causes and meaning of the conflict. "What and how we remember, what carries weight for us in the future, will help to determine what we become," wrote Karl Jaspers soon after the war's end. In their self-appointed role as teachers and interpreters, the intellectuals hoped to make the defeat of 1945 a turning point in Germany's political consciousness. "Politics has to do with experience," observed the journal *Die Gegenwart*. "With experience, that is, whose cause and effect have been understood."[3]

The need for understanding was all the more urgent in the confusion and uncertainty that followed Germany's unconditional surrender. In many ways the emotional climate was reminiscent of France in 1940; French soldiers who arrived with General Koenig's occupation forces were struck by the parallel. "We have a German Vichy," reported Pierre Courtade. "Around us [are] the German people, unknown, unreachable, made sullen by the immense shock they have received, preoccupied solely with learning news of their kin and with assuring themselves a tenuous means of subsistence."[4] Like the French underground a half-decade before, German intellectuals felt that they could offer moral leadership in this spiritual vacuum. They could attempt to provide the sense of purpose that their own Resistance movement—weak, divided, and uncertain—had been unable to sustain during the war. Some viewed the failure of the German Resistance to overthrow Hitler by force as a hidden blessing, since it left National Socialism without a martyr and freed Hitler's opponents from the onus of contributing to their country's defeat. It was now essential to make the most of these presumed advantages.

One major obstacle threatened to prevent the postwar German intellectuals from appealing to their countrymen with the same effectiveness as the writers of the French Resistance during the war. The object of their efforts was not to rouse the populace against a regime imposed from without, but rather to acquaint the individual with his conscience. The French experience of occupation had offered clear, if difficult, choices and a kind of moral exaltation. The German intellectuals demanded instead a confrontation with guilt, with moral responsibility for the past, and with the ways most Germans had evaded that responsibility. If the intellectuals dwelt on these themes with stubborn insistence during the first eighteen months of peace, it was because they were well aware that the learning process would be neither swift nor universally welcome.

Behind their efforts lay a belief in Germany's capacity to liberate itself inwardly now that National Socialism had been overthrown by foreign intervention. Freedom born of understanding was what the intellectuals desired above all. This was the deeper, political meaning of their wish to inform, to explore, to criticize. The immediate postwar period they saw as a time of preparation for independent thought and judgment. Their aims could be described by Kant's definition of enlightenment: "The emergence of man from his self-imposed minority."[5]

The Postwar Press

During the first two years of Allied occupation, when travel remained difficult, books a luxury, and personal contacts among friends and colleagues rare, German intellectual life was sustained above all by the press. As the Allies relaxed their initial restraints on German publications in the fall of 1945, under a new system of indirect control through licensing, a public starved for information devoured whatever came to hand. One contemporary observer recalled: "After weeks of total uncertainty, when rumors rolled through the streets like avalanches and the few news reports from still functioning radio sets were generally passed on in distorted form, the appearance of a newspaper was like a light in the darkness. Everyone remembers with what relief and fascination often long outdated copies were read, shared, critically studied, and discussed."[6]

The editors of the new postwar papers were fully aware of their responsibility. In an article entitled "Our Task," *Die Zeit* noted that "the years that lie behind us, especially the six years of war, have shut off the German reader from the world and surrounded him with a fog of propaganda." The words "a free press," it continued, thus signified "a great privilege and an even greater duty" toward the public. The intellectuals did not intend merely to preach, however. The press would provide a conduit for their own views, and might in addition stimulate a public response that would end the isolation they had suffered during the war. Their aim was to begin a dialogue that would benefit all its participants. "We can speak publicly with one another once again," Jaspers commented in the first issue of *Die Wandlung*. "Let us see what we have to say."[7]

The desire for what Jaspers called "mediation and discussion" following the enforced silence of the Hitler years was felt with special intensity by those journalists who had contributed to the "camou-flaged" opposition press during the Third Reich. Now at last they were able to move from insinuation to an open statement of principles. The impatience of such veterans to resume writing in these new cir-cumstances could be judged from the speed with which they gained leading positions in the postwar press. From the old staff of the *Frankfurter Zeitung* alone came editors of three prominent journals: Dolf Sternberger directed *Die Wandlung* in Heidelberg; Walter Dirks cofounded the *Frankfurter Hefte* in Frankfurt; and their former col-leagues Benno Reifenberg and Albert Oeser supervised *Die Gegenwart* in Freiburg im Breisgau.[8]

The majority of Germany's postwar publications appeared in smaller provincial cities. Of the more than two hundred papers and journals eventually licensed by the Allies, few reached more than a regional audience. Newsprint rationing and zonal frontiers restricted their distribution and encouraged a return to the decentralized pattern of cultural life that had existed in Germany before Berlin's rise to ar-tistic pre-eminence in the 1920s. But although no single paper could claim an authority comparable to that of *Combat* in France, their strong local roots fostered a sense of community between readers and editors and prompted the latter to view their publications as coopera-tive enterprises. The *Frankfurter Hefte* wrote in its inaugural issue: "We expect 'reflective' readers. We believe that we are thus performing a service for the renewal of Germany—we, meaning the editors, staff, and readers included. The darkness around us shall brighten. We wish to help all to clarify the opaque and the enigmatic, insofar as that is permitted . . . to us as we emerge from the depths." Like many weekly and monthly journals, the magazine hoped especially to attract a clientele of "lively, questioning" persons from "all social strata, age groups, and currents" of thought.[9]

To gain and hold such a readership, it was necessary to earn its respect. Many Germans, however eager for news, remained wary and cynical after their exposure to Goebbels's propaganda. Memories of Nazi journalism, as well as the need to avoid incurring Allied censor-ship, encouraged sobriety and editorial caution. *Die Gegenwart* noted: "The tone of contemporary journalism strikes a realistic, if subdued note. The fact that the soft voice of . . . objectivity follows the infernal clamor that filled a whole land for twelve years is one of the few compensations that our misfortunes have afforded us till now." Such "objectivity" meant a preference for stressing problems rather than offering solutions and for an inductive approach that made no claims to superior insight or omniscience on the part of the editors. Instead, postwar journalists adopted a posture of self-conscious humility. "None of us is a leader," wrote Jaspers in *Die Wandlung*, "no one is a prophet who says in binding fashion what exists and what is to be done."[10]

The assumption behind the initial phase of postwar journalism was nonetheless an optimistic one. Given unbiased information, the reader could be expected to form opinions rationally and independently, free from prejudice or the pressures of conformism. To provide such information, a number of journals devoted considerable space to documents and summaries of current events. *Die Wandlung*, for example, published the complete text of the Potsdam Agreement in its first issue; in its second, the texts of the Atlantic Charter and the Teheran Conference declaration. Under the rubric "Zeitregister" ("Index of the Times"), *Die Gegenwart* provided a digest of trends and decisions likely to affect Germany in the coming months, while its feature "From the Newspapers of the World" offered glimpses of foreign opinion from publications still unobtainable in Germany.[11] In addition to information concerning politics and daily life, postwar journals brought news of cultural events abroad—the first that many of their readers had received since the beginning of the Third Reich. The *Frankfurter Hefte* carried one report on "literature and society in the U.S.A.," another on the Italian novelist Ignazio Silone; *Der Ruf* printed excerpts from works by Silone and Beauvoir and from Koestler's *Darkness at Noon*. These offerings signaled a small step toward overcoming what one journalist termed "the spiritual desolation in which we have been forced to live for many years."[12]

The feature of the postwar press that best exemplified the search for truth and the attempt to broaden readers' perspectives was the *Reisebericht*, or travel account. This typically took the form of a first-person narrative recounting journeys to other cities or into other zones, conversations with fellow travelers, and details of living conditions, interspersed with philosophic or historical reflections and presented in a loose, anecdotal style. One journalist noted in 1946: "A new genre, one might say, has arisen in the publications of all zones —the kaleidoscopic report of travels through Germany. On these wanderings reality is recovered, still very impressionistically, dot by dot, movement by movement."[13] The *Reisebericht* balanced the neutral, factual side of postwar journalism with a personal and subjective component. It related a series of adventures, dominated by the contingent and the unexpected, whose narrow focus provided narrative intensity at the expense of overall perspective. It conveyed fragments of a broader picture yet to be completed—fragments more convincing because they made no claim to final judgment. In this respect the *Reisebericht* conformed to Borchert's admonition that the first task of the postwar observer was to "add, reckon the total, draw a balance, note things down."

The author of a *Reisebericht* also served as eyes and ears for the mass of readers who were still unable to travel freely. His observations broadened the experience of the stay-at-homes, providing standards by which to assess their own misfortunes. There was, in fact, a curiously anachronistic flavor to these accounts, reminiscent of the importance assigned to travelers' tales in the preindustrial age. At the same time, they continued from the previous decade the tradition of the novel of exploration and discovery, transposed to a now unfamiliar homeland. The shock of confronting the reality of postwar Germany was a recurring theme in the *Reisebericht*. Dolf Sternberger, in "Travels through Germany—Summer 1945," described the sight of his gutted home in Frankfurt as triggering a sensation "like an amputation that touches one's innermost tissues and fibers." "I was no longer the same person," he added, "as I turned away."[14]

As Sternberger's remarks suggest, the traveler underwent a change in the course of his journey; he returned altered both by his observations and by his contact with others. Debate and shared experience were as much a part of the *Reisebericht* as independent discovery. In the crowded freight cars that most often served as transport for these reporters, Germans from all classes and backgrounds were brought together at random. Hans Werner Richter observed in *Der Ruf*: "The network of rails that run criss-cross through a land is the pulse of a people . . . Thousands of conversations take place along its length between persons who have never met before and who will never see one another again. The conversations spring to life and subside, come and go . . . But all contain a portion of truth." The dislocation brought by the war and its aftermath permitted new patterns of interaction to replace fixed routines and circles of acquaintance. "It is still possible," Sternberger concluded, "to accept lessons and to give lessons." The *Reisebericht*, by implication, invited its readers to do the same.[15]

Familiarity with current events and with the judgments of others helped the individual to test ideas and to reach conclusions on his own. Yet postwar journalists hoped to move beyond the sphere of private opinion, to encourage public debate as a part of everyday life. Such a move, however, presumed a tolerance for diversity and conflict that challenged the traditional German view of community. In 1945 Germany still lacked an alternative civic culture to that of the *Volksgemeinschaft*. Such an alternative culture not only required a willingness

to view disagreement as inevitable and even valuable; it also assumed
that the citizen could now judge and decide matters formerly referred
to the state. The ideal of the search for knowledge as a common enterprise thus could not be separated from an inquiry into basic democratic values: tolerance, the rights and limits of opposition, belief in
the political competence of the individual. From being the preserve of
a "constant higher power," as the nineteenth-century legal theorist
Rudolf Gneist had once defined it, politics became a concern of all.[16]

How could a new civic culture be achieved? Joseph Mannhardt,
writing in the first issue of the *Deutsche Rundschau* in April 1946,
observed that German indifference toward political issues was
endemic and long-standing. "We are—one can no longer minimize the
fact—an unpolitical people, were and remained so even after we attained national unification. Not that we had no political personalities
in our midst. But they always met with extreme difficulties . . . since
we lacked the spiritual-political atmosphere without which both political thought and action occur in a vacuum." For Mannhardt, the German university offered one hope for reversing this situation. "The intensified focus on politics," he argued, "is essential. It will add a new
value to higher education alongside the old." He proposed to expand
the university's role as a place of debate and training for the young.
The *Frankfurter Hefte* agreed, and urged that the university curriculum "not be unpolitical, but on the contrary . . . furnish an important contribution to the alloy of spirit and politics."[17]

Yet while educational reform engaged the attention and sympathies
of many journalists, few saw it as a wholly adequate answer to Germany's need for a more mature and informed "spiritual-political atmosphere." The *Frankfurter Hefte* qualified its support for the
university's role in a civic education, observing that the classroom
should serve "as a place for a preparatory training, not for action."[18]
Moreover, no matter how successful such training might prove, its
scope would necessarily remain restricted to the student minority.
What was needed in addition was civic education on a broad scale,
devoted to practice rather than theory—an exploration of abstract
democratic ideals that would relate them to the daily affairs of the
citizen. This task the postwar journals undertook themselves by offering their readers what can best be described as a primer in the political
process.

One of the most active and successful popularizers in the domain of
civic education was Dolf Sternberger. In an article entitled "The Rule
of Freedom," he discussed the nature of individual rights; in another
he explained the relative advantages of various voting procedures.
Through a series of biweekly radio talks he illustrated lessons in
political conduct with examples drawn from history and from every-

day life. The bully who tried to elbow his way into a crowded streetcar demonstrated how freedom could be misused; courteous behavior, by contrast, was for Sternberger analogous to the orderly functioning of a community that respected the rights of all. These illustrations were more than mere analogies; they represented politics at its most basic level, human interactions that gave expression to values and attitudes linking the sphere of government with the actions of the citizen. "Everyone can easily see that we all participate in politics," Sternberger insisted, "every day, every hour, knowingly or unknowingly. It was and is a basic and dangerous error to believe and teach that politics begins only with the state."[19]

In their efforts to explain the practical meaning of democracy, journalists like Sternberger could not avoid confronting once again the issue of Allied political controls. Though the signatories of the Potsdam Agreement had pledged to "prepare for the eventual reconstruction of German political life on a democratic basis," individual and civil liberties were to remain "subject to the necessity for maintaining military security" as defined by the zonal authorities.[20] This unresolved conflict in Allied policy posed a serious problem in the area of civic education. Germans might explore the principles of self-government in small matters, and so begin reshaping their attitudes toward authority. Yet was it possible to create a true sense of responsibility among a captive populace? Could they be convinced of the virtues of freedom while they were denied a chance to enjoy its full expression?

It seemed to many Germans as if authoritarian Allied government had merely been substituted for totalitarian Nazi rule, leaving the ordinary citizen with few more rights than before. "Only when one acknowledges clearly and soberly that we are dealing with a military dictatorship in Germany," *Der Ruf* observed in September 1946, "does our situation appear in its true perspective." But it added: "The fundamental difference between Fascist dictatorship and the Allied military government is the fact that under the latter, one can at least demand freedom." As this remark suggested, even while political action remained restricted, it was still possible for journalists to encourage a constructive dissent that had too long been absent in Germany. Alfred Andersch explicitly linked the sharp and vigorous criticism of authority with the practice of true democracy: "The term 'opposition' may seem frightening. But it frightens only those who have not understood the essence of democratic opposition and thus of democracy . . . The inner precondition of democracy . . . is attained solely through the vital interplay of opposing forces, pros and contras, positive and negative tendencies."[21]

Some observers feared that encouraging dissent would only invite the unrestrained attacks on democratic institutions that had raged during the Weimar years, or the "negative tendencies" that had fueled National Socialist support. *Der Ruf* was accused of promoting "opposition at any price" and of receiving "applause from the wrong side" —that is, from unreconstructed Nazis. Andersch and his colleagues did not share this pessimism. The potential for freedom existed, they believed, and must be nurtured. "A living democracy needs time in order to grow," Eugen Kogon noted in the *Frankfurter Hefte*, "a great deal of time and a great deal of practical exercise, especially as long as an unavoidable military government partly promotes, partly hinders it."[22] The presupposition behind the call for criticism was less a belief in its impact on others than a faith in the positive effects it would have on those who exercised it. *Der Ruf* answered those who questioned the wisdom of this course: "Perhaps the example of *Der Ruf* will make many young Germans aware for the first time that they no longer live in a world dominated by government propaganda alone. In other words, we are providing young Germans with the fundamental experience they need in order to arrive at their own conclusions—the experience of *liberty*. Democracy does not exist if those who are to create it have not yet taken part in this basic experience."[23]

Nuremberg and the Question of Guilt

Late in November 1945, amid the chill ruins of Nuremberg, the most famous of Europe's postwar trials began. In a city where National Socialist leaders had harangued cheering crowds at the party congresses of the 1930s, many of these same leaders now stood as prisoners before the International Military Tribunal convened by the Allies. The human drama of "the mighty called to judgment," as one correspondent termed the tribunal's proceedings, dominated the attention of the onlookers.[24] Yet the deeper significance of the trial lay elsewhere. At Nuremberg it was not simply victors and vanquished who confronted one another, but two opposing conceptions of law. To what legal and moral standards should the individual be held accountable? That was the question raised by the Latin motto above the judges' bench: *Fiat justitia*. "Let justice be done."

Before the advent of National Socialism, German legal theory had been governed largely by the principle of the *Rechtsstaat* ("state of law"). This concept differed from those of natural rights or Anglo-American common law in providing a detailed codification of norms, fixed in advance, which (at least in theory) protected the citizen against arbitrary use of force. The range of individual initiative remained narrow; legislation or administrative edict regulated most aspects of daily life. Yet the interests of the individual, though entrusted to a bureaucracy or the courts, were recognized as real and legitimate. Nazi law, in contrast, embodied a radical shift of emphasis in favor of the *Volksgemeinschaft*. "The National Socialist revolution in legal thinking and legal philosophy," wrote the Nazi jurist Hans Frank in 1936, "consists to a large degree in replacing the individualistic principle of law with the idea of a national community." Those excluded from the community on racial or political grounds forfeited their claims to equal protection under law. And even within the privileged precincts of the *Volksgemeinschaft* that protection remained uncertain; the boundary between legal and illegal acts proved to be exceedingly fluid. As Frank declared: "Criminal activity, if it merits punishment according to the fundamental spirit of the legal code and the sound feeling of the people, is punished even when it is not explicitly declared to be subject to legal penalty."[25] The Nazi state, as arbiter of the "sound feeling of the people," was thus bound neither by universal principles nor by its own statutes. It could invoke the good of society to justify any action it deemed expedient.

For Germans living under the Third Reich, Hitler's promise to free justice from the trammels of written statutes and learned technicalities had a genuine appeal. The Nazis exploited a widespread conviction that law and justice were at odds and that the legal protections of the Weimar Republic, like its political institutions, remained too remote from daily needs and realities. J. P. Stern has observed that the Nazis succeeded in creating "the myth of a law that is uniquely capable of identifying and justly evaluating the authentic subjectivity of the offender, that which he 'really' is, and meting out punishment accordingly."[26] The practical consequences of this myth were less reassuring. Since law remained in constant flux, interpreted variously and arbitrarily by the Führer and his associates, the citizen lost the assurance that he could judge between legal and illegal acts. Faced with the power of a police state and denied the certainty of formal law consistently applied, most Germans limited their sense of personal accountability to following orders as meticulously as possible.

In its extreme relativism and its overt subordination to politics, Nazi legal practice accorded the state unlimited power to define and to punish criminal behavior. The International Military Tribunal made a different claim. It necessarily asserted the existence of universal standards of conduct, since without these it could not defend its competence to judge the accused—men who claimed innocence under Nazi law. But the legal philosophy that informed the proceedings at Nuremberg was more than a tactical expedient. It reflected a belief in natural rights and moral absolutes shared by Hitler's opponents in the Resistance. The French prosecutor, François de Menthon, was both a Resistance veteran and a former Minister of Justice who had overseen the early phase of the purge trials in Paris. Speaking before the Nuremberg court as an "interpreter of the martyred peoples of Western Europe," he suggested that the tribunal's principal service would be to affirm "a moral order that is accepted by all." Menthon told the judges: "When you have declared that a crime is always a crime, whether committed by one national entity against another or by one individual against another, you will thereby have affirmed that there is only one standard of morality which applies to international relations as well as to individual relations, and that on this morality are built prescriptions of law recognized by the international community."[27]

The charge that most clearly implied the existence of universal moral standards was that of "crimes against humanity." Menthon argued that this article of indictment could be defined simply as "the perpetration for political ends and in a systematic manner, of common law crimes . . . that are provided for and punishable under the penal laws of all civilized states." Yet its application on an international scale was an extraordinary step. The tribunal charter stipulated that offenses ranging from religious persecution to genocide should be declared illegal, "whether or not in violation of domestic law of the country where perpetrated."[28] Natural law—protecting all equally—took absolute precedence over existing statutes.

Because of the novel breadth and uncertain legal standing of the charge of "crimes against humanity," the prosecution sought to marshal overwhelming evidence to support its case. "The proof of the actual facts," presiding Justice Lawrence later declared, became a "fundamental purpose of the Trial." For ten long months, the courtroom ringed with military police listened to a chronicle of horrors that gathered weight with each succeeding witness. Conditions in the concentration camps, plans for war, and Nazi exploitation of conquered territories were spelled out in minute detail. The trial transcript ran to forty-two volumes, offering what *Die Gegenwart* termed "an unprecedented documentation of an unprecedented era." When the final verdicts were handed down, condemning Göring, von Ribbentrop, and nine others to death, the judges were able to affirm that "the case . . . against the defendants rests in a large measure on documents of their own making."[29]

The Allies' stated aims at Nuremberg won a positive response from most German intellectuals. They interpreted the trial as a sign that natural law might be made relevant to politics through a structure of international controls. "At Nuremberg," wrote the *Frankfurter Hefte*, "the foundation for a new world order has been laid . . . The 'aggressor' becomes a criminal; the time of justification by success is gone." The educational goals of the trial also won their warm support. And yet, in contrast to the dramatic effect and sense of participation generated by Hitler's rallies, the Nuremberg trial was an event that to many Germans seemed alien and remote. "The attitude of the average German," reported the *Süddeutsche Zeitung* a month after the proceedings had begun, "is generally an attitude of apathy, at best of skepticism."[30]

The Germans could remain passive and aloof because they were not prosecutors at the trial, only defendants and observers. Evidence of Nazi atrocities, though profoundly disturbing to some, failed to provoke as deep a shock as might have been expected because the crimes were simply too great to comprehend. The *Neue Zeitung* observed in November 1945: "The human capacity for understanding is limited. Things that exceed a certain measure can scarcely be taken in. During a single hearing on a 'normal day' of the trial . . . one hears of so much guilt and so many demonic crimes that one runs the danger of becoming numbed." The sheer volume of evidence introduced and the haze of legal argument raised by the defense also robbed the alleged offenses of their immediacy and meaning. Even anti-Nazi Germans who were allowed access to the courtroom found it difficult at times to disguise their sense of estrangement from what they saw. "As the session finally came to an end," one reporter wrote, "I myself returned from a far-off, foreign world, out of abstraction into reality. I stood up with a feeling of relief."[31]

When the circle of accusation broadened to include those not present in the Nuremberg courtroom, however, apathy gave way to anger and resentment. While the International Tribunal pursued its deliberations into the fall of 1946, other, local proceedings were simultaneously begun—in accordance with the Potsdam Agreement—against millions of Germans suspected of active complicity with the Third Reich. The effects of "denazification," as it came to be known, soon threatened to destroy what remained of the Germans' willingness to accept guilt. So vast a bureaucratic operation inevitably proved slow, arbitrary, and open to abuse. The shifting criteria used for establishing guilt and the inequalities in punishment meted out in the four zones of occupation led to widespread disillusionment and cynicism. American reliance on documents attesting to a person's character, for example, gave rise to a flourishing cottage industry that produced "Persil certificates"—attestations of (fictitious) past good works, which, like the soap of the same name, were used to launder compromising records. The results of the protracted rounds of hearings and appeals, *Der Ruf* noted critically, were a "continually expanding war of paper" and growing sympathy for its victims.[32]

Still greater protest greeted the Allied theory of collective guilt. This blanket accusation, reminiscent of the much-disputed guilt clause in the Versailles Treaty of 1919, was directed at the German people as a whole. Allied posters showing piles of emaciated corpses in the concentration camps bore the message "You are to blame for that!" At its most extreme, the collective guilt theory took on racist overtones reminiscent of Nazi propaganda, reducing the "master race" to a race of criminals incapable of reform. *Die Gegenwart* asked pointedly whether "an entire people can be so rapidly and summarily judged" by means of a "simple formula."[33] Such a charge commanded no respect from those who had struggled to maintain an inner distance from the *Volksgemeinschaft*, nor from the smaller number who had risked their lives in active opposition.

Though a majority of intellectuals supported the general goals of denazification and atonement in some form, they were unanimous in attacking the shortcomings of Allied practice. Walter Dirks, who briefly assisted the Americans as a judge in the local courts (*Spruchkammern*) created to try former Nazis, spoke for many colleagues when he later concluded that "denazification was one of the greatest mistakes" of the occupying authorities. The intellectuals' concern with education caused them to speak out against the bureaucratic rigidity and judicial clumsiness of an anti-Nazi purge in which the accused were graded and sorted like goods on an assembly line. How, they asked, could Germans learn to value the dignity of the individual when so many were treated as a commodity of little worth?[34] Walter Kolbenhoff protested against the "belief in an unchanging, odious German mentality and the pointlessness of any attempt to alter it," and defended those Germans who "are now attempting, with great difficulty, after bitter disappointments and painful blows, to find a new path."[35]

The Allies judged as outsiders. While this gave their views a claim to objectivity, many Germans felt that only those who had experienced the Third Reich directly could weigh German guilt and motives with any degree of fairness. The *Frankfurter Hefte*, taking note of the "atmosphere of resentment and repression" that now existed in Germany, suggested that German intellectuals should take the lead in helping their countrymen assume responsibility for judgment. "Our task now is . . . to offer the prerequisites for forming one's own opinion and for private reflection."[36] The *Frankfurter Hefte* also offered a second, more radical proposal. True moral insight, its editors believed, could not be compelled from without, but should come voluntarily from within. The review therefore urged that the act of judgment be entrusted to the individual concerned rather than to an external authority. Major Nazi criminals should continue to be tried and punished. But apart from such exceptional cases, each individual German should determine in what measure he was guilty; he should be both defendant and prosecutor in a private trial whose outcome was known to him alone.

Freedom was thus seen as an indispensable prerequisite for contrition. Without it, the *Frankfurter Hefte* insisted, men and women ceased to feel morally accountable for their actions. The Nazi state had robbed its citizens of the responsibility for independent judgment, while the Allies, despite a desire to restore respect for standards of conduct systematically violated under the Third Reich, questioned the Germans' willingness and capacity to accept these standards of their own accord. To reverse this long-standing pattern of constraint and to promote a measure of individual initiative, the *Frankfurter Hefte* advocated retreat to the citadel of privacy. Walter Dirks touched on this theme in the summer of 1946: "We demand no public confession of sin . . . What we must demand of ourselves is first of all a secret but unrelenting examination of conscience." Others echoed his view: "The more quietly and secretly the 'I have sinned' is admitted in one's inmost heart, the more genuine is its worth."[37]

The themes of guilt, self-knowledge, and the difficulty of facing one's conscience dominated Borchert's most famous work, the radio drama *Draussen vor der Tür* (*Outside the Door*, 1946). Its principal character, Lieutenant Beckmann, returns to his native Hamburg after three years as a Russian prisoner of war, only to find himself an outcast. He is "one of those who come home and yet do not come home, because a home for them no longer exists." His parents have committed suicide rather than face the consequences of denazification. Among the living, he finds neither comfort nor absolution. In scene after scene, Beckmann seeks to re-establish contact with other human beings, to reintegrate himself into the community. To no avail. The isolation of his Siberian exile is prolonged by a continuing isolation "outside, at night in the rain, on the street." At length, like the narrator in "The Dandelion," Beckmann is forced to confront "the one being he fears the most"—himself. Here, Borchert argued, lay the true source of help for his hero. Guilt must be acknowledged and accepted; only this self-acceptance could lead to a new beginning.[38]

Borchert's message, however, raised a disturbing possibility. If all norms were declared invalid save those defined by the individual, the way lay open for an absolution pronounced without rigor or guidance. The continuing German respect for qualities extolled and exploited by the Nazis—obedience, loyalty, bravery, hard work—made such an outcome seem all the more probable. Germans might feel a sense of betrayal, even horror, when they surveyed the legacy of the Third Reich, yet still consider themselves blameless for having loyally served the regime. What was needed was a moral framework that linked these subaltern virtues with the ends they served, one that led each person to recognize that he shared responsibility with his superiors, yet at the same time defined levels of complicity with greater precision than did the collective guilt thesis. "Guilt must be determined concretely," Dirks wrote, "clearly defined and precisely differentiated. Guilt must be localized; we must know exactly where it exists. It must be named; we must be told exactly in what it consists."[39]

Karl Jaspers attempted to provide this guidance for introspection in a series of lectures at Heidelberg University during the winter of 1945-46. The discussion of guilt, he maintained, suffered from a mixture of concepts and points of view." Remorse was inadequate if it did not lead to an "objective view of what can be known and pondered." Jaspers therefore distinguished four progressive stages of guilt and responsibility, ranging from the criminal to the metaphysical. Criminal guilt resulted from acts committed "in clear violation of the law." The two intermediate categories of political and moral guilt he associated with specific actions that, while technically legal, were in practice inhumane. Specifically rejecting the argument that atrocities carried out under orders were permissible acts, he endorsed the concept of common responsibility for the political deeds of a nation's leaders. "Government," he stated, "is each man's business." The final category, metaphysical guilt, was the most comprehensive, for it applied to each individual insofar as he failed to act against evil. Jaspers noted: "There exists a *solidarity* among men as men which renders each individual accountable for all the wrongs and injustice in the world, particularly for crimes that occur in his presence or with his knowledge. When I do not do what I can to prevent them, then I share responsibility for them."[40]

In the course of his lectures, Jaspers succeeded in redefining collective guilt in a manner that dispelled much of its ambiguity yet remained consistent with the universal principles to which the Nuremberg trial aspired. "There can be no doubt," he maintained, "that we Germans, that each German is in some manner guilty." But not all were guilty in equal degree. More important, the concept of guilt itself had to be distinguished from that of "political accountability (*Haftung*)." The Allies had been prone to confuse the two. Though it was true that the German people were collectively responsible for the Third Reich and its crimes, an individual was guilty only insofar as he failed to respect a common standard of conduct based on a common humanity. Germans who rightly rejected the Allied claim that they belonged to a pariah nation fundamentally different from others should therefore be prepared to "take on the guilt . . . that speaks to us from our conscience."[41]

The German intellectuals' response to the question of guilt thus proposed a reconciliation between universal precepts and the individual conscience—a solution very close to Beauvoir's "ethics of ambiguity." In this view, each man was responsible to others; it was his duty to respect their rights as equal to his own. But no higher authority could presume to dictate his actions or pass judgment on their worth. This assumed harmony between absolute standards and moral autonomy also answered the ideal many Germans had vainly sought in Nazi law—judgment that "evaluated the authentic subjectivity of the offender"—while avoiding the pitfalls of relativism or nationalistic idolatry of the state.

Yet repentance for past sins, even if attained in full measure, would not in itself prevent the recurrence of National Socialism. As long as its root causes were not understood, they could not be sought out and dealt with. It was necessary to move beyond the inner moral universe and to confront recent German history. The goal of education, which the intellectuals had sought to achieve through a "secret examination of conscience," was now broadened to include the collective experience of the previous decade. Insight into the forces that had brought the nation to disaster appeared an essential complement to the self-knowledge advocated by Jaspers. As *Die Gegenwart* noted, "We must understand and reject this period [of our history]. No other way to overcome it exists."[42]

The Causes of Catastrophe

It soon became clear that Hitler's reign presented a major challenge to the way Germans were accustomed to view their nation's past. "Will we ever," the historian Friedrich Meinecke asked in 1945, "fully comprehend the monstrous events that befell us during the twelve years of the Third Reich?"[43] Meinecke's doubts were shared by many other intellectuals. The phenomenon of National Socialism seemed to mock efforts at rational comprehension. It was the antithesis of measure, clarity, and logic. An additional barrier to understanding Nazism, however, lay in the traditional assumptions of German historiography. The first postwar efforts to interpret the Third Reich led to the realization that these assumptions should be revised.

Central to the established conventions of German historiography had been the belief, inherited from the previous century, that history embodied a definite meaning and purpose. According to the doctrine of *Historismus*, elaborated by the nineteenth-century scholar Leopold von Ranke among others, each culture obeyed an inner drive for self-expression, progressively realizing its distinctive spiritual character in the realm of power politics. As Ranke observed: "In power itself there appears a spiritual substance, an original genius, which has a life of its own, fulfills conditions more or less peculiar to itself, and creates for itself its own domain. The task of history is the observation of this life." Applied to Germany and German aims, such a view took on nationalistic overtones. In Prussia's successful struggle for pre-eminence in Europe, patriotic historians discerned signs of a unique and providential national destiny. Heinrich von Sybel, a spokesman for this faction, argued that military success revealed a harmony between the goals of the state and some greater design: "He who sides with the nature of things is always victorious."[44]

Historismus, like German political theory as a whole, reserved a special role for the state as the agent of order and purpose in history. "The state," Hegel had insisted, "is the reality of the moral idea." Culture and authority, morality and politics found their integration in a single corporate body above the mass of citizens. The many statues of "Germania" erected throughout the Reich after 1871 did not merely portray an allegorical figure, but reflected the German tendency to see the state as an actual person. Historians ascribed a special morality to this collective being, distinct from the code governing individual conduct. They accepted the state's actions as necessarily good by invoking a circular reasoning: since the state alone gave shape to the nation's spiritual values, power and ethics could not be in conflict. "Individual states," wrote the young Meinecke in 1908, "can be understood only if they are granted the unconditional right to act solely in accordance with their own nature and profit." For, he added, "Nothing can be immoral that derives from the most profoundly individual nature of a being."[45]

Both the belief in history as the realm of coherence and necessity and the identification of the state with a higher morality began to be questioned after Germany's defeat in World War I. The "crisis of historicism" that attracted scholarly attention in the 1920s was only a mild prelude, however, to the far deeper crisis precipitated by the fall of the Third Reich. A historicist interpretation of Nazism seemed patently unacceptable to most intellectuals, since it would compel them to admit that Hitler's career had been in some way foreordained—worse still, that the National Socialist state embodied the quintessence of the German spirit. But the alternative prospect of declaring the past to be void of meaning was equally unpalatable.

When Meinecke sought in 1946 to address the "deeper causes of the frightful catastrophe that has broken over Germany," he did so as a reluctant critic of the historicist school in which he had been reared. There were few observers at the war's end whose experience, like Meinecke's, bridged both the founding of the Reich and its final collapse three-quarters of a century later. *Die deutsche Katastrophe* (*The German Catastrophe*), published·in the author's eight-fifth year, was a notable retreat from the self-confident nationalism that had characterized his earlier attitude toward Prussia and its beneficent role in uniting Germany. A current of pessimism first apparent in his *Idee der Staatsräson* (*The Doctrine of Reason of State*, 1924) now emerged to dominate a work in which he castigated Nazi militarism, power politics, and totalitarian rule. "The German conception of the power state (*Machtstaat*), whose history began with Hegel," he concluded, "was destined to experience its most destructive . . . climax and exploitation under Hitler."[46]

Yet beyond a clear perception that the synthesis between spirit and power had come apart with disastrous consequences, Meinecke's diagnosis of how Germany had failed was ill defined. His perplexity revealed itself in a vacillation between opposing explanations. On the one hand, he portrayed the Third Reich as the inevitable consequence of the "two mass movements of the age"—nationalism and socialism. On the other hand, he also believed that accident had favored Hitler's bid for power. Despite "circumstances and facts of a general nature" that might have shaped National Socialism, he found himself compelled to ask whether "chance did not aid . . . Hitler in his rise and final accession to the office of Chancellor."[47]

Meinecke thus remained suspended between a deterministic view of history as dominated by impersonal forces and one that abandoned the notion of historical causality altogether. "Who can ever distinguish clearly between the personal or accidental," he asked, "and the universal [factors] arising from the depths of national life?" In the end, he seemed ready to subordinate the whole problem of explanation to what he considered the equally urgent need for hope. He was prepared to use the past, not as a warning, but as an invitation to recover the virtues of an earlier, more innocent age in German history—the classic age of Idealism so revered by the *innere Emigranten*. "Our task as a people," he wrote, "can now be simply to work . . . at purifying and deepening our spiritual being." Meinecke's final recommendation called for a return to Goethe as a source of inspiration in the nation's time of trial. "Goethe Societies," he hoped, would offer "the most noble German music and literature" to those seeking sustenance, and thus "bring living testimony of the great German spirit into the listeners' hearts."[48]

The one level of explanation on which Meinecke achieved some consistency was emotional. Scattered throughout *The German Catastrophe* lay hints of a dark "satanic principle" whose presence had characterized the Hitler years. "The effect of our experiences on historical thinking," Meinecke wrote, "has been to reveal the demonic dimension of man's historical existence in a more shocking manner than ever before." Others of Meinecke's generation shared this view. Thomas Mann, writing from American exile, also associated German history with the demonic. His dense and demanding novel *Doctor Faustus*, begun in 1943 and completed four years later, employed the legend of Faust's temptation by the devil to explore Germany's descent into Nazi barbarism. In an essay written while *Doctor Faustus* was in progress, Mann observed: "The devil, Luther's devil, Faust's devil, seems to me a very German figure. The pact with him, the written bondage to the devil in order to receive all the treasure and power in the world for a time in exchange for the welfare of one's soul, seems to me peculiarly appropriate to the German being."[49] The career of a modern Faust, the composer Adrian Leverkühn, became for Mann a symbol of the unrestrained ambition that had driven his homeland into the night of the Third Reich. Leverkühn contracts syphilis in exchange for the devil's promise of heightened musical creativity; he attains a lonely and short-lived artistic triumph, only to perish of the disease that both inspires and consumes him.

References to a half-religious, half-romantic conception of the demonic, the metaphor of sickness, Meinecke's contradictory attempts at explanation—all these illustrated the abandonment of rational causality as an appropriate tool for understanding the Nazi period. A vision of Hitler as Satan was an evocative symbol for the suffering caused during his regime; yet its timelessness obscured the specific features of National Socialism. Satan, like "Germania," gave an artificial coherence to a bewildering succession of events that neither Mann nor Meinecke could otherwise explain. For the historian, the major lesson taught by the Third Reich appeared to be resignation to a world of elemental forces beyond man's ken.

Younger intellectuals drew a different conclusion. In contrast to Meinecke's generation, they attempted to focus rational analysis on specific features of the Nazi regime. Chief among the advocates of this modest empiricism was Eugen Kogon. His review of Meinecke's *The German Catastrophe* in the *Frankfurter Hefte*, though respectful of the elder historian's "brave attempt to move beyond old points of view," expressed deep reservations at the results: "The attempt to explain Hitler's concrete ascension with all manner of 'accidents' . . . does not seem at all convincing. 'Chance in history' is certainly an interesting topic, but in no way implies the existence of a sort of *deus ex machina*, a 'demon' or 'hand of fate.'" What required explanation,

Kogon asserted, was less the accidental or demonic aspects of National Socialism than the political climate in which they occurred: "The spiritual rebirth of Germany presupposes a basic change in the way its history is perceived, a backward glance that indicates the forces behind the catastrophe, so that they cannot continue to operate undiscovered in the future."[50]

Pursuing this aim, Kogon published in 1946 a now-classic account of the Nazi concentration camps, *Der SS-Staat* (*The SS State*), as well as a series of studies in the *Frankfurter Hefte* dealing with German history and with popular reactions to the Third Reich. By focusing on the camps, Kogon confronted the aspect of Hitler's New Order that was most "demonic," but also, he felt, most important for revealing Nazi methods and goals. He wrote in the introduction to *The SS State*: "An objective report on the system of German concentration camps, the conduct of all categories of prisoners within them and the attitude of the nation toward this complex . . . can initiate the process of clarification more readily than any other theme."[51] Kogon had survived seven years of captivity at Buchenwald and had become a leader in the prisoner underground, a position that allowed him to "learn every detail of camp conditions." Shortly before American troops arrived to liberate the camp in April 1945, he was placed on a death list by the SS, but he escaped (with the complicity of an SS doctor) concealed in a crate of medical supplies. When the American authorities decided to prepare a report on camp conditions for use at the Nuremberg Trial, they chose Kogon to supervise the task. The resulting book, as its author felt obliged to warn, stood "at the edge of the ethically permissible" in its revelations.[52]

Kogon's analysis recalled Rousset's study of Buchenwald, *The World of the Concentration Camps*, in several respects. Pieced together from his own observations and corroborating accounts from other prisoners, supported with statistics and a mass of detail, *The SS State* showed the camps as an integrated, well-ordered "system of domination through terror." Both Kogon and Rousset adopted a sociological perspective from which to view their appalling experiences, thereby gaining the minimal distance from their subject that permitted them to write at all. Both emphasized the unwritten rules of conduct that governed the prisoners' lives, as well as the perverted logic that dictated their masters' brutality. The Buchenwald system, Kogon asserted, "was well thought out. It effectively met the purpose it was expected to fulfill."[53]

But whereas Rousset presented an emotionally charged account that blended anecdote, analysis, and moral judgment, Kogon dissected the camp system with icy patience and thoroughness. Comparing the two approaches, Rousset later observed that he had attempted to "recreate the movement" of camp life, while Kogon "isolated each element" as if "viewed through a microscope." This contrast reflected in part the different expectations of the audiences for whom these works were intended. The Occupation had prepared the French for subsequent disclosures concerning Nazi atrocities. The Germans, on the other hand, disputed the assertion that their own countrymen could be guilty of such barbarity or that Nazi violence was anything but an occasional (and often merited) response to the enemies of the Reich. Kogon's aim was to overcome his readers' resistance, soberly and methodically, knowing that they would not readily abandon their illusions. The book jacket of the first German edition cautioned: "This book serves no propaganda purpose and does not intend to appeal to sensationalism; it presents a systematic, objective account."[54]

Kogon attempted to show that the "demonic" possessed an internal logic of its own. In his view, the camps were a primitive but potentially stable form of political and economic organization based on slave labor. Not only had they destroyed the "racial enemies" of National Socialism and neutralized its political opposition with frightening efficiency; they had also helped to finance the SS and had increased Germany's war production through a network of satellite factories. "There is no doubt," Kogon concluded, "that had Germany won the war, [Himmler] would have succeeded in . . . extending a tight, effective, permanent [camp] network throughout Germany and across Europe."[55]

This conclusion marked the first step in Kogon's argument. However demented the Nazis' aims, the means they employed to gain them were the product of rational calculation. "Through reason," Kogon summarized in 1948, "the irrational is erected into a system, science is transformed into inhumanity." The German reaction to the camps, on the other hand, displayed a rational pattern of a different sort. Here it was not conscious, but unconscious motives that Kogon emphasized. German claims that the nation had been unaware of the camps, he asserted, could not be taken at face value; yet they were an important key to the truth. Kogon, like Freud, sought to establish a logic of behavior hidden from the actor himself. The reactions he discerned could be understood in Freudian terms as denial and transference, though he avoided such labels. He proposed to free Germans from the "complex" they suffered concerning the camps by bringing their psychological defenses into full view, relying, as Freud had, on "the power of truth" to effect a cure.[56]

What did the average German know about Buchenwald or Auschwitz? Kogon readily acknowledged that only a minority had been eyewitness observers of the camps. A larger number had observed incidents directly related to the arrest or deportation of prisoners, despite Nazi attempts to conceal these actions from public view. Yet indirect knowledge, Kogon insisted, was widespread. In fact, it was because they were not entirely blind to the camps that many Germans refused to accept the guilt of knowing and steadfastly denied their existence. "There was no German who did not know that the concentration camps were there. No German who considered them sanatoriums. No one who was not afraid of them. Few Germans who did not have a relative or an acquaintance in the camps, or at least know that certain people were prisoners there." A few individuals, such as those involved in the July 20 conspiracy, had attempted to dispose of the regime by force, but they had been too few and had acted too late. The majority of Germans instead had shifted the blame for the camps from the Nazis to the prisoners. "Their almost limitless belief in authority led the Germans, even under a dictatorship, to view the captives, not the captors, as lawbreakers." Because they "idealized community of whatever sort," their sympathies went to the many against the few.[57]

In directing his readers' attention toward a general, group attitude of this sort, Kogon pointed to yet a third level of rational explanation for the events of the past decade. Concepts such as *Volksgemeinschaft* and the *Machtstaat* were not spontaneous creations; their acceptance depended on a long-standing political and cultural tradition. But only after abandoning the belief that a benevolent hand guided Germany's destiny would Germans be able to see the state in a different light. Kogon explored that prospect in June 1946 in an article entitled "The Third Reich and Prussian-German History," in which he proposed to "search out the roots that bound the Hitler regime to the German past." The focus of his analysis was the state.[58]

Kogon insisted on historical continuity as a key to the German past. The Third Reich was not an aberration, he maintained, but "the direct and debased inheritance of the conception of goals and methods characterizing the Bismarckian and Wilhelmine eras, which continued underground in the Weimar Republic until they could surface again in a horrible new form." At the center of the "goals and methods" inherited by Hitler lay a foreign policy conceived to promote Germany's "mission for dominating central Europe," carried forward for over a century and a half by Prussia. Whereas in 1946 Meinecke still retained enough of his Prussian patriotism to praise "Bismarck's caution and wise circumspection," Kogon's Austrian upbringing encouraged him to judge what he termed the chancellor's "Machiavellian deceitfulness" with less piety and deference. Prussia's policies of centralization, the creation of a strong military and a dependable bureaucracy, and willingness to use force to achieve political ends were all established well before Hitler came to power. In Kogon's view, the Prussian state's "repellent features simply emerged with greater clarity" after 1933.[59] He thus reversed the positive image of the *Machtstaat* defended earlier by the historicists: far from representing a synthesis of political order and spiritual values, it was an active agent of disorder and a constant threat to ethical goals. The coherence of German history lay, not in Meinecke's "testimony of the great German spirit," but in a Prussian state that had become a prisoner of its own amoral conception of power.

Such an assault on the idols of Prussian history invited criticism for its partisanship. Certainly one risk of Kogon's analysis was that it excluded consideration of trends or events that could not be interpreted as a preface to National Socialism. To argue that the recent German past led inexorably to the Third Reich meant simply to replace one teleology with another, so that the outcome still appeared fore-ordained. Yet while the extent of Bismarck's contribution to Hitler's rise remained a widely debated topic during the late 1940s, the need for a new approach to the German past, sharper in its judgments and less prone to self-congratulation, was increasingly accepted among German historians as the decade moved to a close. Even so conservative a figure as Gerhard Ritter, in an address to the German Historical Conference in September 1949, called upon his colleagues to initiate an "unsparingly critical review of our traditions." Ritter acknowledged the errors of an "often extravagant exaltation of the state (*Staatsfreudigkeit*) in our historiography."[60] Compared to the German historians' eagerness to exonerate their country of responsibility after World War I, this was a new and promising development. It indicated that they were willing to dispense with the particularism nurtured by *Historismus*, and instead to accept a standard of historical judgment common to all.

The birth of political science as a recognized academic discipline in Germany, distinct from history or sociology, was another sign that study of the Third Reich from an "unsparingly critical" viewpoint might be realized at last. Kogon, who with Dolf Sternberger was named to two of the first chairs of political science in the Federal Republic, saw this new field as an additional safeguard against dictatorship. "A people enlightened through the knowledge of politics," he wrote in 1949, "will not easily fall victim to charlatans." Such teaching should be conducted "inductively, not deductively, grounded in practical experience" rather than remaining in the realm of pure theory.[61] This profession of faith summed up the spirit in which Kogon had approached the Third Reich. The rational analysis of Nazi tactics, popular reactions, and historical antecedents to Hitler's regime, he believed, yielded a body of knowledge that could now be further refined and disseminated. The intellectuals' insistence on the need for civic education would find gradual implementation as a discipline on the university level.

Yet in the short run, the German public all too often accepted the intellectuals' efforts at education as a substitute for self-scrutiny. Jaspers's calls for atonement and Kogon's pleas for a more critical examination of Germany's past were taken by their audiences as sufficient in themselves, absolving others from undertaking similar initiatives on their own. Guilt and preoccupation with National Socialism were kept compartmentalized, safely outside the bounds of conscience, the concern of a self-selected minority.[62] Amid the hunger and suffering of the bleak postwar months, most Germans turned their energies toward the fight to survive in the present. The fact that the intellectuals' goals were largely negative—recognition of wrongdoing, rejection of the past—further diminished their appeal to the population at large. Nazi emphasis on unity, on Germany's special mission, on individual salvation in a movement with religious overtones ("our movement will be like a holy order," Rudolf Hess proclaimed in 1934) had stirred hopes for which rational analysis could provide no substitute. The emotional void created by the collapse of the Third Reich remained to be filled.[63]

Socialism and the "Young Generation"

The winter of 1946-47 brought renewed hopes for significant economic and social reforms in Germany. Prospects for German self-government and for a common socialist program brightened as the Allies loosened direct control over their respective zones and gave German political parties a greater voice in national affairs. A broad consensus about the measures needed for social change—including provisions for state planning, nationalization of basic industries, and worker participation in management decisions—emerged from party platforms drafted in anticipation of the upcoming *Land* elections. Just as Camus had noted with a touch of irony in 1944 that "everyone in France is a socialist," *Der Ruf* observed two years later that "socialism has suddenly become fashionable."[64] Support for this trend extended across the political spectrum to include the relatively conservative Christian Democratic party, which proclaimed in the so-called Ahlener Programm of February 1947 that "the era of uncontrolled domination of private capitalism is past."[65]

The agreement—at least in principle—that the state must assume greater responsibility for the economic well-being of its citizens came in response to Germany's worst economic crisis since the Great Depression. More than a year after the war's end, millions of Germans continued to live in stark misery. During the Nazi occupation of Europe they had been fed largely through the spoliation of conquered territories; now their turn had come to suffer hunger and want. Victor Gollancz, a British publisher who made a tour of the industrial Ruhr area in the fall of 1946, reported widespread cases of tuberculosis, edema, and other symptoms of malnutrition. "The health of the population as a whole," he concluded, "is being undermined with such startling rapidity that, unless radical measures are taken to effect an improvement, the toll in one, two, or three years' time will be appalling."[66] A majority of families in severely bombed cities like Hamburg and Cologne shivered in damp cellars or gutted apartment blocks. Wartime destruction of industry, followed by Allied dismantling of many factories to meet demands for reparations or disarmament, brought further unemployment to a country whose working population was already swollen by demobilization and by refugees from the East. As inflation continued to erode the value of the old Reichsmark, black markets sprang up in nearly every town, where family heirlooms were bartered for eggs or coal.

In the face of such conditions, it was imperative to organize and distribute the nation's meager resources as quickly and as fairly as possible. While Gollancz and others attempted to induce the occupation authorities to reverse policies that crippled German efforts at reconstruction and to introduce aid programs for the indigent in their own zones, many German intellectuals hoped that the emerging political parties would take the lead in pressing for socialist measures to achieve the same ends. Confiscating private fortunes appeared a long overdue step in this direction. The fact that some of Germany's most powerful industrialists had both supported and profited from the Third Reich made their expropriation seem not merely economically expedient but also morally justified. The *Frankfurter Hefte* wrote in 1946: "We urge the transfer of this property to common ownership for two reasons pertaining to the welfare of all: in order to prevent the repeated misuse of economic power . . . and in addition to restore the economic basis for secure family life . . . to the destitute mass of millions of our people."[67]

Thus in the intellectuals' view Germany's economic collapse created the possibility of a radical new beginning. Despite the suppression of the Antifa movement, steadily worsening conditions made a revolutionary reshaping of the nation's economy seem, if anything, closer at hand a year later. "Germany," *Der Ruf* proclaimed in October 1946, "possesses in the unbelievable advantage of total defeat the strength for total change." The critique of capitalist institutions, which had formed the cornerstone of left-wing doctrine in the past, could now give way to the elaboration of a program for the socialist future. What was needed, Walter Dirks argued in the *Frankfurter Hefte*, was a "productive utopia" derived from "the given facts and currents" of the contemporary situation. Around this vision, the Left could at last unite.[68]

The intellectuals' certainty that the era of socialism had arrived did not imply an equal assurance that its outlines were fixed or its leaders already chosen. On the contrary, the question of how to tap creative energies commensurate with the opportunity now at hand was a topic of intense discussion. Most intellectuals agreed that the doctrinaire Marxism of the Weimar years demanded revision. But from what quarter would its successor come? The two groups who might contribute most decisively to formulating a "productive utopia," Dirks believed, were the working class and the Catholics. Such a partnership, reminiscent of Mounier's prewar program in *Esprit*, promised, in Dirks's opinion, to revitalize the German socialist movement. Like Mounier, Dirks had preached the need for a fusion of socialist and Catholic principles in the early 1930s. His first journal articles, collected in *Erbe und Aufgabe* (*Legacy and Duty*, 1931), included a plea for "understanding between Catholics and Socialists" on the basis of a common anticapitalism and concern for human welfare. The SPD under the Weimar Republic, Dirks wrote at the time, "consists for the most part objectively of petty bourgeois with . . . antisocialist aims." In this situation, he concluded, "Catholic shock troops certainly have much to offer" the socialist cause. The Catholic socialism that the *Frankfurter Hefte* now proposed to its readers in 1946 was thus a return to the familiar strategy of synthesis favored by the apostles of innovation between the wars. "With this hope," Dirks concluded, "we can go to work—we must."[69]

Dirks's disillusionment with the traditional parties of the Left did not lead him to question the need for organized politics. In a *Frankfurter Hefte* article entitled "Party and State," he bluntly described parties as a "necessary evil." Dirks protested against the contempt with which intellectuals traditionally regarded the parties' political role, and argued that a "serviceable standard" for evaluation should replace much current "misunderstanding." Yet he was forced to admit that the revived parties' postwar performance fell short of even these moderate expectations. "Instead of a start in working together we have learned of much rivalry and personal politics, instead of the originality we wished for we have seen routine, and what we have experienced in the elections and read in the party press . . . pleases us not at all and impresses us even less." With Kogon's help Dirks turned his energies toward building a local Christian

Democratic party in Frankfurt that would "create a socialism from the Christian perspective in order to have a third socialist party alongside the two others." But he was to see his hopes subsequently founder amid continuing rivalry and routine.[70]

These failings fostered a skepticsm toward party politics among the younger generation of intellectuals. While they sympathized with Dirks's scorn for the apolitical German middle class, they distrusted political organizations and their functionaries just as intensely. A rebirth of socialism, for them, meant adopting a spirit of experimentation and tolerance that seemed threatened by the narrow exclusivity of doctrine and party loyalty. Only by rejecting the confines of party discipline altogether would they be free to fashion a true "productive utopia." The most eloquent protest against abandoning politics to the politicians appeared in the columns of *Der Ruf*. Its editorial for November 1946 warned that parties that had "lost a battle in 1933 and perished due to their own mistakes are now beginning all over again." "What has been restored," wrote *Der Ruf*, "is what least needed restoration in a world of visible and invisible ruins, namely the German political parties of the Weimar Republic with all their errors and weaknesses."[71]

One major reason for *Der Ruf's* hostility toward the sclerosis of party doctrine and its equally deep commitment to the transformation of socialism lay in the early political experience of its two editors. Both Alfred Andersch and Hans Werner Richter had been active members of the German Communist party before 1933. And both had soon developed strong reservations concerning the KPD's ideology and tactics. Years later, Andersch commented bitterly on the party's failure to close ranks with the Socialists and its misplaced confidence in the inevitability of Hitler's downfall: "No one could explain the laws of the dialectic with such precision as the Central Committee of the Communist International. Its historical predictions had the exactitude of a clock mechanism. Yet no one was so incapable of grasping the fact that the dialectic of history is shaped by human beings as were the leaders of the Communist party."[72] The general distrust of Weimar parliamentary practice—an attitude that Richter and Andersch shared with many other intellectuals of their generation—was thus accompanied by growing condemnation of a more ruthless but equally unproductive style of politics espoused by the extreme Left. During the Hitler years, Richter later recalled, he and his friends passed through a "mood of political disillusionment," and "sought to find the errors [underlying] this debacle." Slowly and painfully, they revised their views.[73]

The conception of socialism that emerged from the disillusionment of the 1930s emphasized doctrinal flexibility and individual freedom.

Andersch and Richter shared a desire to liberate German politics both from "the totalitarian demands of doctrine" and from "empty abstractions"—from an outlook that was either too mechanistic or too theoretical when confronted with the reality of the "concrete." Their alternative vision was set forth in the first issue of *Der Ruf*, where Andersch called for a synthesis between "economic justice . . . that can only be accomplished in socialism" and "a new humanism departing from all traditions." "Europe's youth is humanist in its inexhaustible hunger for freedom. Humanism means for it the acknowledgment of the worth and freedom of man—no more, no less. It would be ready to leave the camp of socialism if it were to see human freedom abandoned in favor of that old orthodox Marxism which postulates the determination of man by his economy and denies man's free will." This program differed little in its essentials from that espoused by Camus in *Combat* or Sartre in *Les Temps Modernes*. Andersch's reference to "Europe's youth" showed that he made no claim to originality. Instead, he stressed the international dimension of a "European reawakening" and saw in it a sign that "the great lesson that European youth have drawn from the experience of dictatorship" had led them to similar conclusions.[74]

But even if the war had given the concept of freedom a new and deeper meaning and had shattered the limits of "old orthodox Marxism," the twin goals of liberty and social justice were not easily integrated. Richter acknowledged this difficulty in November 1946 in an article entitled "The Transformation of Socialism and the Young Generation." Echoing Andersch, Richter insisted that the end of the Nazi regime made it imperative to "bring new order to the state and the economy in the midst of [our] economic, spiritual, and moral chaos and at the same time win the human freedom that has previously been denied." Yet, as he admitted, "When we are forced to view our conceptions in concrete terms, seemingly unbridgeable contradictions arise. The concept of a free, economically independent, and happy man—the goal of which all socialists dream—comes into conflict with the practice of socialist planning, which must control human beings as well as the economy." Richter saw the same danger in an expanding state bureaucracy that *Combat* had warned against when discussing the French nationalization program. He, too, observed that unless a "practical path leading away from the suffocating bureaucracy of a totally planned society" could be discovered, socialism would remain incompatible with the intellectuals' humanist goals.[75]

Richter offered few suggestions as to where such a path might be found. *Der Ruf* had earlier cited the American Tennessee Valley Authority—modest in scale, responsive to local opinion, and successful in improving living standards in the rural South—as proof that a "decentralized socialism" remained a genuine possibility.[76] Yet despite his admiration for the TVA, Richter believed that the Germans would have to create a socialism that was distinctively their own. Those whose potential contribution to the "search for new possibilities" appeared greatest were the young veterans returning from war and imprisonment. They had seen the conditions that made socialism imperative. They were, in effect, a new proletariat. "Property [for this generation] is the shoes they do not have, the bed that is not there, the food they seek. They are hungry, and want to still their hunger . . . They know that they can still their hunger only if the economy is organized according to a plan." This generation had also borne the brunt of the regimentation imposed by the Third Reich; much of their lives had been spent in "mass organizations, work camps, war, the front."[77] From this double experience of poverty and servitude, Richter argued, the "young generation" would emerge determined to gain both material security and freedom. They, of all Germans, best understood the costs if that synthesis should fail.

As in earlier movements such as the Junges Deutschland group of the 1830s or Das jüngste Deutschland of the 1880s, the concept of youth advanced by *Der Ruf* was synonymous with a new elite. Andersch and Richter defined the group for whom they spoke as "the men and women between 18 and 35, divorced from their elders by not being accountable for Hitler and from those younger than they by experience at the front and in captivity." The trials and losses they had sustained in the war, as well as their limited political role prior to 1933, absolved them from complicity with National Socialism. These same war experiences also fostered a pragmatic, skeptical attitude toward abstract notions of honor and duty, rather like Nizan's outlook in favor of "piercing secrets" in *Aden, Arabie*.[78] Both Andersch and Richter thus attempted to derive their image of a new elite from the insights acquired through action rather than through contemplation.

Der Ruf's emphasis on the special wisdom the "young generation" had gained during the war stemmed from a need to find a German equivalent for the French Resistance experience on which to found hopes for renewal. What common ground existed between the *Wehrmacht* soldier and the *résistant*? Andersch discovered it in the concept of "engagement."

Sartre and the young fighters of the Resistance call for the reconciliation between action and thought, a unified existence. From this attitude there stretches a thin, precarious line across an abyss to another group of young Europeans, who in recent years also risked their lives with absolute dedication. We mean the young Germans. They stood for a false ideal . . . But they stood [for it] in the existentialist sense as conceived by Sartre and his young French companions.[79]

The parallel, as Andersch himself admitted, was a forced and "precarious" one. But its very implausibility suggested how strongly the younger German intellectuals yearned to salvage something positive from the six wasted years of military service under Hitler. The new Germany could not be built on repentance alone. To defend courageous conduct (*Haltung*) as praiseworthy in itself, divorced from the ends it served, was to make a virtue of necessity.

A similar desire to discover a basis for renewed confidence in the present situation underlay *Der Ruf's* insistence that Germany enjoyed a unique advantage as a "bridge between East and West." In an article that appeared in October 1946 Richter emphasized the positive aspects of the growing ideological confrontation between the Allies. The rival programs of the United States and the Soviet Union as occupying powers, each engaged in "re-education" stressing one or the other term of a needed synthesis, gave the Germans an opportunity to learn from both.

> The young generation . . . can build anew. It has the socialism of the East and the democracy of the West in its country. From experiences with both orders it can recognize the mistakes it must avoid . . . It must begin at the point where both orders come together; it must simultaneously democratize socialism and socialize democracy. Thus this young generation of Germans can build the bridge that leads from West to East and from East to West.

Mediation, not domination, would characterize Germany's special role in the Europe now taking shape. In this manner the division of Germany might be forestalled as well. Already in 1945, writing in the journal *Die Lagerstimme* while a prisoner in the United States, Richter had foreseen this danger and offered a similar solution: "Since the two great movements of this age—socialism from the East and democracy from the West—are breaking in upon us, we should attempt to see what they have in common and not what separates them; we should always seek synthesis where antithesis threatens to divide us."[80]

Richter advocated a set of national political goals that would preserve German initiative and independence and provide an outlet for that same messianic spirit which the Nazis had once exploited. The current situation, he believed, held abundant promise. Germany's contact with American democracy and Soviet socialism, its ability to initiate reconstruction unencumbered by an aging industrial plant, and the experience of its young generation all provided grounds for hope. Their emphasis on the preconditions for change, their distrust of theory, and their faith in the truths revealed by experiment allowed the editors of *Der Ruf* to sidestep a direct answer to the question of what shape these hopes would assume. But a foundation for change had been laid. That was the certainty with which Richter and Andersch faced the chill of the Cold War.

6
The Road
to Restoration
1946-1949

Creative initiatives! That was it. That at the very least, we thought, would remain open to the Germans: the opportunity to nurse our own spiritual and material illness with our own creative initiatives. The hope has failed. The illusions are swiftly fading from sight.
Alfred Andersch, 1947

The Cold War affected Germany more directly than any other nation in Western Europe. Just as the intellectuals had begun to recover a measure of self-confidence and optimism concerning the future, it forced them to confront once again the narrow limits that circumscribed their freedom of action. At the moment when *Der Ruf* proposed that a defeated Germany mediate between the ideologies of the victors, a growing mutual distrust rendered the United States and the Soviet Union suspicious of German initiatives that might tend toward accommodation with the other bloc. A synthesis between democracy and socialism proved unacceptable to both camps, though for opposite reasons.

The point at which preliminary skirmishes over the implementation of the Potsdam Agreement escalated to a level that might properly be termed the Cold War is still a matter of dispute.[1] But it is clear that the year 1947—the year of the acrimonious Moscow and London Ministers' Conferences, of the announcement of the Truman Doctrine and the Marshall Plan—marked a turning point for Germany's relations with both East and West, just as it did for France. The limited consensus on Germany's future reached at Potsdam and the joint supervision of the Nuremberg Trial had seemed to promise an era of close cooperation in peace; they now appeared to be the final efforts of an alliance threatened with impending rupture. Meetings of the Allied

Control Council in Berlin increasingly became the scene of recrimina-
tions in which the Russians accused the British and Americans of
obstructing the flow of promised reparations, while the Americans
countered with charges of Russian duplicity. From the former capital
of the Reich, the American Military Governor, Lucius Clay, could see
signs that "the Iron Curtain was being lowered inch by inch and day by
day."[2]

As in France, the initial German reaction to the Cold War was a
refusal to side wholeheartedly with either of the two major an-
tagonists. The German position was rendered more difficult than the
French, however, by the far greater control exercised over the country's internal affairs by the Allies. As the intellectuals watched the vise
of East-West confrontation tighten, they hoped that they might yet be
able to exert some counterpressure. "We still have time to go to work,"
Eugen Kogon wrote in January 1948, "not much, but still a few
minutes of the world-historical hour in which we live, [and] in which
we will yet perish . . . if we let them slip away."[3] The consequences of
failure seemed ominous indeed. An armed conflict between East and
West, should it occur, threatened to complete the destruction of Germany. Soviet and American occupation troops now on German soil
could easily transform the country once again into a theater of war. A
more immediate threat, however, lay in the political dismemberment
of the former Reich. The Cold War seemed to portend a permanent
division of Germany into smaller units, each dependent on one of the
superpowers for its survival.

An amputated and divided nation, the intellectuals believed, would
have little choice but to place its fortunes in the hands of more
powerful neighbors, and hence forfeit any chance of pursuing an
independent course. *Der Ruf* argued that however illegal the annexations made by Hitler, his crimes did not excuse a second wave
of annexations at Germany's expense: "It is unjust to make the
average German responsible for all of Hitler's injustice. We
young Germans believe that the new [territorial] settlements and
peace treaties must give recompense for previous wrongs, but
should not use the cause of justice to conceal wrongs done to Germany."[4] This appeal to universal standards of conduct in a patriotic
cause reflected the intellectuals' undiminished faith in moral suasion.
They continued to believe that the Resistance could educate the nation
and defend its interests.

The Idea of Europe

"The precept with which [youth] sets forth," Alfred Andersch wrote in the first issue of *Der Ruf*, "is the demand for European unity."[5] For *Der Ruf's* editors, as for their intellectual colleagues, a united Europe meant peace. The national rivalries that had fed two major conflicts within a half-century could not be allowed to revive and bring the risk of yet another war. A new spirit of understanding and cooperation would both prevent aggression and facilitate reconstruction. Like the vision of socialism, with which it was often joined, the "idea of Europe" seemed dictated by idealism and common sense alike.

The Nazis, of course, had professed their own devotion to European unity. Hitler made skillful use of its appeal among potential collaborators in occupied France. For Frenchmen like Drieu la Rochelle, who had long hoped that Europe would "triumph over the nations that divide her," a powerful Reich appeared the chosen instrument for unifying the continent. But the Führer's deep-seated distrust of France and his open contempt for Germany's weaker satellites rendered such hopes illusory.[6] Although Hitler insisted in 1941 that he sought "the security of Europe and thereby the salvation of all," his war of conquest aimed to create a continental empire of vassal states. He envisioned, as he told Hermann Rauschning, "a confederation, but naturally not of equal partners, a confederation of subordinate peoples (*Hilfsvölker*), without an army, without their own politics, without their own economy."[7] In the hierarchy of European nations, Germany claimed the right to first place.

Despite Nazi attempts to portray a united Europe as synonymous with the wartime Reich, European Resistance movements enthusiastically adopted the goal of unity. Léon Blum, writing in 1941, took pains to distinguish between the two visions of integration: "When Hitler and Goebbels talk of organizing Europe, when French 'collaborators' echo them, one knows what they mean and what they desire. Their European order, in reality, is nothing other . . . than total subjection to Hitler's rule. The same words thus come to signify diametrically opposite ideas. When we say 'European order' . . . we do not imagine a common slavery under a tyrannic hegemony, but an equal federation of free nations."[8] The Resistance appeared to many of its adherents as a forerunner of a true federation founded on a shared recognition that Europe's nation-states could no longer afford the rivalries that had weakened their response to Hitler's aggression. Henri Frenay was among those who stressed the role of the underground as a framework for continued international cooperation once victory had been achieved. "The men of the European Resistance," he declared in *Combat* in late 1943, "will be the builders of a new Europe tomorrow. Already, the men of the French Resistance extend their hands to men of other nations." The Italian Altiero Spinelli, whose "Ventotene Manifesto" of 1941 was one of the first Resistance declarations devoted to European unity, observed: "The collapse of most European states under the German war machine has already reduced most peoples of the Continent to a common fate . . . Attitudes are already much more favorable toward a new, federative European order. The brutal experiences of the last decade have opened the eyes of the unbelievers."[9]

Of all the former belligerents in 1945, Germany stood to gain the most from a European federation and was at the same time the least able to effect it. After exploiting other European states for its own national purposes, Germany now saw itself a pawn in the struggle among conflicting Allied aspirations. This enforced passivity was especially galling to Germans who, like Andersch and Richter, sought not only a federated Europe but a socialist, neutral Europe as well, a "bridge between East and West." As Richter wrote in January 1947: "[The Germans] have not abandoned their own nationalism merely to take the chestnuts out of the fire now for other imperialist interests. They not only say 'Europe,' they mean it as well. They not only talk of peace, they live it . . . But what they now see is a narrow-minded, petty nationalism that attempts to ensure its own security by supporting separatist movements in Germany. What they see is the arrogance of the victors."[10] Richter's remarks were occasioned by French attempts to annex the Saarland, and more generally by the slowness of the Allies' moves toward integrating the occupied zones. In both Cold War camps he perceived a desire to maintain a divided Germany, and thus to prevent the development of a new European socialism that might upset the emerging balance of power.

The German intellectuals were more successful during the mid-1940s in establishing cultural contacts with other European nations than in promoting political integration. Their search for a positive mission of their own, as noted earlier, led them to idealize the French Resistance and the intellectual *résistants*. Richter devoted a special issue of *Der Ruf* in October 1946 to French cultural topics, including discussions of *Esprit*'s "political Catholicism" and French postwar journalism, and a long excerpt from an essay by Beauvoir on existentialist ethics. The literature that the French Resistance had produced under the most adverse conditions was viewed as an example for German writers to emulate. "What was created in the underground there," Nikolaus Sombart wrote, "is precisely what we need . . . We place our hope in France."[11]

French intellectuals, in turn, were torn between bitterness against their former captors and an earnest desire to contribute to Germany's spiritual rebirth. Once it became clear that France would join the occupying powers east of the Rhine, the intellectuals devoted increasing attention to the opportunities created by this reversal of roles. As early as October 1944, *Combat* warned that "the occupation of Germany must not represent vengeance for our side. It should simply help us to come to know this people better and to awaken in it whatever can still serve the interests of Europe." Joseph Rovan, writing in *Esprit*, argued that the French occupation of Germany would be a decisive test for the Resistance spirit. "The question is whether the respect for human rights and human dignity constitutes the living and tested doctrine of the Resistance, or merely so much talk." But this did not mean that the French should impose their standards on an unwilling populace with serene confidence in their own cultural superiority. "The French who will participate in German re-education in the name of the principles that France believes in," Rovan insisted, "are obliged by these very principles to honor, respect, and cherish the German spirit entrusted to their care."[12]

Rovan's idealism took on a special meaning in light of the fact that he had spent the last year of the war as a Nazi prisoner at Dachau, arrested for his Resistance activities. Yet his internment there had actually strengthened his belief in the possibility of Franco-German understanding. As he later recalled: "If there was one place where it was unthinkable to confuse anti-Fascism with an anti-German spirit, it was the camp, since it was filled with anti-Fascist Germans." When Rovan returned to Germany in 1946 as head of the Bureau de la Culture Populaire—one of a number of cultural projects undertaken in the French Zone—he was able to give his hopes genuine substance. Alongside such traditional offerings as touring orchestras, lecturers, and dance groups, opportunities were provided for international youth conferences, adult education, and other projects designed to promote contact and reconciliation between the two countries. A conference for writers and journalists that Rovan helped to organize at Lahr in 1947 brought Mounier together with Dirks and Kogon for the first time, giving rise to a friendship based on mutual esteem and a common Catholic socialism.[13]

The French also extended unofficial aid to German intellectuals in other zones. When the American authorities used financial pressure to muzzle the review *Ende und Anfang* in Munich, Rovan provided its editors with funds to carry on. The same "conspiratorial temperament" that he and his colleagues had displayed in the Resistance now proved an asset in circumventing military regulations for the benefit of the Germans. "We continued to feel that we were *résistants*," he recalled, "operating now in a different context." The acceptance and understanding that German intellectuals discovered in their dealings with the French in Rovan's circle came as a confirmation of goals shared in common. "Since they maintained close relations with us and shared our views on many subjects," Richter later observed, "they helped us a great deal."[14] This willingness for friendship on both sides lessened the German sense of isolation and seemed to promise still greater unity in the years ahead.

Yet for some French intellectuals, contact with the new Germany brought a reminder that the old wounds of distrust and discord had not fully healed. Vercors, visiting the newly reopened university at Mainz in 1948, delivered a speech of warning. He had not come, he told his audience, "to bring you words of amnesty and absolution, and to suggest falsely that former enemies can now simply embrace." On the contrary, Vercors found the German fascination with the French culture of the war years a disturbing sign. "In thinking this way, the young German displays the greatest weakness of his people. Once again, he waits for someone to show him a path. He refuses to search for it himself. Once again, he waits for someone to furnish him a teacher." German readers, he argued, had responded favorably to his *The Silence of the Sea* in part because it depicted a "good German" devoted to France. But that was to misread the novel's message. For in the end, "this best of all possible Germans . . . far from revolting, discovers his duty in submission to his masters." Far too many Germans, Vercors believed, still lacked the courage to adopt an attitude different from that of their compatriot in *The Silence of the Sea*. The true lesson of the French Resistance was that one should refuse such blind obedience. "To be men or slaves," he concluded, "depends on you and on you alone."[15]

The same themes of freedom and choice were emphasized by the writer who became the single most important representative of the postwar French intellectual scene for younger Germans—Jean-Paul Sartre. In 1947 the French occupation authorities sponsored performances of *The Flies* in Baden-Baden and Saarbrücken; the play was later given in a German translation to audiences in Hamburg and Berlin. For these occasions Sartre wrote a short preface to the work that emphasized the similar problems faced by French and Germans under their respective occupations: "The future [in 1943]—even though an enemy army occupied France—was new. We had a hold on it, we were free to make of it a future of defeated men or, on the contrary, of free men who refused to believe that defeat means the end of everything that makes human life worth living. Today, for the Germans, the problem is the same."[16] *The Flies* spoke directly to the German situation. It reinforced the demand for independent judgment and personal reckoning with the past made by intellectuals such as

Dirks and Jaspers in response to the question of guilt. Set against the long German tradition of individual subordination to the state, Sartre's argument seemed if anything more radical than it had in France. When Sartre visited Berlin in early 1948 to participate in a discussion of *The Flies*, one speaker insisted that "liberty must have a goal." "I have been asked what freedom is for," Sartre replied. "To ask such a question is to show that you understand nothing of its deeper meaning. . . If you wish to give men their freedom, it should at least be a freedom without limits, linked to a responsibility without limits." His answer brought a storm of applause.[17]

These successes in Franco-German cultural relations could not offset the difficulties of achieving a broader European integration. Contacts between the Soviet Zone and the rest of Germany diminished, and it became increasingly apparent that occupied Germany was not free to initiate a rapprochement with the East without forfeiting the support of the West. During the winter of 1946-47 *Der Ruf*'s initial optimism about Germany's role as mediator began to wane. In its place there appeared a new bitterness, a sharp and critical denunciation of both sides in the Cold War. Time was running out. Richter and Andersch feared, correctly, that the Allies would institute irreversible changes before the intellectuals could bring some influence to bear on their decisions. What influence on Allied military government did the intellectuals in fact possess? National security, as perceived in Washington and Moscow, overrode any consideration of German interests not in harmony with the victors' aims.[18]

The German intellectuals' dream of a European federation that would preserve their homeland intact while linking it to both their eastern and their western neighbors was not fulfilled. Instead, between 1947 and 1949 West Germany achieved integration within a much smaller European community that was to become the nucleus for the Common Market. The price for this union was the abandonment of German neutrality. What Hans-Peter Schwarz has called the "politics of ambivalence" earlier pursued by the United States, which both galled and encouraged the German intellectual Left, was superseded by a clear anti-Soviet strategy that made Germany's role as a "bridge" appear an anachronism. The "idea of Europe" advocated by *Der Ruf* receded into the realm of lost illusions.[19]

The Group 47

Der Ruf itself proved to be one of the first German casualties of the Cold War. In April of 1947 the American Military Government forbade further publication of the journal under the editorship of

Andersch and Richter on the grounds of "nihilism." Journalistic pro-
vocation, the "democratic opposition" promoted by the review, could
no longer be tolerated. *Der Ruf* continued to appear until 1949 under
a new editor, Erich Kuby, but in a considerably tamer and more obe-
dient version than before. All mention of socialism and criticism of
the Western Allies gradually vanished. Richter, in response to an
earlier warning from the U.S. Army's Publications Section, had explicitly condemned this sort of accommodation: "We . . . live in a
political climate where opportunism appears to be celebrating its
greatest triumph. More narrow-minded and petty than ever, it offers
new ways to leave dogma undisturbed . . . It is not opportune to
discover fresh, unencumbered perspectives toward the future, so one
stands by the old." It was symptomatic of the worsening relations between the review's founders and the Americans that this article was
suppressed by order of the military government. "Let them do what
they want," Andersch remarked as he and Richter left *Der Ruf's* offices for the last time. "We'll stand by our own writing."[20]

What would the forum for their writing be, now that they had lost
Der Ruf? The initial reaction of the group around Andersch and
Richter was to found another journal. But despite Richter's ingenuity
and persuasiveness, he was unable to secure either the financial backing or the Allied publishing license that this enterprise demanded. Instead, he kept the circle of former colleagues intact by other means. In
September 1947 a dozen friends met at Richter's invitation in the
secluded rural setting of the Bannwaldsee near the Bavarian Alps. It
was, Wolfdietrich Schnurre recalled, "practically a substitute editorial
meeting for the forbidden *Ruf*". Texts were read and debated, still in
the hope that Richter might find a way to publish them. Though he
eventually abandoned these efforts, the participants continued to meet
at regular intervals.[21] The sessions of the Group 47, as it came to be
known, supplied badly needed contact and continuity to writers dispersed in a nation without a dominant cultural center. Richter noted:
"Only [the possibility of] communication within one's own circle remained—reading aloud and criticism as substitutes for a journal that we
did not possess and for a literary public that did not exist."[22]

Superficially, the Group 47 seemed a return to the traditional German *Dichterkreis*—a band of initiates gathered at the feet of a poet
whose work they applauded and revered. The circle around Stefan
George at the turn of the century, with its devotion to "the Master,"
had epitomized this spirit of literary discipleship. Central to the purpose and appeal of the Group 47, however, was a very different atmosphere of sharp, unsparing criticism among equals—a spirit that
remained faithful to the opposition stance formerly cultivated by *Der
Ruf*. As one participant at the Bannwaldsee meeting remembered:
"We squatted in unconventional fashion . . . on the floor, smoked

tobacco that did not always smell very good, and read from our works . . . What the debaters lacked in subtlety of formulation they redeemed with their ruthless but friendly candor. No one took offense at another, since we were united in a common goal: to indicate a new, realistic path for German literature, free from false emotional outpourings."[23] The judgments of the Group 47 were categorical; those who read from the "electric chair," as the lectern was called, received a sign of either thumbs up or thumbs down from the assembled critics. There was no middle term.

Many members of the Group 47 had independently evolved similar literary styles. Even writers who had not been directly connected with *Der Ruf* displayed broad agreement in their literary judgments. Wolfdietrich Schnurre, whose short story "The Funeral" was the first work read at Bannwaldsee, recalled the surprise he felt at finding himself in the company of a "dozen unfamiliar but still friendly young people, who differed little in their basic experiences, hopes, and attitudes." They shared a taste for honest, economical writing, and were quick to challenge one another at the first sign of overrefinement. Workshop sessions allowed authors to exchange advice on technical problems such as narrative voice or the treatment of dialogue.[24] An emphasis on the artisanal rather than on the ethereal, on "practical work through practical example," in the words of another observer, reflected the group's desire to bring the writer down to earth. At the same time, the sense of common enterprise generated by the Group 47 extended to the pioneers of the "new realistic path" who had been at work in the early postwar months. Borchert's death was commemorated—"without false ceremony"—at a meeting in 1948. When a prize was introduced two years later for the best presentation made before the group, the first recipient, not surprisingly, was Günter Eich.[25]

Beyond fulfilling these literary aims, the Group 47 was also an experiment in self-government. If its members felt little inclination to accept the directives and discipline of party politics, they eagerly accepted the chance to participate in a direct democracy of their own. What Richter described as "the experience of new-won freedom that makes everything possible" led to a style of personal relations characterized by spontaneity, informality, and mutual respect. The Group 47 thus represented a self-conscious rejection of the hierarchy and bureaucracy that its members had known in the *Wehrmacht* and the first phase of denazification, as well as of the starched protocol of previous writers' associations such as the Prussian Academy of Poetry. "There was no program, no theme, no welcoming speeches, no rules, no ceremonial dinner, no treasurer's report." At Bannwaldsee, the guests had to fish for their dinner in the nearby lake. The necessary minimum of organization and leadership were supplied unobtrusively by Richter, whose warmth, tact, and quiet energy were admirably suited to this task. Richter himself was anxious to create an atmosphere where readers and critics alike behaved according to "unwritten rules of the game." "My model here," he noted, "was Anglo-Saxon democracy."[26]

The Group 47, it may be argued, for all the "intensity and enthusiasm" of its discussions, signaled a withdrawal from the optimistic political journalism of *Der Ruf* into a new and more inward-looking attitude. Richter, at least, has rejected this interpretation. Looking back from the perspective of the mid-1970s, he observed:

> For those in the *Ruf* circle who had spent their early youth in the 1920s — and this is especially true for Alfred Andersch and myself — the value of literature was different from that of politics. First came literature and then politics; at the beginning was the word, not the deed. We still believed — differently from today — in the effect of the written word, in literature as the great, irreplaceable tool of enlightenment. Thus the supposed flight into literature was no escapism, but a shifting of weight, a change in emphasis. What had been taken from us on the one hand through the banning of *Der Ruf* . . . we believed we could replace on the other hand through turning to literature.[27]

The former editors of *Der Ruf* continued to make their views known in other journals. Andersch's articles appeared regularly in the *Frankfurter Hefte* for several years after 1947, while Richter contributed to the columns of *Neues Europa*. Equally significant was Andersch's growing involvement with German radio as a staff member of the Hessischer Rundfunk. There he attempted to create a German equivalent of the BBC Third Programme, and secured the participation of a number of young intellectuals in writing plays, reports, and comments for a growing radio audience.

Yet despite both continuity and new initiatives in journalism, Richter's allusion to a simple "change in emphasis" leaves much unsaid. If not an outright retreat, the shift to greater reliance on literary "tools of enlightenment" represented a postponement of hopes for swift political change. Even more than in France, the audience of the Resistance intellectuals in Germany was now confined to other young, anti-Nazi writers like themselves. They were for the most part preaching to the converted. The elite that *Der Ruf* had once defined to include an entire generation was increasingly restricted to a tiny minority of that generation among the intellectuals. Richter himself, in attempting to characterize the goals of the Group 47, described them as follows: "(a) To form a select group favorable to democracy [working] in the field of literature and journalism. (b) To demonstrate repeatedly the democratic method used in practice among a circle of individualists with the hope of [stimulating] a long-range effect and perhaps a much later and broader influence on the masses."[28] This strategy of patient building and deferred influence, ironically, had been foreshadowed in the very first issue of *Der Ruf*. Arthur Koestler, contributing as a guest author, had written there of a "community of pessimists" whose chief aim should be to "create oases in the desert of the interregnum" that would follow the war.[29]

The commitment to enlightenment and community that Andersch and Richter brought to the Group 47 had been strengthened in the very country that was now restricting their liberties. Captured on the Italian front in the summer of 1944, *Der Ruf's* two principal editors had spent the final year of the war as prisoners in the United States. The experience of internment led them to discover—in different ways—the value of group solidarity and the transforming effect of positive example on the attitudes of those around them.[30]

The American authorities selected Andersch to participate in an "experimental administrative school" at Fort Getty, Rhode Island. There a small but distinguished faculty—headed by Thomas Vernon Smith and including Howard Mumford Jones of Harvard and Arnold Wolfers and Fritz Mommsen of Yale—offered a two-month course in basic spoken English, German and American history, and the outlines of American Military Government administration in occupied Germany. With its New England setting, select student body, and eminent instructors, Fort Getty was less a POW camp than an unacknowledged member of the Ivy League. What impressed the German prisoners most was the spirit in which the Americans approached the enterprise. Andersch later recalled the impact made on him by their "unspoken belief in the possibility of change through teaching." And Thomas Vernon Smith, unconsciously echoing Koestler's language, wrote in evaluating the program: "It is not unlikely, nor from the over-aim of the enterprise unwholesome, that this strange interlude . . . will appear in retrospect for most of [the prisoners] an oasis of sanity in the desert of years . . . wasted in Nazism and worse than wasted in war."[31]

Richter had not been so lucky. He was first sent to a camp in Illinois, where he immediately became involved in a struggle among the prisoners between supporters and opponents of the Third Reich. Under the terms of the Geneva Convention, camp discipline remained the province of German officers, who were often strongly National Socialist in outlook, until May 1945. Their American supervisors intervened only in cases of grave disorder. As a result, Nazis in Richter's camp were able to impose a secret terror on their fellow prisoners, accompanied by denunciations and beatings that the German camp leaders did little to prevent. Richter opposed this campaign indirectly through his activities as camp librarian, teacher of German literature, and editor of the camp newspaper, *Die Lagerstimme*. His activities caught the attention of the American military authorities, and in the autumn of 1945 he was placed on the staff of another German-language newspaper, produced in Fort Kearney, Rhode Island. This paper, *Der Ruf*, later provided the direct inspiration for its German namesake. Andersch, too, had briefly served as an editorial assistant before his move to Fort Getty. But whereas Andersch could look back on his American experience as a relatively untroubled "oasis of sanity," Richter's captivity challenged him to define a strategy for resistance and a basis for hope to orient him on his return.[32]

The most successful of the literary works produced by the Group 47 in the late 1940s was Richter's novelistic account of this captivity—*Die Geschlagenen* (*The Defeated*, 1949)—which one critic acclaimed in that year as the "best war novel to date." *The Defeated* is a *Bildungsroman* set in wartime. It tells the story of a young German soldier whose ordeals during the last days of fighting in Italy and the first months of internment in the United States reflect Richter's own. The opening chapters portray the sense of futility and helplessness that overcomes the protagonist, Private Gühler, as defeat nears for him and his comrades. He despises both the army and the cause for which it fights, yet he cannot break with either. When captured, however, Gühler refuses to disclose the location of other German emplacements to the Americans in order to protect the lives of his fellow soldiers. "I am a German and a socialist," he tells the officer who interrogates him. "For me there is only one possibility—to carry through with my ideas in my country. But not against my country. Not for foreign interests."[33]

Gühler's first true act of defiance is thus directed against his new captors, not his old. As a prisoner, he discovers that his deepest loyalties dictate that he not deny his German origins any more than his socialism. He must attempt to fight Nazism on his own ground, without seeking help from the Americans, and must do it in his own way. During the months of confinement in an American POW camp, he holds himself apart from the Nazis, and survives. With considerable courage, he begins to teach evening classes in German literature to some of his fellow prisoners, hoping to open their eyes to what in the corpus of German classics is still unsullied by National Socialism. He directs the camp library and is eventually entrusted with editing the camp newspaper. All the while he attempts to "carry through his ideas," he must struggle against the temptation to escape from the continuing Nazi terror in the camp by requesting a transfer to a special facility like Andersch's Fort Getty.

"I'm staying here," said Gühler.

"You're staying with the Nazis?"

"I'm staying where I belong . . . I'm staying with the Germans."

"Even if they do you in?"

"Even then," said Gühler.[34]

Gühler's courage includes the willingness to endure isolation and to defer hopes of victory. He has no faith in the transforming effect of his activities in the camp within the near future, nor in American understanding or support. Richter's own struggle with the U.S. authorities is reflected in the final pages of the novel, where the prisoners discuss the future that awaits them after repatriation to Germany:

"Man, we need a revolution," said Schmidt, "a real revolution."

Gühler motioned with his head toward the watch towers where the guards stood.

"They'll stop it," he said. "They'll stop everything."

But Gühler does not give up. The novel's final message is one of patience rather than of resignation. "Things can't go on like this forever," Gühler muses. "At some point we'll get free of this whole, dirty machine."[35]

Böll and the Memory of War

When Heinrich Böll received the Group 47 literary prize in 1951, he was virtually unknown to the German reading public. Yet Böll's early fiction now appears an especially faithful evocation of the restrained mood and modest hopes of the German intellectuals in the late 1940s. His novellas and short stories, like Richter's *The Defeated*, represent an attempt to explore the lessons of the war and to seek some guidance for future conduct. Böll, however, distrusts heroism — even the quiet heroism of a Private Gühler. It is rather the unheroic, the unexceptional, the antithesis of Nazi bravura that attracts his sympathies.

Böll was born in 1917 in Cologne, the son of a Catholic woodworker and sculptor. The "rather anarchistic tradition of . . . Cologne and its environs," he later recalled, was as important as the Catholic faith and the decidedly anti-authoritarian atmosphere at home in shaping his early aversion to National Socialism. During the first years of the Third Reich, his parents provided shelter in their apartment for illegal meetings of Catholic youth groups that Böll attended. His adolescence was spent in the shadow of a conviction, voiced repeatedly by family and friends, that "Hitler meant war." "Naturally we all knew from 1934, 1935 that war would come and that we would take part in it . . . It was only a matter of time." The period from the Depression until the war's end appeared in retrospect to Böll as a continuum, marked by a feeling of defenselessness balanced against an "inner resistance" that grew in proportion to the danger without.[36]

After being drafted, Böll served until 1943 in France, where his special assignments included translating for his superior officers and overseeing military brothels. As the *Bordellaufseher* in towns along the Atlantic coast, he played parcheesi with the prostitutes, searched for German deserters hidden on the premises, and experienced the realities of daily contact between the occupying forces and a captive population. The loneliness, boredom, and shabby pleasures shared by soldiers and civilians were themes that he was to stress heavily in his early postwar writing. Then in the summer of 1943, Böll's unit was ordered to the Russian front. He arrived just as the German armies were beginning the long retreat westward after Stalingrad; in the following months he witnessed the progressive disintegration of army discipline and morale. Repeated injuries caused him to be evacuated first to Odessa, then to Jassy in Rumania, then to a military hospital in Hungary. With the help of forged documents and a talent for malingering that would have aroused admiration in the good soldier Shwejk, Böll subsequently evaded military service until the final days of the war. Captured by advancing American forces in the spring of 1945, he spent six months in an American POW camp in France, then returned to the rubble of his native Cologne.[37]

Böll had begun to write before the war. In an interview with Horst Bienek in 1960, he admitted to having composed "four or five, maybe even six novels, of which three were destroyed by fire in a Cologne attic during the war, the others put somewhere in the cellar." During his military service, however, he found it impossible to continue. After his liberation from the prisoner of war camp he felt he could begin again, but his first attempts to transpose his wartime experiences into fiction proved unexpectedly difficult. As he told Bienek: "We were few [writers then], and that did not make things any easier. Style develops through contact with one another, and such contact did not exist."[38] It was not until after he had surmounted these problems that Böll became aware of the Group 47. In the meantime, he read Camus, Faulkner, and Hemingway for the first time, and reread the German classics. Out of this combination of influences there gradually evolved a voice and a vision that were recognizably his own. His first short stories—"Friend with the Long Hair" and "The Message"—appeared in 1947. His finest and most telling evocation of the war, nine inter-related studies entitled *Wo warst du, Adam?* (*Adam, Where Art Thou?*), did not appear until 1951.

Böll's fictional treatment of the war differs in a number of impor-tant respects from the Weimar novels about World War I, such as Erich Maria Remarque's well-known *All Quiet on the Western Front* (1929). Rather than focusing on battles, Böll depicts life behind the lines. Rather than shocking the reader with graphic scenes of bloody encounters, he describes the fear, isolation, and constantly frustrated attempts to establish relations with others that are the lot of the com-mon German soldier. His characters lack firm standards and secure knowledge of what goes on around them. "There is nothing certain," thinks the protagonist of *Der Zug war pünktlich* (*The Train Was on Time, 1949*) "nothing certain at all, only total uncertainty." The soldiers hope for the war's end, for the minimal assurance of defeat, but no one can say when it will come. "How long will the war go on? It could last another year, before everything gives way once and for all in the East, and if the Americans and British don't attack in the West it will be two more years before the Russians reach the Atlantic."[39] The result is general resignation and passivity. One can only accept one's lot and try to stay alive.

Böll's perspective is distinctively that of the common soldier. Of-ficers appear in his fiction only rarely, and never in sympathetic guise. The atmosphere of confusion and insecurity is thus reinforced by a loss of any overall view of the war. Orders for advances or retreats ar-rive from an unseen source, for unknown reasons, and with unpredic-table results. Men are moved back and forth across the continent like pieces on a giant chessboard as the German military situation worsens in the years 1943-1945—the period in which virtually all of Böll's war fiction is set. His characters are forever at the mercy of new orders that call them away from barely familiar surroundings. In this con-stant movement, trains and railway stations play a central role. The train is a mechanical, inhuman threat to fragile personal ties; it is never late, it never waits, it is in the literal sense an engine of war. Its military passengers have no contact with the countryside through which they pass, and which they will never see again. They wait in gray stations for a train that will take them to another station, there to board another train bound for distant points with mysterious Slavic names: Przemysl, Stryj, Cernowitz.

Böll's style in these early stories underlines the uncertainty and loss of perspective felt by his characters; it is descriptive, seldom analytic. His prose registers the world without comment. The opening lines of the story "Wanderer, Should You Come to Spa . . ." (1950) are typical:

> As the truck came to a stop, the motor idled for a while. Somewhere outside, a large gate was thrown open. Light fell through the shattered window into the interior of the truck, and I now saw that the lightbulb on the ceiling was also in pieces. Only its threads were still fixed in the socket, a few glistening wires with glass fragments. Then the motor stopped idling, and outside a voice cried: "Bring in the dead! Do you have any dead with you?"[40]

A constant tension exists between the precision with which individual objects are depicted and the absence of any similar precision concerning their relation to other objects. "Somewhere" a large gate is opened, a cry is heard "outside," a light suddenly comes from an invisible and unexplained source. Böll's world is reduced to fragments without a context. Significantly, he writes with little use of causal conjunctions. "Thus," "therefore," "hence" have no place in a disordered universe, but are replaced by temporal connectives that merely tell us in what order a series of disconnected events occurs.[41]

The one certain value in Böll's war stories—fleeting but real—is love. Some critics have objected to what they regard as an overly sentimental treatment of this theme, one that seems to clash with Böll's unsparing realism in depicting the human costs of war.[42] Yet it is precisely the unfulfilled promise of happiness that reveals the true misery of Böll's characters, through its contrast with the wasted existence most are forced to lead. Men and women come together for the space of a few hours, only to be separated again by the winds of war like the lovers in Dante's *Inferno*. Their brief encounters are a form of protest against the war that governs their lives, a protest doomed to failure yet stubbornly repeated time and again. Böll's sympathies clearly lie with these furtive couples; their stolen moments of happiness suggest an alternative to the silent resignation of many of his other characters.

All these themes are united in *Adam, Where Art Thou?*—an episodic account of the retreat of German armies from Russia during the months from summer 1943 to spring 1945. The central figure is Private Feinhals, an architect by trade, attached as orderly to a medical unit that slowly disintegrates in the course of the long withdrawal. Communication breaks down, disorder spreads, and cooperation gives way to mistrust: "Telephone conversations were no use any more, since the personnel with whom you were accustomed to speak either no longer existed or existed somewhere where they could not be reached . . . The threads were jumbled or knotted, and the one solution was to save your own skin each day." At one of the way stations on this retreat, Feinhals meets Ilona, a Jewish girl who teaches in a convent that the Germans have requisitioned as a hospital. The two fall in love and experience a single afternoon's happiness. Ilona, however, insists on returning to the town ghetto at nightfall to reassure herself of her family's safety: "'Stay here,' he said, 'or let me come along. No matter what happens . . . You don't know the war, or those who are waging it. It is not good to part, even for a moment, when it isn't necessary.' 'It is necessary,' she said. 'Do understand.'"[43] But Feinhals's premonition proves accurate. They do not meet again. Ilona dies in a concentration camp, Feinhals in the street at the moment when he finally reaches home.

Böll's dominant attitude toward his characters is one of compassion. His anger is reserved for the generals, the ambitious time-servers, the brown-shirted fanatics of the German army. Because Böll restricts his narrative focus to the plight of their victims, soldiers and civilians alike, he is unable to investigate the war's causes, the nature of National Socialism or the question of guilt. But his intent is not to address these issues for their own sake, in the manner of Jaspers or Kogon. Rather, he deals with the destruction and the suffering caused by a conflict whose meaning his characters cannot understand, and which appears as a natural force against which men and women must take shelter as best they can. His attitude is most reminiscent of Camus's. Both see history as mysterious and malignant, and both refuse to speculate on its outcome. Like Camus, Böll believes that one can do no more than "take the side of the victims in order to limit the damage." Feinhals and the dying narrator of "Wanderer, Should You Come to Spa . . ." bear as little guilt for the fate that befalls them as does the stricken populace of *The Plague*, and receive a similar absolution.[44]

At the same time, Böll emphatically defends the private virtues displayed by his characters in their daily lives. His humanist vision represents a complete inversion of Nazi values. As the critic and historian J. P. Stern has written: "Where the National Socialists proclaimed the glory of the embattled nationalist collective, Böll proclaims the absolute value of the unprotected individual; where they exalted the will and political power, his favorite characters are full of doubt and uncertainty, and he invariably sees power of any kind as evil; where they excelled at organizing people, he favors gentle anarchy."[45] Thus the disintegration of the army and the helplessness of Böll's soldiers and civilians in the face of war are not only an accurate description of Germany in defeat but also an indirect endorsement of the "absolute values" that are denied by the Nazi state. He does not suggest that they will triumph, merely that an irreducible part of man's nature will ensure their survival, despite times of darkness like the era from which Germany had recently emerged.

Böll first came to the attention of the reading public in a time of growing material abundance, when Germans appeared disposed to forget the values revealed in the "limit situation" of war. His fiction, with its emphasis on the primacy of human bonds when all else has been stripped away, lost none of its relevance amid the distractions of the "economic miracle" (*Wirtschaftswunder*). Böll's characters embodied a moral critique appropriate to the postwar scene; they held fast to essentials while the nation sought its security in the impermanent world of things.

The "Economic Miracle"

When Germany began its dramatic economic resurgence in the late 1940s, many intellectuals greeted the signs of returning prosperity with surprise and a sense of foreboding. Capitalism, with its material inequalities and social divisiveness, they had believed a thing of the past. Just as the hunger, unemployment, and general misery of the early postwar years were shared by all, so the intellectuals hoped that recovery would benefit all equally. They looked forward to a spirit of sharing and sacrifice in the work of reconstruction. Walter Dirks called upon the Germans in the summer of 1947 to "take on poverty as a *common* fate," and to join in "the decision for an honest sharing of burdens." A "new arrangement of social relationships" — Dirks's expression for a Christian-socialist alliance — would "initially transform scandalous poverty into a bearable [poverty], then into a modest living standard."[46]

But the change in the nation's fortunes, when it occurred, rapidly attained a tempo that was anything but "modest." The signal for recovery came with the currency reform of June 20, 1948, initiated by the occupation authorities. The banking sytem of the American, British, and French zones had already been unified in March of that year through the creation of a Bank Deutscher Länder in Frankfurt. Under the umbrella of this coordinating agency, the old inflated Reichsmark was abolished and the total amount of money in circulation reduced by a factor of ten. The effect of a more stable currency on the availability of goods proved immediate and astonishing. As one economic historian has described it: "Literally from one day to the next fresh vegetables appeared in the windows of food stores empty for years; shoes, clothing, and underwear, unobtainable for money the Saturday before, could once more be bought. It now made sense to supply the markets with hidden goods and subsequently to produce goods for these markets. To achieve output and offer it in exchange for money promised a reward."[47] This reward was a potent stimulus. Barter and the use of the cigarette as the unofficial medium of exchange vanished overnight, along with the shadowy underworld of the black market.

In their place came evidence that traditional German efficiency and diligence had by no means been exhausted by the rigors of the war. By the end of 1948, industrial production had risen by more than half; during 1949 it rose another 25 percent. Added to these internal stimuli was the impact of Marshall Plan aid from abroad, which began reaching Germany at significant levels during these same months. "The United States," Marshall had declared in his famous Harvard Commencement speech of 1946, "is opposed to policies which will continue Germany as a congested slum or an economic poorhouse in the center of Europe."[48] The American government feared that Communist parties would increase their following in Western Europe unless immediate steps were taken to alleviate the region's economic distress. Germany, already subject to partial Soviet occupation, was the central focus of U.S. concern, and a principal beneficiary of assistance intended to transform a recent enemy into a new ally in the Cold War. Marshall's speech announced a relief effort that attained its goal. Although real German prosperity was not to be achieved until the mid-1950s, the postwar "hunger years" were over.

German economic recovery was achieved through policies that ignored the intellectuals' demands for socialist planning. Hans Werner Richter later admitted that "capitalism revealed itself to be a far more dynamic force behind reconstruction than an economy controlled by the state could ever have been." Yet the single-minded vigor with which Germans pressed forward in pursuit of their "economic miracle" was disquieting. Behind such industrious behavior, in the view of many intellectual observers, was a narrow selfishness that ignored the need for solidarity and sharing. The practical effect of prosperity was to reward private interests at the expense of the public good, and to make material comforts a matter of greater concern than spiritual renewal. As Eugen Kogon subsequently noted, Germany had again embarked on "an economically very successful system of unrestricted personal gain," and in so doing had diverted the nation's energies from a reckoning with the Nazi past.[49]

The monetary reform and the flood of available goods that followed meant that culture now vied with other commodities for a share of an ever more crowded marketplace. One unexpected effect of the

Wirtschaftswunder was a dramatic decline in the circulation of postwar journals. The public preferred to acquire the many small luxuries it had gone without for so long rather than continue to purchase reviews whose editorials attacked such self-indulgence. The lifting of Allied licensing restrictions in the West after 1949 was a further blow to the existing press, since the legal monopoly under which it had operated since the early postwar months was now succeeded by competition with a second generation of avowedly "popular" papers. Some journals such as the *Frankfurter Hefte* survived this change in climate; *Die Wandlung* and *Die Gegenwart* were among the many that did not.[50]

Three years after Dirks had called for moral regeneration in the midst of austerity, he reluctantly concluded that his fellow countrymen had "chosen the path of least resistance." "Fear, the need for security, and comfort," he wrote in 1950, "were stronger than courage, truth, and sacrifice." As a consequence, he continued, "we live in an age of restoration."[51] "Restoration" did not signify for Dirks a complete return to the past, but rather a revival of old habits and prejudices within a new context. Prosperity swelled the ranks of the middle class, while at the same time strengthening the respect for discipline, hard work, and political conformism on which the Nazis had capitalized with such success. Ostentation, jealousy, and a growing segregation that divided the rich from the relatively less fortunate now replaced the enforced equality of the "hunger years". As the middle class returned to prominence in the nation's business life, the familiar antibourgeois rhetoric of the late 1920s reappeared among its intellectual critics. Restoration took many forms.

One promising development that offset some of the intellectuals' disillusionment was the progress made toward unity in Western Europe. The Union Européenne des Fédéralistes, which held its first congress in the Swiss city of Montreux in August 1947, brought Henri Frenay, Altiero Spinelli, and Eugen Kogon into a close partnership as leaders of the movement during the next five years. Other congresses followed in rapid succession. German delegates often discovered that they shared more views with their foreign counterparts than with their compatriots, and entered into a fruitful dialogue, renewed during visits to Paris, Geneva, or Rome. Kogon wrote from Paris in February 1949: "An important milestone on the way toward European unification has been reached more rapidly than we dared hope . . . This is a victory for Europe's political avant-garde and its tireless efforts." Kogon's optimism was confirmed in a meeting that same month in Brussels, where the UEF and a dozen other groups signed an accord. They pledged to uphold a series of "basic guidelines for European politics" whose Resistance inspiration was explicitly acknowledged: "The love of liberty, opposition to totalitarianism of whatever kind, the modest and conscientious search for truth, and, above all, respect for the human person, for the individual as an individual—these are the fundamental characteristics of the true European spirit . . . These moral values, which . . . have been confirmed anew in the resistance against Nazism and Fascism, must guide the organization of Europe."[52]

But the enunciation of such principles did not ensure their adoption. The same Cold War pressures that led European intellectuals to renew their call for unity revealed the fragility of moral values as "basic guidelines for politics." While the foundations of the future Common Market were being laid in the West, events in the East were heading toward an open conflict between the two superpowers. On March 31, 1948, the Soviet blockade of Berlin began; Russian authorities announced that the Helmstedt-Berlin Autobahn linking the city to the West would be closed indefinitely for "repairs." Late in June, all surface travel and transport to and from Berlin were effectively halted. The beleaguered city became a symbol of East-West conflict, dependent for its survival on the American "air bridge" that successfully defied the blockade for over a year before the Russians gave way. In such an atmosphere, even the democratic socialism proposed by Richter and Andersch seemed a dangerous concession to Soviet propaganda. Neutrality in the Cold War was impossible. Germans in the Western zones looked with apprehension at the threat from the East. They were more inclined to revive Goebbels's warnings against the "Bolshevik menace" and to take pride in a renewed mission as guardians of the West than to remember the responsibility they bore for the Russian presence in Berlin. The physical partition of Germany in 1949 caused the last vestiges of an ideological middle ground to disappear; as in France, there was no center to occupy.[53]

The year 1949 saw a cultural debate that dramatized West Germany's movement in the direction of the tried and the familiar. It was the "Goethejahr"—the two hundredth anniversary of Goethe's birth. A dispute arose over plans to reconstruct the house in Frankfurt am Main where the poet had spent his early years, recorded with loving detail in his autobiography, *Dichtung und Wahrheit* (*Poetry and Truth*, 1831). The area had been badly bombed during the war, and only charred remnants of the building still stood. To some, its reconstruction was an act of piety incumbent on Goethe's spiritual heirs. To others, this project seemed an attempt to efface the memory of the war and its terrible consequences. As Dirks observed in the *Frankfurter Hefte*: "Connections exist between the spirit of the Goethe house and the circumstances of its destruction . . . The German nation of "poets and thinkers"—under the influence of Idealism and the classics, and under Goethe's influence as well—allowed the economy and [political] power to pass from their control, relinquishing them to the more mighty . . . In other words, there is a bitter logic in the fact that Goethe's house lies in ruins." Dirks suggested that the ruins remain undisturbed. They were now part of "German and European cultural history," and the verdict of history should be respected.[54] But the supporters of restoration prevailed. So meticulously was the house rebuilt, in time for the bicentenary, that it appeared untouched by the war.

The *Goethehaus* episode symbolized the intellectuals' situation at the end of the decade. They found themselves isolated, an elite without followers, determined to bear witness to the recent past yet unable to overcome the collective silence of their countrymen. As in France, they resigned themselves to a role of permanent opposition and sought refuge in a strategy of dissent that preserved their ideals and dignity intact, though its practical effects remained slight. They continued to speak out, moved by a determination not to resume the silence they had been forced to maintain during the Hitler years. Their attitude of undiminished resistance was exemplified in the closing lines of Günter Eich's radio play *Träume* (*Dreams*), broadcast for the first time in 1950:

> No, do not sleep, while the organizers of the
> world are at work.
> Be mistrustful of their power, which they
> pretend they must gain in your interests.
> Be sure that your hearts are not empty, when
> they count on the emptiness of your hearts.
> Do the impractical, sing the songs that they
> do not expect from your mouths.
> Be uncomfortable; be sand, not oil, in the
> machinery of the world.[55]

ANNO III · N. 4 · Una copia lire UNA   MILANO, Venerdì 27 aprile 1945

L'ITALIA LIBERA
Quotidiano del Partito d'Azione
"GIUSTIZIA · LIBERTA'.

Iniziativa di popolo: fonte della rinascita

Gli Alleati dilagano nell'Alta Italia
Resa senza condizioni dei nemici!

LA FINE dell'incubo

La battaglia di Berlino nella fase finale

Liberazione e libertà

IL VENTO DEL NORD

Le ultime battaglie in Italia
nel flammeggiare dell'insurrezione

Le truppe alleate alle porte di Milano - La marcia oltre l'Adige iniziata nel Veneto - Brillante azione delle formazioni "Giustizia e libertà"

Il corteo dei gerarchi soffoca alla ricerca di un asilo

Il terzo soggiorno estraneo di Mussolini - Le ultime leggendarie gesta di Graziani - Turismo obbligato di Claretta e Luisa

Un nuovo governo sarà nominato dopo la totale liberazione

Churchill denuncia le atrocità naziste a Buchenwald

Inizio dei lavori alla Conferenza di San Francisco
Protesta dell'Italia per l'esclusione

Internati italiani in Alto Adige maltrattati dai nazisti

Popolo rientrato in Francia

7
From Fascism to Resistance
1930-1945

*The war intensifies the experience of life
because it shapes everyone's inner feelings in accord with an extremely simple
framework—the two camps—while the
awareness of ever-present death gives
even the most trivial actions the stamp
of extraordinary gravity.*
Cesare Pavese, 1944

      The experience of Italian anti-Fascist intellectuals from
the early 1930s until the end of World War II bore similarities to the
separate dramas played out in Germany and France. Like the Germans, Italian writers and thinkers suffered the rule of a dictatorship
that at first enjoyed broad popular support, and were slow to emerge
from an attitude of "inner emigration." Like the French, they endured
a period of Nazi-imposed occupation and participated in a strong,
well-organized Resistance movement. They shared hopes for radical
change at the war's end with both their French and their German colleagues, and surpassed either in the share of power they won in their
country's first postwar government.[1]

This intermediate position between Germany and France makes
Italy—aggressor and victim, Fascist and free—a useful point of
reference in establishing common patterns for the intellectual
Resistance as a whole. The moral origins of revolt against an established regime, the attempt to integrate humanist and socialist principles in a vision of society that would succeed the Fascist order, the
discovery of a new trust and comradeship among members of the
underground, and the preference for direct democracy are all present
in the Italian *resistenza*. The Italian example, moreover, provides a
sort of test case, a control for any attempt to understand the conditions that favored or impeded Resistance activities in Western Europe.

The Italian intellectuals bore the weight of Fascist rule for two full decades without losing their will to dissent. The very length of Mussolini's reign permitted signs of Fascist corruption to appear with greater clarity. Nor was the regime successful in molding youth to conform with its ideals. Despite the propaganda resources of the Italian Fascist party and its repeated efforts to bring the country's educational establishment to heel, men and women who had spent virtually all their adult years as a captive audience for Mussolini's oratory at length rebelled.

The three factors most important in determining the extent of resistance in France, Germany, and Italy seem to have been the quality of leadership furnished by the intellectuals and their allies, the relative strength of the government they opposed, and the degree of support for open dissent offered by the populace. None of these preconditions existed in Italy during the 1920s, but by the 1940s all were in evidence. The opposition that surfaced with such surprising vigor in 1943 resulted from a gradual but far-reaching change in political loyalties.[2] How did this shift come about?

The 1930s proved a key decade in the formation of the Italian intellectual Resistance, for it was then that the first generation of Mussolini's opponents was joined by a younger group of dissidents. Some gravitated to the Resistance as soon as they reached their teens, influenced by the example of teachers or older friends. Others progressively discovered the failure of Fascism to live up to its early promises. They had been attracted by the party's break with middle-class convention, its hostility toward parliament and toward economic liberalism. But in time their enthusiasm waned. Following a period of growing discontent, Mussolini's Ethiopian adventure and the Spanish Civil War jolted many into active condemnation of the Fascist state. Contacts with foreign cultures and regimes—the positive example of America and the negative one of Nazi Germany—also helped to crystallize alternatives to the official faith.[3]

The protest awakened in these different ways culminated in the so-called Resistenza Armata ("Armed Resistance") of 1943-1945 and created support for a true revolution after the war. The long duration and the heterogeneous sources of the Italian Resistance movement gave it deeper roots in the population than in Germany, and a broader appeal than in France. Its achievements won respect from both French and German observers, who saw the Italian underground as an exemplary effort in training future citizens of the republic. As Alfred Andersch wrote in retrospect: "The Italian spirit emerged from the war into the world more intact than the German. Italy had already regained its self-possession. It could appeal to a tradition of resistance, and it did so."[4]

Fascism and Culture

By the beginning of the 1930s much of the earlier drive and dynamism of the Italian Fascist movement had been lost. Bureaucratic lethargy began to sap the energies of the regime as it entered its second decade of power. At the very moment when Mussolini's definition of Fascism appeared in the *Enciclopedia italiana*, with its claim that the Fascist "conceives of life as duty and struggle and conquest," stagnation and cynicism were rapidly undermining his boasts of Italian renewal. The "living faith" of which Mussolini proudly spoke was showing signs of age.[5]

Nowhere was the exhaustion of Fascist ideals more apparent than in the realm of culture. The official goal of the regime in the 1920s had been to create a "cultural autarky" of purely Italian inspiration. But what this recourse to *italianità* meant in practice, besides a rejection of foreign models, remained unclear. The eclectic nature of Fascist ideology was reflected in the regime's attitude toward the arts, which vacillated between a respect for ancient Roman grandeur and a desire for innovation. Mussolini's remarks to the Perugia Academy of Fine Arts in 1926 testified to this confusion: "Now on the field thus prepared [by the triumph of Fascism] a great art can be born again, which can be traditionalist and modern at the same time. We must create, otherwise we will be the exploiters of an old patrimony; we must create the new art of our times, Fascist art."[6]

To acquire its own *stile fascista* became a matter of prestige to the regime. In a sense, the 1920s were a propitious time for Italy's new leaders to impose their own style, amid the cultural vacuum that followed the deaths of such major figures as the painter Amedeo Modigliani, the sociologist Vilfredo Pareto, and the composer Giacomo Puccini in the years 1921-1924. Yet positive examples of Fascist art were more difficult to produce than programs of intent. When Mussolini attempted to set the tone by composing plays, few were inspired to follow suit. Given the Fascist movement's glorification of action and power, its impatience with "cold rationalism" and preference for the more direct testimony of blackjacks and castor oil, the concept of "Fascist culture" seemed a contradiction in terms.[7]

Giovanni Gentile, who emerged in the mid-1920s as self-appointed theorist and intellectual spokesman for the new order, argued the contrary. In language that anticipated similar claims by Brasillach and Drieu la Rochelle, Gentile asserted that Fascism's doctrinal incoherence was a sign of its spiritual vitality. "Fascism," he noted in 1925, "is a spiritual attitude rather than a certain content of thought." At the same time he protested against the "legend of a Nietzschean, barbaric Fascism, despising and trampling upon culture." In a country whose art and literature had long been sources of patriotic pride, Fascism was obliged to declare itself heir to the national genius; an openly proclaimed anti-intellectualism could only damage its standing at home and abroad. Gentile therefore called for a truce between artists and the regime. But he was also aware that the "new Italian culture created by Fascism" of which he spoke had a practical use as a means of political propaganda. Art existed to serve the state. If the state extended a welcoming hand to the artist, as Gentile proposed it should, its gesture was hardly a disinterested one.[8]

Fascist culture was pre-eminently a collective enterprise. The proliferation of organizations dedicated to the arts in the 1920s provided a semblance of creative vigor, while also serving to check any unwelcome independence in the intellectual community. A Fascist Institute of National Culture, presided over by Gentile, was inaugurated in December 1925. A Fascist Academy, whose purpose was "to preserve for our intellectual life its national character according to the genius and tradition of our race, and also to favor its expansion abroad," held its first meeting four years later.[9] During the years 1927-1929, artists were brought into official unions, amid a swell of propaganda comparing the new *sindicati* to the old medieval guilds. The most conspicuous Fascist contribution to a "new Italian culture"—the *Enciclopedia italiana* (1929-1937) of thirty-two volumes—exemplified this same collective spirit. Gentile saw the *Enciclopedia* as a vehicle for the intellectuals' fruitful cooperation in a national effort: "Italians of today . . . in contrast with the Italians of yesterday, no longer shut themselves off . . . in a self-centered individualism. Even scholars feel that they must cultivate a sense of national duty, which carries with it obligations of organizing and of solidarity . . . at the cost of personal sacrifice, for the honor and for the good of their own country."[10]

Despite this massive drive to enroll the intellectuals in the Fascist cause, the pressures for conformity exerted by the Italian state remained a good deal less brutal than those of the Nazi *Gleichschaltung*. One measure of this comparative leniency was the small number of intellectuals who chose to emigrate during the two decades of Mussolini's rule. Dissidents might experience social ostracism or bureaucratic harassment, but for most these inconveniences seemed preferable to the unknown perils of exile. The hundreds of contributors to the *Enciclopedia italiana* included many known anti-Fascists, whose presence was officially ignored and unofficially tolerated.[11] Tolerance extended in both directions, however. During the period 1929-1934, which the historian Renzo De Felice has termed the "years of consensus," overt hostility to the regime was rare. Intellectuals compromised more often than they protested; many practiced prudent self-censorship. The writer Corrado Alvaro observed in 1930: "We write a bare minimum to those with whom we correspond, very clearly so that an unseen censor will not misunderstand. Thus the letters that we write and receive seem dictated in the presence of witnesses . . . When we close the envelope we ask ourselves in a flash whether we have not committed some indiscretion."[12]

One of the few intellectual figures who refused to compromise during this period was the philosopher Benedetto Croce. Croce had been slow to criticize Mussolini — whom he hoped might bridge the gulf between the working classes and the nation — after the Duce's rise to power in 1922. Only in 1925 did he begin to speak out against the Fascist party. When Gentile presented the public with a "Manifesto of the Fascist Intellectuals" in that year, Croce countered with a blistering attack on the party, which he described as offering "an incoherent and bizarre mixture of appeals to authority and demagoguery, of proclaimed reverence for and [actual] violation of laws, of ultramodern concepts and moldy rubbish, of absolutist attitudes and bolshevist tendencies, of disbelief and overtures to the Catholic Church, of loathing for culture and sterile groping toward a culture without a basis, of mystic sentimentality and cynicism."[13] Croce utterly rejected Gentile's claim that Fascism had a cultural mission. But the grounds for his contemptuous dismissal lay equally in a general distrust of the subordination of art and philosophy to political ends. Like Benda, Croce believed that culture and politics should remain separate spheres of activity. The intellectual might enter the political arena — Croce in fact did so as a member of the Italian Senate from 1910 on, and in 1920-1921 as a cabinet minister under Giolitti — but his true allegiance must be to universal ideals, not to national interests.

Croce gave his highest allegiance to liberty. His was a classic European liberalism. Liberty, he insisted, remained both the "explanatory principle of the course of history" and the "moral ideal of humanity." In his review *La Critica* and in the five major works of history he completed during the Fascist period, he attempted to hold this value before his readers as a constant standard by which to judge Italian history.[14] At the same time, Croce was determined to maintain contact with the world of thought beyond Italy's borders. Each issue of *La Critica* devoted a third of its space to reviews of the latest publications in France, Germany, and England as well as at home. Despite this measured defiance of *italianità*, *La Critica* was not censored or suppressed. Until 1933 its regular subscribers included a majority of Italian universities and a number of secondary schools, where it found an audience among the young.

It was by force of personal example, however, that Croce exercised the greatest influence in Fascist Italy. Upright, independent, unmoved by threats or criticism, he grew in moral authority as the regime's prestige declined. Piero Calamandrei, the future editor of *Il Ponte*, recalled Croce's unseen presence during this period: "In certain decisive moments of action, in certain choices between cowardice and self-respect, it happened that we asked ourselves how he would have judged us. Within ourselves, without his knowledge, we asked his advice. It was he who during the past twenty years, even when it seemed that he was speaking of some other matter, counseled us to resist . . . For many of us the Resistance had its beginning in him."[15] No single figure in France or Germany commanded comparable respect under the Occupation or the Third Reich. Yet Croce's stance encouraged not only an ethical rigor that later served to strengthen the Resistance but also a cultural aloofness that resembled that of the *innere Emigranten*. His defense of cultural freedom centered upon the artist's duty to oppose the forces of political regimentation. It was in the sphere of art that liberty could be kept alive.

The two genuinely innovative Italian literary movements of the 1920s developed outside the orbit of Fascist culture. Both were indebted to foreign literary models of the prewar era. The school of poetry temed *ermetismo* favored a dense and laconic style, free in meter and rich in images, that took its inspiration from the French Symbolists. It marked a deliberate retreat to a world far from politics and ideological engagement, in which metaphysical problems of human existence were treated with studied indirectness. Among the best hermetic poets were Eugenio Montale and Salvatore Quasimodo, both in their twenties as the Fascist era began. Quasimodo's *Acque e terre* (*Waters and Lands*), published in 1929, began with a brief poem:

> Each person stands alone on the heart of the earth
> Pierced with a ray of sunlight.
> And it is suddenly evening.[16]

The bare simplicity of these lines recalls the postwar poetry of Günter Eich. But whereas Eich strives to put his surroundings in sharper focus, Quasimodo conveys a poetic self-containment. His metaphors evade precise definition, leaving the reader to interpret the meaning of "the heart of the earth" and "evening." The poem's chief strength lies in ambivalence.

Ermetismo was clearly a poetic style destined for an elite. Since the means adopted to protect the artist's autonomy from Fascist censorship also blocked access to a wide audience, the Italian writers faced a dilemma similar to that of the German inner émigrés. The price they paid for independence was self-imposed isolation. As Montale recalled: "Novelists and poets had a certain freedom, in the sense that they were not subjected to excessive demands. They were less free, even slaves, when one thinks how much they had to suppress within themselves . . . They could converse with their own transcendent ego, in a veiled manner . . . They were in no way permitted to react directly to their own era, to criticize it, denounce its customs, mock its vices."[17] Montale's remarks concerning *ermetismo* apply equally well to *decadentismo*, the second literary movement of note during this decade. The *decadenti* were neoromantic aesthetes and psychological novelists who sought to probe the hidden contours of the human consciousness in the manner of Proust or Thomas Mann. The inward-looking, self-absorbed character of most of this writing was again related to a conscious refusal to subordinate art to politics, a desire to remain aloof from troubled times. Yet to the extent that Italian society was itself growing "decadent" and self-absorbed under Mussolini, more interested in sensual pleasure than in service to the Fascist state, such literature conveyed a muted social commentary.

The outstanding example of *decadentismo* is Alberto Moravia's *Gli indifferenti* (*The Time of Indifference*), which was published in 1929 and ran rapidly through four editions. The novel deals with a middle-class Roman family fallen on hard times and the cynical, self-possessed, and ultimately triumphant outsider who bends them to his will. Michele, the son of the family, is too weak to oppose Leo, the manipulating adventurer, with more than an empty gesture when he learns that Leo has seduced his sister after tiring of a long liaison with his mother. At the novel's close Michele finds himself entangled in a situation from which he is powerless to break free: "An opaque disgust oppressed him . . . The falseness and humiliation that filled his soul he saw in others as well, always. It was impossible to be rid of that discouraging, impure spectacle . . . which interposed itself between him and life. A bit of sincerity, he repeated to himself, clutching at his old fixed idea, a bit of faith."[18]

The indictment presented in *The Time of Indifference* was moral, not political. Moravia attacked the bourgeoisie in terms that Nizan or the young Goebbels would have found congenial. While Leo's confident self-assertion and unscrupulous dominance might seem to fit him for playing the role of a Fascist hero, Moravia undercut their appeal by placing Leo squarely within the world of capitalist finance. Leo makes his money by playing the stock market and manipulating real estate with the proceeds, and nourishes designs on Michele's house as well as on his sister's virtue. This coexistence of bourgeois decadence and Fascism could be interpreted by Moravia's readers as a judgment on the Duce's failure to bring about promised changes in a corrupt society. Similarly, his repugnant portrait of Michele's mother, Maria-grazia, seemed an oblique and ironic attack on the Fascist idealization of family and motherhood.[19]

The Time of Indifference was a work of transition between *decadentismo* and the Italian turn to neorealism in the 1940s. Moravia's concern for honesty and his impatience with sentimentalism and mannered writing provide links with later writers such as Pavese and Vittorini, just as his concern with psychology and inner landscapes issues from an earlier tradition. As the 1930s progressed, the moral message of his novel attracted greater attention than its psychological acuity. Yet though Moravia documented the hypocrisy and spiritual bankruptcy that continued under Fascism, he did not attempt to offer an alternative faith. In *The Time of Indifference* he presented a diagnosis but not a cure.[20]

The counterproductive nature of Mussolini's "cultural autarky" was revealed by the growing prestige of foreign literature during the 1930s. That which was forbidden became avidly sought after, while the official culture languished. The simple-minded nationalism that underlay the concept of *italianità* betrayed a sense of inferiority, a hidden fear that Fascist culture could not compete with its rivals. As the atmosphere of repression grew, despite Gentile's earlier calls for mutual tolerance, young Italian intellectuals increasingly looked beyond Italy's borders for relief from the stuffy platitudes and hollow sloganeering of official art. Mussolini himself turned abroad for inspiration during this period. The Duce's admiration of Hitler—symbolized by his state visit to Germany in September 1936—was a tacit admission that Fascism required schooling by a fellow dictator. His vow to "prussianize" Italy, his introduction of anti-Semitic legislation in 1938, and the Pact of Steel he signed with Germany in the same year were all attempts to infuse new vigor from across the Alps into a faltering enterprise. Mussolini's opponents, too, sought foreign inspiration. But whereas Mussolini looked to Germany, the anti-Fascist writers turned to a land most of them had never seen—America.

Pavese and the Discovery of America

The stratagem of indirectly criticizing one's own country by praising a foreign land has a long and venerable history. Voltaire, for example, applauded the London Stock Exchange, "that place more respectable than many royal courts," whose openness and freedom from religious intolerance he implicitly contrasted with the religious persecution in eighteenth-century France following the revocation of the Edict of Nantes.[21] Europeans living under Fascism could look to America for similarly instructive contrasts. The extraordinary outburst of literary talent in the United States during the 1920s combined with America's traditional ideals of liberty and democracy to create a strong interest in its writing. Sartre later recalled the "black market for American books" in Paris during the war, when "the reading of Faulkner and Hemingway became for some a symbol of resistance." Some Parisians "believed they could demonstrate against the Germans by reading *Gone with the Wind* in the Metro."[22]

It was in Italy that American fiction found its earliest appeal and greatest resonance among European intellectuals. To Moravia's generation, it offered a possible source of a new "sincerity" and "faith." In November 1930, a year after the appearance of *The Time of Indifference*, the young writer and critic Cesare Pavese published an essay in the Turinese review *La Cultura* that marked the beginning of both a covert protest against the *stile fascista* and a new movement in Italian literature. Reviewing the novels of Sinclair Lewis, the recent Nobel laureate, Pavese praised the vitality so clearly absent from contemporary Italian writing, "the spectacle of a changeable and variegated reality, full of testimony of a life lived with much — perhaps with too much — enthusiasm." "In our country," he noted, "nothing resembling this has ever been written." In Lewis's portrait of America Pavese found "a protest against a social order that suffocates and negates life." "Basically," he concluded, "these characters have but a single thirst: liberty. Liberty for individuals in opposition to the irrational chains of society."[23]

Yet this protest remained centered on the individual, and emphasized flight rather than combat. Authors like Lewis, Sherwood Anderson, and the young John Dos Passos portrayed characters whose energies are directed toward emancipating themselves from their stolid, provincial milieu. Like George Willard in Anderson's *Winesburg, Ohio* (1919), these characters do not attempt to change society, they simply withdraw. What one critic has termed the "theme of secession" in such novels provided an alternative mode of escape for Italian writers dissatisfied with the purely aesthetic response of *ermetismo* or the paralyzing disenchantment of *decadentismo*, while preserving the essentially personal and negative features of both.[24] This underlying continuity helps to explain the facility with which the new American literature was assimilated by Italian intellectuals like Pavese. Fiction that implicated society without demanding collective opposition, and that recognized the frustrations as well as the heroism of individual secession, reflected the dilemma of the artist in an authoritarian state.

Pavese was born near the northern industrial city of Turin in 1908, in the town of San Stefano Belbo, where his family kept a small country house. All his life he remained attached to the Piedmontese countryside, with its landscape of hills, canebrakes, and vineyards, seeing in it a symbol of peasant simplicity and strength, qualities that he later came to associate with the American Midwest. Yet his adolescence was a conventional middle-class, urban experience: classical studies at the Liceo Massimo D'Azeglio in Turin, followed by the less orthodox choice of American literature as his field of study at the University of Turin. There, in 1930, he received a degree in letters with a thesis on the poetry of Walt Whitman.

At the Liceo Massimo D'Azeglio Pavese fell under the spell of Augusto Monti, a teacher who was to influence both his conception of literature and his political outlook. Monti's role in forming a generation of northern Italian intellectuals—including Leone Ginzburg, Vittorio Foa, Norberto Bobbio, and Carlo Levi—can be compared with Alain's influence on Sartre and his friends at the Lycée Henri IV. In fact, there was a good deal of the traditional French republican pedagogue in Monti's approach to teaching. Fiercely anti-Fascist, convinced of the ethical superiority of the classics and of the high moral calling of the writer, Monti became a second father to Pavese, and Pavese his favorite student. Their common Piedmontese ancestry provided an additional bond. The young man's confiding yet respectful letters to his former teacher, in whom he loved "something more than a teacher," suggest Monti's importance for an entire "fraternity" of his students who, like Sartre's *bande à part*, continued to see themselves as a special group long after their studies ended.[25]

Turin in the 1920s was the most anti-Fascist city in Italy. Its heavy concentration of industry (especially automotive concerns such as Fiat and Lancia) gave it an unusually large working-class population. Many of its workers—disciplined, socialist, and implacably opposed to Mussolini—were former members of the metallurgical unions whose aspirations had been championed by Antonio Gramsci in *L'Ordine Nuovo* immediately after World War I. The middle and upper-middle classes, liberal supporters of Giolitti or admirers of the young radical Piero Gobetti (another of Monti's students), were no less adamant in their condemnation of Fascism. Fascist repression in Turin was correspondingly severe. In such a politically charged environment, even a timid and apolitical student like Pavese could not help taking sides.[26]

Pavese's expertise in American letters gave him a means to criticize the regime without risking arrest. Between 1930 and 1935, Pavese translated works by Melville, Lewis, Anderson, Dos Passos, and Faulkner. His translation of *Moby Dick* in 1932 was a major stimulus to Italian interest in writing from the New World. He also published enthusiastic essays on these and other writers, including Whitman, Edgar Lee Masters, and Theodore Dreiser, in *La Cultura* and *La Nuova Italia*. His reviews conveyed a sense of "the anguish and the fervor and the constantly revived pleasure" that he received from American fiction.[27]

For the younger generation of Italian writers, such translations and reviews provided one of the few sure means of support during the 1930s. Publication of their own works was restricted by censorship, and employment in the liberal professions, now run as guilds under the aegis of the Corporate State, was severely limited. Only one out of every two hundred graduates from the faculties of law, for example, was able to secure admission to the bar at this time.[28] The period of tightening controls over intellectual life forced the writers into a cat-and-mouse battle with the Fascist establishment in which the *terza pagina*—the third page of Italian newspapers, devoted to literature and the arts—provided a welcome outlet. It is not clear why a regime dedicated to the principle of "cultural autarky" should have permitted extensive translation from foreign sources. By 1938 Dostoevsky, Turgenev, and other "Bolshevik" authors were put on the Fascist index and circulation of their works was prohibited. German writers, for obvious reasons, escaped this ban. But so did the Americans.[29]

Pavese's spirited apologetics on behalf of American literature occasioned critiques from the older generation of specialists in this domain (*americanisti*). Carlo Linati, writing in 1932, heaped scorn on the idea that American culture had anything to offer Europe besides a superficial "ability to construct machines or to amuse oneself without cares." "Europe," he declared, "desires in the end merely to remain Europe, to remain true to its foundations, to stand by its moral traditions."[30] A decade later, Emilio Cecchi published his *America amara* (*Bitter America*), an unflattering account of a journey through the United States, whose extremes of poverty and rampant materialism, of Harlem and Hollywood, he interpreted as signs of growing crisis and decay. Cecchi's pessimistic and hostile diagnosis of an America devoid of spiritual grandeur, where emotional and material security provided "the one true American ideal," was in part a product of the Depression years. Whereas Pavese's literary studies introduced him to the sleepy towns and boisterous cities of the flapper era, Cecchi witnessed the fears and uncertainties that followed the Crash of 1929. But their contrasting outlooks were also rooted in a generational difference. As another of the younger admirers of America, Giaime Pintor, wrote in 1943: "Where Cecchi has scrupulously assembled a museum of horrors, where he has isolated sickness and decadence and recognized a world in which he cannot believe, we have felt a voice profoundly close [to us], that of true friends and of our first contemporaries."[31]

In addition to petty sniping from Italy's cultural nationalists, Pavese's work exposed him increasingly to the danger of a direct attack from suspicious government officials. Although he joked that by altering the title of Masters's *Spoon River Anthology* to read *Antologia di S. River* he would convince credulous censors that it was a collection of pious writings by Saint River, the margin of tolerance that he enjoyed was narrower than his bravado suggests.[32] In 1935, after mass arrests that netted the entire staff of *La Cultura*, he was exiled for a year to the tiny Calabrian town of Brancaleone. But upon his return to Turin, he resumed his translation and essays as before.

By the late 1930s Pavese and the other young *americanisti* who followed in his footsteps had created their own mythical America. Its initial appeal was doubtless tied to the suspicion it aroused among the Fascist authorities, a response that rendered all things American desirable and faintly scandalous. On a deeper level, however, American culture came to symbolize a world untouched by the moral leprosy of Fascism; its health and vibrancy were an inspiration to Mussolini's opponents. Pavese summed up the significance of this image of America for his contemporaries in 1947:

> Toward 1930, when Fascism began to be "the hope of the world," it happened that a few young Italians discovered America in its books—a difficult and barbaric America, happy yet quarrelsome, dissolute, creative, burdened with the entire past of the world yet young, innocent . . . This new fashion aided not a little in perpetuating and strengthening the political opposition, however vague and futile, of the Italian public "who read." For many people contact with Caldwell, Steinbeck, Saroyan, and even old Lewis unveiled the first glimpse of liberty, the first suspicion that not all culture in the world ended with Fascism.[33]

A third and final reason for the influence of American fiction was its suggestion of the possibility of a literature that provided a close link between the writer and society. The use of slang, the simple style, the depiction of everyday situations that Pavese applauded in his 1930 essay on Lewis seemed to speak to the average man in a more direct manner than either Fascist rhetoric or the symbolism of *ermetismo*. Not only did Lewis's *Babbitt* and Steinbeck's *Tortilla Flat* depict real social problems; they were written in a language that accurately reflected the milieu they portrayed. In Italy, where no literary mean existed between provincial dialects and an artificially refined style, the possibility of fusing the two came as a revelation. In these works

Pavese perceived "not a crude dialect still too local—like that of our specialists in dialect here who always retain something petty even in their best work—but a new blend of English, shot through with American idioms, in a style that is no longer *dialect*, but *language*, rethought and recreated."[34]

A language that could mediate between the isolated world of the intellectual and the political concerns of the nation was a first step toward redefining the writer's role in Italy. American writing provided, as Pavese observed, a "rethought and recreated" medium that demonstrated both the possibility of a "renovation" in art that might eventually be extended to other spheres and the possibility of basing such a renovation on respect for the common man. It was this humanistic aesthetic that gave American literature its claim to universality. As Giaime Pintor put it in 1943: "This America has no need of [a] Columbus; it is discovered within us. It is the land toward which strives, with the same hope and the same faith of the first emigrants, whoever is resolved to defend at the price of weariness and errors the dignity of the human condition."[35]

The Italian concern for language, stimulated by contact with American literature, occupies a place within the broader scheme of moral and ontological questions raised by Merleau-Ponty and Sartre, Eich and Böll. But whereas the French intellectuals approached language as a problem of communication between conflicting freedoms and the Germans saw in it the key to the perception of reality, Italians like Pavese and Pintor saw it as the symbol of a gap between an aristocratic and a popular culture. Perhaps because of the long rhetorical tradition in Italy, they accepted the artifice inherent in literary expression of any kind. Symbolism and allegory appeared to them necessary poetic tools. Nevertheless, they aspired to create a literature that would speak to the masses and to the intellectuals alike, that would be inclusive and not exclusive. In a country riven by regional, political, and cultural differences, they would find a common tongue for men of goodwill.

Vittorini's Spiritual Pilgrimage

The intellectuals' hope of establishing relations with a broader public was destined to remain frustrated during the 1930s. As in France during the first months of the Occupation and in Germany under Hitler, Italian anti-Fascists were split into a patchwork of individuals and small groups with no regular communication and little scope for common initiatives. The "exceptional laws" passed by the Fascist Council of Ministers in November 1926 had driven the organized political opposition underground by outlawing all parties but the Fascists. The clandestine cadres of Communists and Socialists were gradually crippled by arrests and infiltration by Mussolini's secret police, while attempts of such groups as the Paris-based Giustizia e Libertà to create a coherent resistance network from outside Italy enjoyed only limited success.[36] Those who remained in Italy under Fascist rule might administer journalistic pinpricks in the reviews that escaped the censors' scissors, or deride the Duce among their friends; they were still isolated in their efforts to spread the flame of resistance.

The path traveled by Italian intellectuals from isolation to collective dissent, beginning in the 1930s and ending in World War II, emerges clearly in the autobiographical fiction of Elio Vittorini. His writing also traces the transition from antibourgeois to anti-Fascist sympathies among some "left-wing Fascists" of the younger generation. Vittorini and his comrades believed in socialism, moral renewal, and personal sacrifice, but they distrusted Croce's conservative liberalism. They became supporters of the regime out of misplaced idealism, and for a time attempted to defend the official goals of the Corporate State against the corruption and cynical compromise that were the reality of Fascist practice. Italian Fascism appeared the sole means of realizing their vision in a "concrete" manner. Not until the mid-1930s did they fully realize their error; then the same motives and values that had led them to join the Fascist party prompted their departure.[37]

Vittorini spent his early years in Sicily, the son of a minor railway employee, living on the malarial coast in a succession of "tiny railway stations with metal screens on the windows and emptiness all around." His schooling was minimal. From an early age he read stories of escape and fantasy, his favorites being *The Arabian Nights* and *Robinson Crusoe.* Like Camus, whom he resembled in other ways as well, Vittorini all his life retained an emotional attachment to the Mediterranean world of his youth. As he later wrote: "I know the joy of a summer afternoon spent reading a book of cannibal adventures, half-naked in a chaise-longue by a house on a hill that overlooks the sea . . . of hearing infinite sand-existences crack and collapse in the sand; or of rising before dawn in a world inhabited by chickens and swimming, alone in all the water of the world, near a pink beach."[38]

At age fourteen, while a student at the Syracuse Istituto Tecnico, Vittorini joined local anarchist groups in protesting the new Fascist government's repressive labor policies. Three years later, he left Sicily for good, anxious to "see the world" that his reading had opened up to him. He found temporary employment with a construction company near the Yugoslav border, but his real interest was writing. Curzio Malaparte, a left-wing Fascist with populist sentiments, encouraged Vittorini's early literary efforts and printed a number of his essays in the review *Conquista dello Stato*.[39] In 1930 Vittorini moved to Florence, joined the staff of the Florentine daily *La Nazione* as a proofreader, and became acquainted with the circle of dissident writers around the literary review *Solaria*. "I became a *solariano*," he later recalled, "a word which, in the literary circles of that time, meant anti-Fascist, Europeanist, universalist, antitraditionalist."[40]

Yet Vittorini's political views in the early 1930s were far more ambivalent than his retrospective account acknowledged. A member of the Fascist party, he contributed articles to the local Fascist review, *Il Bargello*, alternately praising the revolutionary potential of the movement and decrying the conservatism and narrow-mindedness of its leaders. As his friend Romano Bilenchi recalled: "We shared with each other the fruits of our reading, our preoccupations, our disappointments. We had both hoped . . . that Fascism might be an anti-bourgeois revolution, a new form of socialism. The year 1933 . . . brought us greater doubts, and fears."[41] Straddling the two worlds of *Solaria* and *Il Bargello*, Vittorini explored the possibilities of cautious dissent within the party and at the same time took the initial steps toward a more aggressive critique.

In 1933 *Solaria* brought out the initial installment of Vittorini's first novel, *Il garofano rosso* (*The Red Carnation*), a study of young schoolboys simultaneously encountering the adult world of sexual adventures and the violence condoned by Fascist authorities. The novel's greatest interest lay in its depiction of the spirit of revolt that inspired the young to make common cause with the Fascists. "We want true liberty," declares one of the principal characters, "because we want to destroy all privileges—those of Freemasonry, of the monied interests, of 'moral propriety,' of judicial institutions." Difficulties with the censor prevented publication of *The Red Carnation* in full. As the author noted in a preface to the 1948 edition: "The book did not succeed in getting through because the censors . . . did not wish even allusions to reasons for being Fascist that were not the official ones, and to juvenile enthusiasms for the criminal aspect of Fascism . . . for its bloody and violent sides, or for its noisy boldness which, in the eyes of us boys, unfortunately signified vitality."[42]

The ambivalence toward Fascism that Vittorini depicted in his young protagonists, who "adhere to Fascism and make trouble from within," was dispelled in large measure by two developments during the 1930s. The first was the finding of an opposing cultural ideal: Vittorini's discovery of American literature, which he pursued with an enthusiasm similar to Pavese's. While still at *La Nazione*, Vittorini began to teach himself English by translating *Robinson Crusoe* with the aid of a dictionary, one word at a time. When lead poisoning from the paper's typographic fonts forced him to quit his job in 1933, he had mastered the new language sufficiently to support himself by translating. His translation of Lawrence's *The Virgin and the Gypsy* appeared in 1935, and was followed by Poe's *Tales* (1936), Faulkner's *Light in August* (1939), Steinbeck's *Tortilla Flat* (1939), and Caldwell's *God's Little Acre* (1940). In 1940 the Milanese publishing house of Bompiani commissioned an anthology of American fiction with a series of critical prefaces by Vittorini. When it appeared, *Americana* was seized by the authorities and purged of these compromising prefaces, which too openly presented America as all that Fascist Italy was not. A few of the original copies survived, rescued by friends who circulated them in the anti-Fascist literary underground. One of them found its way into the hands of Pavese, who in 1942 wrote to Vittorini: "Here you have brought the tension and the cries of discovery of *your own* literary history . . . with the result that here a whole century and a half of America is reduced to the basic dimension of a myth that we all experienced and that you are retelling to us."[43]

The second force behind Vittorini's reappraisal of Fascism was political. Mussolini's invasion of Ethiopia in 1935, and especially his intervention in the Spanish Civil War the following year, changed the attitude of his left-wing critics within the party from disillusionment to opposition. The republican forces in Spain received their increasingly enthusiastic support. Italian volunteers in the Garibaldi Battalion were fighting Fascist conscripts in the Italian army on Spanish soil, turning the struggle into a civil war among Italians. Vittorini found himself totally absorbed by the events in Spain. As he later recalled: "The first news of Madrid and Barcelona, of Andalusia, Estremadura, the Basque cities, halted me in front of the newspapers . . . as if in front of the lowered bars of a grade crossing. In the following days I could do nothing else (apart from the hours of translating with which I earned my bread at the time) but read newspapers."[44] A plan to join the republican forces in Spain came to naught. But a final article in *Il Bargello*, calling on Italian Fascists of truly revolutionary temper to support the republicans against Franco, brought about Vittorini's expulsion from the Fascist party in the fall of 1936.

By 1938, when word reached Vittorini that *The Red Carnation* had been definitively rejected by the censors, he was already at work on a far subtler and more profound indictment of Italian Fascism. Entitled *Conversazione in Sicilia* (*Conversation in Sicily*), his new work portrayed a largely autobiographical character whose human sensibilities had been dulled by the corrosive atmosphere of Mussolini's Italy. Silvestro Ferrauto, a typographer who has spent his last fifteen years in exile from his native Sicily in a large northern Italian city, falls prey to despair during a cold, rainy winter: "I bowed my head. I saw screaming headlines in the papers and bowed my head. I saw friends for an hour, two hours, and stood with them without saying a word and bowed my head . . . Life in me [was] like a mute dream, without hope, silent."[45] Silvestro's physical exile in the North is thus at the same time a spiritual exile from his fellow men. His alienation at length becomes unbearable; "haunted by abstract furies," he impulsively resolves to seek release from his silence by returning home to visit Sicily.

Silvestro's journey is a pilgrimage, a quest for self-knowledge and inner peace that eventually reconciles him with himself and with others. A series of encounters lead him from an initial sense of exclusion to a feeling of community. As he approaches Sicily by ferry across the Straits of Messina, he strikes up a conversation in dialect with Sicilian peasants returning from a vain attempt to sell their oranges on the mainland. There is something wrong with the fruit, they say, some "poison" that has infected it. Significantly they refuse to recognize Silvestro as one of them, and ask if he is an *americano*, an emigrant returning from abroad. On the train ride through Sicily that follows, Silvestro meets a tall man identified as the Gran Lombardo, who speaks of the "stink" caused by two portly Fascists standing nearby in the third-class carriage and confesses that "he would have liked to acquire other knowledge, that's how he put it, other knowledge, and to feel himself different, with something new in his soul."[46] Silvestro begins to understand that others are suffering from the same frustrations and dissatisfactions, that in his alienation from Fascist Italy he is not alone.

The major part of the novel, as its title suggests, is devoted to Silvestro's conversations with his mother and the other inhabitants of the small town of his childhood. The familiar sights and smells reawaken his senses; a new intimacy with his village restores a lost feeling of peace and innocence. As he accompanies his mother, a nurse, on her rounds, ministering to patients who are also her friends, he glimpses the possibility of acquiring the "other knowledge" and assuming the "other duties" to which the Gran Lombardo alluded. The novel's climax comes in a visionary scene when Silvestro is briefly reunited with a brother killed abroad fighting for Mussolini:

I said: "Do you suffer much?"
"A great deal," he said. "Millions of times."
I: "Millions of times?"
He: "For every word printed, for every word spoken, for every millimeter of bronze raised [as a statue]."

I: "It makes you cry?"
He: "It makes us cry."

The sufferings of the war dead, like the sufferings of the peasants who cannot sell their produce or who lie sick awaiting his mother, make Silvestro's unhappiness pale into insignificance, and at the same time unite him with others. It is those who suffer on this earth, he comes to believe, who are most human, most like true men: "But perhaps not every man is a man; and not all the human race is the human race . . . Kill a man; he will be more a man. And thus a sick man is more a man, and a starving man [as well]. A more human race is the human race of those who die of hunger."[47]

The message of *Conversation in Sicily* is thus one of moral reawakening through fraternity with the victims of suffering. On one level, as a critic has noted, this best-known of Vittorini's works is "the novel of the 'turning point' of 1936-37, the novel of the 'abstract furies' that exploded in Vittorini (and in other intellectuals) with the war in Spain, and which subsided in a rediscovery of his Sicily."[48] But one finds a more general message here as well. By setting his novel in the timeless Sicilian countryside, Vittorini was able to give his descriptions symbolic overtones that raised the suffering of its peasants to universal significance. This symbolic dimension is reinforced by the operatic repetition of key words and phrases throughout the novel: "other duties" (*altri doveri*) "much suffering" (*è molto soffrire*), "more a man" (*più uomo*). They bind together the separate episodes, enriched with additional meaning in every new context, like a litany that emphasizes the basic similarities uniting the fates of individual men.

The polyphony and symbolic resonance of *Conversation in Sicily* suggest another aspect of American literature that found an appreciative response among Italian writers of the 1930s — the exploration of moral themes in a pastoral setting, typified by the work of Herman Melville. At the time when he wrote his novel, Vittorini recalled, "we thought that with the help of American freshness, we would perhaps enter into a poetic maturity and into a poetic tradition of the novel." Giaime Pintor, in a review of Vittorini's book published in 1941, observed: "In no recent novel has the pain or anguish — the human element, in sum, which underlies creation — appeared so plainly, so little obscured by the literary framework. For this reason *Conversation in Sicily* has the absolute value of an allegory."[49]

But if Sicily emerged in Vittorini's novel as an island haven from the "abstract furies" of Fascism, the mainland from which Silvestro fled remained in the hands of the enemy. Solidarity among a few was achieved at the price of continued isolation from the many. The opposing worlds of country and city suggested the deep estrangement between anti-Fascist intellectuals and the masses still content to "believe, obey, and fight" for Mussolini. The anti-Fascists' hopes for a popular response to their ideals went unfulfilled until June 1940. In that month, the Duce decided to honor his Pact of Steel with Hitler, and by belatedly attacking France, tipped both Fascists and their opponents into war.

The Armed Resistance

World War II was unpopular in Italy from the start. Having fought two wars in Ethiopia and Spain in less than four years, the Italian people desired nothing so much as peace in the summer of 1940. They submitted to the prospect of yet another conflict with weary resignation. "The news of war surprises no one," Count Ciano, the Italian foreign minister, noted in his diary on June 10, "and does not arouse excessive enthusiasm. I am gloomy, very gloomy. The adventure begins. God help Italy."[50]

Mussolini gambled on a short campaign. Mindful of the price exacted by Italy from its French and British allies for entry into World War I, and impressed with the German successes in the field, the Duce was moved by the hope of further territorial gains to cast his lot with the probable Nazi victor. But the gamble failed. Deficient in troops, leadership, and materiel despite brave boasts to the contrary, the Italian armies suffered humiliating reverses in Greece and North Africa. As the war dragged on, morale deteriorated. Food shortages and a widespread black market became routine in Italian cities. The crescendo of discontent culminated in March 1943, when an estimated 100,000 Turinese workers struck to express their disgust with the Duce and the war. Carmine Senise, the head of the police, noted with surprise that "all participate, Fascists and anti-Fascists." The regime found itself deserted on all sides.[51]

On the night of July 24, 1943, with half of Sicily occupied by Anglo-American forces and an invasion of southern Italy imminent, the Fascist Grand Council bowed to the inevitable and voted to depose Mussolini.[52] While crowds demonstrated their joy in the streets, negotiations over armistice terms were initiated with the Allies. In the meantime the Germans, rightly suspecting that their tottering partner was on the brink of defection, rushed troops south across the Alps. When the new prime minister, Marshal Badoglio, finally capitulated to the Allies on September 3, the Germans retaliated by occupying Italy as far south as Naples, while the king and his ministers fled

Rome in disarray. Mussolini was soon freed on Hitler's orders and permitted to reign over the so-called Republic of Salò in the North, where he found that the Germans conceded him less real power than they had granted Pétain at Vichy. The Italian people, who had anticipated a speedy liberation by the Allies, were confused and divided. Some advocated a policy of *attesimo*, a watchful wait-and-see attitude calculated to give offense to neither side. But a growing minority viewed such a posture as both cowardly and short-sighted. They formed the core of the Resistenza Armata, the armed Resistance movement that sprang into being in German-held territory beginning in the fall of 1943, which was to contribute in no small measure to the liberation of central and northern Italy in the months to come.[53]

The Resistance movement involved large numbers of ordinary Italian men and women in the political life of their country for the first time since the days of the Risorgimento, when Garibaldi's ragged volunteer army had opened the way for national unification with its victories over the foreign dynasty ruling Naples and Sicily. Italian patriots rediscovered their revolutionary heritage in 1943, much as the French Resistance would with the liberation of Paris in 1944. Whereas many had been discontented but passive before Mussolini's fall, the conditions of life under the Germans and faith in a coming Allied victory now elicited a far more vigorous response. Resistance groups in the Apennine hill country and the mountains of the North launched sabotage missions against railway lines and communications centers, and partisan operations against German troops and Mussolini's own makeshift army. Though made up chiefly of former soldiers (so-called *sbandati*) and youths seeking to evade compulsory labor or military service, their social composition was unusually broad. A survey of one group in Piedmont revealed workers, peasants, industrialists, students, members of the professions, and four priests living and fighting together.[54] They were united by a common sense of shame at the failure to stand firm against the Germans in September 1943, and a common hope that by participating in Italy's liberation they might win the right to help to determine its future once hostilities ended. They were resolved, in Winston Churchill's phrase, to "work their passage home."

The Resistenza Armata dissolved the barriers that had previously isolated the intellectuals from a repressive regime and an indifferent populace. As one partisan leader, the widow of Piero Gobetti, later wrote, the "bond of solidarity, based not on ties of blood, of the fatherland, nor of an intellectual tradition, but on the simple human relationship of feeling oneself one with another among many, appeared to me the inner significance . . . of our battle."[55] Two different groups of intellectuals joined the Resistance — the younger generation of Vittorini and Pintor, and exiles returning from abroad such as Aldo Garosci, Leo Valiani, and Franco Venturi. Their cause drew recent defectors from Fascism as well. An officer who had fought with the Fascist forces in Spain, Davide Lajolo, discovered in the Resistance the "true face" of the Italian people: "Beaten, abandoned, betrayed, they still knew, on their own, how to find the proper path of revolt—alone, without propaganda, in a rush of faith . . . I was becoming, perhaps only now, a true soldier of Italy." The mood of the intellectuals was expressed by Giaime Pintor in a letter to his brother shortly before the Resistance mission that would claim his life: "We musicians and writers must renounce our privileges in order to contribute to the liberation of all . . . Today all the possibilities of the Risorgimento are open to the Italians once again."[56]

A sense of suddenly widening horizons, of fluid possibilities and beckoning change, accompanied and complemented the warmth of fellowship discovered in the Resistance. Altiero Spinelli, liberated from a long captivity in August 1943, wrote that freedom appeared to him "the fount of every possibility" and a "magnificent uncertainty" rather than a "restful conclusion" to the anti-Fascist struggle.[57] The months that followed were difficult but exhilarating. Each small victory against the Germans and Mussolini's rump republic confirmed the Resistance faith in man's power to shape events as he desired; each defeat brought renewed determination that it should be the last. Italian intellectuals rejected passive acquiescence to the present as decisively as had Sartre in *The Flies*. Now, at last, they saw a promise of creating a nation that was truly their own.

A year before the start of the Resistenza Armata, Vittorini had consummated his break with Fascism by joining the Communist underground in Milan, where he helped to edit the clandestine Communist party newspaper, *L'Unità*. This activity led to his arrest and imprisonment in July 1943; but he was released in September after Badoglio's armistice with the Allies. Under the German occupation, Vittorini slipped once more into the ranks of the Resistance, living the precarious life of a fugitive from the Gestapo while actively contributing to the underground press and founding a short-lived paper of his own. In February 1944, while in Florence to rally support for a general strike against the Germans, he barely escaped capture. Forced to seek refuge in the mountains, he set to work on a new novel directly inspired by the Milanese underground, which, as one historian observes, was "the most prestigious underground . . . in the North."[58] The title that Vittorini chose for this work, *Uomini e no* (*Men and Not*), was derived from Steinbeck's *Of Mice and Men* (*Uomini e topi* in Italian translation), and reflected his earlier interest in those who were "more men" in *Conversation in Sicily*. The structure of the novel was again built around a few central and recurring themes: happiness, solidarity, and liberation. But whereas the earlier novel recounted a single individual's liberation from his doubts and fears, *Men and Not* dealt with engagement in a Resistance enterprise aimed at the liberation of all.

A large part of the interest of *Men and Not*, apart from its evocation of the dangers and heroism of the underground, lies in Vittorini's attempt to probe the ethical grounds motivating the men of the Resistance to risk their lives in Milan. The answers emerge in a series of dialogues whose lesson is underscored by the author's favored device of ritual repetition. An elderly partisan sympathizer asks the hero: "'Can't we desire that a man be happy? We are working in order that men may be happy. What meaning would our work have if it did not serve to make men happy? That is what we are working for. Is that not what we are working for?' 'It is for that,' [he] said." A second answer appears during a conversation between the heroine, Berta, and a beggar. Both have seen Resistance hostages lying dead in the street, their bodies guarded by German soldiers.

> "But what should we do?" she asked him.
> "Oh!" the old man replied. "We must learn."
> "Learn from the dead?"
> "Of course. From whom can one learn if not from them? They alone teach."
> "Teach what?" said Berta. "What do they teach?"
> "That," said the old man, "for which they died."
> Berta asked the old man what he meant, and the old man said he meant that for which everything happened and for which people died, he said, even if they were not fighting.
> "Liberation?" said Berta.
> "Certainly," the old man replied.[59]

For Vittorini's generation, as for Sartre and his friends, the Resistance brought a release from the isolation they had experienced during the 1930s. Their engagement was prompted by a variety of circumstances and motives: a war they could not evade, a regime they could not accept, a solitude they could not justify. It was also a response to more positive goals of fraternity, hope, a shared humanism that transcended their individual lives. The sacrifices imposed on the members of the Resistance had figured prominently in Beauvoir's novel *The Blood of Others*. In *Men and Not* the main character, like Beauvoir's Hélène Bertrand, dies a martyr while serving others. He is the archetypical intellectual who renounces the privilege and safety of a sheltered position in society and is rewarded for this decision with a deeper sense of purpose and community. In an aside, the author comments: "[Our hero] is an intellectual. He would have been able to struggle without ever experiencing desperation if he had continued to struggle as an intellectual. Why did he wish to change the kind of struggle [in which he was engaged]? Why did he want to change weapons? Why did he leave his pen and take a pistol in hand?"[60]

The answer, Vittorini suggested, was that while "one loses oneself" alone, "one fights together." As he wrote in a eulogy for his friend Eugenio Curiel, from whom the portrait of the novel's hero was partly drawn, "we have a great deal ahead of us. We have to . . . fight for this 'great deal,' certainly, intensify our struggle, and close ranks among ourselves." The struggle intensified in early 1945. That April, as Mussolini was making his unsuccessful bid to pass on the mantle of authority to Resistance leaders in Milan, popular insurrections in Genoa, Turin, Milan, and other northern cities brought Fascism's reign to an end.[61] The creation of a new political system based on humanistic ideals was the next task of the Italian Resistance intellectuals. In the course of this attempt, as in France and Germany, their faith and idealism were to be severely tried.

8
A Season of Hope
1945-1946

*Will we ever have a culture that is able
to protect man from suffering instead of
limiting itself to consoling him? A
culture that prevents [suffering], that
exorcises it, that helps to eliminate
exploitation and slavery and conquers
need—that is the culture into which we
must transform the old.*
Elio Vittorini, 1945

In the spring of 1945 the energies that had been mobilized for the liberation of Italy were directed toward the task of
reconstruction. Giorgio Amendola, a leader of the Piedmontese
underground, remembered the new mood that gripped the inhabitants
of Turin that Easter: "There were many happy groups already
celebrating the end of the terrible incubus. This spectacle . . . was a
proof of the courage of men and women of the people, with their will
to overcome the disasters of the war, to live, to build."[1] It was fitting
that the expulsion of the last German troops from Italian soil should
coincide with the first signs of spring. A spirit of renewal, a flowering
of hopes long dormant during the Fascist winter, accompanied the
battles fought in the marshes and the mountains of the North. As in
France, the Resistance inspired hope in its participants not only
because its initial goal had been secured but also because its institutions and ideals seemed to furnish a model for the new Italy now taking shape.

After twenty years under Fascism, the Italian people had proved
themselves capable of self-government and could claim a new political
maturity. A volunteer force of 200,000 men and women—the largest
partisan movement in Western Europe—had struggled for twenty
months against the enemy. The result was civic education on a mass
scale. The voluntary nature of the enterprise, which bound partisans

with ties of trust rather than with discipline imposed from above, as well as the need to make rapid decisions on the spot, which followed the Nazi disruption of communications in central and northern Italy, accentuated the independent, self-governing character of the Resistance. Whereas anti-Fascist intellectuals such as Leone Ginzburg had noted with sorrow that Italy was "a country without a political heritage" during the 1930s, few such fears were expressed in the underground press after 1943. "The Italian people," Ginzburg himself wrote with evident satisfaction, "have now taken their place among the peoples who struggle for liberty."[2]

But the Resistance was more than an exercise in civic responsibility. It was a political experiment marked by a return to local autonomy and the rise of a new elite to positions of real influence. It not only seemed to make good the omissions of the earlier Risorgimento but also promised to sweep away the authoritarian constraints of the Fascist state and the paternalism of a discredited monarchy, thereby allowing genuine popular involvement in politics and the creation of "natural" associations without force. In contrast to Mussolini's claim of "everything for the state, nothing outside the state," the Resistance aspired to dismantle the state bureaucracy and to place liberty and equality before power and hierarchy. The Partito d'Azione, whose members included many leading Resistance intellectuals, stated in a manifesto in 1944: "The Partito d'Azione aspires to found a society of free men, in which political and social equality of the citizens signals the end to all oppression of man by man . . . Characteristic of this struggle will be the intense participation of the popular masses, from whose autonomous intervention . . . new institutions of liberty will arise, which the people [will] recognize and defend as their own."[3]

Underlying the Resistance hopes for a *taglio netto*, a clean break with both the compromises of the old parliamentary system and the Fascist cult of power, was thus a vision of human dignity that had been revealed in the recent struggle. As one Resistance veteran later recalled: "The Italian people found during these years new values and forgotten values, not so much buried in the tradition and the history of our country as present in the soul of each individual." Resistance against the Fascists, ironically, fulfilled a number of aims that the Fascists themselves had professed two decades before. The suppression of class antagonisms in a common effort, the renunciation of narrow self-interest, the confirmation of military valor in the Italian *maquis*—these were at last realities that promised further changes to come. But whether the Resistance was strong enough to ensure continued loyalty to its ideals in liberated Italy was an open question. Ada Gobetti later remembered: "In a confusing way I sensed, however, that another struggle was beginning: longer, more difficult, more tiring, even if less bloody. It was no longer a question of fighting against arrogance, cruelty, and violence—easy to identify and to reject—but . . . of not allowing that little flame of solidarity and fraternal humanism, which we had seen born, to die in the calm atmosphere of an apparent return to normal life."[4]

Political Reconstruction and the Vento del Nord

At the center of the Resistance attempt to fashion new institutions for Italy were committees that composed the Comitato di Liberazione Nazionale (CLN), which had emerged during the brief period of hope and confusion between Mussolini's fall from power and Badoglio's armistice. On September 9, 1943, as news of the government's flight from Rome spread, Ivanoe Bonomi and others who had previously formed an anti-Fascist committee in Rome met to discuss ways of filling the political vacuum that seemed imminent. The group's purpose was stated as follows: "At the moment when Nazism is attempting to restore [to power] its Fascist ally in Rome and in Italy, the anti-Fascist parties are forming a Committee of National Liberation to summon Italians to struggle and resist, and to win for Italy the place it deserves in the assembly of free nations."[5] It was decided that each major city would form its own CLN, with the Roman committee as central coordinating body. The committees in the North gradually assumed a separate identity as the Comitati di Liberazione Nazionale d'Alta Italia (CLNAI), with headquarters in Milan.

These committees, like their French counterparts, formed a structure of parallel governments in the occupied areas of the country. As the Liberation progressed northward, they emerged to nominate local officials and to assume administrative responsibilities. The CLNAI declared in one of its earliest proclamations: "There will be no room among us tomorrow for a regime of disguised reaction or for a lame democracy. The new political, social, and economic system cannot be other than a pure and effective democracy. The CLN of today is a prefiguration of the government of tomorrow."[6] As in France also, Liberals, Catholics, and the Left appeared to suspend political rivalry in a new spirit of national unity. The Roman CLN, for example, frequently held meetings as the guest of the Vatican in the Lateran Seminary. The cabinet formed by Bonomi in July 1944 revealed the same trend toward cooperation: it included as ministers without portfolio both the conservative Liberal Benedetto Croce and the head of the Italian Communist party, Palmiro Togliatti.

The CLN differed from the French Conseil National de la Résistance in both composition and political competence, however. Whereas the Resistance movements in France formed the core of the CNR and tolerated the representatives from the prewar parties with mixed disdain and apprehension, the Italian parties were the sole participants in the CLN. The opprobrium directed against politicians in France, whom many considered responsible for both the French defeat in 1940 and the sabotage of the Third Republic, was aimed in Italy at King Victor Emmanuel III, who had named Mussolini as head of government in 1922. The Italian parties' anti-Fascist credentials made them acceptable to the intellectuals as vehicles for political reform. The Partito d'Azione was in fact largely a party of intellectuals, less concerned than Sartre and his circle to avoid traditional political channels in pursuing their goals. Nor were the Italian Resistance forces confronted with a powerful rival returning from exile abroad. The French CNR was forced to assert its rights against the claims of de Gaulle; its collective Italian counterpart enjoyed an uncontested position as the sole and legitimate leader of the Resistance.

All parties represented in the CLN were united in their opposition to Fascism. A similar consensus was lacking, however, concerning the future of the monarchy, the purge of government officials, and the political role of the CLN itself. It is possible to identify three major divisions within the complex tangle of ideological differences and tactical alliances: North versus South, Left versus Right, and partisans of autonomy versus defenders of unity. In general, those favoring autonomy tended to be leftists from the North, while those favoring unity were more conservative and from the South. The Left pushed for abolishing the monarchy, vigorously purging the Fascists, and expanding the powers of the CLN; the Right urged caution in all three areas.[7]

The differences in regional attitudes should serve as a reminder that the effects of the Resistance were not felt with equal force throughout the Italian peninsula. The military campaign against the Germans and their Fascist allies from 1943 until the spring of 1945 created very different wartime experiences in the North and South. With the exception of a brief popular insurrection in Naples, southern Italy was liberated entirely by the Allies. No clandestine committees appeared to challenge the German occupation, and the political parties that surfaced in 1943 were at first subjected to controls by the Allied Military Government similar to those later imposed in Germany. Attitudes in central Italy were mixed; though Rome and the Albine Hills were active Resistance centers, the surrounding countryside remained largely passive. It was in northern Italy that the Resistance lasted longest and gained the broadest support. The war thus widened the traditional gulf between two distinct and rival nations within Italy's borders: a politically advanced, industrial North and a backward, agricultural South. The insistence on autonomy in local government so prevalent in the North reflected both a de facto independence from Rome and a distrust of the conservative attitudes that prevailed there.[8]

The major exception to this alignment within the CLN was the Communist party (PCI). Returning in early 1944 from a long Russian exile, Togliatti immediately initiated a radical shift of tactics that brought the PCI into close cooperation with the Right for the balance of the war. Victory over Fascism was a more immediate Communist concern than the future revolution. As Togliatti told a Communist audience in Naples on April 11, 1944: "We are the party of unity. Unity of the working class, unity of the anti-Fascist forces, unity of the entire nation in the war against Hitler's Germany and against the traitors in its service. We are the party whose special duty it is to ward off the attempts, from whatever quarter, to shatter the unity we need for our salvation."[9] This strategy undermined the CLN's attempt to initiate national political and institutional changes before the end of the war. While the combat continued, there could be little progress toward resolving the debates within the Resistance, which remained frozen for the duration.[10]

During the next twelve months, as the Allies moved slowly northward and the Italian partisans behind the lines gained in numbers and courage, the most significant political activity of the Resistance occurred at a local level. The CLNAI, though subordinate in theory to the orders of the Allied Military Government, acted in practice as a sovereign power wherever the Fascists were in retreat. Local groups enjoyed their period of greatest influence during the spring of 1945. Liberation committees decreed the suspension of Fascist legislation, ordered the beginning of purge trials against the most notorious of Mussolini's supporters, and took steps to ensure continuity in public services much as the Antifas were to do in Germany after Hitler's defeat. These measures were accompanied by more ambitious projects that looked toward the future. In the large industrial cities of the North, workers' councils received formal recognition and encouragement from the CLNAI as a step toward giving their members a share in the control of local factories. Agricultural cooperatives obtained similar support. The Corporate State, in the view of the Resistance intellectuals, would have its institutions progressively replaced by a loose confederation of independent centers of self-management, whose powers the new national government would find it difficult to abrogate once faced with a fait accompli.[11]

The final liberation of northern Italy in early 1945 strengthened the forces calling for change. This spirit of political and social renovation, termed the "wind from the north" (*vento del nord*), seemed as if it might blow away the haze of compromise and immobility that had settled over Rome during the tenure of the second Bonomi cabinet. Supporters of the CLNAI fully expected their views to prevail in the deliberations that were soon to begin. They were moved by an optimism and a sense of mission that overcame all party barriers, while reinforcing their belief in the opposition between a dynamic North and stagnant South, between a morally pure CLNAI and a tepid CLN. As in France and Germany, a dualistic mode of thinking was evident in their speeches and writings, which associated youth, courage, and moral vigor against the declining powers of age, division, and facile compromise. The time was propitious for reform, and throughout Europe the Left was gaining strength. Leo Valiani wrote in the journal *Nuovi Quaderni di Giustizia e Libertà* soon after the Liberation: "The partisan war, the overwhelming victories of the Red Army and the armies of the Anglo-Americans, the popular insurrections in France and Italy, the triumphs of the Labour party in the British elections, have pushed Europe to the Left. This is the moment to put into practice the programs of advanced democracy, of radical social reform, that compose the ideological and political message of all modern popular parties."[12]

Events in May and June of 1945 seemed to confirm these hopes. The CLNAI succeeded in forcing the resignation of Bonomi, whose increasingly open monarchist sympathies made him a symbol of the old order. No sooner was he gone from office, however, than the anticipated disagreements broke out concerning his successor. The Socialists and Communists proposed Pietro Nenni, while the Christian Democrats supported Alcide De Gasperi. The deadlock was finally resolved by the nomination of Ferruccio Parri, the leader of the Partito d'Azione in Milan and former military chief (with Luigi Longo) of the Resistance forces in the North. While this choice was widely regarded as a victory for the ideals of the Resistance, it reflected equally the current stalemate between the mass parties of the Left and the Christian Democrats. In this sense it was as much a negative decision, a temporary expedient pending further consolidation of the two blocs, as a positive endorsement of the *vento del nord*.

The election of Parri was nevertheless highly significant for the fortunes of the Liberation in Italy. Unlike de Gaulle, whose preference for order appeared to outweigh his sympathies toward change, Parri was sincerely dedicated to achieving fundamental political and social reforms. His very lack of political experience seemed a virtue; he owed no political debts, was tied to no financial interests. His sole qualifications to lead Italy in this critical period were a shining Resistance record and lofty personal integrity. "He was considered a saint," recalled one man who had known him during the Resistance years. "He was a man whose authority was . . . not political, not even ideological, but certainly moral."[13] Parri's impatience with rhetoric, his distrust of authority, his obvious sincerity and sense of duty illustrated the moral strength as well as the political limits of the northern Resistance.

Parri's accession to office symbolized both the Resistance continuity with prewar anti-Fascism and the innovations possible in the postwar climate of experiment and change. That a political outsider should be named prime minister demonstrated the possibility of a break with the past. Parri represented the new elite that derived its prominence from a heroism demonstrated in the Resistenza Armata. At the same time, he was firmly rooted in the liberal socialism associated with the Giustizia e Libertà movement from the 1930s. The movement had been founded by his friend Carlo Rosselli, a member of a prominent Jewish family whose forebears had distinguished themselves during the Risorgimento. Rosselli and Parri belonged to the first generation of Italian anti-Fascists, who struggled first in Italy and then in exile to organize support "for liberty, for the republic, for social justice."[14] They had arranged the escape of the aging Socialist leader Filippo Turati from Italy in 1926, for which they were exiled to the island of Lipari off the northeastern coast of Sicily. There they held long discussions concerning the future of socialism, and with other political prisoners explored the possibilities of broadening the framework of orthodox Marxism to include a new emphasis on individual freedom. As Parri later recalled: "Rosselli said that if the *Communist Manifesto* of 1848 had been the revolutionary gospel of a century, after the bitter experience of Fascism there was need for new promise, more human and richer in its emphasis on liberation than mechanical Marxism."[15]

While still confined on Lipari, Rosselli began to distill his thoughts in a manuscript, which he concealed from his captors in an old piano and subsequently published in Paris in 1930, a year after he escaped from detention. *Socialismo liberale* (*Liberal Socialism*) began by tracing the "slow but fatal erosion of Marxist socialism," and concluded with a summons to "a revolutionary struggle in the name of the principle of liberty." Rosselli's emphasis on the revolutionary aspects of liberty came in direct response to the suppression of human rights under Mussolini. At the same time, it reflected his desire to renew Marxist doctrine by grafting liberal principles to a socialist stock. As he wrote: "The formula 'liberal socialism' grates on the ears of many who are used to the customary political terminology . . . Yet socialism is simply the logical development of the principle of liberty in its utmost consequences. Socialism, understood in its broadest meaning and judged by its results—that is, the movement for the concrete emancipation of the working class—is liberalism in action." Most important, in Rosselli's view, was the need to reject Marxist determinism in favor of a faith in personal initiative. The responsibility for making freedom a concrete reality rested with the individual. "Without free men," he wrote, "a free state is impossible."[16]

Rosselli's message was to prove particularly suited to the Italian Resistance movement during World War II, with its moral idealism and stress on the ability of men and women to secure these ideals through their own actions. Indeed, as Aldo Garosci has noted, there is a perceptible strain of existentialist ethics in Rosselli's works. Yet his attempt to link the goals of freedom and of socialism implied the same contradiction later noted by Richter in *Der Ruf*. Was it possible to achieve social justice without restricting individual liberties? After socialism was freed from a Marxist view of historical inevitability, the task of imposing coherence on a multitude of potentially conflicting wills remained.

The Partito d'Azione inherited both Rosselli's belief that social change was intimately bound with the liberation of the individual and his reluctance to confront the problems raised by the attempt to give each equal weight. In the short run, this ambiguous position proved an advantage. Parri's stance midway between Marxism and its liberal critics made him acceptable to both, and thus gave the Resistance a chance to inaugurate its own program in the summer of 1945. As Parri told a congress of the CLNAI soon after taking office, his would be a "policy of mediation." The Resistance press was less cautious in its predictions. "It is fortunate for us that the Fascists did not succeed in killing all those like Parri," commented *Il Ponte*. "The men who remain are all we need for the renewal of Italy."[17]

The Parri Government

In late 1945 Italy alone among the countries of Western Europe was governed by a Resistance leader who shared the ideals of the non-Communist Left. Parri's accession to office inspired optimism among his supporters that the ethical concerns of the Resistance would at last find effective political expression. But in Italy, as in Germany and France, those who strove to keep alive the Resistance ideals were powerless without the support of the country's ruling groups and the populace at large. Many Italians had won new privileges under Mussolini's regime and were determined to retain them. As one

Resistance veteran later noted: "We continue to call the movement of liberation in Italy a 'resistance'; but let us not forget that it was not a resistance, but an attack, an initiative, an ideal innovation, not an attempt to preserve something."[18] Those with "something to preserve" understandably proved hostile to the Resistance call for reform.

Parri's program embraced far-reaching changes. He opposed the monarchy and favored a republic. He sympathized with proposals to decentralize the government, a move foreshadowed by the virtual autonomy of many local CLNAI committees in the North during the spring of 1945, reversing the policy of tight control from the center that had characterized Italian administration since the Risorgimento.[19] He called for a redistribution of power from large concentrations of capital such as the Confindustria, which united Italy's most powerful enterprises, to small and medium-sized businesses overshadowed in the past. He supported increased worker participation in the management of industry, on the pattern of the management councils (*consigli di gestione*) created by the CLNAI in the factories of Milan and Turin in April 1945. To slow inflation and to reduce the government deficit, he repeatedly called for currency reform. Finally, he intended to resume and accelerate the program of purges initiated a year earlier by the first Bonomi cabinet, but since allowed to lapse. Together these measures would contribute toward Italy's "material and moral reconstruction" and "lay the foundations for a new society."[20]

Faced with the overwhelming task of reconstruction, the Parri government inevitably appeared to fall short in its performance. The very fact that it represented an experiment in Italian politics led its supporters to anticipate miracles. In this sense Parri was the victim of the hopes he inspired. Working long hours in the Viminal Palace with often as little as three hours' sleep a night, attending to a host of administrative details that a more experienced or less conscientious head of government might have left to his subordinates, Parri nevertheless began to find himself accused of inaction by both Right and Left. Growing unrest among the unemployed and the homeless caused conservatives to call for strong countermeasures against demonstrators and to cast nostalgic glances at Mussolini's "strong state," where such disorders had been held in check.[21] Spokesmen for radical change, on the other hand, predictably felt that Parri was moving too slowly toward his stated goals.

The resumption of the purges, which Parri thought would contribute to Italy's moral regeneration, prompted the same conservative critics who protested his inaction in maintaining public order to accuse him of excessive rigor, claiming that he was willing to sacrifice the stability of institutions for the sake of moral goals. For the lower middle class, which had profited greatly by Mussolini's expansion of the Italian administration, the renewed purges exacerbated a general feeling of insecurity caused by growing unemployment.[22] As in Germany, a large group of minor functionaries, compromised by a formal adherence to Fascism, felt simultaneously guiltless of wrongdoing and vulnerable to inquiries into their past.

The upper middle class felt more threatened by Parri's economic reforms. The government's plan to break up the large industrial combines was resisted by the Liberals as a direct attack on free enterprise. Many small producers, who would have benefited from this plan, interpreted it as a conspiracy against private property and opposed it bitterly. The management councils created in the North further alienated many businessmen, who considered them but the first stage of a Communist campaign to capture the "commanding heights" of industry. The prospect of monetary reform stirred passionate opposition from those who feared that their bank assets would be frozen or confiscated. The result was a tacit alliance among Liberals, Christian Democrats, and the Confindustria that shattered the unity of the Resistance by dividing the middle and working classes on the issue of personal liberty versus social justice. The two terms of the equation that Rosselli and Parri had struggled to unite threatened to dissolve once again into conflicting alternatives.

Parri has been seen as a high-minded but inept figure, an idealist adrift in the savage world of politics.[23] It is true that he agonized over decisions that a more experienced politician would have made without regard for ethical niceties, at a time when rapid action was needed on several fronts. He also fundamentally mistrusted the civil servants who staffed the vast bureaucratic apparatus of which he was the designated head. Both his reluctance to delegate power, which contributed to his government's apparent paralysis, and his moves toward decentralization and a revival of the purges, which aroused such protest, were attempts to circumvent a central administration whose loyalty he doubted.

Yet Parri's weaknesses as a leader in time of crisis, like those of Léon Blum and the French Popular Front of 1936, were compounded by his being forced to govern without the secure backing of either Right or Left. To the extent that Parri's social reforms overlapped with those proposed by the Italian Communist party, the Communists regarded him as a rival. To the extent that they threatened the vested interests of the middle class, that class saw him as an enemy. The Allied Military Government continued to exercise control over the Italian North, where Parri might have counted on the greatest support. Lacking a strong mass base for his own party, unable to win the support of the larger parties in the coalition on which he continued to depend, Parri was forced to resign after barely five months in office. At a final press conference called to announce his resignation, he candidly admitted the "insufficiencies, errors . . . indecision in the work of the government." But his sense of betrayal was apparent when he attacked both Liberals and Christian Democrats for failing to place the interests of the nation before their own partisan advantage, and for preparing a "coup d'état" that could only favor the "resurgence and reorganization of Fascist and reactionary forces, sabotaging the democratic future of Italy."[24]

The winter of 1945-46 brought increasing signs that the wave of reforms so confidently expected or widely feared during the previous autumn was not likely to materialize. Economic conditions, the attitude of the Allies, and the nature of the government that succeeded Parri all combined to block further movement toward Resistance goals. Parri's tenure in office, rather than heralding a permanent change in Italian political habits, now appeared to have been simply an interregnum, a brief burst of innovation favored by the uncertainty of the first months following the Liberation. In the minds of many it was an aberration, not a precedent.

The man who replaced Parri as prime minister symbolized the return to normality. Alcide De Gasperi, leader of the Christian Democratic party, was in many ways the antithesis of his predecessor. Parri had been a newcomer to politics, but De Gasperi's political experience on a national level reached as far back as 1919, when he had been Don Luigi Sturzo's lieutenant in the ranks of the Catholic-oriented Popular party. During the war years, when Parri had worked in the North, directing the military operations of the CLNAI, De Gasperi had been in Rome, participating as the Christian Democratic delegate in both the central CLN and Bonomi's two cabinets. And whereas Parri, the political outsider, had distrusted the state, preferring to lean on the local CLN committees wherever possible, De Gasperi, the insider, possessed a "sense of the state," a ready appreciation of the prerogatives of a national government, as well as an understanding of those areas in which it should not attempt to interfere.[25]

De Gasperi's sense of purpose, backed by the power of a mass party, allowed him to dominate a cabinet whose composition differed little from the one Parri had been unable to control. Despite the continued presence of Communists, Socialists, and Actionists, De Gasperi gradually engineered a shift to the Right. The results of this general reorientation were first visible in the economic sector. In December 1945 worsening inflation led the single Italian trade union (CGIL) to conclude an agreement with the Confindustria covering all workers in the industrial triangle of Genoa-Turin-Milan. It provided for a standard minimum wage, a sliding scale of pay raises to correspond with future increases in the cost of living, and equality of pay for men and women. But these concessions were obtained at a price: the CGIL lost the right to representation on the "management councils" that had formed a cornerstone of the Resistance labor program.[26]

Meanwhile the Western Allies showed clearly that they preferred the new premier to the old. In January 1946 the United Nations Relief and Rehabilitation Administration agreed to increase aid to Italy almost ninefold—from $50 million the previous year to $435 million for the period through June 1947. The Allies also transferred full control of the northern provinces to Italian authorities. As of December 31, 1945, the last area under the jurisdiction of the Allied Military Government returned to Italian sovereignty. De Gasperi immediately suspended all purge trials in those provinces and allowed earlier verdicts to be appealed, thus bringing that aspect of Parri's moral and administrative reform to an end. In addition, he requested that local officials who had been placed in office by the CLNAI either regularize their positions by joining the state civil service or cede their posts to career officials appointed by himself.[27]

De Gasperi's ending of the purge and his move to co-opt or dismiss the CLNAI administration were aspects of a general attempt to give power back to the central government by restoring its former provincial representatives and making them dependent on Rome. Like de Gaulle, De Gasperi viewed the local CLN Resistance groups as temporary manifestations of a popular anti-Fascism. Their continued existence after the final phase of the Liberation would pose a threat to the legitimate government, for it would provide a power base from which the Left—and especially the Communists—might extend control to other sectors of the government.[28]

Although the Partito d'Azione continued to participate in succeeding political coalitions through 1946, its ability to shape policy was necessarily limited, and it lacked the power to prevent the reversal of many of Parri's initiatives. Resistance intellectuals in Italy thus found themselves in the same position as their French and German colleagues. Having moved further and more rapidly than either group toward the elusive goal of national leadership, they were obliged to abandon both the premiership and the local CLN alternative with equal haste. Their last line of defense remained the journalism to which the intellectuals in France and Germany also retreated. During the period of waiting and apprehension that followed De Gasperi's accession to the premiership, the Resistance press took on added importance as the chief guardian of the *vento del nord*.

Journalism and Liberation

Comparatively few Italian Resistance publications survived the war in their original format. They were superseded by a score of new journals that appeared during the years 1944-1946, recalling the similar creative outburst in the postwar German press. Compared with contemporary German reviews, however, the Italian journals showed a greater self-assurance and ideological diversity. Neither the burden of defeat nor the pressures of Allied censorship restrained their debate. From Croce's new *Quaderni della Critica* on the Right to Togliatti's *Rinascita* on the Left, all displayed a common desire to complete Italy's emancipation from Fascism and to intensify the political discussion surrounding the nation's future.[29]

Characteristic of this new journalism was the monthly *Il Ponte*, published in Florence from the beginning of 1945. Its editor was Piero Calamandrei, a participant in various anti-Fascist groups in the 1920s and later a member of the Partito d'Azione.[30] *Il Ponte*'s emphasis on moral regeneration, its distrust of party politics, its broad humanism, and its faith in continuing Resistance unity all typified the determination to keep the spirit of the *vento del nord* alive in postwar Italy. The journal declared its intention to "contribute toward rebuilding moral unity after a period of profound crisis." "We believe," wrote Calamandrei in its first editorial, "that it is necessary now to struggle in all fields to reconstruct . . . the moral sincerity of man." At the same time, the editors of *Il Ponte* followed the unfolding political drama in Rome with rapt interest mingled with ill-concealed anxiety. Calamandrei was particularly adamant in his opposition to the monarchy and in his insistence on the "stern necessity, imposed by the situation in which Italy now finds itself, *to be not the epilogue, but the prologue of a social revolution.*"[31]

The social revolution that Calamandrei intended to encourage would be achieved by consent rather than by force. Echoing *Combat* and *Der Ruf, Il Ponte* placed its faith in the "new class tempered in the struggle" against Fascism, and searched for evidence that it would succeed in winning over a reluctant nation. A month before Parri's fall from office, it was still possible to be optimistic about the outcome, though Calamandrei and his associates were clearly affecting more confidence than they felt. Like Camus, Calamandrei wrote in a major key whose rhetorical swells compensated for a diminishing impact on events. "From the suffering [of the war] will be born another greatness," *Il Ponte* proclaimed in the autumn of 1945, "another more humane civilization. Accept it, since this is the price, and do not give up. Do not despair. Do not weaken."[32]

The chief focus of journals like *Il Ponte* was not political, however, but cultural. Whatever the outcome of the party struggles in Rome, it seemed that the revolution could be advanced by pursuing the vision of a "new culture" inspired by the Resistance. Franco Fortini described the hope then generally shared among the intellectuals: "Just as there existed a common political program of the anti-Fascist Left, so there should exist a revolutionary and progressive tradition of philosophical, scientific, historical, literary, and artistic thought—above individual political factions—to be passed along to newcomers in the ranks."[33] A "CLN culture," as some termed it, would preserve and enhance the values inherited from the Italian underground, while at the same time assimilating contemporary cultural achievements from abroad. It would be synthetic, innovative, and accessible to all. It would continue to unite those who had come together in the Resistenza Armata and ensure that the poison of Fascism did not seep back into Italy.

Yet the Resistance cultural legacy was anything but tidy. It included a number of currents at variance with one another, just as the political creeds of the member parties clashed at times within the CLN. To define a "new culture" meant to catalogue, test, and choose among these rival claimants. In particular, it meant to confront the influence of Italy's reigning intellectual, Benedetto Croce. Some younger critics considered Croce's late nineteenth-century humanism too static, too timid, above all too elitist to serve as a basis for cultural experimentation in 1945. His liberalism belonged to the world of pre-Fascist Italy—dignified, serene, and ineffectual. They had no wish to see it revived.

Croce did not dispute the moral impact of culture on political life. In fact, he saw the intellectual elite as the "active element . . . which alone represents the nation." But he never fully explained how the elite was to succeed in converting the masses to its own values; nor did he present much evidence that the elite was truly an "active element." In 1945 in the first issue of *Quaderni della Critica*, the successor to his celebrated *La Critica*, Croce referred to the Marxist concept of history shaped by the masses as a "myth," and concluded that the only real force for change was a creative minority. "History," he declared, "proceeds from above toward the lower strata, not the reverse."[34]

Croce's position as a southerner and a leader of the conservative Italian Liberal party provided further reason to construe his idealist philosophy as an elegant defense of the status quo. As the Liberals became more outspoken in their support of the propertied classes and the monarchy, the Left was increasingly moved to attack Croce's views. In the summer of 1944 Togliatti's Communist journal, *Rinascita*, had published excerpts from Antonio Gramsci's prison correspondence that were extremely critical of Croce. The final letter stated: "Placed in a historical perspective—of Italian history, naturally—Croce's activity appears the most powerful engine for 'conforming' the new forces to its vital interests (not merely immediate, but also future) that the dominant group possesses today and which I believe it fully appreciates, despite superficial appearances."[35]

Although Croce had been respected for his anti-Fascist stand during Mussolini's reign, it seemed to many in retrospect that his immunity from censorship had been purchased with a tacit agreement not to go too far in his attacks. The careful balance and equanimity of judgment that he had maintained now came under fire from the Marxists. Croce, who had demonstrated the shortcomings of Marxism and renewed the Italian philosophic tradition with his own derivative of German idealism in the years before World War I, now fell victim to the very ideological forces that he believed had been laid to rest long before.[36]

The impetus for a more critical evaluation of Croce came in large part from the rediscovery of Gramsci, a decade after his death. Gramsci believed that the retarding effects of liberalism had prevented the Risorgimento from becoming a popular revolution. He also disagreed with Croce over the role of the intellectual in society. For Croce, the intellectual was the voice of conscience, the preserver of principle in a world of political hypocrisy and demeaning compromise. His moral force depended in large measure on his independence from the political process—an independence that had ensured Croce's own symbolic leadership of the anti-Fascist intellectuals during Mussolini's reign. Gramsci saw the intellectual's role as both more overtly political and more consciously activist. While rejecting the "rhetorical heroism" of "intellectual elites separated from the masses," he argued that an important contribution could be expected from "intellectuals who are conscious of being linked organically to a national-popular mass."[37]

Gramsci's attitude toward the intellectuals was echoed by Vittorini in his review, *Il Politecnico*. Published first as a weekly, then as a monthly, *Il Politecnico* spanned the decisive period from September 1945 to December 1947, during which Italy passed from reform to restoration. Vittorini launched the journal in the hope of linking the intellectual with society through a popular tradition along the lines suggested by American literature. His ideal was a culture that could constitute an active force for social reform. In his first editorial in *Il Politecnico*, Vittorini called for "a culture that no longer consoles in the midst of suffering, but a culture that protects from suffering, that combats and eliminates it." He attacked the Italian literary tradition for its isolation from popular concerns and its failure to resist the rise of Mussolini. Although "there was no crime committed by Fascism that this culture had not taught us to condemn long ago," its moral strictures were ignored with impunity. For the poets of *ermetismo* and philosophers of the spirit, art had assumed a compensatory role, providing illusory solace for real ills. Yet the high priests of this culture continued to preach their familar message. "Will we continue," Vittorini asked, "despite this, to follow the path that even today the Thomas Manns and the Benedetto Croces point out to us?"[38]

As a first step toward defining a more potent alternative, *Il Politecnico* proposed to inventory contemporary culture. The review introduced its readers to a broad repertoire of literature, interviews, special reports, and current events that bore witness to its editor's omnivorous curiosity. In a weekly feature entitled "Encyclopedia," it attempted to inform on all areas of human endeavor: politics, the arts, economics, science, religion, and philosophy. The first issue, for example, carried articles on contemporary Spain, unemployment in Italy, Manzoni's novel *I promessi sposi* (*The Betrothed*), the Chinese theater, and Lenin; a first installment of Hemingway's *For Whom the Bell Tolls* in Italian translation; and an explanation by the physicist James Jeans of why the sky appears blue.[39] When in May 1946 financial difficulties forced Vittorini and his publisher, Giulio Einaudi, to transform *Il Politecnico* into a monthly publication, a slightly more rigorous selection resulted. But an underlying principle of nonspecialization, shared with *Les Temps Modernes*, continued to guide its choices. The thirst for contact with other cultures that had led to the fascination with America in the 1930s had not yet been satisfied.

Especially close ties linked *Il Politecnico* with the French Resistance intellectuals. Two issues of the journal were devoted largely to postwar culture in France; Sartre's opening manifesto for *Les Temps Modernes*, Beauvoir's essay "Moral Idealism and Political Realism," an article by Mounier, and poems by Eluard all appeared in its pages. "The relations between us and these young Frenchmen," Vittorini noted, "given the similarity of our engagement, can only be those of collaboration." When Beauvoir and Sartre visited Milan in the summer of 1946, they exchanged views with the editorial staff of *Il Politecnico*, which later published parts of the conversation in the form of an interview. *Les Temps Modernes* reciprocated by printing excerpts from *Il Politecnico*, which complemented its own offerings. As Beauvoir later remarked, "Our publications were very similar."[40]

A major and revealing difference between the two reviews, however, lay in their conception of their audience. Whereas *Les Temps Modernes* appealed chiefly to the same Parisian intellectual elite from which its staff was drawn, *Il Politecnico*, especially during the period when it appeared as a weekly, aspired to reach readers from all social classes. This policy echoed Gramsci's faith that every person had an intellectual vocation and would take an active part in cultural affairs if given the proper stimulus.[41] Few postwar reviews proved as successful at combining intellectual substance and an open, popular style as *Il Politecnico*. The journal nurtured debate by presenting opposing points of view within the same issue. Vittorini's initial editorial concerning a "new culture" drew many replies, both hostile and enthusiastic, which were answered or reprinted.[42] In its pursuit of journalistic pluralism, *Il Politecnico* set high standards indeed.

Vittorini's goal remained a culture that was both practical and creative—a culture that made a difference in men's lives. The title of his review reflected this preoccupation; the original *Il Politecnico* was a Milanese journal that, under the inspired guidance of Carlo Cattaneo, had played a prominent role in supporting the ideals of the Risorgimento in the mid-nineteenth century.[43] Vittorini saw his new venture as heir to the struggles for liberation that had been waged in the past. How a review that aspired to be creative and iconoclastic could also muster the discipline for sustained combat was not a question that greatly concerned him. At the time when *Il Politecnico* appeared, the clouded prospects for immediate political change made Gramsci's notion of cultural "hegemony" singularly attractive. Vittorini expressly equated cultural and political change when he wrote that "culture should at long last 'seize power.'"[44]

The Vittorini—Togliatti Debate

Il Politecnico was unofficially, if not formally, a Communist undertaking. Vittorini had joined the PCI during the war after discovering that among his companions in the Milanese Resistance "the most honest, the most serious, the most sensitive, the most decisive, and at the same time the happiest and most lively" were Communists.[45] He continued his association with the editorial team of the Communist daily, *L'Unità*, after Milan was liberated, and served as its director until deciding to devote himself to *Il Politecnico*. This decision, though made with party approval, placed Vittorini in a potentially ambiguous position. As a party member, he could be expected to give first priority to the interests of the PCI. But because *Il Politecnico* was not an official party organ, it enjoyed a measure of freedom to explore and innovate independently.

Vittorini was at first inclined to exaggerate the extent of that independence. His view of the role *Il Politecnico* could play was unorthodox from a traditional Marxist perspective. His adherence to the PCI, he later noted, had been motivated by admiration for its members rather than by an understanding of its doctrines. His careful study of Marxist writings had followed, not preceded, this emotional commitment, and he had never fully accepted some of the basic tenets of Marxist thinking. The question of the relations between culture and politics to which *Il Politecnico* addressed itself was a central one in Marxist ideology. But Vittorini was not content to view culture as a simple "auxiliary force" used to support a political struggle; he assigned the two equal weight.[46]

The Fifth Congress of the Italian Communist party, meeting in 1945, appeared to support Vittorini's latitudinarian approach by affirming that the party would not in the future place "ideological obligations" on its members.[47] Despite the narrow sectarianism of some party leaders such as Bordiga in the 1920s, the Italian PCI had been spared the worst effects of Stalin's "class against class" strategy during the decade 1925-1934 through being forced underground. Togliatti himself, as his offer to cooperate with the monarchists showed, both temperamentally and tactically favored a more flexible approach. As long as the policy of maintaining good relations with the anti-Fascist coalition continued, the PCI had every reason to welcome *Il Politecnico*'s diverse and many-sided appeal. But while less absolute in its demands for ideological conformity than the French or German Communist parties after the war, the PCI did not fully accept the principle that its members could support or attack whomever they wished in the interests of a "search for truth." In the climate of growing hostility between Left and Right that accompanied De Gasperi's arrival in office, heterodoxy in a nominally Communist publication was bound to give offense.[48]

In December 1946, just as *Il Politecnico* was about to go to press, its editorial office received an issue of *Rinascita* that contained an open letter to Vittorini from Togliatti. Togliatti reproached Vittorini and his staff with having lost sight of their original goal of forging a closer bond between culture and contemporary society: "The direction announced was not followed coherently, but was superseded little by little by something else, by a strange tendency toward a sort of encyclopedic 'culture.' An abstract search for novelty, for the different, for the suprising took the place of coherent choice and inquiry with an end in view, and news and information . . . overwhelmed thought." The lapse into "superficiality," Togliatti wrote, was regrettable. Far more serious, however, was the danger that *Il Politecnico* might lend itself to "supporting fundamental mistakes of ideological orientation," which Togliatti affected to believe was surely "the precise opposite of your intentions."[49]

Togliatti implicitly reasserted the primacy of politics over culture. He agreed with Vittorini that the two were interrelated and influenced each other. Yet by relating cultural developments to the realm of political strategy, Togliatti intimated that art was too important for the party to leave to the artists. He explained that the "affirmation or development of a specific artistic movement" could have "the most profound repercussions on the rate of progress or even on the success of a political current such as our own."[50] Togliatti was putting the Communist readers of *Il Politecnico* on notice that its political reliability had been corrupted by an injudicious choice of contributors (such as Sartre), and that it should henceforth be approached with caution.

The following issue of *Il Politecnico* carried Vittorini's response. In a rambling statement nearly six times the length of Togliatti's critique, Vittorini confessed to superficiality and philosophical confusion and thanked Togliatti for his "great kindness" in bringing such faults to his attention. This display of contrition, however, was overshadowed by Vittorini's refusal to admit Togliatti's major premise. After an autobiographical preface emphasizing the unfinished state of his political education and a reference to the Fifth Party Congress's sanction of free individual exploration in the cultural realm, Vittorini went on to insist that a political system must remain open to new ideas to survive. Culture provided the arena in which such new ideas were born.

> Culture, that is to say, must unfold its work on two fronts. On the one hand [it must] develop in such a way that the masses remain involved in it . . . On the other hand, [it must] develop in such a way that halts in its progress and changes in its character do not occur because of the cultural backwardness of the masses . . . Politics can adjust itself to the level of maturity reached by the masses, even mark time, even halt altogether, precisely because something else—culture—continues to forge on ahead.[51]

Vittorini was unwilling to abandon his intellectual autonomy. He refused to "play the flute for the revolution"—to allow political criteria to be the sole standards for judging art—and attacked those who maintained that Hemingway was an inferior writer merely because he lacked respect for the French Communist party.[52] Vittorini argued that a bourgeois background did not necessarily blind artists to the deficiencies of capitalism, and that their contribution toward social change was not dependent on their political views. The line that separated progress and reaction in art was of a different nature from the same line in politics. Marx, after all, had admired Balzac—despite the French novelist's royalist sympathies—because he wrote the truth.

In this way, Vittorini was able to lead the argument back to the separation between culture and society. A closed political creed, he noted, remained as far removed from contemporary life as traditional Italian culture. Both were guilty of being "arcadian": "Arcadia is the art that the Victorian age and the Second Empire desired—the art of conformity. I say that it does not 'teach' because it teaches nothing that it finds by itself, discovers by itself in life, because it has nothing to say on its own, because it limits itself to repeating 'lessons' that common morality, or custom, or politics, or the Church already teach."[53]

Vittorini's ideal, like Gramsci's, was still an art that reached the masses and improved and enriched their existence. But rather than emphasizing the need for communication as he had in the past, Vittorini now stressed the "second front" of art as a privileged mode of political and philosophical insight into problems of common concern. Sartre, it will be remembered, similarly assigned a major role to the creative imagination in *Being and Nothingness* and in his discussions of the RDR platform. Although Vittorini more than once obscured his own message through a clumsy and undifferentiated use of abstract concepts such as "culture" and "society," his reply to Togliatti was unambiguous in its insistence that the intellectual could best serve society by maintaining his independence from pragmatic political considerations.

Vittorini remained under the same pressure to align himself with the Left or the Right that weighed upon Sartre and Camus in France and Richter and Andersch in Germany. In a bitter war between two ideological blocs, a "two front" position held independently of either was too exposed to be defensible for long. Vittorini recognized that "party writers" like himself must be prepared to "limit our work, the day that [this] should prove indispensable for the construction of a classless society."[54] But the defensive posture adopted by the PCI with the onset of the Cold War did not, in his view, bring with it the same obligations to observe party discipline as would the ultimate "day of revolution." The gulf between intellectuals and society, bridged during the Resistance, was now being reopened by the Communist party itself. Rather than permitting the intellectuals to act directly on their own, it claimed to mediate between the intellectuals and the masses. In December 1947, tired of the struggle, Vittorini suspended publication of *Il Politecnico* with its thirty-ninth issue. His departure from the ranks of the PCI soon followed.[55]

Vittorini was in many ways as suspicious of the distorting influence of "political passions" as Benda had been; he at length retreated to an elitist position that neither Benda nor Croce would have disavowed.

Vittorini's argument that culture must preserve itself from the "backwardness of the masses" is understandable only in the context of his fears that the PCI would use its role as champion of the working class as a polemical weapon to obtain his conformity. The demands of organized politics became for him a threat to be resisted, just as he had earlier resisted the pressures of the Fascist hierarchy to renounce his unorthodox ideas.

Like Camus, Vittorini held an essentially moral view of the "revolution." "We find ourselves in a moment of moral creativity," he wrote in the penultimate issue of *Il Politecnico*, "in which a moral system is beginning to take shape apart from the historical process that is still generating it, and begins to act itself on history with its own force." Yet the manner in which morality as he conceived it could in fact be said to "act on history" continued to elude Vittorini. Just as Parri's experience had demonstrated the difficulty of translating an ethical vision into administrative practice, so Vittorini's foray into postwar journalism forced him to recognize the distance that remained between culture and politics. His first published work of fiction to follow *Man and Not—Il Sempione strizza l'occhio al Frejus* (*The Simplon Winks at Frejus*, 1947)—continued the exploration of ethical problems but dispensed with a political framework altogether.[56] In this novel his characters suffer hunger, poverty, and sickness; but they are stoic and isolated, not ardent and united as before. The bond of hope that Vittorini tried to forge with *Il Politecnico*, that Parri tried to realize with the help of the *vento del nord*, has touched them not at all.

9
The Triumph
of the State
1946-1949

*At the beginning we wanted a world
revolution, then we were satisfied with a
revolution in Italy, then with some
reforms, then with participation in the
government, then not to be driven from
it. Henceforth we will find ourselves on
the defensive.*
Carlo Levi, 1949

Barely a year after the liberation of northern Italy, the Resistance intellectuals were in retreat. The *vento del nord* gradually saw its political strength decrease as the local CLN committees surrendered their prerogatives to the De Gasperi government. All that was left to the Resistance was the moral prestige derived from its sacrifices during the struggle against Fascism. With no institutional base save the weak and now divided Partito d'Azione, and with no other resource than their own journalism, the intellectuals had slight chance of converting these moral assets into tangible reforms. As *Il Ponte* noted in January 1946, Italy was ruled once again by an "old order of politicians" hostile to Resistance goals.[1]

The one bright spot for the intellectual Resistance in an otherwise depressing picture of stagnation and reaction was the constitutional referendum held in the summer of 1946. Voters blocked a complete return to the past when they agreed—by a margin of 60 to 40 percent—to abolish the Italian monarchy and to create a republic in its stead. But even this event brought reminders of unsolved problems and new reasons for concern. The continuing ideological split between North and South emerged clearly in the regional pattern of the voting: most of the support for the monarchy lay south of Rome, whereas the republican majority came from the North. In the accompanying vote for party representation in the Constituent Assembly the Partito d'Azione suffered losses even in the areas of its previous strength. It trailed the mass parties of the Left and the Christian Democrats badly, receiving barely one percent of the vote.[2]

As in post-Liberation France, Italian intellectuals viewed the evident change in public mood with grave misgivings. The comforting belief that the nation had been spiritually transformed by the Resistenza Armata could no longer be sustained. The urge to abandon the struggle for a new Italy — *la desistenza*, as the atmosphere of lethargy was termed — had overcome allegiance to reform. Whereas *Il Ponte* had earlier affirmed that "a new people remains, though Parri has left," its view after the referendum was far more somber: "Today we seem to sense around us and within ourselves the symptoms of a new dissolution . . . The danger lies . . . in this ease of forgetfulness, in this refusal to bear the logical consequences of the experience [we have] suffered, in this return, with lazy nostalgia, to the blind and easy vices of the past."[3] As in France and Germany, observers discovered that the mood of the Resistance could not be recaptured in its former intensity once it began to wane. To base hopes for change on popular consent required that all, not merely a small band of visionaries, remain loyal to the dreams of the Liberation. The divisions between the intellectuals and the nation, which had seemed healed in the spring of 1945, were opening once again.

What choices remained for the intellectuals? They could not, as Bertolt Brecht once suggested with some irony, "dissolve the people and elect another." Nor did they wish to abandon the moral vision defended at such cost in the battle against Fascism. They continued to see themselves as the champions of the silent and the oppressed. But the group with which they now most closely identified their aims was one that Piero Gobetti had dismissed in 1924 as "condemned by history to a conservative function" — the Italian peasants.[4] Like the intellectuals, the peasants lived beyond the sheltering institutions of the state. They received no benefits from the politicians in Rome, just as they had received none from Mussolini. Their very conservatism, scorned by Gobetti, could be viewed as a guarantee of their incorruptibility. Thus in attempting to maintain a link with a cause beyond their own, the intellectuals idealized another sort of resistance displayed by the Italian peasant community.

At the same time, the notion of community became increasingly important as an alternative to the political order represented by De Gasperi. By the late 1940s intellectuals who wished to keep the hopes of the Resistance alive worked to disassociate their vision from politics altogether, and to seek its fulfillment instead within civil society. Friendship, cooperation, sincerity were all values that they believed could be more fully achieved by independent groups, at liberty to shape their lives as they wished. The promise of companionship and direct democracy that Richter discovered in the Group 47 was one the Italians cast in a pastoral mode—peasants and intellectuals living in harmony with nature, close to the land. This solution, with its obvious overtones of defeat and withdrawal, testifies to the intellectuals' incapacity to make their peace with political institutions more complex than the village or the Resistance underground.

Levi and the Two Italys

The disillusionment, self-criticism, and resignation that gradually overcame the Resistance intellectuals during 1946 gave rise to a renewed distrust of the state. This reversal of attitudes is traced in Carlo Levi's documentary novel *L'orologio* (*The Watch*), begun in 1947 and completed two years later. *The Watch* portrays Parri's fall from office with the advantages of critical hindsight. The prime minister's farewell news conference becomes the focal point for a rich panorama of anecdotes, impressions, and personal portraits telescoped by Levi into the space of three days. Politicians, intellectuals, prostitutes, black marketeers, Allied soldiers, and ex-Fascists provide a range of contrasting reactions to the cabinet crisis. Conscious of the fragility of the Resistance hopes for reform, Levi isolates the moment when these hopes passed into history. His vivid evocation of Rome—its crumbling palaces, heraldic statues, and millennial monuments—serves as a counterpoint to the stream of proposals for change that his first-person narrator records. Rome, in its venerable age and imperturbable inertia, will overcome the *vento del nord* as it has overcome other movements for change in the past.

Levi was particularly well suited to chronicle the Partito d'Azione's hopes and demise. Born in Turin in 1902, he spent his youth in the atmosphere of political activism and intellectual exploration that characterized the Piedmontese capital during and after World War I. Left-wing sympathies, he later recalled, were a "family tradition"; his mother was the sister of the well-known Socialist Claudio Treves, his father an active Socialist party member. At age sixteen Levi met Piero Gobetti, who soon became "not only a very dear friend, a brother," but also a mentor who conveyed "a certain moral quality of intransigence and refusal of all compromise." While a medical student at the University of Turin, Levi was a key figure in the group of young intellectuals who came under Gobetti's spell, contributed to his review *La Rivoluzione Liberale*, and maintained contacts with Gramsci and his associates on the staff of *L'Ordine Nuovo*. The synthesis between liberal individualism and social reform that Gobetti advocated exercised a profound influence on Levi's thought, and led him to participate in the founding of Giustizia e Libertà four years after Mussolini's suppression of *La Rivoluzione Liberale* in 1925.[5]

Thus Levi, like Parri, was a member of the first wave of Mussolini's opponents, who eventually formed the Partito d'Azione during World War II. Levi's anti-Fascist activities brought about his arrest in 1934 and again in 1935 during a series of raids in which Pavese was also arrested. After a year's confinement in a small village in the South, Levi returned to Turin. He left Italy for France in 1939 and remained in exile until 1941, when he returned to join the clandestine work of the Partito d'Azione in Florence. He emerged as one of the party's local leaders in 1944, and by 1945 he was directing the Actionist paper *L'Italia Libera* in Rome, where he was an eyewitness to the events and the setting described in *The Watch*.

The Watch presents a theory of the defeat of the Resistance, conveyed through a long conversation which Levi assigns to two of his narrator's colleagues, Andrea and Carmina. Soon after Parri's departure, they discuss its consequences: "The people do not yet realize [the situation]. They are completely taken up with everyday matters, and are still thinking of fighting, of winning. But we know it now; the political battle is lost. This is just the beginning, and there is nothing to be done." Andrea inquires into the reasons for this setback, and emerges with a sobering picture of Italian politics. All Italy, he declares, is divided into two enemy groups: the *Luigini* and the *Contadini*. The Luigini are the "crowd of bureaucrats, civil servants, bankers, managing clerks, military men, magistrates, lawyers, policemen, graduates, meddlesome persons, and students"—in short, "parasites." The Contadini, on the other hand, are the peasants, workers, artisans, and, significantly, intellectuals who represent the truly productive elements in society, a large minority on whom the host of bureaucratic parasites feed. "Every Luigino," explains Andrea, "needs a Contadino in order to nourish himself, and therefore cannot permit the stock to become too thin."[6]

The division of society into two groups according to whether or not their labor contributes to the material well-being of society was an old notion, one that Saint-Simon, for example, had explored in his famous parable of 1820.[7] Levi extended the logical consequences of this dualistic view into the realm of politics. The country's institutions, he argued, were irremediably in the hands of the Luigini, since these made up the majority of citizens. "The Luigini have [superior] numbers; they have the state, the Church, the parties, the political language, the army, the courts . . . The Contadini possess none of that. They are not even aware that they exist, that they have interests in common . . . The whole problem is there. The others' language, state, flags, and parties do not suit them . . . They must speak, but in their own way." The means, short of revolution, for gaining political power—parties, patronage, and the like—were tailored to fit the needs of the Luigini. The result was not only that it was difficult to win against them, but also that the very attempt of a group such as the Partito d'Azione to engage in the electoral process forced it to adopt, at least in part, their mentality and techniques. Levi's Andrea notes: "The truth is that the form of our parties themselves is influenced by the Luigini, as are the methods of political struggle and the structure of our state. In order for a movement of Contadini to come alive, it must find its own original forms and living structure."[8]

A further consequence of this imbalance, Levi contended, was that a state run exclusively by Luigini catered solely to their needs. Italy appeared to him "one great charitable organization for [the benefit of] those who belong to it." The state resisted initiatives aimed at helping the peasants and workers, in this analysis, because it was already aiding the millions of Luigini on its swollen payroll. It was not a neutral force in the life of the country; it favored some, and was hostile to others. For this reason Parri, as prime minister, had given the impression of one who was "different, as if an alien."[9] To Levi, Parri symbolized the gulf that separated the Resistance intellectuals and their allies from the other politicians and the bureaucrats. He was a Contadino in a world of Luigini, isolated and alone.

The theme of alienation from the political world of Rome, of living like a stranger in one's own land, had similarly dominated Levi's best-known work, *Cristo si è fermato a Eboli* (*Christ Stopped at Eboli*), published at the end of the war. At the same time that Vittorini was composing *Men and Not* in his mountain refuge, Levi was writing his novel while hiding from the Fascist police in Florence.[10] The two books treat common themes of oppression and liberation. But while Vittorini portrayed the anti-Fascist struggle in the North, Levi turned to memories of his year as a political prisoner among the villagers of the tiny town of Gagliano in Lucania. Gagliano's location on the instep of the boot of Italy, the poorest and most barren region of the entire peninsula, reinforced its inhabitants' feeling of remoteness, of belonging to a different civilization from that of the North. Christ, they said, had come no closer than Eboli, near Naples. Neither Christianity nor the modern era had penetrated inland beyond the rugged hills along the coast; the peasants were left with their superstitions, their malaria, their backbreaking labor and frustrated hopes.

Levi viewed Gagliano from a double distance, removed from his subject in both space and time. He was a northerner, and several years distant from the events he recorded.[11] Yet he identified strongly with the villagers — "my peasants," as he called them. The fact that Levi was a political prisoner, and hence a victim of the state, narrowed the gap between himself and the local populace. Living among them, he was initiated into a community of suffering which tempered the aristocratically intellectual views of Gobetti's circle. Like Sartre, Levi discovered in captivity the importance of human bonds in a direct way. When the inhabitants learned that Levi had been trained as a doctor, they sought him out for consultation and aid, and drew him into their daily concerns. "Their extraordinary, naive faith," he wrote, "called for reciprocation. Involuntarily, I came to assume their ills, to feel them almost as my fault."[12]

Within the feudal social structure of Gagliano, where the mayor, the lawyer, the police, and a handful of other notables scrupulously observed the traditional boundaries dividing them from the peasants, Levi thus found himself on the side of the Contadini. His account of life in their midst, told with a heterodox but striking blend of poetic evocation, journalistic reporting, and sociological analysis, introduced his readers to a society whose contours lay beyond their experience. Levi became a link between two societies: the comfortable middle-class world for which he wrote and in which he had been raised, and the peasants whose problems came as a revelation to many in his audience.

What could be done to ease the suffering of these forgotten people? What possible solutions were there to the "southern problem," whose very existence Mussolini was at pains to deny? For the most part, Levi did not attempt to answer these questions in *Christ Stopped at Eboli*. Instead, through anecdote and detail, he tried to convey a sense of the world as seen by the Gaglianese peasants, who adopted an attitude of stolid acceptance in the belief that there were no solutions to be found. When he asked the villagers what remedy they perceived for their distress, the invariable reply was "nothing": "I thought how many times I used to hear that word repeated every day in all the peasants' conversations . . . 'What have you eaten?' 'Nothing.' 'What do you hope for?' 'Nothing.' 'What can be done?' 'Nothing.'" The other word that recurred like a litany in these overheard exchanges was "tomorrow." "But tomorrow," Levi observed, "means 'never'."[13] The peasant universe was a timeless one, unchanging and uniform, closed and unalterable. The concept of tomorrow, implying change, became synonymous with the unattainable.

Yet beneath this resignation, Levi discovered, lay a stubborn faith in an alternative political order, grounded in the peasants' distrust of the state. "Their opposition to a government [perceived as] foreign and an adversary," he noted, "is accompanied . . . by a natural sense of right, a spontaneous intuition of what, for them, would be a real state: a common will that becomes law." Levi shared this ideal. In the final pages of *Christ Stopped at Eboli*, he recalled his frustrations as he tried to explain to his friends in Rome why their well-meaning solutions to the "southern problem" were impracticable:

> In the minds of all of them, the state should have done something, something extremely useful, beneficial, and providential. And they gazed at me in amazement when I said that the state, in the sense in which they meant it, was on the contrary the fundamental obstacle that prevented anything whatsoever from being done. It cannot be the state that resolves the southern problem, I had said, because what we call the southern problem is none other than the problem of the state.[14]

The lot of the peasants of Gagliano represented for Levi the problems that plagued Italian society as a whole—the helplessness of the Contadini faced with a distant, abstract state that remained deaf to their needs. To identify these needs was a first step, and this Levi attempted to do for one region of the country. But a lasting solution would come, he believed, only when such needs could be expressed and remedies sought by the victims themselves, dispensing with a mediator like himself. The imposition of solutions conceived far from the locale where they were to be applied merely worsened the problems they were intended to correct. A decree from Rome that the goats in Gagliano be slaughtered to prevent overgrazing was an example; so little natural plant cover grew in the region that goats were the only suitable livestock, and their forced destruction represented a senseless loss. Fascism was partly to blame for increasing the estrangement between governors and governed. But Levi saw little hope that the "anarchy and necessary indifference" of the peasants would decrease when the Corporate State was gone.[15]

Levi saw this indifference as a source of strength. For all their backwardness and suffering, the peasants remained a cohesive group. They were morally invulnerable to the appeal of Fascism, just as they had resisted so many other would-be conquerors in the past. Yet the peasant communities of the South, "sober and mistrustful," could not transcend either their poverty or their self-imposed isolation. Where Vittorini's vision of the South in *Conversation in Sicily* revealed the possibility of human understanding in the midst of suffering, Levi's *Christ Stopped at Eboli* showed the limits that prevented understanding from being translated into greater social justice. How could the citizen, alone and unskilled in the ways of the Luigini, protect himself from an alien and predatory state? Though Levi briefly hoped that the

Resistance would furnish an answer, his perception of the "two Italys" locked in mutual hostility was merely confirmed by the events that followed the Liberation. When the experiment in local self-government that the CLNs semed to promise was abruptly halted by De Gasperi, Levi began to accept the peasants' attitude toward the state. Their resignation became his own.[16]

Silone between Marxism and Christianity

Ignazio Silone, like Levi, learned to distrust organized politics in Italy. "Is it possible," one of Silone's characters asks, "to put oneself at the service of a political party and remain sincere?" This was Silone's own problem, one that he tried to solve throughout a "painful and lonely struggle"—first in the Communist underground movement against Mussolini during the 1920s, then in Swiss exile until the war's end, and finally back in Italy once again, alternately a member and a critic of the Socialist party.[17]

Silone was raised in the rugged Abruzzi Apennines east of Rome, the son of a peasant farmer and a mother who supplemented the meager family income by weaving. Like Vittorini, he spent his youth in the countryside among peasants and received only limited schooling. At age fourteen he lost both parents and abandoned his studies to support himself on the land. While still a youth, he was appointed secretary of the agricultural workers for the Abruzzi district and joined Gramsci in founding the Italian Communist party in 1921. Silone observed among the Abruzzi peasants, whose spokesman he became, the same "distrust, diffidence, and skepticism" that Levi later noted in Lucania: "For them, the state became the irremediable creation of the devil. A good Christian, if he wanted to save his soul, should avoid, as far as possible, all contact with the state. The state always stands for swindling, intrigue, and privilege, and could not stand for anything else. Neither law nor force can change it."[18]

At first, Silone believed he had found an alternative in the Communist party. But he soon discovered that "it was not easy to reconcile a spirit of moral mutiny against an unacceptable long-established social reality with the 'scientific' demands of a minutely codified political doctrine." Like Vittorini, he was drawn to the PCI for the sake of humanistic ideals rather than through an intellectual apprenticeship in Marxist theory. When the Comintern expelled Leon Trotsky in 1929, the same "spirit of moral mutiny" led Silone to refuse its demand that he support the move in the name of party discipline. He saw in this demand "a new version of the inhuman reality against which, in declaring ourselves socialists, we had rebelled."[19] The structure of the party seemed in his disillusionment to resemble only too closely that of the state, its tactics to be little different from the cynical manipulation and hypocrisy displayed by its Fascist adversaries.

Thus when Vittorini and Pavese were beginning to discover a cultural response to Fascism in American literature, Silone had already passed into and beyond a more revolutionary commitment. He examined the roots of his disillusionment and explored possible alternatives in a series of novels written in exile in Switzerland during 1930-1940. These works were studies of defeat, written at a time when Fascism still seemed supreme in Italy and support for Mussolini's Ethiopian adventure had replaced the apathy of the late 1920s, when Hitler had just come to power and the Western democracies showed little inclination to oppose him. Their reluctantly pessimistic appraisal of the obstacles barring Italian social renewal anticipated many of the insights that were to emerge in the wake of Parri's failure to implement the program of the *vento del nord*.

The first of these political novels, *Fontamara*, was begun in 1930 as Silone struggled against ill health and poverty in his new life as an exile.[20] It tells the story of an isolated hill village in his native Abruzzi, whose peasants are drawn into an unequal battle with the Fascist authorities in an attempt to preserve their age-old way of life. Alternately tricked and rebuffed by a Fascist entrepreneur nicknamed the "impresario," the peasants gradually become conscious of their own helplessness. "One doesn't argue with those in power" is the bitter conclusion that one young peasant draws from their frustrated efforts at self-defense. "The laws are made by 'city folk,' enforced by judges who all are 'city folk,' and interpreted by lawyers who are all 'city folk.' How can a country peasant be in the right?" For a short time their hopes are fired by a helpful stranger, and the villagers overcome their own fears and divisions in a show of solidarity. But retribution is swift. Fascist forces descend on the village, slaughter its inhabitants, and lay waste to their homes. The villagers of Fontamara have finally rebelled against the "city folk," but at a terrible price. The novel ends with a bleak question voiced by one of the survivors: "What is to be done? After so many pains, so many struggles, so many tears and wounds, so much hatred, so many injustices and so much desperation, what is to be done?"[21]

Silone's next major novel, *Pane e vino* (*Bread and Wine*), written in 1935-1936, explores one man's attempt to "do something" in Fascist Italy.[22] Pietro Spina, an intellectual and former Communist militant, returns to his native Abruzzi region after several years abroad. To shield his identity from the police while recovering from a grave illness, he assumes the role of a priest and takes up residence in the small town of Pietrasecca. The isolation he seeks and his forced inactivity as a convalescent lead him to reflect on his past and to compare the theoretical precepts of Marxism with the actual needs of the peasants among whom he now lives. In his private notebook Spina asks himself: "Has truth not become for me a party truth, and justice a party justice? . . . Where has my old enthusiasm gone? Was not the primacy of the political faculty over all the remaining faculties and the other needs of the spirit an impoverishment for me, a withering of my life? Has it not been an estrangement from more profound concerns?"[23]

Spina's sojourn in the country restores a lost appreciation for "more profound concerns." He rediscovers his roots, and in so doing he breaks with the party that has hitherto been the center of his life. Like Levi in Gagliano, he is impressed with the "otherness" of the peasant world, a world equally far from the Fascist state and from the goals of a conspiratorial political apparatus such as the PCI. Both Fascism and Communism threaten to enslave man through an oppressive political order, he concludes. The answer to that threat is not to substitute one system for another, but to resist both. Even a single act of disobedience has the power to shake popular faith in a dictatorship. "Dictatorship is based on unanimity," he explains to one of his new friends. "It suffices for one person to say NO and the spell is broken."[24]

The reverence in which the peasants still hold the church allows Spina, in his priest's disguise, to combine a Christian care of souls with a Marxist emphasis on attaining social justice in this world. The second half of the novel recounts Spina's experiences as a new sort of holy man, preaching a gospel of individual liberty and human compassion through the force of personal example. The power of goodness, as exemplified in the life of Christ, seems to offer an alternative to the abuses of politics, and Spina's return to the Abruzzi, rather than signifying a retreat from political concerns, results in a new and deeper sense of commitment. Compassion, he believes, is meaningless if it does not find expression in action, just as action is meaningless without ethical content.

The form this action takes is the creation of a small community of friends. Like the French Resistance intellectuals (and their German counterparts), Silone views political change as embodying above all a new mode of human relations. *Bread and Wine* ends on another note of defeat when Fascist authorities brutally disperse Spina's circle of admirers, but its sequel presents a more fully articulated vision of community, seen as a delicate balance between individual morality and organized insurrection. *The Seed beneath the Snow*, completed in 1940, deals, in the words of one critic, with the "radical distinction between two societies—a false society and a true one."[25] The duality between town and country that Silone had explored in *Fontamara* is here transposed and concentrated within the single town of Colle into a duality between the Fascist notables—corrupt, jealous, and fearful of losing their status—and Spina's picturesque assortment of friends assembled in a hovel on the outskirts. While the Fascist society is progressively rent with feuds and bitter rivalries, Spina's group attains an ever deeper understanding and coherence. It is a human nucleus that will continue to bear witness to Spina's ideals even after Spina, in an act of self-sacrifice, gives himself up to the authorities to save the life of a friend.

Silone emphasizes two allied themes in *The Seed beneath the Snow*: language and friendship. In *Fontamara* town and country are separated by a linguistic barrier. "A city man and a peasant," comments the narrator, "can understand each other [only] with difficulty." But for Silone language is not only a symbol of social divisions; its use and abuse also carry moral connotations. The lawyer Don Circostanza cheats the *fontamaresi* of their water rights by legalistic casuistry. For Spina, on the other hand, as for the postwar German writers such as Borchert, the ideal language is characterized by clarity, simplicity, and a rejection of the linguistic accretions of the past: "For our old Baroque culture it would be an immense good fortune if we could start from the beginning, recommence with fresh straw and clear water, if we would pick our way gingerly, putting the big words (*paroloni*) through a sieve one by one."[26]

A shared idiom is a prerequisite for friendship. Conversely, the use of language to manipulate others signifies a willingness to play on ties of trust to gain one's own selfish ends. "The real revolution of our era," an old acquaintance tells Spina's grandmother, is the disappearance of friendship from Fascist Italy. "In place of friendship there are so-called relations, which endure as long as they are useful." The themes of language, friendship, and a return to first things are woven together in Spina's account of teaching the deaf-mute Infante to speak. "'Company' was . . . the first new word that Infante learned from me," he recalls. "He already knew how to say 'bread' (*pane*), which he pronounced 'paan.' And I explained to him with gestures that two people who share the same bread become 'cum-pane,' companions."[27]

The circle of friendship is extended to include nature as well. "The word 'earth,'" Spina observes, "is now for me the name of a close acquaintance." Spina, Infante, and outcast Simone-la-faina eventually move from Colle to the hill town appropriately named Acquaviva. There they help the peasants with the spring chores in the vineyards, a spiritual freemasonry of brothers living close to the earth, in voluntary poverty, exploring a "new way of being friends." Theirs is an application of "the old Christian message of equality and fraternity," as Silone later explained in an interview. This scene conveys a buoyant lyricism which is new to his work, with only a hint of the menace that weighs on the surrounding countryside: "The peasants working among the vines appear encircled with tiny clouds like the blessed in paradise. But it is a pastoral paradise . . . a paradise of small landowners, in separate compartments . . . The atmosphere is green like a tender meadow, but on the horizon, above the mountains, are building heaps of clouds, like sacks full of grain in a rich granary."[28]

Silone's "pastoral paradise," a landscape fashioned from memories of the preindustrial world in which he was raised, may appear at times to verge on a literary escapism little different from Wiechert's *The Simple Life*. There is certainly an element of revolt against modernity in Silone's fiction, accompanied by nostalgia for the natural and the elemental. Yet violence and suffering are never absent from Silone's novels as they are from all but a few works by the *innere Emigranten*. Political forces constantly intrude upon the life of the peasants, requiring them to choose submission or resistance. The earth is hard and barren, demanding constant toil to sustain a population for whom each harvest is a victory. Ever-present danger gives brief moments of peace such as the interlude in Acquaviva their true value and meaning.[29]

Nature, for Silone, both challenges man and reveals his basic strengths. It strips him of the illusion that he can subsist alone, as it rewards those who unite in a common effort. The emphasis on labor and solidarity, and the analysis of the struggle between rich and poor, suggest the Marxist elements that continued to inform Silone's writing long after his break with the PCI. At the same time, his concern with love, suffering, and redemption shows the Christian roots of his inspiration. Silone's Catholic faith, maintained despite his hostility to the church as an institution, and his search for companionship in a hostile environment recall the postwar fiction of Heinrich Böll. No less than Böll, Silone attempted to portray values that reversed those of Fascism. As he wrote to a friend in the autumn of 1941: "Pietro Spina cherishes all that Italian society despises, and rejects all that it promotes."[30]

Silone went further than Böll, however, in his wish to define the spiritual power of exemplary acts. In the figure of Pietro Spina, he was proposing an idealized alter ego for his readers to emulate. It was not possible, he concluded, to serve a political party and remain sincere. And of the two, sincerity was the more important. The seed, if pure, would germinate in time. In his Swiss exile, Silone strove simply to keep it alive.

The Communal Ideal

The evolution of Silone's thought in exile thus is traced in his three major novels of this period. *Fontamara* is a call to battle; *Bread and Wine* describes the uncertainties of a false start; and *The Seed beneath the Snow* captures a new inner peace and certainty in an ideal community whose goal is to overcome injustice through the solidarity and virtues of its members. In view of this final message, it is surprising that the pattern of Silone's life abruptly diverged from Pietro Spina's solutions in favor of an unambiguous return to politics. In 1940, the year he finished *The Seed beneath the Snow*, Silone ended a decade of solitary writing to engage once more as a militant in the struggle against Fascism and in the preparation for the social order that would succeed it.

Silone's new activism was not the complete break with his earlier positions that it might appear. He did not cease to believe that the state and the Communist party multiplied constraints on the individual citizen. If anything, he saw that the war was likely to provide new opportunities for both to extend their powers, and hence he turned to action partly to block their future incursions. It is significant that he now enlisted his talents on the side of the Italian Socialists, rather than returning to the Communist fold. During the war leading members of the PCI attempted to induce him to reconsider his apostasy. Although they considered him a heretic, his growing literary prominence abroad rendered him *récupérable* in the eyes of the party.[31]

Silone refused these veiled offers of amnesty. His active participation in party politics from 1940 to 1949 — participation that encompassed roles of journalist, Socialist deputy in parliament, and party official — was guided by two main aims. First, he sought an Italian Socialist party distinct from and independent of the Communists, and therefore worked against the Socialist faction led by Pietro Nenni that counseled fusion with the PCI. Secondly, he attempted to integrate this movement into a European federation of states.[32]

In advocating Socialist independence, Silone was in fact urging a return *ad fontes*, to a socialism uncorrupted by Stalinist rigidity and imbued with the humanitarian spirit and idealism of Joseph Proudhon, Carlo Cattaneo, and above all Giuseppe Mazzini, a selection of whose works he edited in 1938. As he noted in his introduction to that volume:

> The conservative elements in society [have been able] to revive many outmoded issues of the past century, such as the nation-

ality question or . . . projects of government control . . . This strange and contradictory situation lends a most striking freshness to many forgotten pages of Mazzini, and the interest is only intensified by the fact that, in a number of European countries, today as a century ago, the spirit of freedom is forced to seek refuge in underground conspiracy.

The following year, in an interview with the American art critic Clement Greenberg, Silone called for the establishment of a "third front" to renew this effort of emancipation under the socialist banner: "Real peace depends today on the rapidity with which revolutionary workers all over the world regain their political autonomy and resume the struggle to overthrow capitalism." Yet the Soviet experience cautioned against assuming that such a negative goal sufficed in itself. "Socialism rids us of one enemy of human liberty," he noted, "but it can also introduce new ones, unknown to past history."[33]

In a sense, Silone was echoing the call for a via media between capitalism and Stalinism that had already gained favor on the non-Communist Left. The coming war, as he explained to Greenberg, would make it "easier to create revolutionary situations in Italy and Germany, but these situations would have to be exploited by Italian and German revolutionaries themselves, and by no one else." Russia's claim to lead the forces of socialist progress, he felt, had been forfeited under Stalin.[34] Silone's position in favor of an international "third front" also provided evidence of his continued hostility to the state. But here again, 1940 had brought a shift of emphasis. Just as the Communist party was to be counterbalanced by a second socialist party rather than by a series of loosely organized "communities," the power of the state was to be balanced by its inclusion in a group of other states. In both cases, Silone now chose to curb excessive control on the level of institutions, rather than on the level of the individual.

These ideas were spelled out in thirteen "Theses for the Third Front," which Silone published anonymously in the underground Zurich newspaper *Avvenire del Lavoratore* in August 1942. The third thesis reaffirmed that "the sole adversary capable of overcoming Fascism on the third front is socialism." Another thesis claimed that "political unification should express the real unity of European society; the old, reactionary system of national sovereignty must be destroyed." Silone voiced his belief in the power of socialism and federalism to act in concert against the rule of the Luigini: "The European federation must not be a limited and perpetually weak union of sovereign states, but a grouping of free peoples, among whom associations directed by the producers will have reabsorbed a good part of the functions currently monopolized by big capital and by the state bureaucracy."[35]

Despite the utopian, Proudhonist elements in this declaration, its combined militancy and optimism strike a very different tone from the gentle exhortations of Pietro Spina. They suggest the new sense of urgency and the new wave of hope that inspired Silone's second foray into politics during the war years.

At the time the "Theses" were published, Silone had for two years been in charge of the Foreign Center (Centro Estero) of the outlawed Italian Socialist party in Zurich. When the PSI enlarged its base in 1943 by fusing with other groups such as the Movimento di Unità Proletaria to form the PSIUP (Partito Socialista Italiano di Unità Proletaria), Silone was deeply disturbed by the evident support among his colleagues for further alliances on the Left, this time including the Communists. When he returned to Italy in October 1944 he joined the governing circle of the PSIUP in the hope that he might influence future party strategy. Silone, Giuseppe Modigliani, and Giuseppe Saragat formed the core of opposition to fusion with the Communists. In 1945 Silone was elected a Socialist delegate to the Constituent Assembly from the Abruzzi, and also assumed direction of the Socialist daily, *Avanti!*, in Rome.[36]

Silone was credited by some observers with blocking a union with the PCI that seemed imminent after the two parties renewed their "Pact of Action"—first concluded in 1934 during the era of the Popular Fronts. Ernesto Rossi, for example, wrote in 1945: "Had Silone and Modigliani not arrived in Rome, I believe that the Socialists would have followed the Communists." But this victory was not achieved without a bitter struggle within the PSIUP; the fusionist faction clearly intended to renew its offensive at a more opportune time. Such infighting seemed to Silone a regrettable diversion from the more basic problems of elaborating a general program for future socialist action in the spirit of his earlier "Theses." On the eve of assuming his post on the staff of *Avanti!*, he wrote: "In the broadest and most permanent sense, socialism is the aspiration of the poor toward social justice and equality, with the suppression of economic and political privileges. In the labyrinth of ideological 'isms' this basic and potent tendency of socialism risks becoming lost, weakened, compromised with spurious and entirely extraneous elements."[37]

In his mistrust of party rigidity and his desire for an ideological synthesis that would "preserve in social democracy the Christian and liberal values of which it is the principal heir," Silone was far closer to the ideals of the Partito d'Azione than to those of the Socialist left wing. With the fall of the Parri government in November 1945, he sensed that his position as a spokesman for an independent stand between an increasingly doctrinaire Left and Right was becoming untenable. Silone had hoped to initiate a dialogue on fundamentals, only to find that maneuvering among party factions took precedence over a reassessment of socialist goals. He had assumed that a shared anti-Fascism and desire to liberate political discourse from authoritarian propaganda would lead to a common language of reason even in disagreement, but found that no understanding was possible beyond "the banal repetition of 'hurrah' and 'down with.'"[38] Like Camus and Vittorini, like Andersch and Richter, he discovered that a journal seeking to re-examine basic questions could not also maintain support for immediate political aims. Eight months after Parri's resignation, in July of 1946, Silone resigned his editorship of *Avanti!* He feared that Italy was in danger of succumbing to a "partitocrazia" of which he wanted no part.[39]

With the failure of the experiment in Socialist unity, Silone faced a dilemma. His anti-Communism could not fail to contribute "objectively" to a strengthening of the Right in Italy, however much he might disagree with the conservative point of view. As the Cold War led the United States to support De Gasperi's Christian Democrats with growing infusions of money and advice, disunity began to appear a luxury the Left could ill afford, and Nenni's attempts at fusion seemed justified in retrospect. Unwilling to abandon his independent stance despite the political logic of choice between East and West, Silone sought a counterweight to both blocs within a broader European framework. During the years 1947-1949 he intensified his efforts in support of an international socialism, which he believed might still overcome the setbacks suffered in Italy. He founded and directed the review *Europa Socialista*, which served as a rallying point for Socialists opposed to Nenni's policy, and participated in a number of groups, such as Adriano Olivetti's Comunità, that espoused European integration.[40]

Typical of this activity was a speech given by Silone in the autumn of 1947 at the invitation of the Movimento Federalista Europea (an Italian affiliate of the Union Européenne des Fédéralistes) in Rome. The same occasion served as a forum for other Italian intellectuals—among them Parri, Calamandrei, and Gaetano Salvemini—to criticize the interparty struggles that dominated Italian politics and to affirm their belief in the need for a broader political vision. As Silone noted: "Today in our country there exists a general disorientation, a rather dispirited tone of life, a sterile insistence on secondary or empty questions. There is an abyss separating the true and essential problems of well-being from . . . the daily preoccupations of the greater part of those who mold our public opinion." The cure for the disorientation that had succeeded the hopes of the Resistance, he suggested, lay in the prospect of a United Europe:

In these difficult conditions of ours, to speak once more to the Italian people concerning European unity is to pose an essential problem—a true, authentic, fundamental problem—and to prevent their attention for a moment from becoming fixed on harmful struggles for abstract or imaginary goals . . . A renewal of the struggle for European unity is a vital necessity for the free countries of the old continent; it is the sole path toward their salvation.[41]

The specific role of the intellectual in helping to transcend the limits of the nation was the subject of another address Silone delivered that same year to the International PEN Club conference at Basel. There he began by evoking the international character of the Resistance, "that invisible, underground country without frontiers that we created, together with some who are with us today and others who are no longer alive, during the long years of persecution; that country of which we wish to remain free and loyal citizens." But there was a darker side to the wartime role of the intellectual: "To be perfectly frank, I do not know if, in recent years, there has been a single country or a single party where the intellectual has not been degraded to the humiliating function of an instrument of war."[42]

Silone's plea for a moral commitment that avoided the narrow limits of party persuasion echoed the calls for nonalignment voiced by Camus, the RDR, and *Der Ruf*. Neither side in the Cold War held a monopoly on truth, and hence neither side could be supported uncritically against the other. "At every congress of writers is there not some significant allusion to new and inevitable ideological crusades? But these zealots must be told firmly that there can be no graver threat to moral values in any period than to regard them as historically bound to the old political and social forms. Only by the sacrifice of intellectual honesty is it possible to identify the cause of truth with that of an army." The intellectuals' true allegiance, Silone claimed, must be to mankind irrespective of party affiliation.[43]

In the late summer of 1949, Silone finally conceded defeat in his efforts to overcome the double threat of the parties and the state. At a meeting of the Comunità movement in Milan, he drew up a balance sheet of postwar Italian politics. The Resistance had, he confessed, been engaged since the war in a struggle on two levels—"an immediate struggle within the bounds of the existing political order to resist the dangers of a totalitarian revolution," and at the same time a "more radical critique that involves the political and social structure of the nation itself." Neither had led to success. "We were under the illusion of being able to renew the traditional parties from within. We were under the illusion of being able to prevent Italian politics from dividing into two camps, one under American protection and the other under that of the Russians. We had the illusion that in this postwar period, the Church could be spared and could occupy a position other than its traditional one. These hopes of ours have failed."[44]

Faced with mass parties locked in a bitter struggle for power, Silone proposed a return to the old ideal of small communities that would act as leavening agents in the political life of the country. It was a concept illustrated a decade before by Pietro Spina and his disciples in *The Seed beneath the Snow* and later embodied in the Comunità movement. Silone now reluctantly abandoned the ideal of a united Socialist party. As he had during his Swiss exile, he foresaw a long period of deferred hopes, and called for the intellectuals to husband their strength for the future: "It is important that we not allow ourselves to become exhausted on the level of immediate political action . . . We need to keep alive the hopes nourished during the period of the Resistance, those which express our deepest political beliefs . . . It is important that . . . there be groups of free men who . . . confront the present state of things . . . with a libertarian, humane ideal."[45]

Journey's End

During the late 1940s, as the spirit of the Resistance suffered successive defeats, the myth of America associated with the first stirrings of that Resistance also underwent a change. The mystery, the innocence, the spirit of novelty once promised by American literature had vanished. It was no longer a symbol of liberty or of "life lived with enthusiasm." "Gone are the days when we discovered America," Pavese wrote in 1947. "From its people will no longer come anything resembling the names and revelations that excited our prewar generation."[46]

The immediate reasons for this change of attitude lay in the presence of American troops in Italy and in American foreign policy. Contact with the soldiers inevitably brought its share of misunderstanding and antipathy. No occupation army could escape the stigma of its privileged situation, not even one that saw itself as a friend and an ally of the people. After the initial euphoria of liberation had passed, the contrast between the American soldier with his spam and his jeep, well-fed and mobile, and the hungry and dislocated population understandably aroused jealousy and resentment among the Italian intellectuals. The apparent spiritual superiority of America they had admired from afar. Now its overwhelming material superiority evoked a far less favorable judgment.

The realization that this material superiority could be used for political ends directly opposed to their own increased the intellectuals' alienation from America. The differing responses to Parri's and De Gasperi's appeals for economic assistance were a case in point. America's strongly anti-Communist stance after 1947 seemed to many intellectuals a sharp denial of their own hopes for greater social equality in postwar Italy. Fearing that the Resistance might bring a Communist regime to power, the United States intervened in Italian domestic affairs even after the Allied Military Government relinquished formal control. The link between the Christian Democrats and Washington — giving the DC a strong foreign ally in addition to its already solid support from the Vatican at home — promised to bury once and for all the hopes for achieving any major portion of the *vento del nord* program.

In fact, the late 1940s saw the replacement of one myth of America by another. In the minds of many intellectuals, the young, vigorous, innovative land of opportunity became a middle-aged, sated, inflexible champion of the status quo. One of the few American authors accorded a sympathetic reception during these years was Richard Wright. As a black writer, a former Communist, and an expatriate, Wright symbolized the critique of America in its most uncompromising form.[47] Within the Manichaean world that had replaced the old moral universe of Fascists and anti-Fascists, the United States took its place among the hosts of darkness. To be anti-American was almost as common among Italy's leftist intellectuals by 1947 as to be anti-Fascist had been a few years before. The reassessment of views on both sides of the Atlantic obeyed a curious symmetry. American policymakers and Italian intellectuals each assigned to the other the villain's role that both had formerly reserved for Mussolini.

An analogous trend could be observed in France and Germany. The articles that Sartre had written for *Combat* during his visit to the United States in early 1945, though not uncritical, revealed his underlying admiration for the sheer scale and power of its industry, the breadth of its countryside, and the diversity of its population, all so much in contrast with the narrow, fearful, bourgeois France he continued to detest. But two years later, in Beauvoir's *Amérique au jour le jour: 1947* (*America Day by Day*), this same strength became a cause for alarm. America was generous in its aid to Europe, Beauvoir admitted; yet she found its Cold War diplomacy disquieting. "One would say," she wrote of the Americans, "that they believe it possible to settle the future of Europe with shipments of canned food. Is it their purpose to ignore their true responsibilities and to forget, among other things, that the decision between peace and war is in their hands?"[48] German intellectuals such as Andersch felt their dependence on a strong but unpredictable ally even more directly. As Germany's need for a military shield against the Soviet Union increased, so did the intellectuals' apprehension at the loss of control over their nation's destiny.

If America ceased to inspire European intellectuals with admiration, however, its cultural influence persisted. The closer link between the writer and society exemplified by the vernacular style and earthy subject matter of Steinbeck and Hemingway now found expression in the Italian neorealist school of the late 1940s. A wave of literature that rivaled the French "existentialist offensive" in vitality and surpassed it in number of practitioners brought the earlier attempts at creating an anti-Fascist culture to a triumphant conclusion. Its subject, embodied in novels such as Vasco Pratolini's *Cronache di poveri amanti* (*A Tale of Poor Lovers*, 1946), was the lives of ordinary men and women. The drama and dignity of their existence emerged from a narrative style that avoided excess and attempted to capture the reality of the everyday, unretouched and undisguised.

The most successful ventures in the neorealist style occurred in film. Using untrained actors and natural lighting, shooting on location, a new generation of movie directors brought Italy to the center of international attention with such early postwar works as Roberto Rossellini's *Open City* (1945) and Vittorio De Sica's *The Bicycle Thief* (1948). The art of neorealist film consisted in its apparent absence of illusion. The footage for *Open City*, a harsh depiction of the final days of the Resistance in Rome, included scenes of German soldiers taken secretly from rooftops at the actual time of their departure. The documentary character of these efforts to transcribe reality directly conformed to the intellectuals' wish for "concrete" works with a claim to literal truth. Each spectator became an eyewitness to scenes of courage or suffering which, it was hoped, might stir greater understanding and compassion for experiences that were the concern of all.[49]

Yet the simple depiction of simple lives was not what most Italians wished to read or to view in the late 1940s. The neorealistic novels of Pratolini and films of Rossellini and De Sica were—like Parri's brief tenure in office—exceptional and isolated events that did not reach a broad audience. Ironically, some of the most popular films of the period were Hollywood imports whose lavish sets and cotton-candy optimism were the antithesis of the sobriety and realism that had so impressed Pavese and Vittorini in American literature a decade before. The Italian public wished to forget the hardships of everyday life, just as the American public had wished to forget the trauma of the Depression. Rather than bringing the artist closer to the people, Italian neorealism seemed to isolate him all the more.[50]

The theme of isolation dominates the novels that Pavese wrote in the late 1940s. It is as if he sensed that his own growing distance from friends and society was a general phenomenon, that the unity and common purpose of the Resistenza Armata were giving way to fragmentation and mutual incomprehension once again. Even the Resistance, seen in retrospect, appeared to him a more ambiguous experience than the fraternal and heroic adventure portrayed in Vittorini's *Men and Not*. In Pavese's novella *La casa in collina* (*The House on the Hill*), written in 1947-1948, the narrator, Corrado, is unable to overcome his inner paralysis and self-doubt sufficiently to join the Resistance at all. He remains in the hills near Turin, symbolically poised between two women — his former mistress, now implicated in a Resistance network, and the Fascist daughter of his landlady. The natural beauty of the countryside and the affection of his dog provide his only emotional security in this web of conflicting loyalties. When the resisters are captured in a police raid, Corrado flees, first to a sheltering monastery, then back to his boyhood town. There the true depth of his isolation and its roots in a desire to escape responsibility are finally borne home: "I now realize that all this year, and also before . . . I have lived one long isolation, a futile vacation, like a boy who while playing hide-and-seek enters a thicket and enjoys it in there, who looks at the sky through the leaves and forgets ever to come out again."[51]

Pavese's last novel, *La luna e i falò* (*The Moon and the Bonfires*, 1950) also deals with a homecoming. Here the mythic overtones of the natural world that Pavese had admired in the work of Melville and Hawthorne give an added dimension to the book's political and autobiographical themes. The narrator returns from America to the tiny town nestled in the Turinese hills that he left before the war. He departed penniless and an outcast because of his illegitimate birth; he returns a rich man of considerable social standing. But this outward success hides an inner emptiness. America has not satisfied his need for roots. Like Silvestro Ferrauto in Vittorini's *Conversation in Sicily*, he hopes to lay claim to a part of himself abandoned long ago and enshrined in the familiar landscape of his youth.

Yet he finds his village and acquaintances, especially his boyhood friend Nuto, changed by the war. While he was abroad seeking his fortune, the Resistance sowed seeds of guilt and hatred at home that have not yet died. The narrator's search to recover the past centers on the three daughters of a local landowner for whom he worked as a boy, and whom he had desired at a distance. In the climactic last scene of the book, Nuto tells his friend of the night when he executed the youngest and most beautiful of the three for betraying Resistance fighters to the Germans, then burned her body in a bonfire. The fire

symbolizes both violence and purification. It is also the echo of a peasant ritual, a fertility rite intended to assure a bountiful harvest. But
the harvest of the Resistance has been robbed of its promise; the
purification is incomplete. Nuto will never be totally free of his past,
just as the narrator will never be able to join him across the barrier of
the Resistance experience they do not share. "The old beauty has been
destroyed but the new order does not appear."[52]

On August 27, 1950, four months after the publication of *The
Moon and the Bonfires*, Pavese died in Turin, unable to emerge from
his isolation, a victim of suicide. His death marked the symbolic end
of the Resistance era in Italy.

Conclusion: The Resistance Legacy

Whatever our personal failings may be, the nobility of our calling will always be grounded in two obligations that are difficult to fulfill: the refusal to lie about what one knows, and resistance against oppression.

Albert Camus, 1957

If *Combat*'s slogan, "From resistance to revolution," had summed up the hopes of the Liberation period, the prevailing attitude of many Europeans during the 1950s was expressed in German Chancellor Konrad Adenauer's 1957 election motto, "No experiments." Economic reconstruction and political conservatism went hand in hand. Despite the continuing menace of the Cold War and domestic inflation, Western Europe settled into a stable pattern of life, free from the sudden upheavals that had punctuated the two preceding decades. Not since the nineteenth century had the continent experienced so long a period of peace and sustained growth as the one that began within ten years after World War II.[1]

The 1950s confirmed and accelerated the trend toward "restoration" against which the Resistance intellectuals had warned in the late 1940s. While Europe returned to prosperity, their fundamental goal of "spiritual revolution" remained unfulfilled. Probably no course of renewal could have fully satisfied the hopes the intellectuals had cherished in 1945; but the high standards they set accentuated the modest character of postwar achievements. The advances made in this period seemed dwarfed by what was yet undone. "The true sin of the restoration," Walter Dirks commented in 1950, "is the sin of omission."[2] The creative possibilities present during the first years of peace had vanished and appeared unlikely to return.

Disappointed by the restoration, yet aware of its entrenched strength, the intellectuals continued to attack specific features of postwar society without aspiring to introduce fundamental reforms. Theirs was essentially a critical posture, that of moral censors whose judgments were heard but not heeded by the public at large. This attitude left many intellectuals prey to frustration and mild self-contempt. *Esprit* observed in December 1953 that analysis and criticism of the present were poor substitutes for more direct influence on national affairs: "Like the petty bourgeois who seek consolation for their powerlessness in interminable discussions at the local café, we drown our despair . . . in oceans of universal lucidity."[3]

This sense of becoming outsiders once again, confined to the margin of events, was reinforced by a shift in cultural orientation for which the intellectuals were ill prepared. During the late 1940s art and politics had followed different courses; the political climate favored the Right, while the message conveyed by literature and film remained overwhelmingly sympathetic to the Left. In many ways, as in the case of *Il Politecnico*, a "new culture" became the last refuge of the revolution. By the mid-fifties, however, art ceased to bear a political stamp. Increasingly, writers were drawn toward a private, formalistic literature freed from utilitarian constraints, epitomized by the French *nouveau roman*. What Sartre characterized as a new "antinovel" abandoned the conventions of engaged literature altogether in favor of a self-conscious hermeticism that necessarily restricted its appeal to a small circle of initiates. In Germany Gottfried Benn, whose enthusiastic embrace of National Socialism no longer barred him from public acceptance and esteem, defended "the absolute poem, the poem without belief, the poem without hope, the poem directed at no one."[4] Art was its own justification, an ideal transcending place and time. It had ceased to be a weapon, a lesson, or a cry of protest.

Looking back across the intervening decade, Resistance intellectuals sought to define and to perpetuate the memory of an experience whose uniqueness—in terms of both risk and promise—was now apparent. Amid signs of indifference or hostility to the Resistance heritage, intellectuals who had formerly wished to distance themselves from Europe's bourgeois past discovered new virtue in the task of preserving a record of the war years. The survivors of the Resistance became its first historians. On the tenth anniversary of the liberation of Paris, the inaugural volume in a series entitled Esprit de la Résistance was published in France. Georges Bidault, in a laudatory preface, stressed the need to "enlighten our citizens" and to "educate young Frenchmen" concerning the accomplishments of the underground.[5] The German Institut für Zeitgeschichte and the Istituto Storico della Resistenza Italiana in Milan pursued similar projects during the 1950s, testifying to a shared recognition that the Resistance now belonged to the past.

"From a certain point of view," commented *Il Ponte* in 1954, "the Resistance is history and will not recur, just as we will not see the return of those who ten years ago gave their lives for ideals that are more vital than ever, since in large part they have yet to be accomplished."[6] The contrast between living ideals and fragmentary achievements suggests the contradictory nature of the Resistance legacy as perceived in the decade of "restoration." Its greatest contribution remained a moral one: the defeat of nihilism and the creation of an ethical consensus based on the principle of human dignity. Its most serious failure was the inability to implement its values in the political or social sphere. How, then, was the intellectual Resistance to be judged? What had been its effect on those who now tried to chart and record its course? What changes had it brought to European culture as a whole?

Resistance Humanism

World War II forced the intellectuals into a confrontation with the concrete that was both more intense and more widely shared than the political mobilization of the 1930s. "Without the war," wrote Giaime Pintor in 1943, "I would have remained an intellectual with primarily literary interests . . . The war alone has resolved the situation, overturning certain obstacles, sweeping away many convenient shelters, and placing me brutally in contact with a hostile world."[7] A conflict that engulfed soldiers and civilians alike, that was fought in occupied cities and the *maquis* as well as on the battlefield, offered no refuge from a "hostile world." The choices it imposed could be neither evaded nor postponed.

The decision to resist during the war was an act of both self-discovery and self-affirmation. Like all commitments to a cause, it brought the individual's loyalties into sharp relief. But unlike adherence to Nazi or Fascist doctrine, encouraged by the fervor of mass rallies or enforced by intimidation and fear of arrest, entry into the Resistance depended on a solitary choice justified by no external authority. Opponents of Fascism challenged not merely a political creed but the habitual deference to a nation's leaders and to majority opinion that kept many of their countrymen loyal to Mussolini, Hitler, or Pétain. The moment of decision has often been described by Resistance intellectuals as a private victory, an inner rejection of constraints in defiance of the state. Alfred Andersch wrote in 1952 of his desertion from the German army: "I simply thought, with a tremendous sense of triumph, of the freedom that I had created for myself."[8]

Yet the dissolution of the familiar social landscape in the war, the confrontation with Pintor's "hostile world," at first proved profoundly disorienting. Conscription, exile, deportation all disrupted the effort to comprehend the present. Thus it is perhaps not surprising that the "limit situation" in which many intellectuals at last returned to both perceptual and moral clarity occurred not in the midst of action but in captivity. For Sartre in his German stalag, for Borchert in his Nazi cell, for Levi in Gagliano, a forcibly simplified existence led to a new understanding of the world around them and of their own inner resources. The truths they discovered were at first fragmentary, but precious nonetheless. As Sartre later wrote: "Because the Nazi poison was introduced into our thoughts, each accurate thought was a conquest."[9]

Intellectuals who succeeded in defining a moral basis for revolt tended to organize values as pairs of opposites: positive and negative, evil and good. In a situation of deep ethical uncertainty, the most basic schema exercised the strongest attraction. This binary approach also prolonged the pattern of creating ideals through opposition to prevailing norms—a pattern evident in the 1930s, when the intellectuals rejected first middle-class standards and then Fascist doctrine. Resistance, in a strict sense, meant opposing what existed in the name of its contrary. Camus's journalism, with its contrasting abstractions, the two communities in Silone's *The Seed beneath the Snow*, Böll's unheroic heroes—all illustrate this process. The result was a universe in which moral choices were simplified to exclude all but two alternatives.

Such a Manichaean universe mirrored the Fascists' rhetorical approach. They, too, dealt in stark and simple alternatives, choices for and against. Here opposition came close to a mere inversion of terms. As Klaus Mann had argued in 1938, what the Fascists praised, their opponents would attack; what the Fascists attacked, they would defend. For each side, the presence of an enemy offered a crucial point of reference. But since the Resistance was the younger of the two movements, the issues on which it differed with the Fascists were already fixed. It had merely to react.

Resistance intellectuals had a more compelling reason to prefer such conceptual simplicity, however. They believed that the most basic truths possessed an absolute, unqualified character. "Purity" was the term often used to describe the moral revelations of the underground. The approximate, the embellished, the complex or contradictory seemed false by definition. The desire to purify language of the muddy distortions of propaganda—a goal shared by Camus, Borchert, and

Silone among many others—reflected this attitude. Whatever was perceived clearly could be conveyed in a direct, simple manner. André Malraux remarked in 1937 that the twentieth century was "the age of fundamentals"—a statement with which few Resistance intellectuals would have disagreed.[10]

Such an outlook relied on the specific data of personal experience as the basis for defining reality. This view received a theoretical justification in existentialist thought, with its emphasis on an inductive rather than a deductive approach to discovering the "concrete." Similarly, the special role played by the *Reisebericht* in postwar journalism in both Germany and Italy revealed the intellectuals' continuing desire to plunge directly into the present and to report their findings. Trusting the individual observer did not mean a return to the purely subjective or solipsistic; Resistance faith in the testimony of personal encounters was supported by an equally firm belief in reason. Both the individual and the rational elements of their approach are exemplified in Eugen Kogon's *The SS State*—an account based exclusively on eyewitness reports of the concentration camps, intended to produce a detailed, accurate record of a demented world.[11]

Just as a series of independent moral choices converged in the common enterprise of the Resistance, so the testimony of separate observers would, it was assumed, fuse into a satisfying whole. Sartre argued in *Les Temps Modernes* for a "synthetic anthropology," while Dolf Sternberger adopted a similar stance in the final issue of *Die Wandlung*: "A secret, connecting thread almost always bound the poetry, essays, and directly political pieces. The editors often recognized with pleasure that contributions from the most opposed genres came together in a meaningful union within a single issue."[12] What gave this eclecticism its unity was the belief, repeatedly stated by the Resistance intellectuals, that both ethics and epistemology were centered on the individual. Man remained not only the one sure source of knowledge but also the one sure value.

"How many times the word 'man' recurs in my writing," Nizan had observed in *Aden, Arabie* in 1931. "But there is no other. The real problem is to define what meaning it contains."[13] The intellectual *résistants* believed they had found the solution to this problem. They had rediscovered humanism at first hand; it ceased to be "abstract" for them and took on the shape of the friendship, sacrifices, daring, and fulfillment of the underground. Man's basic worth and dignity were ideals they defended against the moral relativism preached by the Fascists, and relied on for sustenance and inspiration in their daily lives.

A faith in the basic goodness of human nature may appear a strange response to the realities of dictatorship and war. Racial prejudice, the mass hysteria aroused by Hitler and Mussolini, the instances of cowardice and opportunism that occurred even in the ranks of the Resistance, all suggested much more negative conclusions about man's capacity for virtuous action. How is it that the intellectuals did not develop a more cynical view, or at least a melancholy resignation to man's penchant for barbarism such as Freud expressed during World War I? The answer lies in their willingness to trust in their own experiences. Because some individuals had responded to the pressures of war with heroism and selflessness, because they themselves had withstood the demands of Fascism, the intellectuals believed that, in human nature as a whole, virtues to which they could appeal lay dormant.

Resistance humanism implied both respect for the individual and a commitment to social change. Individual needs dictated the shape of the new order that the intellectuals hoped to realize after the fall of Fascism. Regimes that had proven hostile to the human spirit, denying human freedom and personal fulfillment, would yield to an alternative society in which those values were honored. The standards that the *résistants* invoked were "natural" ones, in contrast with the "artificial" constraints imposed by totalitarian rule. Here again, a binary approach made itself apparent, with a significant consequence. If good and evil were drawn with exaggerated profiles, the distance between various types of good appeared to diminish in proportion. All positive and "natural" goals were presumed to be mutually supportive and compatible. Those who contrasted freedom and oppression also minimized the potential conflict between freedom and socialist planning. The old desire for synthesis remained.

Yet to predicate a future social order on values derived from "man" and his needs was to assume not only that such needs were in harmony with one another but also that they were universally shared. The Resistance intellectuals supported the tenets of natural law—moral principles valid for and binding on all—and at the same time defended the individual's right to choose as he wished. As Sartre wrote in the inaugural issue of *Les Temps Modernes*: "We openly affirm that man is an absolute." He immediately qualified this statement, however, by adding that the individual possessed an absolute value "in his time, in his milieu, on his own ground."[14]

The potential conflict between universal ideals and an unbending individualism was resolved by the intellectuals on a theoretical level through their concept of a moral elite. They assumed the existence of moral leaders, recognized by the nation at large, who agreed among themselves on how specific ethical norms might be implemented and whose agreement would serve as an example to all. The peculiar conditions imposed by clandestine opposition during the war contributed to the intellectuals' tendency to view themselves as part of this elite. The small circles of *résistants*, isolated from one another and from society in daily life but united by a warm glow of common purpose, encouraged a style of political participation that was at once lonely, morally elevated, and heroic. Writing for the underground press and the first postwar journals, or sharing his thoughts with a few close confidants, the intellectual could imagine himself as the spokesman and example for thousands of his countrymen condemned to silence by occupation or defeat. He became a "representative," in Bonhoeffer's term, one whose voluntary actions redeemed the congregation of the oppressed.[15]

This style of participation had an obvious appeal. It was both elitist and uncompromising, firmly subordinating political expediency to the dictates of conscience. If society as a whole was unable to act in the defense of freedom and social justice, the intellectual and his Resistance companions were called to act alone. They functioned as advocates for other groups whose cause they adopted: the nation, the peasantry, the industrial proletariat, the "younger generation." By encouraging the intellectuals to identify their interests as individuals with those of a group or groups, the Resistance and the Liberation made possible a momentary resolution of essentially incompatible desires. The intellectuals could retain their former elite status yet speak for the masses, preserve their independence yet advance social change. No longer hostile or mutually uncomprehending, they and the nation were one.

Thus World War II required Resistance intellectuals to confront the problem of choice but enabled them to evade the difficulties posed by their social vision. It encouraged a state of moral exaltation coupled with political passivity—prolonged in Germany under the Allied occupation—in which planning social change took precedence over implementing it. Yet in 1945, it was not at all apparent to most Resistance intellectuals that their recent experiences had simply masked, rather than resolved, the potential conflict among their ideals. The voluntarist spirit of the Resistance, its faith in man's power to create as he wished, diverted them from such a harsh assessment. On the contrary there seemed no limit to what they might achieve with the coming of the Liberation.

The "Spiritual Revolution"

The war demonstrated that change was indeed possible. A society in which human capabilities were suppressed—whether by Nazi terror or by the slow stagnation that French intellectuals viewed as endemic to the Third Republic—had been swept away. The advent of Fascism had earlier revealed that the structures of the old Europe were not immutable. Now the victory of anti-Fascist forces in 1945 opened the way for the transformations desired by the intellectual Resistance, and confirmed its members in their belief that they could shape events.

The moral elite, in the intellectuals' view, would guide the changes to come. Its force was centered in local groups such as the Comités Départementaux de Libération in France, the German Antifas, and the Italian CLN committees. The intellectuals participated in this elite through the small circles of associates that characterized the staffs of *Combat* and *Les Temps Modernes, Der Ruf* and *Il Politecnico*—groups whose importance increased after the initial defeat of the Resistance committees by the post-Liberation government in each country. The international links within the moral elite, typified by the RDR and the Union Européenne des Fédéralistes, provided an equally exemplary mode of organization. The intellectuals' ideal, inspired by their Resistance experience, was thus a network of local voluntary associations, vehicles of direct democracy, united within a European federation.[16] The old nation-states, bellicose and unresponsive to the needs of their citizens, were to be superseded at both a lower and a higher level by more responsible institutions. As Silone had argued in his "Theses for a Third Front," local autonomy and international cooperation would form a complementary whole.

Of these two elements, the local community was the more important and the more fully realized in the intellectuals' Resistance past. Its origins were those of a community founded on opposition. From a position on the periphery of the political order, such groups would now move to occupy the center, but would continue to follow the "natural" pattern of free human associations. The intellectuals' desire for flexibility in government reflected a concern for remaining close to life. Rules, conventions, bureaucratic rigidity should be discarded in favor of improvisation, contact, and consensus. For the same reason, they wished those affected by decisions to have a hand in their making. The recourse to *cahiers* of grievances in the RDR offered one example of this consultative goal.

Institutions that remained faithful to these "natural" guidelines would prove welcome to all. Thus the notion that armed force might be required to impose the "revolution," once the Resistance had triumphed, the intellectuals never seriously entertained. Instead, they believed they could secure popular support through persuasion. Their Resistance experience led them to view the essence of social change as the moral conversion of society. Their passage from an aristocracy of intellect to an aristocracy of ethical and political commitment was

analogous to a religious conversion both in the depths of the transformation it induced and the feelings of personal election that resulted.
Sartre's trilogy *Roads to Freedom,* Beauvoir's *The Blood of Others,*
Camus's *The Plague,* Richter's *The Defeated,* Vittorini's *Man and
Not,* Silone's *The Seed beneath the Snow,* all revolve around the
theme of personal commitment. In all these works, the action centers
on a moral crisis precipitated by the war or Fascism; the crisis is
resolved through a choice that is presented as an example or an admonition. It is a literature that celebrates the author's own conversion
to an ethic of social responsibility and aims to provoke a similar experience in his readers. Like a medieval saint's life, it points the way to
salvation.[17]

The literature of "unveiling," to use Sartre's term, was thus a prime
tool for the intellectuals' attempts at persuasion. Their desire to act
directly on the consciences of their readers was one reason for the conservative literary style of these writers during the 1940s—their emphasis
on a clear narrative line, objective description, and an unambiguous
message. Technical experiments would have created a gulf of
misunderstanding between themselves and the public. Only when innovation promised to bring literary language closer to popular speech,
as in Italy, was it adopted by the intellectuals with any enthusiasm.
Memories of Fascist propaganda led them to stress both the reasoned
and the reciprocal nature of their contact with an audience that they
wished to convert to their views. Their ideal—illustrated by titles such
as "Conversations on Politics" and *Conversation in Sicily*—was
dialogue, not the manipulation of sentiment.

One attitude that dialogue was to encourage was a critical view of
the past, a recognition of wrongdoing and an acceptance of guilt. To
the extent that Fascism had drawn its strength from popular consent,
the majority of citizens in France, Germany, and Italy were implicated
in its crimes. Atonement would come through introspection, a willingness to admit the need for change in one's values and behavior.
Complementary to this goal was that of civic education—the acceptance of dissent, tolerance, and the individual's right to follow the dictates of conscience. Finally and most important, the intellectuals
hoped for a change in the relations among citizens: the creation of
bonds of trust and mutual respect such as they had experienced in the
Resistance, exemplified in the "natural" community.

The intellectuals based their hopes on the human capacity for
reasoned understanding and discourse. Human error they regarded as
willful error. It is significant that Sartre, for one, refused to accept the
notion of an unconscious beyond man's control. The intellectuals concentrated their efforts on dispelling the prejudices that distorted and
darkened the present, and on pointing to moral truths which, they

judged, would be acknowledged as both evident and desirable. Their failure to concern themselves with practical politics was grounded in this confidence in their role as teachers. If politics was a series of moral choices made by rational, self-directed citizens, it followed that they should concern themselves with guiding choice rather than with shaping institutions. "The possibility of change through teaching," as Alfred Andersch noted about his experiences as a prisoner of war in the United States, "presupposes a faith in the positive forces in man."[18]

This optimism did not extend to the realm of government institutions. Indeed, the Resistance approach to politics was reminiscent of the anarchist belief that all government is bad. A deep hostility toward the state, part of the legacy of antiparliamentary attitudes inherited from the 1920s and reinforced by the subsequent contact with Fascism, posed major problems for the Resistance intellectuals after the war. Time and again it prevented them from identifying within the government potential allies with whom to join in the pursuit of concrete goals. Their distrust of the state and of corporate interests within the state—parties, the bureaucracy, pressure groups—was consistent with their defense of the individual, but it robbed them of the opportunity to seek organized political expression of their ideals after 1945. The one significant exception to the intellectuals' suspicious attitude toward interest groups was their sympathy for the proletariat and, especially in Italy, the peasantry. But here again, their sympathy rested on the perception that the peasants themselves were hostile to the state, and that the Communist party distorted the workers' true interests for its own political ends.

This anarchist tendency can be seen in the uneasiness with which the intellectuals viewed not only the activities of the Communists but also the prospect of assuming the burden of government themselves. Communist leaders saw the state as a prize to be captured and exploited. . The Resistance intellectuals were not so confident. In Italy, where the forces of the CLN held power for a brief five months in 1945, the discomfort felt by many intellectual members at exercising governmental authority can be read in their response to Parri's fall. Faced with a conservative assault on Italy's central administration, they promptly acknowledged defeat, abandoned their posts, and withdrew.[19]

Although the Resistance intellectuals made detailed and perceptive critiques of contemporary problems and attitudes, and although they were generally agreed on the synthesis of freedom and economic reforms as their ultimate political goal, they failed to supply a link connecting present and future. They elected to look below, or above, but not *at* the social institutions with which any attempt to change society (even by abolishing these same institutions) would eventually have to deal. Their approach illustrated what Leonard Krieger has analyzed as a "pattern in which the initial reality is firmly apprehended, the final goal generally envisaged, and the connecting social means entirely confused."[20] Their preferred strategy for social change was to transform personnel rather than structures, as in the call for purges that arose at the war's end.

In their fear of corrupting the Resistance legacy, the intellectuals retreated from the center of political life. Yet even then, they made clear their own deep reluctance to subordinate their independence or to compromise their goals in the discipline of a common cause. It is interesting to note the frequency with which they used the metaphor of a bridge to explain their role; Sartre's RDR, *Der Ruf, Il Ponte* all proposed to act as mediators, touching but not coalescing with other social groups. They would remain teachers and guides, possessing influence but not power, fostering attitudes in their fellow citizens from which social change—desired and accepted by all—would follow in due course.

Perceptions and Realities

This brief summary of the intellectuals' assumptions at the time of the Liberation does not, of course, do full justice to the nuances of their doctrine or to their personal differences of opinion. Yet their agreement on basic principles remains more striking and more significant than their controversies. If *Les Temps Modernes* carried articles reprinted from *Il Politecnico,* if *Der Ruf* published excerpts from the works of Beauvoir and Silone, it was because Resistance intellectuals shared similar aspirations and felt themselves to be part of a common venture. The wartime experience that molded this unity, however, also hindered their understanding of the conditions under which their hopes had now to be realized. The intellectuals' consensus was not shared beyond their circle; the support and acquiescence they sought were refused by their countrymen at large.

One line of argument rejects altogether the notion that Europe's future could be shaped by purely European initiatives in 1945 to more than a modest degree. The capacity of the two superpowers during this period to impose measures dictated by their own national security requirements, the argument goes, far outweighed the capacity of an exhausted, impoverished, and disorganized continent to pursue an independent course of reconstruction and renewal. The goals of the intellectuals, insofar as they diverged from the wishes of the United States and the Soviet Union, were not so much mistaken as irrelevant.[21]

This assessment cannot be dismissed lightly. In Germany, the occupying powers exercised a decisive influence on domestic affairs during the late 1940s. Italy, to a lesser degree, was also subject to the American Military Government's control from 1943 to 1946 and to indirect economic and political pressures from Washington thereafter. In both countries the United States was able to reward its friends and appreciably hamper those it considered its enemies, such as the journalists of *Der Ruf* or Ferruccio Parri, during the early stages of the Cold War. As Europe's banker, America influenced the course of reconstruction through the Marshall Plan. Even in France, as Léon Blum's 1946 trip to Washington in search of credits showed, economic dependence on a foreign power was a fact of life that government leaders were forced to acknowledge.[22]

This Cold War explanation of the intellectuals' failure to promote genuine social change, however, overlooks the strong domestic current of conservatism after 1945. It helps to put the developments tending toward "restoration" in context, but alone it cannot explain why de Gaulle was as hesitant to embark on full implementation of the CNR charter in 1944 as Truman was to allow French Communists to exercise ministerial powers in 1946. The defeat of the Resistance program occurred relatively soon after the close of hostilities, well before the Cold War reached its height.[23] It must therefore be asked whether domestic forces were not equally decisive in curbing proposals for change that were seen to threaten their economic and social interests.

Fear of "revolution" preoccupied conservative opinion in all three countries. There was considerable activity aimed at tempering the more radical Resistance proposals—including purges and nationalization programs—in conservative circles after the war. The participation in the wartime Resistance of elements from the military, the industrialists, the Catholic church, and other members of the traditional (as opposed to the Fascist or Nazi) Right allowed its spokesmen to take their place alongside delegates of the Left in the coalition governments that followed. The economic difficulties encountered during the first phase of the Liberation were resolved as much by open favoritism toward private economic interests as by nationalization and state control of vital industries—a tribute to the influence of those interests within the halls of government.

The Communist party, meanwhile, was cautious, to say the least, about supporting revolutionary aims during the very period when they might most easily have been achieved. As Alfred Rieber and others have observed, until 1947 the Communist parties of both France and Italy were a restraining rather than a militant force on the Left, more concerned with consolidating wartime gains in membership and with maintaining the Soviet-Western alliance than with attempting a seizure of power that was judged by Stalin to be both impracticable and inopportune.[24] It was the French Communist party leader, Thorez, who demanded that the Communist *milices patriotiques* surrender their arms and that the French miners refrain from strikes that might harm the national interest. It was the Italian Communist chief, Togliatti, who urged the PCI to cooperate with Marshal Badoglio's government in 1943 and who similarly opposed industrial unrest during the first months of the Liberation. Both the Right and the Communist Left, in fact, saw greater tactical advantages in order than in change. The Resistance intellectuals, free from the constraints of economic interests or party discipline, thus emerged as the most consistent advocates of a thorough restructuring of society immediately following the war. Not until after the Soviet break with the West in 1947 did the Communist party of either France or Italy revert to a revolutionary stance more in keeping with its origins. By that time the stability the Communists had previously sought was well on its way to becoming a reality, and their reversal came too late.

Postwar stability was further enhanced by the emergence of a trio of strong national leaders whose style of government departed markedly from the ideals of consultation and consensus favored by most Resistance intellectuals. De Gaulle, who guided France from late 1944 until early 1946, and Adenauer and De Gasperi, whose tenure in office proved considerably longer, stood for a centralization of political power that appeared desirable to many in the midst of the formidable difficulties of reconstruction. France, Germany, and Italy emerged from the war as republics, but republics that inherited much of the administrative authority formerly vested in the totalitarian state. Just as after World War I, executive dominance of parliament continued for a time with the return to peace.[25]

The choice of order over radical change suited the general public as well as the organized group or party interests. The succession of economic, political, and military blows that had shaken France, Germany, and Italy since the first decades of the century had awakened what one historian termed "a basic and highly conservative longing, however inchoate, to return to peace and stability."[26] Despite the widespread hope that a better society would arise from the ruins of war, the populace was unwilling to face further disruptions. They preferred to entrust the affairs of government to others, and to return to their private concerns. However sympathetic to the ends proposed by the intellectuals, they drew back before the self-scrutiny and sacrifice required to realize them. Instead they worked toward more modest, and more material, goals.

The gulf between the intellectuals' expectations about conditions in postwar Europe and the reality of foreign pressure, conservative

resistance, and popular indifference could hardly have been more profound. The intellectuals, unable to foresee the strategic constraints imposed by first the Soviet-Western alliance and then the Cold War,
believed that Europe would be free to pursue an independent course
between capitalism and Stalinism. They assumed that the parliamentary and economic elites of the past had either abandoned their pretensions to power or been converted to the Resistance cause. They trusted
that the momentum of change begun by the war would sweep a willing
populace into supporting a total renewal of society. They underesti-
mated or ignored precisely those phenomena that in 1945 proved the
greatest barriers to change.

Yet the Resistance intellectuals' inability to secure the adoption of
their program after the Liberation was not evidence of diminishing
political power or a sudden loss of influence. They had never controlled the fortunes of the Resistance, much less the outcome of the
war. Although the intellectuals had participated in the underground
and rendered valuable services to its cause, it was the Allies who had
defeated Fascism. That these same foreign powers should have influenced the course of postwar Europe was scarcely surprising. That
domestic interests should have reasserted their dominance over questions of national policy might also have been predicted. The Resistance had been a coalition drawn from many quarters. Agreement on
the negative aim of defeating Fascism could not guarantee a continuing agreement about positive measures to be pursued once victory had
been attained. Some well-organized groups such as the Communist
party emerged from the war with their power enhanced; others such as
the Catholic church and the Italian Confindustria survived with their
former authority damaged but intact. There were many rivals for
power in 1945, of whom the Resistance intellectuals, as it proved, were
least able to make good their claims.[27]

The intellectuals had never intended to direct their countries'
destinies alone. Instead, they had looked to the other groups in the
Resistance for cooperation and support. They believed that the war
would change the values and expectations of their countrymen, and
they were ready to guide that change by distilling the war's lessons in
their writings. Their error was not so much to overestimate the impact
of this experience as to misunderstand its ambiguous character. Many
of its survivors wished to forget the trauma of the war rather than to
draw on it as a source of ideals for the future. The work of physical
reconstruction in all three countries, as the *Goethehaus* controversy
suggested, often aided the repression of painful memories by effacing
the evidence of destruction. Those whose wartime activities had been
criminal or shameful—an unfortunately large number—preferred a
guilty silence to public atonement.

The intellectuals adjusted their views during the 1940s not by abandoning their goals but by revising their estimate of the time required to achieve them. By 1948 they had decided that the task of education must be undertaken in the long term. Paradoxically, the very slowness of the change in attitudes that they now foresaw seemed a guarantee of its permanence once achieved. They would continue to extend their network of contacts and to win supporters just as they had during the wartime Resistance. As Alban Vistel observed in *Héritage spirituel de la Résistance* (*Spiritual Legacy of the Resistance*, 1955):

> We must bring new, living communities into existence, determined to remain vigilant and, if necessary, to take up revolt. We must seek out, man by man, woman by woman, those who refuse to become victims of an anonymous plot to dull our senses . . . Let us create, in the midst of growing noise and confusion, islands of lucidity, of meditation, of intransigence against lies. The same values are menaced [as during the war], and our defeat this time would be irreparable.[28]

Thus the Resistance intellectuals were able to use the dissident community as a refuge after the war. A basically defensive strategy, evolved at a time when they feared Fascist or Nazi persecution, proved equally well adapted to the needs of survival in the postwar era. The late 1940s saw the intellectuals shift their attention from journalism alone to the founding of more voluntary associations—some of which, like the RDR, soon perished, while others, like the Group 47, continued for over a decade.[29] The metaphor they used to describe their aims shifted as well; from a "bridge," it became an "oasis" or an "island."

The Resistance intellectuals increasingly focused on fidelity to the past. They were the guardians of a memory that provided them with continuing inspiration. Their faith in the power of extreme conditions to reveal man's capabilities survived the setbacks and disappointments of the late 1940s. Few agreed with Merleau-Ponty that the Resistance experience had been too exceptional to be a guide to action after 1945. On the contrary, the exceptional nature of the Resistance, they felt, gave it a special claim to truth. What was superficial or transient had been stripped away by the ordeal of the war, leaving behind an irreducible core of ethical certainty.

The moral force of the Resistance had resided in its unbending posture in the face of pressures for compromise. Revolutionaries have long known the value of intransigence. Opposition based on an ideal that permits no concessions, that demands absolute fidelity in the struggle with an enemy portrayed as evil incarnate, is more likely to succeed in periods of unrest than is the voice of moderation. Just as in the French Revolution Robespierre's rhetoric prevailed over the more temperate proposals of the Gironde, so the intellectual Resistance proved victorious over the cautious temporizers of World War II. The same unwillingness to compromise, however, became a liability in postwar Europe. An attitude supremely suited to opposition could not be adapted to the needs of a period when only halfway measures were attainable. The vision of the future that had sustained the underground in its darkest moments could not be translated into reality without sacrificing the "purity" essential to its appeal. The Resistance tendency to see the good in synthetic terms further diminished its ability to choose among practical goals once peace was at hand. Its habitual insistence on "both . . . and" made resignation to "either . . . or" exceptionally difficult.[30] Thus at the heart of the intellectual Resistance lay an insoluble dilemma: it could not abandon its moral demands without destroying the basis of its mission, and it could not act while remaining true to its ideals. Continued opposition was its only recourse.

Resistance and Enlightenment

In their suppositions concerning the role of the intellectual in society, the men and women of the Resistance resembled their spiritual ancestors of the eighteenth century, the philosophes. Their faith that the ideal social order was one that corresponded to permanent human needs was shared by those who framed the *Declaration of the Rights of Man and Citizen* in 1789, which asserted that "the aim of all political associations is the preservation of the natural and imprescriptible rights of man." The belief of the Resistance intellectuals that true knowledge derived from direct, personal experience rather than from theory was anticipated in Diderot's famous definition of the philosophe, who "shapes his principles according to an infinite number of specific observations."[31] Their hope that man could create a society based on the first principles thus discovered had also fed the stream of social criticism that found expression in the French Revolution.

This eighteenth-century heritage was at times acknowledged by Resistance writers themselves. Sartre invoked the example of Voltaire in the first issue of *Les Temps Modernes*, while *Les Lettres Françaises* and *Combat* called for a return to the ideals of "liberty, equality, and fraternity." German intellectuals pointed with approval to Lessing's religious tolerance, especially the respect shown his Jewish hero in the drama *Nathan the Wise* (1779). In Italy, it was the Risorgimento that provided the most direct inspiration for the efforts of the Resistance, but its Enlightenment roots were not forgotten. The *Declaration of the Rights of Man* received mention in the press of all three countries; the need for a new edict that would preserve and expand the terms of the old was a theme that Emmanuel Mounier addressed in the December 1944 issue of *Esprit*.[32]

What Mounier and his colleagues found congenial in Enlightenment thought was its practical, as opposed to mechanical, use of reason, its critical approach to the world, and its willingness to pose basic questions concerning human nature and the foundations of morality. While they did not share the Enlightenment confidence that a rational order governed all things, they did believe in the power of human reason to order society, and in the ultimate perfectibility of man. Above all, their vision of their own role as moral preceptors, who mediated between a humanistic ideal and an imperfect society by awakening a new respect for universal values, bound the Resistance intellectuals to the tradition of the philosophes. The balance between opposition and optimism attained by the international community of critics in the eighteenth century was their own.

That the intellectual Resistance should have become heir to the Enlightenment—its most eloquent European defender during the first half of this century—few of its participants could have forseeen when they began their attack on liberalism late in the 1920s. Their ideal of creativity demanded the elaboration of new values, not a return to the old. But the coming of Fascism altered their perspective. Its challenge induced the intellectuals to reaffirm their commitment to precisely that role of moral judge and public conscience which Julien Benda had feared would be submerged in "political passions." At the same time, it spurred them to rescue both liberalism and socialism from an onslaught mounted by the Fascist Right.

The dangers that this mission entailed led the intellectuals to see their role as that of heroes as well as critics. They shared with their Fascist opponents an admiration for qualities of courage, enthusiasm, and willingness to endure sacrifice for the sake of an ideal. Both sides professed faith in a "spiritual revolution" that would restore vitality and purpose to an aging continent; both pursued their struggle with the fervor of a crusade. What distinguished the intellectual Resistance from its foe was not a more dispassionate outlook, but an ardent defense of the individual. It opposed Fascism in the name of traditions whose commitment to reason and measure it respected and revived.

The creativity of the Resistance intellectuals was largely confined to attempts at synthesis between these traditions—juxtaposing ideals such as humanism and individualism, freedom and justice. They were preservers rather than innovators; they restated beliefs and testified to their efficacy as guides to conduct. If the "generation of 1914" emerged from World War I in a state of profound disillusionment, the reverse can be said of the Resistance generation, whose values survived and were strengthened by war. Their disappointments came when the role they had assumed during the conflict, which had permitted them to identify their own cause with that of the nation as a whole, did not lead to the social transformation they desired and expected. Their voluntarism was tempered by a respect for history and a resignation to bureaucratic inertia soon after 1945. But they refused to discard the heritage of moral exaltation, warm fellowship, and sense of mission they had found in the Resistance.

The intellectual Resistance did not end in 1949. It lived on in reviews such as *Les Temps Modernes*, the *Frankfurter Hefte,* and *Il Ponte*, and in "oases" of the sort typified by Richter's Group 47. Its effects were felt in the existentialism and the peace movements of the 1950s and in the efforts at European integration culminating in the creation of the European Economic Community in 1957. In Europe's colonial relations with the Third World, where overt suppression of basic liberties continued, the force of the intellectuals' moral message had a more immediate impact. The 1950s witnessed the Resistance intellectuals' growing support for decolonization; in France, most notably, Indochinese and Algerian independence became an important goal for the intellectual Left. They identified the more recent struggles for liberation with the wartime underground.[33]

Resistance empiricism and stress on the importance of man's "concrete situation" also served as a starting point for the reassessment of European social thought undertaken in the 1950s by a younger generation of intellectuals. Their attention was drawn to the field of institutional theory, badly neglected by the Resistance. Sociologists such as Michel Crozier, Ralf Dahrendorf, and Alessandro Pizzorno proposed in the late 1950s to study society with the tools of quantitative analysis in an effort to overcome the limits of the earlier moralistic approach. Their concern for the structure of bureaucracy and the institutional roots of opposition to change replaced philosophical debates over the accountability of the individual. But the Resistance vision of a society that permitted personal fulfillment continued to guide their research. They considered their investigation of existing social systems to be a step toward the elusive goal of humanist reform.[34]

The intellectual Resistance can serve to correct the common assumption that Europe's cultural history in the first half of this century is marked exclusively by themes of despair, skepticism, or moral relativism. What one observer has termed the "decline of the Enlightenment" during these decades remains a part, but only a part, of a more complex pattern of responses to crisis. The Resistance drew its chief inspiration from a faith that this decline could be reversed. Its dissent was based on a reassertion of hope, reason, and firm ethical standards. As Albert Camus observed when he accepted the Nobel Prize for Literature in 1957: "Most of us, in my country and in Europe, rejected this nihilism and began the search for a justification. We had to forge an art of living in a time of catastrophe, to be born again and then to struggle openly against the instinct of death at work in our history . . . This generation, within and beyond itself, has had to recover through resistance alone a little of what gives dignity to life and to death."[35]

Notes

INTRODUCTION: THE ORIGINS OF THE INTELLECTUAL RESISTANCE

1. Henri Frenay, *La Nuit finira: Mémoires de Résistance, 1940-1945* (Paris: Robert Laffont, 1973), p. 559.

2. André Malraux, "D'une jeunesse européenne," in André Chamson et al., *Ecrits* (Paris: Bernard Grasset, 1927), p. 148.

3. Julien Benda, *La Trahison des clercs* (Paris: Bernard Grasset, 1975), pp. 107, 7. For an analysis of this work within the context of Benda's other writings see Robert J. Niess, *Julien Benda* (Ann Arbor: University of Michigan Press, 1956), pp. 144-173. Also Norberto Bobbio's perceptive essay "Julien Benda," *Il Ponte*, 12 (Aug.-Sept. 1956), 1377-1392, and David L. Schalk, "*La Trahison des clercs*—1927 and After," *French Historical Studies*, 7 (Fall 1971), 245-263.

4. Benda, *La Trahison des clercs*, pp. 223, 222.

5. Ibid., pp. 132, 133.

6. Ibid., p. 136.

7. Ramon Fernandez, "Sur *La Trahison des clercs*," *La Nouvelle Revue Française*, 15 (Jan. 1928), 106. Emmanuel Berl reproached Benda in 1929 for displaying a "nostalgia for the cloister." Berl, *Mort de la pensée bourgeoise* (Paris: Bernard Grasset, 1929), p. 32.

8. Karl Mannheim, *Ideologie und Utopie*, 5th ed. (Frankfurt am Main: Verlag G. Schulte-Bulmke, 1969), pp. 49, 50, 177, 179.

9. Ibid., pp. 172, 214.

10. Ibid., pp. 191, 215.

11. Ibid., pp. 216, 217.

12. Ibid., pp. 221, 222, 213.

13. Antonio Gramsci, *Quaderni del carcere*, ed. Valentino Gerratana (Turin: Einaudi, 1975), III, 1550, 1551.

14. Ibid., II, 1378-1379.

15. Ibid., III, 1518-1519. On Gramsci's typology of intellectuals see Maria-Antonietta Macciocchi, *Pour Gramsci* (Paris: Editions du Seuil, 1974), pp. 202-281. Mannheim specifically acknowledged his debt to Hegel in *Ideologie und Utopie*, pp. 174-175.

16. Gramsci, *Quaderni*, III, 1517, 1551; II, 1331-1332. For an excellent discussion of Gramsci's views on hegemony and the role of the intellectual see Norberto Bobbio, "Gramsci e la concezione della società civile," in Eugenio Garin et al., *Gramsci e la cultura contemporanea* (Rome: Editori Riuniti, 1969), I, 75-100.

17. André Malraux, *La Tentation de l'occident* (Paris: Bernard Grasset, 1926), p. 204; Hans Zehrer, "Die Revolution der Intelligenz: Bruchstücke zukünftiger Politik," *Die Tat*, 21 (Oct. 1929), 487.

18. Robert Brasillach, *Notre avant-guerre,* in *Une Génération dans l'orage: Mémoires* (Paris: Plon, 1968), p. 244.

19. Among the many studies of this fin-de-siècle critique, see especially Zeev Sternhell, *La Droite révolutionnaire, 1885-1914: Les Origines françaises du fascisme* (Paris: Editions du Seuil, 1978); and Fritz Stern, *The Politics of Cultural Despair: A Study in the Rise of the Germanic Ideology* (Berkeley: University of California Press, 1961).

20. Piero Gobetti, for example, deplored the conservatism of Liberal circles in Italy and called for a "liberal revolution" that would restore genuine meaning to principles now reduced to "heuristic and rhetorical" use. Gobetti, *La rivoluzione liberale*, in *Opere complete*, I: *Scritti politici*, ed. Paolo Spriano (Turin: Einaudi, 1960), 1040.

21. Kurt Tucholsky, "In Uniform," in *Gesammelte Werke* (Reinbek bei Hamburg: Rowohlt Verlag, 1960), II, 743.

22. For an early critique of Mussolini as heir to bourgeois political practices see Gobetti, "Noi e le opposizioni" (1924), in *Opere complete*, I, 644.

23. Emmanuel Mounier, *Oeuvres*, ed. Paulette Mounier-Leclercq, (Paris: Editions du Seuil, 1961), I, 271.

24. Emmanuel Berl, *Mort de la morale bourgeoise* (Paris: Jean-Jacques Pauvert, 1965), p. 64 (first published in 1929); Norberto Bobbio, "Introduzione," in Leone Ginzburg, *Scritti* (Turin: Einaudi, 1964), p. xxi.

25. Mounier, "Confession pour nous autres chrétiens," *Esprit*, 1 (March 1933), 894.

26. Paul Valéry, *Regards sur le monde actuel* (1929), in *Oeuvres*, II, ed. Jean Hytier (Paris: Gallimard, 1960), 927.

27. Oswald Spengler, *Der Untergang des Abendlandes: Umrisse einer Morphologie der Weltgeschichte* (Munich: C. H. Beck, 1969), pp. 28, 3.

28. Spengler, "Pessimismus?" (1921), in *Reden und Aufsätze* (Munich: C. H. Beck, 1951), pp. 79, 76, 70.

29. Erich Kästner, *Fabian: Die Geschichte eines Moralisten,* in *Gesammelte Schriften* (Cologne: Kiepenheuer & Witsch, 1959), II, 81, 187.

30. Raymond Poincaré, *La Restauration financière de la France* (Paris: Payot, 1928), p. 139. Poincaré's remarks were made in a speech to the Chamber of Deputies on 4 February 1928. Hans Zehrer wrote in December 1929: "The race has begun . . . The starting gun has sounded." "Grundriss einer neuen Partei," *Die Tat*, 21 (Dec. 1929), 41.

31. Claude-Edmonde Magny, *Histoire du roman français depuis 1918* (Paris: Editions du Seuil, 1950), p. 61.

32. For a discussion of Goebbels's considerable borrowings from Goethe and Nietzsche see Marianne Bonwit, *"Michael, ein Roman von Joseph Goebbels, im Licht der deutschen literarischen Tradition,"* in *Deutsche Literaturkritik der Gegenwart,* IV, pt. 1, ed. Hans Mayer (Stuttgart: Goverts Krüger Stahlberg Verlag, 1971), 490-501.

33. Goebbels, *Das Tagebuch von Joseph Goebbels, 1925-26,* ed. Helmut Heiber (Stuttgart: Deutsche Verlags-Anstalt, n.d.), p. 76 (diary entry for 30 April 1926); Goebbels, *Michael: Ein deutsches Schicksal in Tagebuchblättern* (Munich: Verlag Franz Eher Nachfolger, 1931), p. 222.

34. Goebbels, *Michael,* pp. 38, 156, 157. "Socialism, in the deepest sense, is service. Renunciation of the individual and support for the whole" (p. 38). For a discussion of Goebbels's political beliefs at the time he wrote *Michael* see Richard M. Hunt, "Joseph Goebbels: A Study of the Formation of his National-Socialist Consciousness (1897-1926)" (Ph.D. diss., Harvard, 1960), esp. pp. 101-110.

35. Paul Nizan, *Aden-Arabie* (Paris: François Maspero, 1967), p. 62.

36. Ibid., p. 108. Nizan was in Aden from the fall of 1926 to the spring of 1927.

37. Ibid., p. 156.

38. Nizan, *Les Chiens de garde* (Paris: François Maspero, 1971), p. 101. For a discussion of Nizan's critique see David L. Schalk, "Professors as Watchdogs: Paul Nizan's Theory of the Intellectual and Politics," *Journal of the History of Ideas,* 34 (Jan.-March 1973), 79-96.

39. Karl Jaspers, *Philosophie,* II: *Existenzerhellung* (Berlin: Julius Springer Verlag, 1932), 209, 211.

40. Ibid., pp. 244, 231. For a useful analysis of Jaspers's concept of "limit situations" see Charles F. Wallraff, *Karl Jaspers: An Introduction to His Philosophy* (Princeton, N.J.: Princeton University Press, 1970), pp. 141-166.

41. Nicola Chiaromonte, "Idee e figure di André Malraux," *Solaria,* 8 (Jan. 1933), 19.

42. Malraux, *Les Conquérants* (Paris: Bernard Grasset, 1928), p. 266; Malraux, *La Voie royale* (Paris: Bernard Grasset, 1930), p. 268.

43. Malraux, *La Condition humaine* (Paris: Gallimard, 1933), p. 362. "It is difficult to be a man," Malraux noted two years later, "but it is not more difficult to become one by deepening one's solidarity than by cultivating one's individuality—the former nourishes with at least as much energy as the latter." *Le Temps du mépris* (Paris: Gallimard, 1935), pp. 12-13.

44. Zehrer, quoted in Klemens von Klemperer, *Germany's New Conservatism: Its History and Dilemma in the Twentieth Century* (Princeton, N.J.: Princeton University Press, 1968), p. 199. For an analysis of this search for political synthesis in France see Jean-Louis Loubet del Bayle, *Les Non-conformistes des années 30: Une Tentative de renouvellement de la pensée politique française* (Paris: Editions du Seuil, 1969), esp. pp. 329-397.

45. In 1934 Drieu described his political philosophy as being "never completely on the Left nor completely on the Right," but rather as "a continual oscillation." Drieu la Rochelle, *Socialisme fasciste* (Paris: Gallimard, 1934), pp. 244, 245. Roselli's study *Socialismo liberale,* written in 1928-1929, was first

published in a French translation in Paris in 1930.

46. On the successive phases of *Esprit* and the evolution of its political outlook see Michel Winock, *Histoire politique de la revue 'Esprit,' 1930-1950* (Paris: Editions du Seuil, 1975), esp. pp. 198-238.

47. Mounier, *Oeuvres,* I, 179. His remarks appeared in *Esprit*, Dec. 1934, under the title "Révolution personnaliste." Concerning Mounier's analysis of "le désordre établi" see Candide Moix, *La Pensée d'Emmanuel Mounier* (Paris: Editions du Seuil, 1960), pp. 55-80; and Michel Barlow, *Le Socialisme d'Emmanuel Mounier* (Paris: Edouard Privat, 1971), pp. 91-106.

48. Mounier, *Oeuvres*, I, 523, 163.

49. Ibid., pp. 526, 158. The term "engagement" had already appeared in a different context in Nizan's *The Watchdogs*. Mounier, however, was the first to employ it extensively as a synonym for social responsibility. See David L. Schalk, *The Spectrum of Political Engagement: Mounier, Benda, Nizan, Brasillach, Sartre* (Princeton, N.J.: Princeton University Press, 1979), pp. 17-25.

50. Mounier, *Oeuvres,* I, 148, 149.

51. Ibid., p. 149; Thomas Mann, "[Rede vor Arbeitern in Wein]," in *Gesammelte Werke* (Frankfurt am Main: S. Fischer Verlag, 1974), XI, 899.

52. Among the many studies of the shifting perceptions of the Fascist movement see especially Renzo De Felice, *Le interpretazioni del fascismo* (Rome: Laterza, 1969).

53. Benito Mussolini, "Al gran rapporto del fascismo" (14 Sept. 1929), in *Opera omnia,* ed. Edoardo and Duilio Susmel (Florence: La Fenice, 1958), XXIV, 145.

54. For two eyewitness accounts of this congress see Jean Guéhenno, *La Foi difficile* (Paris: Bernard Grasset, 1957), pp. 164-167; and Emmanuel Mounier, "Le Congrès International des Ecrivains pour la Défense de la Culture," *Esprit,* no. 35-36 (1 Sept. 1935), 793-798.

55. André Gide, "Allocution d'ouverture," in *Littérature engagée*, ed. Yvonne Davet (Paris: Gallimard, 1950), p. 84; Klaus Mann, "Der Kampf um den jungen Menschen," first published in *Kürbiskern*, no. 2 (1975), 40, 41-42.

56. Mann, "Der Kampf um den jungen Menschen," 43.

57. Mounier, *Oeuvres*, I, 498.

58. Albert Camus, "Préface à *L'Espagne libre,*" in *Essais*, ed. Roger Quilliot and Louis Faucon (Paris: Gallimard, 1965), p. 1604. Camus wrote this preface in 1946.

1. THE LESSONS OF THE RESISTANCE, 1940-1944

1. Philippe Pétain, "Appel du 17 juin 1940," in *Paroles aux Français: Messages et écrits, 1934-41* (Lyons: Lardanchet, 1941), p. 42.

2. Jean Guéhenno, *Journal des années noires, 1940-1944* (Paris: Gallimard, 1947), p. 59 (diary entry for 30 Nov. 1940).

3. Claude Bourdet, *L'Aventure incertaine: De la Résistance à la Restauration* (Paris: Stock, 1975), p. 34.

4. Léon Blum, *A l'échelle humaine,* in *L'Oeuvre* (Paris: Editions Albin Michel, 1955), V, 412.

5. For Gide's reaction to the French defeat see his *Journal, 1939-1949* (Paris: Gallimard, 1954), especially pp. 25-52. After the armistice Gide confessed regrets at having "stayed on the sidelines" during the traumatic weeks of May and June 1940 (p. 42).

6. Jean-Paul Sartre, "Présentation," *Les Temps Modernes,* no. 1 (Oct. 1945), 5, rpt. in *Situations,* II (Paris: Gallimard, 1948), 9-30.

7. Sartre, *Les Mots* (Paris: Gallimard, 1964), pp. 66, 55. His final verdict is even more severe: "I detest my childhood and all that has survived from it" (p. 137).

8. Ibid., pp. 46, 53. On the literary atmosphere of Sartre's childhood see also his interview with Olivier Todd in *The Listener,* 6 June 1957, p. 915.

9. Paul Nizan, *Aden-Arabie* (Paris: François Maspero, 1967), p. 53.

10. A portrait of Herr during his tenure at the Ecole Normale can be found in Hubert Bourgin, *De Jaurès à Léon Blum: L'Ecole Normale et la politique* (Paris: Arthème Fayard, 1938), pp. 104-132; for a discussion of Herr's last years and the circumstances of his death see Charles Andler, *Vie de Lucien Herr* (Paris: Editions Rieder, 1932), pp. 310-311.

11. Gustave Lanson, *Histoire de la littérature française,* 21st ed. (Paris: Hachette, [1929]), p. ix.

12. Alain, *Politique,* ed. Michel Alexandre (Paris: Presses Universitaires de France, 1962), pp. 110, 138. Concerning the influence of Alain on Sartre's generation see Raymond Aron, "Alain et la politique," in *Études politiques* (Paris: Gallimard, 1972), pp. 75-84; and Simone de Beauvoir, *La Force de l'âge* (Paris: Gallimard, 1960), p. 20.

13. Beauvoir, *Mémoires d'une jeune fille rangée* (Paris: Gallimard, 1958), p. 310.

14. Ibid., p. 335.

15. Léon Brunschvicg, *La Modalité du jugement,* 3d ed. (Paris: Presses Universitaires de France, 1964), p. 235; Sartre, "Une Idée fondamentale de la phénoménologie de Husserl: L'Intentionalité," in *Situations,* I (Paris: Gallimard, 1947), 31-32.

16. Jean Wahl, *Vers le concret: Études d'histoire de la philosophie contemporaine* (Paris: Vrin, 1932), p. 2.

17. Sartre, *L'Imagination,* 7th ed. (Paris: Presses Universitaires de France, 1969), p. 3 (first published in 1936).

18. Raymond Aron, who was close to Sartre during this formative period, believes that "what he found in Husserl and Heidegger was above all a vocabulary. His ideas were already there; what he needed was terms for them." Interview with Raymond Aron, Cambridge, Mass., 11 April 1974. On Sartre's Cartesianism see his interview with Pierre Lorquet, *Mondes Nouveaux,* no. 2 (21 Dec. 1944), 3. Sartre discusses "opaqueness" in *L'Etre et le néant: Essai d'ontologie phénoménologique* (Paris: Gallimard, 1943), pp. 33-34.

19. Sartre, *La Transcendance de l'ego: Esquisse d'une description phénoménologique,* ed. Sylvie Le Bon (Paris: Vrin, 1965), p. 87; Beauvoir, *La Force de l'âge,* p. 35.

20. Beauvoir, *La Force de l'âge,* p. 21.

21. Ibid., pp. 213, 136, 37. Sartre, Beauvoir remarks, "found society loathsome as it was, but did not dislike loathing it." *Mémoires d'une jeune fille rangée*, p. 340.

22. Beauvoir, *La Force de l'âge,* p. 22.

23. Sartre, *La Nausée* (Paris: Gallimard, 1938), pp. 166, 221, 222.

24. Sartre, *Les Mots*, p. 210.

25. Sartre, "Paul Nizan," in *Situations,* IV: *Portraits* (Paris: Gallimard, 1964), 147.

26. Nizan describes Lange, an ex-*normalien* who "always held himself aloof from adventures," planning a novel that anticipates *La Nausée.* "He imagined a book that would describe . . . the relations of a man with a city where people would merely be stage props, that would talk about a man alone, truly alone, like a desert island." *Le Cheval de Troie* (Paris: Gallimard, 1935), pp. 164, 105-106.

27. Interview with Henry Magnan in *Le Monde,* 1 June 1955. See also Sartre's interview with Michel Contat in *Situations,* X (Paris: Gallimard, 1976), 175-179. Sartre's activities during this period are discussed by Beauvoir in *La Force de l'âge*, p. 448.

28. Beauvoir, *La Force de l'âge,* p. 442.

29. Sartre, "Une Idée fondamentale de la phénoménologie de Husserl," p. 35; *La Nausée,* p. 16.

30. Interview with Jean-Paul Sartre, Paris, 22 June 1974.

31. Sartre paints a vivid picture of camp life in his novel *La Mort dans l'âme* (Paris: Gallimard, 1949), pp. 211-281. See also his interview with Claire Vervin, *Les Lettres Françaises* (2 Dec. 1944), 3.

32. Sartre, "Forgers of Myths: The Young Playwrights of France," *Theatre Arts,* 30 (June 1946), 330.

33. Sartre, *Bariona* (Paris: Editions Elisabeth Marescot, 1967), pp. 114,115.

34. Interview with Sartre, 22 June 1974.

35. Beauvoir, *La Force de l'âge,* p. 493.

36. *La France Libre,* 15 June 1941, rpt. in Raymond Aron, *De l'armistice à l'insurrection nationale* (Paris: Gallimard, 1945), p. 91.

37. Sartre, "Paris sous l'occupation," in *Situations,* III (Paris: Gallimard, 1949), 28. For an appraisal of the French mood in defeat see H. R. Kedward, *Resistance in Vichy France: A Study of Ideas and Motivation in the Southern Zone, 1940-1942* (London: Oxford University Press, 1978), pp. 1-46.

38. Pierre Audiat, *Paris pendant la guerre, 1940-1944* (Paris: Hachette, 1946), p. 22. On German expectations see Otto Abetz, *Das offene Problem: Ein Rückblick auf zwei Jahrzehnte deutscher Frankreichspolitik* (Cologne: Greven Verlag, 1951), esp. pp. 122-131.

39. Among many statements of the need for collaboration, see Marcel Déat, "L'Intérêt allemand," *L'Oeuvre,* 19 Aug. 1940; and Pierre Drieu la Rochelle, "Ne plus attendre," *La Gerbe,* 10 Oct. 1940. A general assessment of the collaborationist rationale is presented in Pascal Ory, *Les Collaborateurs, 1940-1945* (Paris: Editions du Seuil, 1976), pp. 36-53.

40. Jacques Benoist-Méchin, *La Moisson de quarante: Journal d'un prisonnier de guerre* (Paris: Albin Michel, 1941), p. 183. Benoist-Méchin joined the Vichy government under Admiral Darlan in February 1941 as secretary of

state for Franco-German relations. The writer Jacques Chardonne offered grounds for similar hopes in his "L'Eté à La Maurie," in *Chronique privée de l'année 1940* (Paris: Stock, 1941).

41. Vercors [Jean Bruller], "Conférence demandée par les universités américaines à l'auteur du *Silence de la mer*," in *Le Silence de la mer* (Paris: Club des Libraires de France, 1964), p. 127.

42. Vercors, *Le Silence de la mer*, pp. 74, 66-67, 94.

43. On the heightening of tension between the German Occupation forces and the French see Henri Noguères et al., *Histoire de la Résistance en France de 1940 à 1945*, II: *L'Armée de l'ombre* (Paris: Robert Laffont, 1969), 69-85, 129-134.

44. Beauvoir, *La Force de l'âge*, p. 496.

45. Maurice Merleau-Ponty, "La Guerre a eu lieu," in *Sens et non-sens* (Paris: Nagel, 1966), p. 266.

46. Beauvoir, *La Force de l'âge*, p. 514.

47. Interview with Sartre, 22 June 1974. On Bloch's Resistance activities see Georges Altman, "Avant-propos," in Bloch, *L'Etrange Défaite: Témoignage écrit en 1940* (Paris: Armand Colin, 1957), pp. 11-18; and Lucien Febvre, *Combats pour l'histoire* (Paris: Armand Colin, 1965), pp. 405-407.

48. Pétain, *Paroles aux Français, 1934-41*, p. 124; Sartre, "Jean-Paul Sartre à Berlin: Discussion autour des *Mouches*," *Verger*, no. 5 (March 1948), 111.

49. Lucien Rebatet, *Les Décombres* (Paris: Denoël, 1942), p. 542. More than 50,000 copies of the book were sold during the first year of publication, and Rebatet received a flood of mail supporting his views. See Rebatet, *Les Mémoires d'un fasciste,* II: *1941-1947* (Paris: Jean-Jacques Pauvert, 1976), 61-65, 79.

50. For a discussion of political allegory in *Les Mouches* see Philip Thody, *Sartre: A Biographical Introduction* (London: Studio Vista, 1971), pp. 62-63.

51. Sartre, *Les Mouches*, in *Théâtre*, I (Paris: Gallimard, 1947), 84: Merleau-Ponty, "*Les Mouches*," *Confluences*, no. 25 (Sept.-Oct. 1943), 515.

52. Edith Thomas in *La Résistance intellectuelle*, ed. Jacques Debû-Bridel (Paris: Julliard, 1970), pp. 60-61; Gabriel Péri in *Deux Voix françaises: Péguy Péri*, ed. André Rousseaux (Paris: Editions de Minuit, 1944), p. 73; Guéhenno, *Journal des années noires*, p. 60 (diary entry for 30 Nov. 1940).

53. Paul Eluard, "Courage," *Les Lettres Françaises*, no. 3 (January-February 1943); rpt. in Eluard, *Oeuvres complètes*, ed. Marcelle Dumas and Lucien Scheler (Paris: Gallimard, 1968), I, 1230-1231. Beauvoir, *La Force de l'âge*, p. 584.

54. *Combat*, in its third issue (May 1942), had already censured Pétain for having "handed over the products of our factories and mines to the enemy, furnished Hitler with the manpower he lacks." Raymond Aron analyzed German aims with remarkable insight in a series of articles published by *La France Libre* during the Occupation and reprinted in *De l'armistice à l'insurrection nationale*, pp. 47-59, 103-116, 224-235, 284-295. See also Jean-Marie d'Hoop, "La Main-d'oeuvre française au service de l'Allemagne," *Revue d'Histoire de la Deuxième Guerre Mondiale*, no. 81 (Jan. 1971), 73-88.

55. Interview with Sartre, 22 June 1974. For the origins of *Les Lettres Françaises* see Jacques Debû-Bridel, "Naissance des *Lettres Françaises*" and

Claude Morgan, "Vingt-trois mois d'action: Comment vécurent *Les Lettres Françaises"* in the 9 Sept. 1944 issue of *Les Lettres Françaises.* The subsequent fortunes of the paper up to the Liberation are described in Louis Parrot, *L'Intelligence en guerre: Panorama de la pensée française dans la clandestinité* (Paris: La Jeune Parque [1945]), pp. 229-277.

56. *Les Lettres Françaises,* no. 2 (Oct. 1942); no. 1 (1 Sept. 1942).

57. François Mauriac, *Le Cahier noir,* in *Oeuvres complètes* (Paris: Arthème Fayard, [1952]), XI, 365. *Le Cahier noir* was originally published during the Occupation by Les Editions de Minuit.

58. Drieu la Rochelle, "Bilan," *La Nouvelle Revue Française,* no. 347 (Jan. 1943), 105; Sartre, *Les Lettres Françaises,* no. 6 (April 1943); *Les Lettres Françaises,* no. 11 (Nov. 1943) and no. 14 (March 1944). Drieu, who felt himself a "hunted prophet," attempted to justify his role in "Entre l'hiver et le printemps," *La Nouvelle Revue Française,* no. 338 (April 1942), 468-479. On Drieu's collaboration see Lionel Richard, "Drieu la Rochelle et la *Nouvelle Revue Française* des années noires," *Revue d'Histoire de la Deuxième Guerre Mondiale,* no. 97 (Jan. 1975), 67-84.

59. *Les Lettres Françaises,* no. 12 (Dec. 1943); no. 7 (15 June 1943).

60. Thomas in *La Résistance intellectuelle,* p. 63. A full list of works published, including contributions from Aragon, Eluard, Gide, and Mauriac, can be found in Jacques Debû-Bridel, *Les Editions de Minuit: Historique et bibliographie* (Paris: Editions de Minuit, 1945), pp. 93-96.

61. "Manifeste des Editions de Minuit," in Vercors, *Le Silence de la mer,* pp. 121, 122; Vercors, *La Bataille du silence* (Paris: Presses de la Cité, 1967), p. 189. Vercors emphasized this point in "Permanence de la pensée française," *La Revue de Paris,* no. 25 (Dec. 1945), 15-27. See also J. H. King, "Language and Silence: Some Aspects of French Writing and the French Resistance," *European Studies Review,* 2 (July 1972), 227-238.

62. Pierre Dunoyer de Segonzac, *Le Vieux Chef: Mémoires et pages choisies* (Paris: Editions du Seuil, 1971), p. 80. The "national revolution" during its early phase is well described in Henri Michel, *Vichy année 40* (Paris: Robert Laffont, 1966), pp. 103-151.

63. *Les Lettres Françaises,* no. 1 (1 Sept. 1942).

64. Les Editions de Minuit, for example, invoking Péguy's "intransigent and revolutionary patriotism," published a collection of excerpts from his writings accompanied by selections from Gabriel Péri in June 1944. *Péguy Péri,* p. 17.

65. Sartre, *Esquisse d'une théorie des émotions* (Paris: Hermann, 1939), pp. 35-39.

66. Sartre, *L'Etre et le néant,* p. 641.

67. Ibid., pp. 99, 98.

68. Ibid. pp. 660, 657-658. As Sartre wrote in 1946: "The free choice that a person makes of himself is rigorously the same as what is called his destiny." *Baudelaire* (Paris: Gallimard, 1947), p. 224.

69. Sartre observed in 1945: "What is common to art and ethics is that in both we have creation and invention." *L'Existentialisme est un humanisme* (Paris: Editions Nagel, 1946), p. 77.

70. Sartre, "Qu'est-ce qu'un collaborateur?" in *Situations,* III, 51-52. For an excellent discussion of the motives leading to collaboration see Stanley

Hoffmann, "Self-Ensnared: Collaboration with Nazi Germany," in *Decline or Renewal? France since the 1930's* (New York: Viking Press, 1974), pp. 26-44.

71. Sartre, "Qu'est-ce qu'un collaborateur?" p. 60. Among the many studies of Sartre's ethical system, see Francis Jeanson, *Le Problème moral et la pensée de Sartre* (Paris: Editions du Seuil, 1965), pp. 233-294; and Mary Warnock, *Existentialist Ethics* (London: Macmillan, 1967), pp. 18-52.

72. Emmanuel d'Astier de la Vigerie in *The Sorrow and the Pity*, filmscript trans. Mireille Johnston (New York: Outerbridge and Lazard, 1972), p. 118; Sartre, "La République du silence" (1945), in *Situations*, III, 14.

73. Beauvoir, *Le Sang des autres* (Pans: Gallimard, 1945), p. 222.

74. Vercors, *La Bataille du silence*, pp. 331-332. Vercors expressed similar sentiments shortly after the Liberation in his article "Nous avons été heureux," *Les Lettres Françaises*, 30 Sept. 1944.

2. LIBERATION

1. Simone de Beauvoir, *La Force des choses* (Paris: Gallimard, 1963), p. 13.

2. Jean-Paul Sartre, "Un Jour de victoire parmi les balles," *Combat*, 4 Sept. 1944; Albert Camus, "Le Sang et la liberté," *Combat*, 24 Aug. 1944.

3. *Combat*, Sept. 1942, rpt. in *Les Idées politiques et sociales de la Résistance*, ed. Henri Michel and Boris Mirkine-Guetzévitch (Paris: Presses Universitaires de France, 1954), p. 144. Spiritual revolution was a common theme in the Resistance press. "It is not a class that we must overcome," wrote one observer in March 1944, "but a spirit . . . We must strike down the bourgeois spirit—timid, chilly, and self-centered." Robert Salmon in *Cahiers de Défense de la France* (March 1944), rpt. in *Les Idées politiques et sociales de la Résistance*, p. 156.

4. *Le Franc-Tireur*, 1 March 1944.

5. Sartre, "La Libération de Paris: Une Semaine d'apocalypse," *Clartés*, no. 9 (24 Aug. 1945); Léon Blum, *A l'échelle humaine,* in *L'Oeuvre* (Paris: Albin Michel, 1955), V, 488.

6. Interview with Henri Frenay, Neuilly-sur-Seine, 14 April 1977.

7. "Programme d'action de la Résistance," in René Hostache, *Le Conseil National de la Résistance* (Paris: Presses Universitaires de France, 1958), pp. 458, 459, 461.

8. "Programme d'action de la Résistance," pp. 461-462. For a discussion of Resistance attitudes toward civil liberties, see Gilbert Ziebura, "Idee der Demokratie in der französischen Widerstandsbewegung," in *Zur Geschichte und Problematik der Demokratie: Festgabe für Hans Herzfeld* (Berlin: Duncker und Humblot, 1958), pp. 355-374. Concerning Vichy legislation and its influence on Resistance thinking, see Stanley Hoffman, "The Effects of World War II on French Society and Politics," *French Historical Studies*, 2 (Spring 1961), 28-43; and Robert O. Paxton, *Vichy France: Old Guard and New Order, 1940-1944* (New York: Alfred A. Knopf, 1972), pp. 210-220.

9. "Programme d'action de la Résistance," p. 462. The corresponding Popular Front demands may be found in the "Programme commun" in Léon Blum, *L'Oeuvre*, IV, i (Paris: Albin Michel, 1964), 227.

10. The one concrete proposal, made in section 3, was that the Office du Blé created by the Blum government in 1936 be expanded to assure protection to all farmers (p. 462).

11. Charles de Gaulle, "Discours prononcé à l'Albert Hall, Londres," in *Discours et Messages*, I: *Pendant la guerre, juin 1940-janvier 1946* (Paris: Plon, 1970), 238. The speech was delivered on 11 November 1942.

12. De Gaulle, "Discours prononcé à la radio de Londres," in *Discours et messages*, I, 4. The General's distrust of the metropolitan Resistance, tempered by admiration for its achievements, is evident throughout his memoirs. Its early operations appeared to him motivated by "romanticism and levity" rather than by any "more serious purpose." *Mémoires de guerre*, I: *L'Appel*, 1940-1942 (Paris: Plon, 1954), 128-129.

13. Stanley Hoffmann, "The Hero as History: De Gaulle's *War Memoirs*," in *Decline or Renewal? France Since the 1930's* (New York: Viking Press, 1974), p. 188.

14. De Gaulle, "Intervention du général de Gaulle à la séance de l'Assemblée Consultative Provisoire," *Discours et messages*, I, 365. These remarks were delivered in Algiers on 10 January 1944. For de Gaulle's maneuverings with the parties of the Third Republic, see his own account in *Mémoires de guerre*, II: *L'Unité, 1942-1944* (Paris: Plon, 1956), 149-186. The view of a critical eyewitness may be found in Henri Frenay, *La Nuit finira: Mémoires de Résistance, 1940-1945* (Paris: Robert Laffont, 1973), pp. 409-430.

15. De Gaulle, *Mémoires de guerre*, III: *Le Salut, 1944-1946* (Paris: Plon, 1959), 95. For an assessment of de Gaulle's attitude toward reform measures see Henri Michel, *Les Courants de pensée de la Résistance* (Paris: Presses Universitaires de France, 1962), pp. 98-107.

16. Léo Hamon in *La Vérité sur la libération de Paris*, ed. Francis Crémieux (Paris: Pierre Belfond, 1971), p. 19. The best general account of the Paris uprising remains that of Adrien Dansette, *Histoire de la libération de Paris* (Paris: Fayard, [1966]), esp. pp. 65-242.

17. The proclamation appears in full in Robert Aron, *Histoire de la libération de la France, juin 1944-mai 1945* (Paris: Arthème Fayard, 1959), p. 415.

18. Sartre, "L'Insurrection," *Combat*, 28 Aug. 1944; "Colère d'une ville," *Combat*, 30 Aug. 1944; "La Naissance d'une insurrection," *Combat*, 29 Aug. 1944.

19. De Gaulle, *Mémoires de guerre*, II, 317. For an eyewitness account of the *fête populaire* that accompanied Leclerc's arrival in Paris see Pierre Audiat, *Paris pendant la guerre, 1940-1944* (Paris: Hachette, 1946), pp. 325-327.

20. *Combat*, 8 Oct. 1944.

21. Emmanuel d'Astier de la Vigerie, *Sept Fois sept jours* (Paris: Editions de Minuit, 1947), p. 215. An ordinance of 22 June 1944, issued in Algiers, provided for the suppression of the collaborationist press. But for the most part "the government ratified, rather than directed, the occupation of newspaper

buildings, which were divided among Resistance papers on the basis of informal agreements they had made among themselves." Peter Novick, *The Resistance versus Vichy* (London: Chatto and Windus, 1968), p. 117.

22. "Critique de la nouvelle presse," *Combat,* 31 Aug. 1944. Camus expanded this conception of the liberated press in "Le Journalisme critique," *Combat,* 8 Sept. 1944 and "Autocritique," *Combat,* 22 Nov. 1944. All three articles rpt. in *Essais,* ed. Roger Quilliot and Louis Faucon (Paris: Gallimard, 1965), pp. 263-268.

23. Marc Bloch paints a very damning portrait of the prewar press in *L'Etrange Défaite* (Paris: Armand Colin, 1957), pp. 186-188, 211-212. On the influence of "monied interests" on French journalism during this period see Jean-Noël Jeanneney, "Sur la vénalité du journalisme financier entre les deux guerres," *Revue Française de Science Politique,* 25 (Aug. 1975), 717-738.

24. Sartre, "Réponse à Albert Camus," *Situations,* IV: *Portraits* (Paris: Gallimard, 1964), 111. For Camus and the role of *Combat* in the underground movement see Marie Granet and Henri Michel, *Combat: Histoire d'un mouvement de résistance* (Paris: Presses Universitaires de France, 1957), pp. 133-149.

25. Camus, "Préface" (1957) preceding *L'Envers et l'endroit,* in *Essais,* pp. 6, 13. Camus further discusses his childhood in the essay "Entre oui et non," *Essais,* pp. 23-30. See also Herbert R. Lottman, *Albert Camus: A Biography* (New York: Doubleday, 1979), pp. 14-59.

26. Sartre, "Explication de *L'Etranger,*" in *Situations,* I (Paris: Gallimard, 1947), 110; Camus, *"La Nausée* de Jean-Paul Sartre," in *Essais,* p. 1419. Camus's review of the novel originally appeared in *Alger Républicain,* 20 Oct. 1938.

27. Camus, "Quatrième lettre," in *Essais,* pp. 239-240, 241.

28. Camus to Roland Barthes, 11 Jan. 1955, rpt. in *Théâtre, récits, nouvelles,* ed. Roger Quilliot (Paris: Gallimard, 1962), pp. 1973-1974; Beauvoir, *La Force des choses,* p. 18.

29. *Combat,* 1 Oct. 1944; 24 Nov. 1944.

30. Among many examples of this rhetoric built on antitheses, see the editorial in *Combat,* 6 Oct. 1944: "For us there is now only one war—the war for truth; during the long years ahead we will feel weakened by duplicity, and strengthened only by the the harsh light of sincerity." Antecedents of this style can be found in the writings of the eighteenth-century *moraliste* Nicolas de Chamfort, for whom Camus expressed admiration. See Camus, "Introduction aux *Maximes* de Chamfort" (1944), in *Essais,* pp. 1099-1109.

31. *Combat,* 9 Feb. 1945; 11 Nov. 1944. The CNR, meeting in plenary session in February 1945, voted a resolution stating that it "declines all responsibility for certain political difficulties that exist in France," because it "has exercised no legal or administrative power in the country since August 25, 1944." *Combat,* 27 Feb. 1945.

32. *Combat,* 29 Sept. 1944; de Gaulle, quoted in Jacques Chastenet, *Un Monde nouveau, 1944-1970* (Paris, Librairie Tallandier, 1970), p. 29. On economic conditions in France during the early months of the Liberation see Georgette Elgey, *La République des illusions, 1945-1951, ou la vie secrète de la IVᵉ République* (Paris: Arthème Fayard, 1965), esp. pp. 56-59.

33. *Combat,* 18 Feb. 1945.

34. Mounier, "La Grande Colère des administrés," *Combat*, 13 Jan. 1945; *Combat*, 20 Jan. 1945. Immediately after the Liberation Camus had referred to the same problem: "Men who have proven admirable in clandestine work may not be suited to occupy ministerial posts. But we have no choice; we must risk new men." *Combat*, 9 Sept. 1944.

35. *Combat*, 16 Jan. 1945.

36. The intellectuals' condemnation of private vengeance is exemplified in Paul Eluard's moving poem "Comprenne qui voudra," *Les Lettres Françaises*, no. 32 (2 Dec. 1944), rpt. in *Oeuvres complètes*, I (Paris: Gallimard, 1965), p. 1261. Pierre Mendès-France has described the doubtful legal procedures used at his 1942 trial for desertion in *Liberté, liberté chérie* (Paris: Arthème Fayard, 1977), pp. 181-205.

37. *Combat*, 22 Aug. 1944.

38. See, for example, Claude Morgan's editorial "La Justice de France," *Les Lettres Françaises*, no. 15 (April 1944); "Now that Pucheu has been executed, the task of justice must be pursued against Flandin, Peyrouton, Boisson, and the other traitors."

39. *Le Figaro*, 17 Oct. 1944, rpt. in Mauriac, *Le Bâillon dénoué après quatre ans de silence,* in *Oeuvres complètes*, XI (Paris: Arthème Fayard, 1952), 421-422. Among the more important contributions to this polemical exchange are Mauriac's in *Le Figaro*, 19 and 22 Oct. 1944, 4 and 14 Dec. 1944, and 7-8 Jan. 1945; and Camus's in *Combat*, 20 and 25 Oct. 1944, 5 and 16 Dec. 1944, and 11 Jan. 1945.

40. *Combat*, 20 Oct. 1944; Camus, "Tout ne s'arrange pas," *Les Lettres Françaises*, no. 16 (May 1944). This essay and Camus's hostility toward "abstractions" are discussed in Roy Pierce, *Contemporary French Political Thought* (London and New York: Oxford University Press, 1966), pp. 124-127.

41. *Combat*, 20 Oct. 1944; Mauriac, "Une Réponse à *Combat*," *Le Figaro*, 22 Oct. 1944.

42. *Combat*, 18 and 20 Oct. 1944.

43. Robert Brasillach, *Notre Avant-guerre*, in *Une Génération dans l'orage: Mémoires* (Paris: Plon, 1968), p. 241; Jacques Isorni, *Le Procès de Robert Brasillach*, 2nd ed. (Paris: Flammarion, [1956]), p. 29.

44. Isorni, *Le Procès de Robert Brasillach,* p. 122; Beauvoir, "Oeil pour oeil," *Les Temps Modernes*, no. 5 (1 Feb. 1946), 823; *Combat*, 20 Jan. 1945. On Brasillach's attitude toward collaboration and the trial see David L. Schalk, *The Spectrum of Political Engagement: Mounier, Benda, Nizan, Brasillach, Sartre* (Princeton, N.J.: Princeton University Press, 1979), pp. 81-109; and William R. Tucker, *The Fascist Ego: A Political Biography of Robert Brasillach* (Berkeley: University of California Press, 1975), pp. 225-273.

45. Isorni, *Le Procès de Robert Brasillach*, pp. 175, 146, 169. Isorni, who was Brasillach's defense lawyer, presents a complete transcript of the proceedings.

46. Beauvoir, *La Force des choses*, p. 32.

47. *Combat*, 5 Jan. 1945.

48. On the internment of prisoners see Robert Aron, *Histoire de l'épura-*

tion, II: *Des prisons clandestins aux tribunaux d'exception* (Paris: Arthème Fayard, 1969), 119-207. For a brief review of measures taken to restrict the availability of collaborationists' works see Novick, *The Resistance versus Vichy*, pp. 126-131.

49. Among the numerous accounts of Pétain's trial, see esp. Jules Roy, *Le Grand Naufrage* (Paris: Julliard, 1966); for details of Laval's trial and execution see Aron, *Histoire de l'épuration*, II, 534-568, and the verbatim transcript in Maurice Garçon, ed., *Le Procès Laval: Compte rendu sténographique* (Paris: Albin Michel, 1946).

50. *Combat*, 30 Aug. 1945.

51. Camus, "Au Service de l'homme," *Résistance ouvrière*, 14 Dec. 1944, rpt. in *Essais*, pp. 1544-1546.

52. Interview with David Rousset, Paris, 4 Feb. 1977; Rousset, *L'Univers concentrationnaire* (Paris: Editions du Pavois, 1946), pp. 105-106. Rousset's book was awarded the Prix Renaudot for 1946. It appeared in English translation as *The Other Kingdom.*

53. Rousset, *Les Jours de notre mort* (Paris: Editions du Pavois, 1947), p. 760. Among the many other accounts of the camp experience published in France during the late 1940s, see Robert Antelme, *L'Espèce humaine* (Paris: Editions de la Cité Universelle, 1947). An excellent discussion of the camp survivors' difficulty in articulating what they had seen and felt is Claude-Edmonde Magny's "La Parabole de Lazare ou le langage retrouvé," *Esprit*, no. 142 (Feb. 1947), 311-321.

54. Gaëton Picon, "Jean-Paul Sartre et le roman contemporain," *Confluences*, no. 8 (Oct. 1945), 887; Sartre, *Baudelaire* (Paris: Gallimard, 1963), p. 21.

55. Beauvoir, *Pour une morale de l'ambiguïté* (Paris: Gallimard, 1947), p. 23. The essay first appeared in four consecutive issues of *Les Temps Modernes*, no. 14-17 (Nov. 1946-Feb. 1947).

56. Ibid., p. 31; Emile Durkheim, *L'Education morale*, rev. ed. (Paris: Presses Universitaires de France, 1963), p. 56.

57. Beauvoir, *Pour une morale de l'ambiguïté*, p. 82.

58. Ibid., p. 102; Immanuel Kant, *Grundlegung zur Metaphysik der Sitten*, in *Werke*, ed. Ernst Cassirer (Berlin: Bruno Cassirer, 1913), IV, 289.

59. Beauvoir, *Pour une morale de l'ambiguïté*, pp. 218, 219, 198, 199-200, 202-203.

60. Camus to Guy Dumur, quoted in Dumur, "Portrait d'Albert Camus," *Confluences*, no. 32 (July 1944), 65; Beauvoir, "Idéalisme moral et réalisme politique," *Les Temps Modernes*, no. 2 (1 Nov. 1945), 266.

61. Hannah Arendt, *On Revolution* (New York: Viking Press, 1963), p. 268.

62. *Combat*, 11 July 1945. The *Combat* editorial of 14 July 1945 noted pointedly that "one is not a revolutionary or a builder just because one adopts these labels; we still have to prove ourselves."

63. *L'Année politique, 1944-45*, ed. Jean-Baptiste Duroselle et al. (Paris: Le Grand Siècle, [1946]), pp. 246-248. For a description of the proceedings see also Alexander Werth, *France, 1940-1955* (New York: Henry Holt, 1956), pp. 265-266.

64. Vercors [Jean Bruller], *Le Sable du temps* (Paris: Emile Paul Frères,

1946), pp. 114-115; Camus, *La Peste*, in *Théâtre, récits, nouvelles*, p. 1328. Vercors's assessment is echoed in Jean Cassou, *La Mémoire courte* (Paris: Editions de Minuit, 1953), pp. 99-100.

65. De Gaulle, *Mémoires de guerre*, III: *Le Salut, 1944-1946* (Paris: Plon, 1959), 284.

66. Jean Bloch-Michel, *Journal du désordre* (Paris: Gallimard, 1955), p. 10.

3. THE LIMITS OF CHOICE

1. Jean-Marie Domenach, "Objectif inchangé," *Esprit*, no. 128 (Dec. 1946), 919.

2. Albert Camus, "Le Siècle de la peur," *Combat*, 19 Nov. 1946, rpt. in *Essais*, ed. Roger Quilliot and Louis Faucon (Paris: Gallimard, 1965), p. 332; Vercors [Jean Bruller], "La Morale et l'action" (April 1947), in *Plus ou moins homme* (Paris: Albin Michel, 1950), p. 101.

3. Emmanuel Mounier, "Situation du personnalisme," *Esprit*, no. 118 (Jan. 1946), rpt. in *Oeuvres*, III: *1944-1950*, ed. Paulette Mounier-Leclercq (Paris: Editions du Seuil, 1962), p. 193.

4. Vercors, "La Fin et les moyens" (1946), in *Plus ou moins homme*, p. 85.

5. Maurice Merleau-Ponty, "Pour la vérité," *Les Temps Modernes*, no. 4 (Jan. 1946), 599-600, rpt. in *Sens et non-sens* (Paris: Editions Nagel, 1966), pp. 301-302.

6. Merleau-Ponty, "Le Héros, l'homme" (1945), in *Sens et non-sens*, p. 330.

7. Among the many contemporary treatments of this topic see Simone de Beauvoir, "L'Existentialisme et la sagesse des nations," *Les Temps Modernes*, no. 3 (Dec. 1945), 385-404, and "Idéalisme moral et réalisme politique," *Les Temps Modernes*, no. 2 (Nov. 1945), 248-268, both rpt. in Beauvoir, *L'Existentialisme et la sagesse des nations* (Paris: Editions Nagel, 1948); also Camus, "Remarques sur la politique internationale," *Renaissance*, no. 10 (1945), rpt. in *Essais*, pp. 1572-1576.

8. Sartre, "La Liberté cartésienne" (1946), in *Situations*, I (Paris: Gallimard, 1947), 319.

9. Beauvoir, *La Force des choses* (Paris: Gallimard, 1963), pp. 50, 52.

10. Sartre, *L'Existentialisme est un humanisme* (Paris: Editions Nagel, 1962), p. 16. "No sooner do you finish his latest book," the critic Claude-Edmonde Magny complained in 1948, "than he immediately hits you with another." Magny, "Le Temps de la réflexion: Jean-Paul Sartre et la littérature," *Esprit*, April 1948, p. 686.

11. Sartre, *L'Existentialisme est un humanisme*, pp. 55, 22; Sartre, "Pour un théâtre de situations," *La Rue*, no. 12 (Nov. 1947), 8, rpt. in *Les Ecrits de Sartre: Chronologie, bibliographie commentée*, ed. Michel Contat and Michel Rybalka (Paris: Gallimard, 1970), p. 684.

12. Sartre had begun *The Age of Reason* before the war and finished it after

his return from captivity in 1941; *The Reprieve* was written in 1943-1944. Beauvoir's play *Les Bouches inutiles (The Useless Mouths)*, whose first staging coincided with the existentialist offensive, was also a product of the war years.

13. Beauvoir, *La Force de l'âge* (Paris: Gallimard, 1960), pp. 576-577; Sartre, "Présentation," in *Situations*, II: *Qu'est-ce que la littérature?* (Paris: Gallimard, 1948), 28. Originally published in *Les Temps Modernes*, no. 1 (Oct. 1945).

14. Sartre, "Présentation," pp. 23, 28, 16.

15. Sartre recalled the "living fellowship" that bound the group together at the start; only gradually did their diverging views become apparent. "Merleau-Ponty vivant," in *Situations*, IV: *Portraits* (Paris: Gallimard, 1964), 209-210.

16. Sartre, "Présentation," p. 16.

17. Sartre, *L'Etre et le néant: Essai d'ontologie phénoménologique* (Paris: Gallimard, 1943), pp. 317-323, 339.

18. Sartre, "Présentation," p. 29. For an excellent discussion of Sartre's aesthetic theory see Benjamin Suhl, *Jean-Paul Sartre: The Philosopher as a Literary Critic* (New York and London: Columbia University Press, 1970), pp. 47-110.

19. Sartre, "Qu'est-ce qu'écrire?" in *Situations*, II, 72; Sartre, "Pour qui écrit-on?" in *Situations*, II, 197. These essays originally appeared in *Les Temps Modernes*, no. 17-22 (Feb. - July 1947), and were intended to answer the criticism provoked by his "Présentation" of October 1945.

20. Sartre, "Pourquoi écrire?" in *Situations*, II, 105.

21. Sartre, *Huis clos*, in *Théâtre*, I (Paris: Gallimard, 1947), 182; Sartre, *Les Chemins de la liberté*, I: *L'Age de raison* (Paris: Gallimard, 1945), 256; Sartre, *L'Existentialisme est un humanisme*, p. 102.

22. Henri Lefebvre, quoted in Dominique Aury, "Qu'est-ce que l'existentialisme? Bilan d'une offensive," *Les Lettres Françaises*, no. 83 (24 Nov. 1945); Roger Garaudy, "Un Faux Prophète: Jean-Paul Sartre," *Les Lettres Françaises*, no. 88 (28 Dec. 1945). Lefebvre admitted to Aury that he had not read Sartre's postwar fiction, but still insisted that "existentialism fills me with disgust."

23. Jean Kanapa, *L'Existentialisme n'est pas un humanisme* (Paris: Editions Sociales, 1947), pp. 102, 118.

24. Sartre in the filmscript *Sartre*, ed. Alexandre Astruc and Michel Contat (Paris: Gallimard, 1977), p. 83; Sartre, "A propos de l'existentialisme; Mis au point," *Action*, no. 17 (29 Dec. 1944), 11.

25. Mounier, "Débat à haute voix," *Esprit*, 14 (Feb. 1946), 164; Edgar Morin, *Autocritique* (Paris: Editions du Seuil, 1970), p. 78. Annie Kriegel, then a student at the women's Ecole Normale Supérieure de Sèvres, recalls making a pilgrimage to the rue d'Ulm with her Communist classmates in order to see "the last Socialist in France, a dinosaur on the verge of extinction." Interview with Annie Kriegel, Paris, 20 June 1974.

26. Sartre, "Matérialisme et révolution," in *Situations*, III (Paris: Gallimard, 1949), 175. The essay originally appeared in *Les Temps Modernes*, no. 9 and 10, June and July 1946.

27. Ibid., p. 139.

28. Ibid., pp. 184, 199, 194.

29. Ibid., p. 215.

30. Ibid., pp. 216, 224.

31. Merleau-Ponty, "La Querelle de l'existentialisme," in *Sens et non-sens,* p. 126; Sartre, "Merleau-Ponty vivant," in *Situations,* IV, 214.

32. Merleau-Ponty, "La Guerre a eu lieu," in *Sens et non-sens,* pp. 245, 259, 265. The essay was completed in June 1945.

33. Ibid., pp. 267, 266.

34. Merleau-Ponty, "La Querelle de l'existentialisme," p. 125; Merleau-Ponty, *Phénoménologie de la perception* (Paris: Gallimard, 1945), p. xvi.

35. Merleau-Ponty, "Pour la vérité," in *Sens et non-sens,* p. 294; Merleau-Ponty, "La Querelle de l'existentialisme," pp. 141, 125.

36. Merleau-Ponty, "Marxisme et philosophie" (1945), in *Sens et non-sens,* p. 234.

37. Karl Marx, *Nationalökonomie und Philosophie* (1844), in *Die Frühschriften,* ed. Siegfried Landshut (Stuttgart: Alfred Körner Verlag, 1964), pp. 281, 235. Concerning the impact of Marx's early writings on Merleau-Ponty's generation see Mark Poster, *Existential Marxism in Postwar France: From Sartre to Althusser* (Princeton, N.J.: Princeton University Press, 1975), pp. 36-71. An older but still valuable study of the same topic is George Lichtheim, *Marxism in Modern France* (New York and London: Columbia University Press, 1966), pp. 84-102.

38. Marx, "Zur Kritik der Hegelschen Rechtsphilosophie" (1844), in *Die Frühschriften,* p. 216.

39. Merleau-Ponty, "Pour la vérité," p. 287.

40. Arthur Koestler, *The Invisible Writing: The Second Volume of an Autobiography, 1932-42* (London: Macmillan, 1969), p. 480; Merleau-Ponty, *Humanisme et terreur; Essai sur le problème communiste,* 2nd ed. (Paris: Gallimard, 1972), p. 42. For Koestler's break with the Communist party and the writing of *Darkness at Noon,* see *The Invisible Writing,* pp. 464-494. The success of *Darkness at Noon* in France was immense; 400,000 copies were sold, and the book received comment from all quarters in the press.

41. Koestler, *Darkness at Noon,* trans. Daphne Hardy (New York: Macmillan, 1941), pp. 243, 100, 260, 255.

42. Merleau-Ponty, *Humanisme et terreur,* p. 57. Three excerpts from this study, entitled "Le Yogi et le prolétaire" (a reference to Koestler's essay "The Yogi and the Commissar" of 1942) appeared in *Les Temps Modernes,* nos. 13, 14, and 17 (Oct. and Nov. 1946, Jan. 1947).

43. Ibid., pp. 41, 66.

44. Ibid., pp. 13, 71.

45. Ibid., pp. 45, 61. "More exactly," Merleau-Ponty noted, "the Moscow Trials are revolutionary trials presented as if they were ordinary trials" (p. 62).

46. Ibid., pp. 70, 73.

47. Ibid., pp. 129, 139, 125.

48. Ibid., p. 161.

49. Ibid., pp. 161, 153, 163.

50. Ibid., p. 186.

51. Ibid., p. 36; Camus, "Le Choix," *Combat,* 22 April 1947.

52. Jacques Fauvet, *La Quatrième République* (Paris: Club des Libraires de France, 1961), p. 84.

53. For an analysis of this strategy see Annie Kriegel, *Les Communismes au miroir français* (Paris: Gallimard, 1974), pp. 163-176.

54. Maurice Thorez quoted in Fauvet, *La Quatrième République*, p. 78. The maneuvers and motives surrounding the Communists' expulsion from the Ramadier cabinet are discussed in some detail in Georgette Elgey, *La République des illusions, 1945-1951, ou la vie secrète de la IVe République* (Paris: Arthème Fayard, 1965), pp. 246-293.

55. [Merleau-Ponty], "En un combat douteux," *Les Temps Modernes*, no. 26 (Dec. 1947), 462-463.

56. Charles de Gaulle, "Discours prononcé à Vincennes" (5 Oct. 1947),in *Discours et messages*, II: *Dans l'attente, 1946-1958* (Paris: Plon, 1970), 127; Beauvoir, *La Force des choses*, p. 108.

57. François Goguel, "Conjoncture politique du néo-gaullisme," *Esprit*, no. 141 (Dec. 1947), 886.

58. Camus, *La Peste,* in *Théâtre, récits, nouvelles,* ed. Roger Quilliot (Paris: Gallimard, 1962), p. 1215; Camus, *Carnets,* II: *Janvier 1942 - mars 1951,* ed. Francine Camus and Roger Quilliot (Paris: Gallimard, 1964), 72.

59. Camus, *La Peste,* p. 1473. Bloch's critique of French indifference is a major theme in "Examen de conscience," the third section of his *L'Etrange Défaite: Témoignage écrit en 1940* (Paris: Armand Colin, 1957): "In a lazy, cowardly manner we let events take their course" (p. 216).

60. Jean Pouillon, "L'Optimisme de Camus," *Les Temps Modernes*, no. 26 (Nov. 1947), 926. Jean Catesson made a similar critique in "A propos de *La Peste,*" *Cahiers du Sud*, no. 287 (1948), 144-149.

61. On the genesis of *La Peste* see Roger Quilliot's comments in Camus, *Théâtre, récits, nouvelles*, pp. 1935-1943. The earliest notes by Camus concerning his novel can be found in his *Carnets*, I: *Mai 1935-février 1942*, ed. Roger Quilliot (Paris: Gallimard, 1962), 139, 165, 229.

62. Camus's explanation, which appeared in *Combat* in Dec. 1948, is rpt. in *Essais*, p. 391; Camus, *La Peste*, pp. 1474, 1426-1427.

63. Camus, "Où est la mystification? Réponse à d'Astier de la Vigerie," *Caliban*, no. 15 (June 1948), rpt. in *Essais*, p. 356.

64. Camus, *Les Justes,* in *Théâtre, récits, nouvelles*, p. 373. The plot of Camus's play was based on an actual incident that occurred in Saint Petersburg in 1905.

65. Camus, *Les Justes,* p. 339; Camus, "Remarque sur la révolte" (1945), in *Essais*, p. 1692.

66 Camus, *L'Homme révolté,* in *Essais*, pp. 579, 708.

67. Sartre, "Réponse à Albert Camus," in *Situations*, IV, 90, 114; Camus, "Le Siècle de la peur," in *Essais*, p. 331. Concerning the celebrated quarrel between Sartre and Camus see Herbert R. Lottman, *Albert Camus: A Biography* (Garden City and New York: Doubleday, 1979), pp. 495-507, and, for a view more sympathetic to Sartre, Beauvoir, *La Force des choses*, pp. 278-282.

68. Beauvoir, *La Force des choses*, p. 163.

69. Sartre quoted by Beauvoir, ibid., p.165.

70. On Merleau-Ponty's participation in the RDR see Sartre, "Merleau-Ponty vivant," in *Situations*, IV, 223-224.

71. "Appel du Comité pour le Rassemblement Démocratique Révolutionnaire," *Combat*, 27 Feb. 1948, rpt. in *Les Ecrits de Sartre*, ed. Contat and

Rybalka, pp. 197-199. The manifesto also appeared the same day in *Franc-Tireur* and in *Esprit*'s March 1948 issue.

72. Sartre, David Rousset, and Gérard Rosenthal, *Entretiens sur la politique* (Paris: Gallimard, 1949), pp. 13-15; Rousset, "Notre programme," *La Gauche*, 15-30 May 1948.

73. Sartre et al., *Entretiens sur la politique*, p. 165.

74. Ibid., p. 204; Sartre, "La Faim au ventre," *La Gauche*, 15-30 May 1948. The RDR's conception of direct democracy was further developed in *Entretiens sur la politique*, pp. 27-35.

75. Sartre et al., *Entretiens sur la politique*, p. 204.

76. Sartre in an interview with Paul-Louis Mignon, "Le Théâtre de A jusqu'à Z: Jean-Paul Sartre," *L'Avant-Scène Théâtre*, no. 402-403 (1-15 May 1968), 34. For the origins of and first reactions to the play, see Beauvoir, *La Force des choses*, pp. 165-168.

77. Sartre, *Les Mains sales* (Pairis: Gallimard, 1948), p. 257. For a discussion of the play and its parallels with *Les Mouches*, see Philip Thody, *Sartre: A Biographical Introduction* (London: Studio Vista, 1971), pp. 90-94.

78. Camus, "Le Témoin de la liberté" and Sartre, "Il faut que nous menions cette lutte en commun," *La Gauche*, 20 Dec. 1948. Camus's speech rpt. in *Essais*, pp. 397-406. *Franc-Tireur* published an account of the meeting and excerpts from the speeches in its issue of 14 Dec. 1948.

79. Interview with David Rousset, Paris, 4 Feb. 1977.

80. Sartre quoted by Beauvoir, *La Force des choses*, p. 194. For an evaluation of the RDR and its impact on Sartre's thinking see Poster, *Existential Marxism in Postwar France*, pp. 139-144; and Michel-Antoine Burnier, *Les Existentialistes et la politique* (Paris: Gallimard, 1966), pp. 63-75.

81. Sartre in an interview with Robert Kanters, "Deux heures avec Sartre," *L'Express*, 17 Sept. 1959.

82. H. Stuart Hughes, *The Obstructed Path: French Social Thought in the Years of Desperation, 1930-1960* (New York: Harper & Row, 1968), esp. pp. 6-9, 294.

4. THE DILEMMAS OF OPPOSITION

1. Joseph Goebbels, *Goebbels-Reden, I: 1932-1939,* ed. Helmut Heiber (Düsseldorf: Droste Verlag, 1971), 109. Goebbels delivered this speech at the Berlin Opernplatz on 10 May 1933.

2. Gottfried Benn, "Der neue Staat und die Intellektuellen," in *Gesammelte Werke*, IV: *Reden und Vorträge* (Wiesbaden: Limes Verlag, 1968), 1004, 1008; Thomas Mann, "Leiden an Deutschland," in *Werke*, XII: *Reden und Aufsätze* (Frankfurt am Main: S. Fischer Verlag, 1974), 692. Mann noted bitterly at the war's end that if the German intellectual community had "risen as one man against the shame [and] declared a general strike," then "much might have turned out differently." *Werke*, XII, 955.

3. H. Stuart Hughes, *The Sea Change: The Migration of Social Thought,*

1930-1965 (New York: Harper & Row, 1975), p. 18. The German literary critic Manfred Durzak has estimated that nearly 2000 writers went into exile in 41 countries. "Literarische Diaspora: Stationen des Exils," in Durzak, ed., *Die deutsche Exilliteratur, 1933-1945* (Stuttgart: Philipp Reclam Verlag, 1973), p. 40.

4. For one unusally effective example of such broadcasts, see Thomas Mann, "Deutsche Hörer! Fünfundfünfzig Radiosendungen nach Deutschland," in *Werke*, XI, 983-1123. For an eyewitness account of German émigré activities in Moscow during the war see Wolfgang Leonhard, *Die Revolution entlässt ihre Kinder* (Cologne: Kiepenheuer & Witsch, 1955), pp. 282-340.

5. Reinhold Schneider, *Verhüllter Tag* (Cologne: Jakob Hegner Verlag, 1950), p. 99; Rudolf Pechel, *Deutscher Widerstand* (Erlenbach-Zurich: Eugen Rentsch Verlag, 1947), p. 35; Dietrich Bonhoeffer, "Nach zehn Jahren," in *Widerstand und Ergebung: Briefe und Aufzeichnungen aus der Haft,* ed. Eberhard Bethge (Munich: Christian Kaiser Verlag, 1964), p. 16.

6. The term "inner emigration" seems first to have been used by the conservative author Frank Theiss soon after the war's end in an open letter defending those who remained in Germany after 1933: "The world from which we inner German emigrants sought support was an interior realm which Hitler, despite all his efforts, never succeeded in conquering." *Stuttgarter Stimme,* 17 Aug. 1945.

7. *Goebbels-Reden,* I, 121. Speech given to NSDAP party members on 16 June 1933 in Hamburg.

8. Adolf Hitler, *Reden und Proklamationen, 1932-1945,* I: *Triumph (1932-1938),* ed. Max Domarus (Würzburg: Schmidt Neustadt, 1962), 233. In his first proclamation as head of government in February 1933, Hitler promised that an "act of reconciliation" would replace the "heartbreaking fragmentation" of the Weimar years (pp. 194, 191).

9. William L. Shirer, *Berlin Diary: The Journal of a Foreign Correspondent, 1934-1941* (New York: Alfred A. Knopf, 1941), p. 18 (diary entry of 5 Sept. 1934); Hitler, *Mein Kampf* (Munich: Franz Eher Nachfolger, 1932), p. 536.

10. *Goebbels-Reden,* I, 134, 135. Speech delivered on 15 Nov. 1933 in Berlin, inaugurating the Reich Chamber of Culture: "We do not wish to restrict artistic-cultural development, but to promote it. The state wishes to shield it with a protecting hand" (I, 139).

11. Goebbels, quoted in Dietrich Strothmann, *Nationalsozialistische Literaturpolitik: Ein Beitrag zur Publizistik im Dritten Reich* (Bonn: H. Bouvier Verlag, 1960), p. 29; Werner Beumelburg, "Vom deutschen Menschen der Gegenwart," *Deutsche Kultur-Wacht,* 1 July 1933, rpt. in *Literatur und Dichtung im Dritten Reich: Eine Dokumentation,* ed. Joseph Wulf (Gütersloh: Sigbert Mohn Verlag, 1963), p. 150.

12. Hanns Johst, *Schlageter* (Munich: Albert Langen/Georg Müller, 1934), p. 83.

13. Ursula von Kardorff, *Berliner Aufzeichnungen, 1942-1945,* 2nd ed. (Munich: Nymphenburger Verlagshandlung, 1976), p. 48 (diary entry of 12 May 1943).

14. Pechel, *Deutscher Widerstand*, p. 39; Ernst Wiechert, *An die deutsche Jugend: Vier Reden* (Munich: Kurt Desch Verlag, 1951), pp. 50, 71. Wiechert's speech was later parodied by younger critics of the inner emigration in "500. Rede an die deutsche Jugend," *Der Ruf*, no. 1 (15 Aug. 1946), 12.

15. Wiechert, *An die deutsche Jugend*, p.73.

16. Wilhelm von Humboldt, *Gesammelte Schriften*, ed. Albert Leitzmann (Berlin: B. Behr's Verlag, 1903), I, 106; Johann Wolfgang von Goethe, *Wilhelm Meisters Lehrjahre*, in *Werke* (Berlin: Aufbau Verlag, 1962), X, 431.

17. Goethe, "Generalbeichte," in *Werke*, I, 89; Friedrich Percyval von Reck-Malleczewen, *Tagebuch eines Verzweifelten: Zeugnis einer inneren Emigration* (Stuttgart: Harry Goverts Verlag, 1966), p. 186 (diary entry of 9 Oct. 1944).

18. Wiechert, *Jahre und Zeiten*, in *Sämtliche Werke* (Munich: Kurt Desch Verlag, 1957), IX, 689; Wiechert, *Das einfache Leben*, ibid., IV, 370, 501, 424.

19. Wiechert, *Jahre und Zeiten*, pp. 328, 689; Werner Bergengruen, *Schreibtischerinnerungen* (Zurich: Die Arche Verlag, 1961), p. 176.

20. Bergengruen, *Schreibtischerinnerungen*, pp. 203, 201, 200. Some observers saw the rash of political jokes as a diversion from more effective opposition. Reck-Malleczewen noted in July 1944: "I would prefer it if German protesters would expend their energy in training partisans rather than in these mildly witty jokes, which only reflect our misery." *Tagebuch*, p. 179.

21. Pechel, *Deutscher Widerstand*, p. 287. This form of opposition was not without its dangers. The *Deutsche Rundschau* was suppressed in 1942 and Pechel interned in a concentration camp; the *Frankfurter Zeitung* was suppressed the following year.

22. Goebbels, *The Goebbels Diaries*, trans. Louis P. Lochner (New York: Doubleday, 1948), p. 91 (diary entry of 17 Feb. 1942); interview with Walter Dirks, Wittnau bei Freiburg, 30 July 1974. See Rudolf Werber, *Die "Frankfurter Zeitung" und ihr Verhältnis zum Nationalsozialismus* (Bonn: Rheinische Friedrich-Wilhelms-Universität, 1965), esp. pp. 160-172.

23. Ernst Jünger, *In Stahlgewittern*, in *Werke* (Stuttgart: Ernst Klett Verlag, 1960), I, 1955; Jünger, *Der Arbeiter*, in *Werke*, VI, 322; Jünger, *Auf den Marmorklippen*, in *Werke*, IX, 209.

24. Jünger, *Auf den Marmorklippen*, pp. 294, 282, 293. The allegorical dimensions of the novel are examined in J. P. Stern, *Ernst Jünger: A Writer of Our Time* (Cambridge: Bowes and Bowes, 1953), pp. 13-14.

25. Jünger, *Auf den Marmorklippen*, p. 283. Jünger's cyclical conception of history allowed him to view martyrdom as a source of renewal as well. "The human order," he noted, "resembles the cosmos in that from time to time, in order to create itself anew, it must pass through fire" (p. 230). Despite the novel's ambiguities, its message was widely understood. "This highly romantic and symbolic story was for us all the parable of the need for resistance." Alfred Andersch, "Achzig und Jünger," in *Öffentlicher Brief an einen sowjetischen Schriftsteller, das Überholte betreffend* (Zurich: Diogenes Verlag, 1977), p. 93.

26. Hans-Peter Schwartz, *Der konservative Anarchist: Politik und Zeitkritik Ernst Jüngers* (Freiburg im Breisgau: Rombach Verlag, 1962), p.

186; Bonhoeffer, *Ethik* (Munich: Christian Kaiser Verlag, 1962), p. 71. Bonhoeffer's editor and biographer, Eberhard Bethge, dates this portion of the manuscript as having been written in September 1940.

27. Himmler, quoted in Karl Dietrich Bracher, *Die deutsche Diktatur: Entstehung, Struktur, Folgen des Nationalsozialismus* (Cologne: Kiepenheuer & Witsch, 1969), p. 453. Bracher notes that Gestapo arrests in the fall of 1941 rose to 15,000 per month — ten times what they had been in 1935-1936 (p. 454).

28. Ulrich von Hassell, *Vom anderen Deutschland: Aus den nachgelassenen Tagebüchern, 1938-1944* (Zurich: Atlantis Verlag, 1946), pp. 92-93 (diary entry of 19 Oct. 1939); Weisse Rose leaflet reprinted in Inge Scholl, *Die weisse Rose* (Frankfurt am Main: Verlag der Frankfurter Hefte, 1952), p.103.

29. Fabian von Schlabrendorff, *Offiziere gegen Hitler: Nach einem Erlebnisbericht*, ed. Gero von S[chulze-]Gaevernitz (Zurich: Europa Verlag, 1946), p. 21; Moltke to James Curtis, 1942, in Ger van Roon, *German Resistance to Hitler: Count von Moltke and the Kreisau Circle*, trans. Peter Ludlow (London: Von Nostrand Reinhold, 1977), p. 377. Van Roon suggests that Moltke's unfavorable assessment of the French Resistance effort was due to the fact that "there was no organized resistance in France before 1942" (p. 210). But French reluctance to enter into contact with Germans also clearly played a role.

30. Pechel, *Deutscher Widerstand*, p. 46; Scholl, *Die weisse Rose*, p. 91; Hassell, *Vom anderen Deutschland*, p. 255 (diary entry of 14 Feb. 1942).

31. Kardorff, *Berliner Aufzeichnungen*, p. 164 (diary entry of 24 July 1944). The conspirators' dilemma is discussed with notable sympathy and insight by Klaus Epstein in "Germans against Hitler," *Modern Age*, 7 (Winter 1962-63), 82-95.

32. Simone de Beauvoir, *La Force de l'âge* (Paris: Gallimard, 1960), p. 556.

33. Bonhoeffer, quoted in Karl Dietrich Bracher, *Das deutsche Dilemma: Leidenswege der politischen Emanzipation* (Munich: R. Piper Verlag, 1971), p. 171; Helmuth von Moltke to Freya von Moltke, 10 Jan. 1945, in *A German of the Resistance: The Last Letters of Count Helmuth James von Moltke* (London: Oxford University Press, 1948), pp. 59-60.

34. Report of the Kreisau Conference of 22-25 May 1942, in van Roon, *German Resistance to Hitler*, p. 329; Moltke to Curtis, 1942, ibid., p. 376.

35. Bonhoeffer, *Widerstand und Ergebung*, p. 27.

36. Bonhoeffer, *Ethik*, pp. 60, 238, 240.

37. Bonhoeffer to Eberhard Bethge, 22 Dec. 1943, in *Widerstand und Ergebung*, p. 129; Bonhoeffer, *Ethik*, pp. 16, 238, 263. Like Camus and Beauvoir, Bonhoeffer rejected an "abstract ethics," but his concept of "representative" responsibility remained in some ways as abstract as Beauvoir's "concrete humanism." See Larry L. Rasmussen, *Dietrich Bonhoeffer: Reality and Resistance* (Nashville: Abingdon Press, 1972), pp. 149-173.

38. Bonhoeffer, *Widerstand und Ergebung*, p. 31.

39. Interview with Walter Dirks, 30 July 1974; Bergengruen, "In dieser Zeit," *Dies Irae* (Zurich: Die Arche Verlag, 1946), p. 16. On verse as a vehicle for dissent, see Charles W. Hoffmann, *Opposition Poetry in Nazi Germany* (Berkeley: University of California Press, 1962), pp. 1-16.

40. Schneider, *Die letzten Tage* (Zurich: Die Arche Verlag, 1945), p. 31;

Schneider, *Apokalypse* (Baden-Baden: Hans Bühler Verlag, 1946), p. 24; Schneider, "Nun stirbt das Volk," *Die Sonette* (Cologne: Jakob Hegner Verlag, 1954), p. 99.

41. Bergengruen, *Schreibtischerinnerungen*, p. 205.

42. Bonhoeffer, *Widerstand und Ergebung*, p. 27.

43. Camus, "La Lutte continue," *Combat*, 21 Aug. 1944; Wolfdietrich Schnurre, "Warum ich nicht wie Swift schreibe," in *Fünfzehn Autoren suchen sich selbst: Modell und Provokation*, ed. Uwe Schulz (Munich: Paul List Verlag, 1967), p. 28.

44. Günter Eich, "Der Schriftsteller 1947," in *Werke*, IV: *Vermischte Schriften* (Frankfurt am Main: Suhrkamp Verlag, 1973), 394; Wolfgang Borchert, *Das Gesamtwerk* (Hamburg: Rowohlt Verlag, 972), pp. 54, 229.

45. Karl Kraus, *Die dritte Walpurgisnacht* (Munich: Kösel Verlag, 1952), p. 11; Hitler, *Mein Kampf*, p. 202. Popular feeling, Hitler noted, "is not complicated, but extremely simple and consistent. There are not many differentiations; positive or negative, love or hate, right or wrong, truth or lies, but never half this way and half that" (p. 201).

46. Moltke, memorandum of 24 April 1941, in van Roon, *German Resistance to Hitler*, p. 319; Gustav René Hocke, "Deutsche Kalligraphie," *Der Ruf*, no. 7 (15 Nov. 1946), 10. Two classic studies of the Nazi impact on the German language are Victor Klemperer, *LTI: Notizbuch eines Philologen* (Berlin: Aufbau Verlag, 1947), and Dolf Sternberger et al., *Aus dem Wörterbuch des Unmenschen* (Hamburg: Claassen Verlag, 1957).

47. Borchert, "Das ist unser Manifest," in *Das Gesamtwerk*, p. 310.

48. One observer wrote in 1946: "This spiritual 'isolation' is revealed as a sudden turning toward what is essential, toward absolute truth, toward self-evident values . . . The impulse toward essentials is expressed most clearly in the poetry of the young." Heinz-Winfried Sabais, "Die Situation der jungen Dichtung," *Deutsche Rundschau*, 69 (Oct. 1946), 77.

49. Hans Werner Richter, "Lyrik der Kreigsgefangenen," *Der Ruf*, no. 3 (15 Sept. 1946), 9.

50. Heinrich Sponsel, "Heimweh," in *Deine Söhne, Europa: Gedichte Deutscher Kriegsgefangener*, ed. Hans Werner Richter (Munich: Nymphenburger Verlagshandlung, 1947), p. 94. An example of this mood of doubt is E. Wörner's poem "Verzweiflung," written in a French POW camp and published in *Deine Söhne, Europa*, p. 105. The first stanza reads:

> My heart gives me no solace.
> Wherever I look I find no meaning;
> I feel bitterly that I am a prisoner
> And restlessness steals all peace from me.

51. Eich, *Werke*, I: *Die Gedichte* (Frankfurt am Main: Suhrkamp Verlag, 1973), 35. "Inventur" is modeled on an earlier poem by Richard Weiner entitled "Jean-Baptiste Chardin" (1916). The German text of Eich's poem reads as follows:

Dies ist meine Mütze,
dies ist mein Mantel,
hier mein Rasierzeug
im Beutel aus Leinen.

Konservenbüchse:
Mein Teller, mein Becher,
ich hab in das Weissblech
den Namen geritzt.

Geritzt hier mit diesem
kostbaren Nagel,
den vor begehrlichen
Augen ich berge.

Im Brotbeutel sind
ein Paar wollene Socken
und einiges, was ich
niemand verrate,

so dient er als Kissen
nachts meinem Kopf.
Die Pappe hier liegt
zwischen mir und der Erde.

Die Bleistiftmine
lieb ich am meisten:
Tags schreibt sie mir Verse,
die nachts ich erdacht.

Dies ist mein Notizbuch,
dies meine Zeltbahn,
dies ist mein Handtuch,
dies ist mein Zwirn.

52. Eich, *Werke*, IV, 441.

53. Ibid., p. 389.

54. Six of Eich's radio plays from the period 1932-1937 are contained in his *Werke*, II: *Die Hörspiele*, 9-133, including a "Weizenkantate" (1936) that shows clear signs of Brecht's influence. Eich's silence during the war was prompted also by *Wehrmacht* regulations against writing.

55. Wiechert, *Das einfache Leben*, p. 525; Jünger, *Kirschhorster Blätter*, in *Werke*, III, 325 (diary entry of 20 Oct. 1944).

56. Eich, *Werke*, I, 10.

57. Ibid., I, 33; IV, 392; I, 36, 30-31, 30, 38

58. Böll, "Die Stimme Wolfgang Borcherts," in *Deutsche Literaturkritik der Gegenwart*, IV, pt. 1, ed. Hans Mayer (Stuttgart: Goverts Krüger Stahlberg Verlag, 1971), 463. An early example of the Borchert cult among the young is Günter Bruno Fuchs, *Der verratene Messias: Essay um den Dichter Wolfgang Borchert* (Düsseldorf: Fladung Verlag, [1953]).

59. Borchert, "Die Blume," in Peter Rühmkorf, *Wolfgang Borchert in Selbstzeugnissen und Bilddokumenten* (Reinbek bei Hamburg: Rowohlt Verlag, 1961), pp. 67-68.

60. Borchert, "Die Hundeblume," in *Das Gesamtwerk*, p. 25.

61. Ibid.

62. Ibid., pp. 33, 39.

63. Urs Widmer, *1945 oder die "Neue Sprache": Studien zur Prosa der "Jungen Generation"* (Düsseldorf: Pädagogischer Verlag Schwann, 1966), p. 197. For a brief discussion of Borchert's debt to Expressionism see Hans Mayer, *Zur deutschen Literatur der Zeit: Zusammenhänge, Schriftsteller, Bücher* (Reinbek bei Hamburg: Rowohlt Verlag, 1967), pp. 301-303. On the links between postwar writing and the immediate past see also Ann L. Mason, "Nazism and Postwar German Literary Style," *Contemporary Literature*, 17 (Winter 1976), 63-83.

64. Borchert, *Das Gesamtwerk*, pp. 81, 311.

65. Ibid., p. 57.

66. Alfred Andersch, "Der Seesack/Aus einer Autobiographie," in *Literaturmagazin, 7: Nachkriegsliteratur*, ed. Nicolas Born and Jürgen Manthey (Reinbek bei Hamburg: Rowohlt Verlag, 1977), pp. 116-117; Richard Brett-Smith, *Berlin '45: The Grey City* (London: Macmillan, 1966), pp. 34, 38.

67. Hitler, quoted in Albert Speer, *Erinnerungen* (Berlin: Propyläen Verlag, 1969), p. 461. The order was given to Field Marshal Jodl on 29 March 1945. Ten days earlier, Hitler had given his so-called Nero Order: "All military, transportation, communication, industrial, and supply installations . . . within the territory of the Reich that the enemy can use for continuing the struggle either now or in the future must be destroyed." *Trial of the Major War Criminals before the International Military Tribunal* (Nuremberg: Secretariat of the Tribunal, 1947), XLI, 430.

68. Speer, *Erinnerungen*, p. 440. On the refusal of Hitler's lieutenants to prepare for defeat see H. R. Trevor-Roper, *The Last Days of Hitler* (New York: Macmillan, 1947), pp. 42-51.

69. Erich Kästner, *Notabene 45: Ein Tagebuch* (Berlin: Cecilie Dressler Verlag, [1962]), p. 196.

70. *Der Aufbau: Organ der Kampfgemeinschaft gegen den Faschismus*, no. 1 (6 May 1945), facsimile reproduced in *Gemeinsam begann es 1945: "Der Aufbau" schrieb das erste Kapitel* (Frankfurt am Main: Röderberg Reprint, 1978).

71. Leonhard, *Die Revolution entlässt ihre Kinder*, pp. 392, 391.

72. Moses Moskowitz, "The Political Reëducation of the Germans: The Emergence of Parties and Politics in Württemberg-Baden (May 1945-June 1946)," *Political Science Quarterly*, 61 (Dec. 1946), 536, 535.

73. The Hamburg program is contained in an excellent study of the Antifa movement, Ulrich Borsdorf et al., *Arbeiterinitiative 1945: Antifaschistische*

Ausschüsse und Reorganisation der Arbeiterbewegung in Deutschland (Wuppertal: Peter Hammer Verlag, 1976), p. 307; *Der Aufbau*, no. 1 (6 May 1945). The scope of Antifa activities was as broad as their mandate was vague. In Marburg "the committee discussed the reactivation of trade unions. It investigated poor-quality work by shoemakers and it ordered the police to close the business of a fortune-teller. It proposed a ban on migration to the city because of the crowded living conditions and the presence of large numbers of American troops. It sought new sources of tax revenue and it reviewed the budget." John Gimbel, *A German Community under American Occupation: Marburg, 1945-52* (Stanford, Stanford University Press, 1961), p. 101.

74. Report quoted in Borsdorf et al., *Arbeiterinitiative 1945*, p. 531. For a discussion of the Antifas' relations with other local authorities in the Stuttgart area see Lutz Neithammer, "Aktivität und Grenzen der Antifa-Ausschüsse 1945: Das Beispiel Stuttgart," *Vierteljahrshefte für Zeitgeschichte*, 23, no. 3 (1975), esp. 298-303.

75. Interview with Oskar Neumann, Munich, 28 March 1977.

76. Leonard Krieger has distinguished between "a pure and a mixed type" of Antifas, the first with no party affiliation, the second a "temporary coalition among preexisting parties." See Krieger, "The Inter-regnum in Germany: March-August 1945," *Political Science Quarterly*, 64 (Dec. 1949), 513-517.

77. *Aufbau*, no. 2 (June 1945). Eleven issues of the paper were published, the last dated January 1946.

78. JCS 1067, in *Documents on Germany under Occupation, 1945-1954*, ed. Beate Ruhm von Oppen (London: Oxford University Press, 1955), p. 17; "Historical Report on the Operations of the Office of Military Government," Office of the Military Governor, U.S. Zone, 1947, quoted in Eugene Davidson, *The Death and Life of Germany: An Account of the American Occupation* (New York: Alfred A. Knopf, 1959), p. 56.

79. Wolfgang Leonhard was given the assignment of disbanding one "lively, exemplary organization" in Berlin as early as mid-May 1945, by his political superior, Walter Ulbricht. *Die Revolution entlässt ihre Kinder*, pp. 393-397.

80. Willy Brandt with Leo Lania, *Mein Weg nach Berlin* (Munich: Kindler Verlag, 1960), pp. 188-189.

5. A FOUNDATION FOR CHANGE

1. Hans Werner Richter, *Briefe an einen jungen Sozialisten* (Hamburg: Hoffmann & Campe, 1974), pp. 92-93; Rudolf Pechel, "Revision der deutschen Legende," *Neue Zeit* (Berlin), 2 Sept. 1945, reprinted in *Deutsche Gegenwart: Aufsätze und Vorträge, 1945-1952* (Darmstadt and Berlin: Im Stichnote Verlag, 1953), pp. 13-17.

2. "Unsere Aufgabe," *Die Zeit*, 21 Feb. 1946.

3. Karl Jaspers, "Geleitwort," *Die Wandlung*, 1 (Nov. 1945), 5; Benno Reifenberg, "Vom Gegenstand der Politik," *Die Gegenwart*, no. 12/13 (24 June 1946), 10.

4. Pierre Courtade, "Un Vichy allemand," *Confluences*, n. s., no. 6 (Aug. 1945), 590, 591.

5. Immanuel Kant, "Beantwortung der Frage: Was ist Aufklärung?" in *Werke*, ed. Ernst Cassirer (Berlin: Bruno Cassirer Verlag, 1913), IV, 169.

6. Hartmann Goertz, "Die Flucht in die Zeitschrift," *Die Neue Zeitung* (Munich), 13 Jan. 1947. For details of American press policies in occupied Germany, see Harold J. Hurwitz, *U.S. Military Government in Germany: Press Reorientation* (Karlsruhe: Historical Division, European Command, 1950), esp. pp. 9-91.

7. "Unsere Aufgabe," *Die Zeit*, 21 Feb. 1946; Jaspers, "Geleitwort," 3.

8. Jaspers, "Geleitwort," 4. The links between the *Frankfurter Zeitung* and this "second generation" of journals are explored in the documentary collection *Als der Krieg zu Ende war: Literarisch-politische Publizistik, 1945-1950,* ed. Bernhard Zeller (Munich: Kösel Verlag, 1974), pp. 64, 79-81, 84-86.

9. "An unsere Leser!," *Frankfurter Hefte*, 1 (April 1946), 2.

10. "Deutsche Publizistik—heute," *Die Gegenwart*, no. 14/15 (24 July 1946), 12; Jaspers, "Geleitwort," 4.

11. "Wortlaut der Erklärung der 'Grossen Drei' auf der Potsdamer Konferenz," *Die Wandlung*, 1 (Nov. 1945), 169-171. The journal *Dokumente*, published in the French Zone by Jean du Riveau, consisted exclusively of documentary material translated for German readers. In introducing the first issue, du Riveau noted: "We in no way intend to take a position; we wish merely to give information . . . through texts, which can serve as a basis for conversation when the time comes." Du Riveau, "Zur Einführung," *Dokumente*, 1 (Sept. 1945), 3.

12. Eduard Schröder, "Literatur und Gesellschaft in U.S.A.," *Frankfurter Hefte*, 1 (July 1946), 79-82; Heinrich von Trott, "Ignazio Silone—Dichter und Politiker," *Frankfurter Hefte*, 1 (Sept. 1946), 79-80; Hermann Uhde-Bernays, "Zeitschriften des Auslandes," *Deutsche Beiträge*, no. 1 (1946), 94. The pieces by Silone, Beauvoir, and Koestler appeared in *Der Ruf*'s issues of 15 Jan. 1947, 15 Oct. 1946, and 1 Jan. 1947 respectively.

13. Gustav René Hocke, "Deutsche Kalligraphie, oder Glanz und Elend der modernen Literatur," *Der Ruf*, no. 7 (15 Nov. 1946), 9. The *Reisebericht* was an established literary genre in Germany during the early nineteenth century, another time of political and cultural provincialism. The most famous example is Heine's *Die Harzreise* (1826).

14. Dolf Sternberger, "Reise durch Deutschland—Sommer 1945," *Die Wandlung* (Nov. 1945), 13-14. Other examples of the voluminous postwar *Reisebericht* literature include Hans Werner Richter, "'Wo sollen wir landen, wo treiben wir hin . . . ?': Skizzen von einer Reise in die östliche Zone," *Der Ruf*, nos. 1 and 2 (15 Aug. and 1 Sept. 1946), 4-5 and 6-7; Karl Zimmermann, "Nach einer Reise in Westdeutschland," *Die Gegenwart*, no. 10/11 (24 May 1946), 28-31; and Ilse Bembé, "Im D-Zug, Sommer 1946, Nachts," *Die Gegenwart*, no. 18/19 (24 Sept. 1946), 31-33.

15. Richter, "Unterhaltungen am Schienenstrang," *Der Ruf*, no. 4 (1 Oct. 1946), 6; Sternberger, "Reise durch Deutschland," 16.

16. Rudolf Gneist, quoted in Leonard Krieger, *The German Idea of Freedom: History of a Political Tradition from the Reformation to 1871*

ₗBoston: Beacon Press, 1957), p. 460.

17. Joseph Mannhardt, "Politik und Hochschule," *Deutsche Rundschau*, 69 (April 1946), 37; Clemens Münster, "Die Universität 1946," *Frankfurter Hefte*, 1 (April 1946), 9. On the intellectuals' attitudes toward the role of German universities in the early postwar years see Rüdiger Bolz, "Ansätze einer Universitätsreform im Spiegel deutscher Nachkriegszeitschriften," in *Zur literarischen Situation, 1945-1949*, ed. Gerhard Hay (Kronberg: Athenäum Verlag, 1977), pp. 63-85.

18. Münster, "Die Universität 1946," 9.

19. Dolf Sternberger, "Herrschaft der Freiheit," *Die Wandlung*, 1 (July 1946), 556-571, and "Über die Wahl, das Wählen, und das Wahlverfahren," *Die Wandlung*, 1, (Nov. 1946), 923-942; Sternberger, *Dreizehn politische Radio-Reden, 1946* (Heidelberg: Lambert Schneider Verlag, 1947), p. 74.

20. Potsdam Declaration of 2 Aug. 1945 in *Documents on Germany under Occupation, 1945-1954*, ed. Beate Ruhm von Oppen (London: Oxford University Press, 1955), p. 43.

21. [Alfred Andersch], "Der grüne Tisch," *Der Ruf*, no. 3 (15 Sept. 1946), 1; [Andersch], "Grundlagen einer deutschen Opposition," *Der Ruf*, no. 8 (1 Dec. 1946), 2.

22. Kogon, "Über die Situation," *Frankfurter Hefte*, 2 (Jan. 1947), 31.

23. "Sorgen im Lager der erhobenen Zeigefinger," *Der Ruf*, no. 13 (15 Feb. 1947), 3.

24. W[ilhelm] E[manuel] Süskind, *Die Mächtigen vor Gericht: Nürnberg 1945-46, an Ort und Stelle erlebt* (Munich: Paul List Verlag, 1963). The continuing tendency to see the Nuremberg Trial in terms of the personalities involved is exemplified in Bradley F. Smith's recent study, *Reaching Judgment at Nuremberg: The Untold Story of How the Nazi War Criminals Were Judged* (New York: Basic Books, 1977).

25. Hans Frank, *Neues deutsches Recht* (Munich: Franz Eher Nachfolger, 1936), pp. 7, 14.

26. J[oseph] P[eter] Stern, *Hitler: The Führer and the People* (Berkeley and Los Angeles: University of California Press, 1975), p. 123.

27. International Military Tribunal, *Trial of the Major War Criminals before the International Military Tribunal* (Nuremberg: Secretariat of the Tribunal, 1947), V, 368, 369.

28. Ibid., V, 372; I, 11.

29. Lord Justice Lawrence, "The Nuremberg Trial," *International Affairs*, 23 (April 1947), 153; "Vor dem Nürnberger Spruch," *Die Gegenwart*, no. 18/19 (24 Sept. 1946), 1; *Trial of the Major War Criminals*, XXII, 413.

30. "Nürnberg und die Geschichte," *Frankfurter Hefte*, 1 (April 1946), 4; Süskind, "Der geschichtliche Augenblick," *Süddeutsche Zeitung*, 30 Nov. 1945.

31. Arthur Steiner, "Das graue Haus von Nürnberg," *Die Neue Zeitung*, 30 Nov. 1945; Robert Haerdter, "Gerichtstag in Nürnberg," *Die Gegenwart*, no. 4/5 (24 Feb. 1946), 20.

32. Richter, "Unterhaltungen am Schienenstrang," *Der Ruf*, no. 4 (1 Oct. 1946), 7. Some American observers were equally critical of the U.S. denazification program. See John H. Herz, "The Fiasco of Denazification in

Germany," *Political Science Quarterly*, 63 (Dec. 1948), 569-594.

33. Robert Haerdter, "Kollektivschuld," *Die Gegenwart*, no. 2/3 (24 Jan. 1946), 11.

34. Interview with Walter Dirks, Wittnau bei Freiburg, 30 July 1974. For a general assessment of postwar denazification from a critical German perspective see Justus Fürstenau, *Entnazifizierung: Ein Kapitel deutscher Nachkriegspolitik* (Neuwied and Berlin: Luchterhand Verlag, 1969).

35. Kolbenhoff, "Brief an Sigrid Undset," *Der Ruf*, no. 4 (1 Oct. 1946), 13. Sigrid Undset, the Norwegian author and Nobel Prize winner, was one of several prominent foreign intellectuals who endorsed the collective guilt thesis. Her article "Die Umerziehung der Deutschen" appeared in *Die Neue Zeitung*, 25 Oct. 1945. Karl Jaspers responded with an "Antwort an Sigrid Undset" in *Die Neue Zeitung*, 4 Nov. 1945, reproving Undset for her systematic hatred of things German but criticizing the Germans for their unwillingness to admit guilt.

36. Eugen Kogon, "Gericht und Gewissen," *Frankfurter Hefte*, 1 (April 1946), 31, 33.

37. Dirks, "Der Weg zur Freiheit: Ein Beitrag zur deutschen Selbsterkenntnis," *Frankfurter Hefte*, 1 (Aug. 1946), 50, 59; Benno Reifenberg, "Archimedischer Punkt," *Die Gegenwart*, no. 1 (24 Dec. 1945), 9. See also "Deutsche Schuld," *Der Ruf*, no. 6 (1 Nov. 1946), 8.

38. Wolfgang Borchert, *Draussen vor der Tür*, in *Das Gesamtwerk* (Hamburg: Rowohlt Verlag, 1972), p. 102. On Borchert's attitude toward self-acceptance and self-liberation see Robert Spaethling, "Wolfgang Borchert's Quest for Human Freedom," *German Life and Letters*, 14 (April 1961), 188-193.

39. Dirks, "Der Weg zur Freiheit," 52.

40. Jaspers, *Die Schuldfrage*, in *Hoffnung und Sorge: Schriften zur deutschen Politik, 1945-1965* (Munich: Piper Verlag, 1965), pp. 76, 77, 77-78.

41. Ibid., pp. 109, 111, 140, 141.

42. Reifenberg, "Epilog zu Nürnberg," *Die Gegenwart*, no. 24/25 (31 Dec. 1946), 9.

43. Friedrich Meinecke, *Die deutsche Katastrophe*, in *Werke*, VIII: *Autobiographische Schriften*, ed. Eberhard Kessel (Stuttgart: K. F. Koehler Verlag, 1969), 323.

44. Leopold von Ranke, "[Historische Erforschung des Einzelnen und philosophische Abstraktion]" (1831), in *Aus Werk und Nachlass*, IV: *Vorlesungseinleitungen*, ed. Volker Dotterweich (Munich: Oldenbourg Verlag, 1975), 89; Heinrich von Sybel, quoted in Georg Iggers, *The German Conception of History: The National Tradition of Historical Thought from Herder to the Present* (Middletown, Conn.: Wesleyan University Press, 1968), p. 118.

45. Georg Wilhelm Friedrich Hegel, *Grundlinien der Philosophie des Rechts*, ed. Johannes Hoffmeister (Hamburg: Felix Meiner Verlag, 1955), p. 207; Meinecke, *Weltbürgertum und Nationalstaat*, ed. Hans Herzfeld (Munich: R. Oldenbourg Verlag, 1962), p. 83.

46. Meinecke, *Die deutsche Katastrophe*, p. 338.

47. Ibid., pp. 325, 383, 386.

48. Ibid., pp. 382, 436, 443.

49. Ibid., pp. 337, 429; Thomas Mann, "Deutschland und die Deutschen" (1945), in *Gesammelte Werke*, XI: *Reden und Aufsätze* (Frankfurt am Main: S. Fischer Verlag, 1974), 1131.

50. Kogon, "Beginn der Geschichtsrevision," *Frankfurter Hefte*, 1 (Nov. 1946), 776, 777; Kogon, "Das Dritte Reich und die preussisch-deutsche Geschichte," *Frankfurter Hefte*, 1 (June 1946), 44. This concept of the "demonic" was more closely bound to a religious meaning as the embodiment of pure evil than the largely amoral definition advanced by Goethe in the twentieth book of his *Dichtung und Wahrheit (Poetry and Truth*, 1831), a definition familiar to most educated Germans.

51. Kogon, *Der SS-Staat: Das System der deutschen Konzentrationslager* (Berlin: Verlag des Druckhauses Tempelhof, 1947), p. 12. Kogon's work has appeared in English as *The Theory and Practice of Hell.*

52. Ibid., p. 6.

53. Ibid., p. 245.

54. Interview with David Rousset, Paris, 4 Feb. 1977; book jacket of *Der SS-Staat* in the edition published by the Karl Alber Verlag, Munich, in 1946.

55. Kogon, *Der SS-Staat*, p. 34. The close relations between the camps and German industry are explored in Joseph Borkin, *The Crime and Punishment of I. G. Farben* (New York: The Free Press, 1978), pp. 95-127.

56. Kogon, "Der Terror als Herrschaftssystem," *Frankfurter Hefte*, 3, (Nov. 1948), 986; Kogon, *Der SS-Staat*, p. 367.

57. Kogon, *Der SS-Staat*, pp. 368, 373.

58. Kogon, "Das Dritte Reich und die preussisch-deutsche Geschichte," 44.

59. Ibid., 45, 53; Meinecke, *Die deutche Katastrophe*, p. 381; Kogon, "Das Dritte Reich," 52, 53.

60. Gerhard Ritter, "Gegenwärtige Lage und Zukunftsaufgaben deutscher Geschichtswissenschaft," *Historische Zeitschrift*, 170, no. 1 (1950), 2, 3. However, Ritter's contribution to this debate, *Europa und die deutsche Frage* (1948), exemplified the very nationalistic bias he was to criticize the next year.

61. Kogon, "Politik als Wissenschaft," *Frankfurter Hefte*, 4 (Nov. 1949), 906. Another significant step toward promoting study of the Nazi past was the founding of the Institut für Zeitgeschichte, planned in the late 1940s and finally brought to term in 1950. See John Gimbel, "The Origins of the Institut für Zeitgeschichte: Scholarship, Politics, and the American Occupation, 1945-1949," *American Historical Review*, 70 (April 1965), 714-731.

62. This point is made in some detail by Alexander and Margarete Mitscherlich in their excellent study *Die Unfähigkeit zu trauern: Grundlagen kollektiven Verhaltens* (Munich: Piper Verlag, 1967), pp. 129-157.

63. Rudolf Hess at the Nuremberg Party Rally, 1934, as recorded in Leni Riefenstahl's film *Triumph des Willens* (1936); Kogon, "Das Recht auf den politischen Irrtum," *Frankfurter Hefte*, 2, (July 1947), 655.

64. Albert Camus in *Combat*, 23 Nov. 1944: [Richter], "Die Wandlung des Sozialismus—und die junge Generation," *Der Ruf*, no. 6 (1 Nov. 1946), 1.

65. "Das Ahlener Wirtschaftsprogramm für Nordrhein-Westfalen" (3 Feb. 1947), in *Dokumente zur parteipolitischen Entwicklung in Deutschland seit 1945*, II: *Programmatik der deutschen Parteien*, 1, ed. Ossip K. Flechtheim

(Berlin: Dokumenten-Verlag Dr. Herbert Wendler, 1963), p. 55.

66. Victor Gollancz, *In Darkest Germany* (London: Victor Gollancz, 1947), p. 51. Gollancz also expressed alarm at the deterioration of private morals under such widespread economic misery. "A technical school in Hamburg," he reported, "is one of the black market centers for that city. 'What does the teacher say?' one of the pupils was asked. 'He's glad if every now and again he gets something out of it himself,' was the reply" (p. 14).

67. Klaus Knappstein, "Die Stunde der Sozialreform," *Frankfurter Hefte*, 1 (June 1946), 1.

68. [Andersch], "Die zwei Gesichter des Charles Bidault," *Der Ruf*, no. 5 (15 Oct. 1946), 3; Dirks, "Die zweite Republik," *Frankfurter Hefte*, 1 (April 1946), 15, 16.

69. Dirks, *Erbe und Aufgabe: Gesammelte kulturpolitische Aufsätze* (Frankfurt am Main: Verlag der Carolus-Druckerei, 1931), pp. 143, 153; Dirks, "Die zweite Republik," 24.

70. Dirks, "Partei und Staat," *Frankfurter Hefte*, 1 (Dec. 1946), 821, 820; interview with Dirks, 30 July 1974.

71. [Richter], "Parteipolitik und Weltanschauung," *Der Ruf*, no. 9 (Dec. 1946), 821, 820.

72. Andersch, *Die Kirschen der Freiheit* (Hamburg: Claassen Verlag, 1952), p. 39.

73. Richter, *Briefe an einen jungen Sozialisten*, pp. 58, 59.

74. [Andersch], "Das junge Europa formt sein Gesicht," *Der Ruf*, no. 1 (15 Aug. 1946), 1, 2.

75. [Richter], "Die Wandlung des Sozialismus – und die junge Generation," *Der Ruf*, no. 6 (1 Nov. 1946), 1, 2.

76. Henry Ehrmann, "Im Vorraum des Sozialismus: Planung und Freiheit – Wesenszüge der zukünftigen Wirtschaft," *Der Ruf*, no. 4 (1 Oct. 1946), 5.

77. [Richter], "Die Wandlung des Sozialismus," 2.

78. [Richter], "Parteipolitik und Weltanschauung," 2.

79. [Andersch], "Das junge Europa," 1-2.

80. [Richter], "Deutschland – Brücke zwischen Ost und West," *Der Ruf*, no. 4 (1 Oct. 1946), 2; Richter, "Ost und West," *Die Lagerstimme*, reprinted in *Der Ruf: Zeitung für Kriegsgefangenen in USA*, 1 Sept. 1945. This concept of Germany as a "bridge" was proposed independently by a number of intellectuals and political leaders, including Jakob Kaiser, the CDU party chief in the Soviet zone. See Hans-Peter Schwarz, *Vom Reich zur Bundesrepublik: Deutschland im Widerstreit der aussenpolitischen Konzeptionen in den Jahren der Besatzungsherrschaft, 1945-1949* (Neuwied and Berlin: Luchterhand Verlag, 1966), pp. 299-344.

6. THE ROAD TO RESTORATION

1. Among the many studies of the Cold War in its infancy see John Lewis Gaddis, *The United States and the Origins of the Cold War* (New York: Col-

umbia University Press, 1972); Lynn Etheridge Davis, *The Cold War Begins: Soviet-American Conflict over Eastern Europe* (Princeton, N.J.: Princeton University Press, 1974); and Daniel Yergin, *Shattered Peace: The Origins of the Cold War and the National Security State* (Boston: Houghton Mifflin, 1977), esp. pp. 221-365. A useful introduction to the controversies surrounding this issue is Charles S. Maier, "Revisionism and the Interpretation of Cold War Origins," in *The Origins of the Cold War and Contemporary Europe*, ed. Maier (New York and London: New Viewpoints, 1978), pp. 3-34.

2. Lucius D. Clay, *Decision in Germany* (Garden City, N.Y.: Doubleday, 1950), p. 127.

3. Eugen Kogon, "Das Jahr der Entscheidungen," *Frankfurter Hefte*, 3 (Jan. 1948), 28.

4. "Nationalstaat, Grenzen, und Völkerrecht," *Der Ruf*, no. 13 (15 Feb. 1947), 4.

5. [Alfred Andersch], "Das junge Europa formt sein Gesicht," *Der Ruf*, no. 1 (15 Aug. 1946), 1.

6. Pierre Drieu la Rochelle, *L'Europe contre les patries* (Paris: Gallimard, 1931), p. 139. Otto Abetz later complained that Hitler's policies meant "a European crusade without Europeans." Abetz, *Das offene Problem: Ein Rückblick auf zwei Jahrzehnte deutscher Frankreichspolitik* (Cologne: Greven Verlag, 1951), p. 199.

7. Adolf Hitler, *Reden und Proklamationen, 1932-1945*, ed. Max Domarus (Würzburg: Schmidt Neustadt, 1962), II, 1731; Hermann Rauschning, *Gespräche mit Hitler* (Vienna: Europa Verlag, 1973), p. 118. See also Paul Kluke, "Nationalsozialistische Europaideologie," *Vierteljahrshefte für Zeitgeschichte*, 3 (July 1955), 240-275. Beneath the "thin shell of propaganda," Kluke finds only a "nationalistic impulse toward conquest and control" in Nazi policies toward their satellites (p. 274).

8. Léon Blum, *A l'échelle humaine*, in *L'Oeuvre* (Paris: Albin Michel, 1955), V, 476.

9. Henri Frenay, "Résistance . . . espoir de l'Europe," *Combat* (Algiers), 12 Dec. 1943, reprinted in *Les Idées politiques et sociales de la Résistance*, ed. Henri Michel and Boris Mirkine-Guetzévitch (Paris: Presses Universitaires de France, 1954), p. 397; Altiero Spinelli, "Das Manifest von Ventotene" (July 1941), in *Europa-Föderationspläne der Widerstandsbewegungen, 1940-1945*, ed. Walter Lipgens (Munich: R. Oldenbourg Verlag, 1968), p. 41.

10. [Hans Werner Richter], "Zwischen Freiheit und Quarantäne," *Der Ruf*, no. 10 (1 Jan. 1947), 1.

11. Nikolaus Sombart, "Junge Franzosen—Jeunes Allemands!," *Der Ruf*, no. 5 (15 Oct. 1946), 2. *Der Ruf* had high praise for the group approach to journalism in postwar France. "The leading French reviews . . . owe their influence far more to their team of collaborators than German reviews, whose importance is largely determined by the editor alone." "Idee und Equipe: Französiche Zeitschriften als Gemeinschaftswerk," *Der Ruf*, no. 5 (15 Oct. 1946), 3.

12. *Combat*, 19 Oct. 1944; Joseph Rovan, "L'Allemagne de nos mérites," *Esprit*, no. 115 (1 Oct. 1945), 532, 539.

13. Interview with Joseph Rovan, Paris, 2 Feb. 1977. The conference at Lahr (Baden-Württemberg) took place on 25-29 Aug. 1947. Dirks and Kogon gave a report on their journalistic activities in Germany and their concept of "enlightenment" through journalism, which appeared as the article "Die Rolle der Publizisten," Frankfurter Hefte, 2 (Dec. 1947), 1169-1199.

14. Interview with Rovan, Paris, 7 Feb. 1977; interview with Hans Werner Richter, Munich, 26 July 1974. Official French occupation policy, whose nationalistic objectives Rovan and his friends often opposed, is outlined in Alfred Grosser, La IVe République et sa politique extérieure (Paris: Armand Colin, 1961), pp. 193-231. See also Richard Gilmore, France's Postwar Cultural Policies and Activities in Germany: 1945-1956 (Washington, D.C.: Balmar Reprographics, 1973).

15. Vercors, "Discours aux Allemands" (1948), in Plus ou moins homme (Paris: Albin Michel, 1950), pp. 227, 249, 241, 254.

16. Jean-Paul Sartre, "A propos de la représentation des Mouches en Allemagne," Verger, no. 2 (June 1947), 12.

17. "Jean-Paul Sartre à Berlin: Discussion autour des Mouches," Verger, no. 5 (March 1948), 115.

18. Alfred Andersch explored this question from the German side in "Aktion oder Passivität?," Der Ruf, no. 12 (1 Feb. 1947), 1-2; as did Richter in "Churchill und die europäische Einheit," Der Ruf, no. 14 (1 March 1947), 1-2; for the conflict between German and American aims viewed from the perspective of the occupying forces see John Gimbel, The American Occupation of Germany: Politics and the Military, 1945-1949 (Stanford: Stanford University Press, 1968), esp. pp. 111-225.

19. Hans-Peter Schwarz, Vom Reich zur Bundesrepublik: Deutschland im Widerstreit der aussenpolitischen Konzeptionen in den Jahren der Besatzungsherrschaft, 1945-1949 (Neuwied and Berlin: Luchterhand Verlag, 1966), pp. 76-77. The phrase was first coined by Manuel Gottlieb in 1960.

20. Richter, "Der Sieg des Opportunismus," in Der Ruf: Eine deutsche Nachkriegszeitschrift, ed. Hans Schwab-Felisch (Munich: Deutscher Taschenbuch Verlag, 1962), p. 296; Richter, "Wie entstand und was war die Gruppe 47?," in Hans Werner Richter und die Gruppe 47, ed. Hans A. Neunzig (Munich: Nymphenburger Verlagshandlung, 1979), p. 71.

21. Interview with Wolfdietrich Schnurre, Berlin, 6 March 1977. A complete list of the dates and meeting places of the Group 47 can be found in Almanach der Gruppe 47, 1947-1962, ed. Hans Werner Richter (Reinbek bei Hamburg: Rowohlt Verlag, 1964), p. 448.

22. Richter, "Wie entstand und was war die Gruppe 47?," p. 87.

23. Hans Friedrich, "Das Jahr 47," in Almanach der Gruppe 47, p. 19.

24. Schnurre in Peter Sandmeyer, "Schreiben nach 1945: Ein Interview mit Wolfdietrich Schnurre," in Literaturmagazin, 7: Nachkriegsliteratur, eds. Nicolas Born and Jürgen Manthey (Reinbek bei Hamburg: Rowohlt Taschenbuch Verlag, 1977), p. 200. The agreement on style did not imply complete agreement on literary content or on the writer's social role, however. Schnurre had been involved in a polemical exchange with Walter Kolbenhoff concerning the "immortality" of art versus the need for social engagement. See Schnurre, "Kunst und Künstler: Unzeitgemässe Betrachtungen eines Aussenseiters,"

Horizont, no. 1 (5 Jan. 1947), 11; Kolbenhoff, "Kunst und Künstler: Eine Antwort," *Horizont*, no. 5 (2 March 1947), 8; Schnurre, "Kunst und Künstler," *Horizont*, no. 11 (25 May 1947), 2-3. Schnurre defended the elite nature of the artist's calling—a thesis not incompatible with Richter's goals for the Group 47.

25. Gunter Groll, "Die Gruppe, die keine Gruppe ist," *Süddeutsche Zeitung*, 10 April 1948, reprinted in *Die Gruppe 47: Bericht, Kritik, Polemik*, ed Reinhard Lettau (Neuwied and Berlin: Luchterhand Verlag, 1967), pp. 31-36.

26. Richter, "Wie entstand und was war die Gruppe 47?," pp. 82, 89; ibid., p. 108.

27. Ibid., pp. 77-78.

28. Richter, "Fünfzehn Jahre," in *Almanach der Gruppe 47*, p. 11.

29. Arthur Koestler, "Die Gemeinschaft der Pessimisten," *Der Ruf*, no. 1 (15 Aug. 1946), 4.

30. On the German prisoners' experience in the United States see the excellent study of Judith M. Gansberg, *Stalag U.S.A.: The Remarkable Story of German POWs in America* (New York: Thomas Y. Crowell, 1977), esp. pp. 120-181. A collection of reminiscences and comments by the prisoners, including excerpts from Richter's novel *Die Geschlagenen*, may be found in Daniel Costelle, *Les Prisonniers: 380.000 soldats de Hitler aux U.S.A.* (Paris: Flammarion, 1975). See also George E. McCracken, "The Prisoner of War Re-education Program in the Years 1943-1946" (declassified report prepared for the Office of the Chief of Military History, Washington, D.C., n.d., 2-3.7 AH C2); and Cummins E. Speakman, "Re-education of German Prisoners of War in the United States during World War II" (Master's thesis, University of Virginia, 1948).

31. T[homas] V[ernon] Smith, "General Comment on the School," in Office of the Chief of Military History, *Re-education of Enemy Prisoners of War* (declassified report, Washington, D.C., 1946, 4-4.1 BB2 C1); Andersch, "Getty oder die Umerziehung in der Retorte," *Frankfurter Hefte*, 2 (Nov. 1947), 1091.

32. Richter's experience, its contrast with that of Andersch, and its consequences for Richter's view of literature are examined in Volker Christian Wehdeking, *Der Nullpunkt: Über die Konstituierung der deutschen Nachkriegsliteratur (1945-1948) in den amerikanischen Kriegs-gefangenenlagern* (Stuttgart: J. B. Metzlersche Verlagsbuchlandlung, 1971), pp. 13-41, 119-135.

33. Friedrich Sieburg, "Das Kriegsbuch" (1949), in *Nur für Leser: Jahre und Bücher* (Stuttgart: Deutsche Verlags-Anstalt, 1955), p. 76; Richter, *Die Geschlagenen* (Munich: Deutscher Taschenbuch Verlag, 1969), p. 125.

34. Richter, *Die Geschlagenen*, p. 223.

35. Ibid., pp. 247, 252.

36. "'Ich habe nichts über den Krieg aufgeschrieben': Ein Gespräch mit Heinrich Böll und Hermann Lenz," in *Literaturmagazin*, VII: *Nachkriegsliteratur*, ed. Nicolas Born and Jürgen Manthey (Reinbek bei Hamburg: Rowohlt Taschenbuch Verlag, 1977), 32; Heinrich Böll and Christian Linder, *Drei Tage im März: Ein Gespräch* (Cologne: Kiepenheuer & Witsch, 1975), pp. 36, 37.

37. These biographical details are drawn from a conversation with Heinrich Böll in Cambridge, Mass., 5 Nov. 1971, and from Christine Gabriele Hoffmann, *Heinrich Böll* (Hamburg: Cecilie Dressler Verlag, 1977), pp. 45-58.

38. Böll in *Werkstattgespräche mit Schriftstellern*, ed. Horst Bienek (Munich: Deutscher Taschenbuch Verlag, 1962), pp. 103, 147.

39. Böll, *Der Zug war pünktlich* (1949), in *Wo warst du, Adam? und Erzählungen* (Cologne: Friedrich Middelhauve Verlag, 1968), p. 10.

40. Böll, "Wanderer, kommst du nach Spa . . .," in *Wo warst du, Adam? und Erzählungen*, p. 330.

41. The role of chance in Böll's fiction of this period, heightening the impression of disorder, was noted by his contemporaries. See Andersch, "Christus gibt keinen Urlaub," *Frankfurter Hefte*, 6 (Dec. 1951), 931-941.

42. For a critique of Böll's sentimentality in his early fiction see Manfred Durzak, *Der deutsche Roman der Gegenwart*, 2nd ed. (Stuttgart: Kohlhammer Verlag, 1973), p. 29.

43. Böll, *Wo warst du, Adam? und Erzählungen*, pp. 201, 206.

44. On this point see Theodore Ziolkowski, "Albert Camus and Heinrich Böll," *Modern Language Notes*, 77 (May 1962), 282-291.

45. J. P. Stern, "An Honourable Man," *Times Literary Supplement*, 10 Jan. 1976, p. 101.

46. Dirks, "Die Stunde der Armut," *Frankfurter Hefte*, 2 (June 1947), 555, 556.

47. Gustav Stolper et al., *The German Economy: 1870 to the Present*, trans. Toni Stolper (London: Weidenfeld and Nicolson, 1967), p. 212. For a contemporary analysis see also Eugen Kogon, Paul Binder, and Walter Strauss, "Die Währungsreform," *Frankfurter Hefte*, 3 (June 1948), 504-519.

48. *New York Times*, 6 June 1947.

49. Richter, *Briefe an einen jungen Sozialisten* (Hamburg: Hoffmann & Campe, 1974), p. 103; Kogon, "Die Aussichten der Restauration—über die gesellschaftlichen Grundlagen der Zeit," *Frankfurter Hefte*, 7 (March 1952), 169.

50. Other reviews that ceased publication in the difficult period that followed the end of licensing included *Deutsche Beiträge* (Munich) and the *Hamburger Akademische Rundschau* (Hamburg), whose last issues both appeared in November 1950. See *Als der Krieg zu Ende war: Literarisch-politische Publizistik, 1945-1950*, ed. Bernhard Zeller (Munich: Kösel Verlag, 1974), pp. 504-518. Though the licensing system was retained in the German Democratic Republic, some journals such as Alfred Kantorowicz's *Ost und West* were suspended by the Communist authorities soon after the monetary reform on political grounds.

51. Dirks, "Der restaurative Charakter der Epoche," *Frankfurter Hefte*, 5 (Sept. 1950), 942.

52. Kogon, "Der Internationale Rat der Europäischen Bewegung: Die deutsche Teilnahme," *Frankfurter Hefte*, 4 (March 1949), 185; "Schlussfolgerungen des Brüsseler Kongresses," in *Einigung und Spaltung Europas, 1942-1965: Eine Darstellung und Dokumentation über die Zweiteilung Europas*, ed. Curt Gasteyger (Frankfurt am Main: Fischer Bücherei, 1966), p. 47. On the origins and subsequent fortunes of the Union

Européenne des Fédéralistes see the brief account in Henri Brugmans, *L'Idée européenne, 1918-1965* (Bruges: De Tempel, 1965), pp. 99-105, 175-180.

53. The events in Berlin are described against the background of Soviet-American relations in W. Phillips Davison, *The Berlin Blockade: A Study in Cold War Politics* (Princeton, N.J.: Princeton University Press, 1958). The effects of the Cold War on the intellectuals' hopes for a neutral, united Europe are analyzed in Schwarz, *Vom Reich zur Bundesrepublik*, pp. 625-638, 664-695.

54. Dirks, "Mut zum Abschied: Zur Wiederherstellung des Frankfurter Goethehauses," *Frankfurter Hefte*, 2 (Aug. 1947), 826. Erich Kästner satirized the pretentions of the coming Goethe festivities in "Das Goethe-Derby" (1949), reprinted in *Gesammelte Schriften*, V: *Vermischte Beiträge* (Cologne: Kiepenheuer & Witsch, 1959), 290-291.

55. Günter Eich, "Träume," in *Gesammelte Werke, II: Die Hörspiele* (Frankfurt am Main: Suhrkamp Verlag, 1973), 322.

7. FROM FASCISM TO RESISTANCE

1. Although Resistance figures such as François de Menthon and Georges Bidault served in de Gaulle's provisional government in France, the sole domestic Resistance leader to head a government after the war in France, Germany, or Italy was Feruccio Parri.

2. Gino Germani attempts to distinguish the chronological phases in this shift in "La socializzazione politica dei giovani nei regimi fascisti: Italia e Spagna," *Quaderni di Sociologia*, 18 (Jan.-June 1969), 11-58.

3. This awakening is portrayed in Vasco Pratolini's *Il mio cuore a Ponte Milvio* (Rome: Edizioni di Cultura Sociale, 1954).

4. Alfred Andersch, "Nachwort," in *Die andere Achse: Italienische Resistenza und geistiges Deutschland*, ed. Lavinia Jollos-Mazzucchetti (Hamburg: Claassen Verlag, 1964), p. 119.

5. Benito Mussolini, "Dottrina politica e sociale" (1932), in *La dottrina del fascismo*, ed. G. Esposito (Milan: Ulrico Hoepli, 1939), pp. 33, 50.

6. Mussolini, *Opera omnia*, XXII, ed. Edoardo and Duilio Susmel (Florence: La Fenice, 1958), 230.

7. Giuseppe Bottai, Mussolini's Minister of Corporations, argued in 1928 that the activist element in Fascism was precisely what was needed to revive Italian culture. See his "Cultura e azione" (an address given at the University of Pisa on 13 November 1928) in *Scritti*, ed. Roberto Bartolozzi and Riccardo Del Giudice (Bologna: Cappelli, [1965]), pp. 64-68.

8. Giovanni Gentile, *Fascismo e cultura* (Milan: Treves, 1928), pp. 49, 46, 55. The occasion of Gentile's remarks was the inauguration of the Fascist Institute of National Culture in Rome on 19 December 1925. On the relations between state and culture during the Fascist era in Italy see esp. Philip V. Cannistraro, "Burocrazia e politica culturale nello stato fascista: Il Ministero della cultura popolare," *Storia Contemporanea*, 1 (June 1970), 273-298; and

Norberto Bobbio, "La cultura e il fascismo," in *Fascismo e società italiana*, ed. Guido Quazza (Turin: Einaudi, 1973), pp. 211-246.

9. Quoted in Denis Mack Smith, *Italy: A Modern History*, 2nd ed. (Ann Arbor: University of Michigan Press, 1969), p. 418.

10. Gentile, *Fascismo e cultura*, p. 114.

11. For a brief discussion of the circumstances surrounding the intellectuals' collaboration on the *Enciclopedia italiana* see Alberto Asor Rosa, *Storia d'Italia*, IV: *Dall'Unità a oggi*, 2: *La cultura* (Turin: Einaudi, 1975), 1483-1486.

12. Corrado Alvaro, *Quasi una vita: Giornale di uno scrittore* (Milan: Bompiani, 951), p. 52. Renzo De Felice discusses the intellecual tenor of this period in *Mussolini il duce*, I: *Gli anni del consenso, 1929-1936* (Turin: Einaudi, 1974), 101-112.

13. Benedetto Croce, "Contromanifesto" (1925), in Emilio Papa, *Storia di due manifesti* (Milan: Mondadori, 1958), p. 95.

14. Croce, *Storia d'Italia dal 1871 al 1915* (Bari: Laterza, 1962), p. 113; Croce, *La storia come pensiero e come azione* (Bari: Laterza, 1957), p. 48. Croce's *Storia d'Italia* was originally published in 1928. Concerning his concept of liberty see Norberto Bobbio, "Benedetto Croce e il liberalismo," in *Politica e cultura* (Turin: Einaudi, 1955), pp. 211-268.

15. Piero Calmandrei, "Benedetto Croce," in *Uomini e città della Resistenza* (Bari: Laterza, 1955), p. 121. Croce's attitude toward the regime and his moral influence on its opponents during the 1920s are detailed in Raffaele Colapietra, *Benedetto Croce e la politica italiana* (Bari: Edizioni del Centro Librario, 1970), pp. 558-692.

16. Salvatore Quasimodo, *Poesie e discorsi sulla poesia*, ed. Gilberto Finzi (Milan: Mondadori, 1971), p. 9.

17. Eugenio Montale, *Auto da fé: Cronache in due tempi* (Milan: Il Saggiatore, 1966), p. 24.

18. Alberto Moravia, *Gli indifferenti* (Milan: Bompiani, 1954), p. 348.

19. Moravia refers to Mariagrazia simply as "la madre" in the novel. On this point see Donald Heiney, *Three Italian Novelists: Moravia, Pavese, Vittorini* (Ann Arbor: University of Michigan Press, 1968), pp. 25-26.

20. "*Gli indifferenti*," wrote Moravia in 1945, "was at most a means of making clear to myself my own situation . . . If the result was an antibourgeois book, that is quite another matter. The fault or merit lies above all with the bourgeoisie, especially in Italy, which possesses little or nothing that inspires . . . admiration or even the most distant sympathy." "Ricordo de *Gli indifferenti*," in Moravia, *L'uomo come fine e altri saggi* (Milan: Bompiani, 1964), p. 66.

21. Voltaire, *Lettres philosophiques*, in *Mélanges*, ed. Jacques van den Heuvel (Paris: Gallimard, 1961), p. 17. A similar use of foreign models is evident in Tacitus's *Germania*, where the rugged virtues of Germanic tribesmen are praised in order indirectly to censure Roman decadence.

22. Jean-Paul Sartre, "American Novelists in French Eyes," *Atlantic Monthly*, Aug. 1946, p. 115.

23. Cesare Pavese, "Un romanziere americano, Sinclair Lewis," in *La letteratura americana e altri saggi* (Turin: Einaudi, 1960), pp. 32, 6, 8.

24. Marcus Cunliffe, *The Literature of the United States*, 3rd ed. (Harmondsworth: Penguin, 1970), p. 278. The limits of the revolt inspired by this American literature are emphasized in Luisa Mangoni's critical review "*Il mito dell'America negli intellettuali italiani dal 1930 al 1950*, di Dominique Fernandez," *Storia Contemporanea*, 1 (March 1970), 190-194.

25. Pavese to Augusto Monti, Aug. 1926, in Pavese, *Lettere, 1924-1944*, ed. Lorenzo Mondo (Turin: Einaudi, 1966), p. 28. On Pavese's relations with Monti, see Dominique Fernandez, *L'Echec de Pavese* (Paris: Bernard Grasset, 1967), pp. 62-66. A respectful and affectionate portrait by one who felt Monti's influence is offered in Massimo Mila, "Augusto Monti educatore e scrittore," *Il Ponte*, 5, no. 8-9 (Aug.-Sept. 1949), 1136-1148.

26. The university in Turin was a center of anti-Fascist feeling in the late 1920s and 1930s. Norberto Bobbio, a student there from 1927 to 1933, recalled that lectures at both the School of Law and the Faculty of Letters were singularly free of Fascist influence. "It was a point of honor not to be considered Fascist." Bobbio, *Trent'anni di storia della cultura a Torino, 1920-1950* (Turin: Cassa di Risparmio di Tornio, 1977), pp. 22-23. A number of professors and students had signed a letter of solidarity with Croce, who made summer visits to the city in order to meet and exchange views with younger anti-Fascist intellectuals.

27. Pavese, "Interpretazione di Walt Whitman poeta," *La Cultura* (July-Sept. 1933), rpt. in *La letteratura e altri saggi*, p. 168.

28. Figures in H. Stuart Hughes, *The United States and Italy*, rev. ed. (Cambridge, Mass.: Harvard University Press, 1965), p. 91.

29. The shifts and inconsistencies of Fascist censorship are described in Maurizio Cesari, *La censura nel periodo fascista* (Naples: Liquori Editore, 1978).

30. Carlo Linati, *Scrittori anglo-americani d'oggi* (Milan: Corticelli, 1932), pp. 64, 66.

31. Giaime Pintor, "Americana," in *Il sangue d'Europa*, ed. Valentino Gerratana (Turin: Einaudi, 1966), p. 150. Cecchi's *America amara* also served as anti-American propaganda during the war. Translated into German in 1942, it proved so popular with the Nazi authorities that they reissued it the following year.

32. This anecdote appears in Donald Heiney, *America in Modern Italian Literature* (New Brunswick, N.J.: Rutgers University Press, 1964), p. 94.

33. Pavese, "Ieri e oggi," in *La letteratura americana e altri saggi*, pp. 193-194. This essay first appeared in the Turinese edition of *L'Unità*, 3 Aug. 1947.

34. Pavese, "Sherwood Anderson" (1931), in *La letteratura americana e altri saggi*, p. 42.

35. Pintor, "Americana," p. 159. The American critic Alfred Kazin, who referred to Anderson and Lewis as the "new realists" of the 1920s, noted: "It was this feeling for common talk and appreciation of common ways . . . that gave the new realists their hold over the popular imagination and made them so significant a cultural influence . . . The new realist made his readers share in the pride of discovering the poignance and the concealed depths to be found in so many prosaic American examples." Kazin, *On Native Grounds: An Inter-*

pretation of Modern American Prose Literature (New York: Reynal & Hitch-cock, 1942), pp. 208-209.

36. For a perceptive discussion of the difficulties encountered in organizing a Resistance movement from outside Italy, with special reference to Giustizia e Libertà, see Aldo Garosci, *Storia dei fuorusciti* (Bari: Laterza, 1953), pp. 26-79.

37. The phenomenon of "left-wing Fascism" among the young is treated in Asor Rosa, *Storia d'Italia*, pp. 1567-1577; and in the classic account of Ruggero Zangrandi, *Il lungo viaggio attraverso il fascismo: Contributo alla storia di una generazione* (Milan: Feltrinelli, 1962), esp. pp. 43-159. See also Renato Treves, "Il fascismo e il problema delle generazioni," *Quaderni di Sociologia,* 13 (April-June 1964), 119-146.

38. Elio Vittorini, *Diario in pubblico* (Milan: Bompiani, 1970), p. 190; Vittorini, *Sardegna come un'infanzia,* in *Le opere narrative,* I, ed. Mario Corti (Milan: Mondadori, 1974), 161.

39. On the political atmosphere in Syracuse during these years see Alfonso Failla, "Con gli anarchici di Siracusa," *Il Ponte,* 29 (July-Aug. 1973), 1068-1069; Vittorini, *Diario in pubblico*, pp. 190, 192.

40. Vittorini, *Diario in pubblico,* pp. 192-193. The literary influences on Vittorini's early work are analyzed in some detail in Anna Panicali, *Il primo Vittorini* (Milan: Celuc, 1974).

41. Romano Bilenchi, *Amici: Vittorini, Rosai e altri incontri* (Turin: Einaudi, 1976), p. 115.

42. Vittorini, *Il garofano rosso,* in *Le opere narrative,* I, 264; Vittorini, "Prefazione alla I edizione del *Garofano rosso*" (1947), ibid., 447.

43. Vittorini, "Prefazione," p. 449; Pavese to Vittorini, 27 May 1942, in *Lettere, 1924-1944,* p. 634.

44. Vittorini, "Nota" (1956), postface to *Erica e i suoi fratelli,* in *Le opere narrative,* I, 566. Vittorini sought to clarify his relations with the Fascist movement during the 1930s in a long letter to the *Partisan Review,* written (but never sent) in October-November 1948, and published in Vittorini, *Gli anni del "Politecnico": Lettere 1945-1951,* ed. Carlo Minoia (Turin: Einaudi, 1977), pp. 211-213.

45. Vittorini, *Conversazione in Sicilia,* in *Le opere narrative,* I, 571. The novel first appeared in installments in the review *Letteratura* during 1938 and 1939.

46. Ibid., pp. 586, 589.

47. Ibid., pp. 695, 646.

48. Gian Carlo Ferretti, "Il romanzo della 'svolta,'" *Rinascita,* 3 Feb. 1967, p. 21.

49. Vittorini, "Prefazione alla I edizione del *Garofano rosso,*" p. 438; Pintor, *"Conversazione in Sicilia,"* *Il sangue d'Europa,* p. 157. Pintor's review originally appeared in the Roman journal *Prospettive,* issue of 15 April-15 May 1941.

50. Galeazzo Ciano, *Diario, 1939-43,* 5th ed., ed. Renzo Trionfera (Milan: Rizzoli, 1971), p. 314. A measure of the war's unpopularity, as one historian has noted, is that "the phenomenon of wartime volunteers, characteristic of [other stages of] Italy's history, was notably absent." Federico Chabod,

L'Italia contemporanea, 1918-1948 (Turin: Einaudi, 1961), p. 103.

51. Carmine Senise, *Quando ero capo della polizia, 1940-1943* (Rome: Ruffolo, [1946]), p. 171.

52. Mussolini was present at the meeting, but manged only a feeble effort at self-defense. For an eyewitness account see Giuseppe Bottai, *Vent'anni e un giorno* (Milan: Mondadori, 1949), p. 302.

53. A comprehensive history of the Resistenza Armata from the Communist viewpoint is offered in Roberto Battaglia, *Storia della Resistenza italiana* (Turin: Einaudi, 1964). Giorgio Bocca's *Storia dell'Italia partigiana* (Bari: Laterza, 1966) provides a needed corrective from a former member of Giustizia e Libertà, while Guido Quazza's *Resistenza e storia d'Italia: Problemi e ipotesi di ricerca* (Milan: Feltrinelli, 1977) is a notable synthesis that incorporates the scholarship of the intervening decade. Charles Delzell's *Mussolini's Enemies: The Italian Anti-Fascist Resistance* (Princeton, N.J.: Princeton University Press, 1961) gives a wealth of detail concerning the Resistance prior to 1943 as well as a more modest treatment of 1943-1945. See also his review article "The Italian Anti-Fascist Resistance in Retrospect: Three Decades of Historiography," *Journal of Modern History*, 47 (March 1975), 66-96.

54. Delzell, *Mussolini's Enemies*, pp. 295-296. The breadth of popular participation in the Italian Resistance is a central theme in Luigi Longo's *Un popolo alla macchia* (Milan: Mondadori, [1947]).

55. Ada Gobetti, *Diario partigiano* (Turin: Einaudi, 1956), p. 13.

56. Ulisse [Davide Lajolo], *Classe 1912* (Asti: Casa Editrice Arethusa, 1945), pp. 57-58; Giaime Pintor to Luigi Pintor, 28 Nov. 943, in *Il sangue d'Europa*, pp. 187-188.

57. Altiero Spinelli, *Il lungo monologo* (Rome: Edizioni dell'Ateneo, 1968), p. 121. German attitudes toward the Italians under occupation are detailed in Silvio Bertoldi, *I tedeschi in Italia* (Milan: Rizzoli, 1964).

58. Delzell, *Mussolini's Enemies*, p. 278. For more details concerning the Milanese CLN see Franco Catalano, *Storia del C.L.N.A.I.* (Bari: Laterza, 1956), pp. 60-67.

59. Vittorini, *Uomini e no*, in *Le opere narrative*, I, 722, 814-815.

60. Ibid., p. 1221.

61. Vittorini, *Diario in pubblico,* p. 205. The eulogy was originally published in the clandestine Milanese edition of *L'Unità* in March 1945. On Mussolini's last days and the fate of his puppet Republic of Salò see F. W. Deakin, *The Brutal Friendship: Mussolini, Hitler and the Fall of Italian Fascism* (London: Weidenfeld and Nicolson, 1962), pp. 775-817; and Giorgio Bocca, *La repubblica di Mussolini* (Bari: Laterza, 1977), pp. 287-339.

8. A SEASON OF HOPE

1. Giorgia Amendola, *Lettere a Milano: Ricordi e documenti, 1939-1945* (Rome: Editori Riuniti, 1973), p. 534.

2. Leone Ginzburg, *Scritti*, ed. Domenico Zucàro and Carlo Ginzburg (Turin: Einaudi, 1962), pp. 6, 34.

3. "Il programma del Partito d'Azione," *Nuovi Quaderni di Giustizia e Libertà*, no. 4 (Nov. - Dec. 1944), 126.

4. Enzo Enriques Agnoletti, preface to *Lettere di condannati a morte della Resistenza italiana (8 settembre 1943 - 25 aprile 1945)*, ed. Piero Malvezzi and Giovanni Pirelli (Turin: Einaudi, [1965]), p. 17; Ada Gobetti, *Diario partigiano* (Turin: Einaudi, 1956), p. 414.

5. Quoted in Ivanoe Bonomi, *Diario di un anno* (Milan: Garzanti, 1947), p. 100. The name of the committee was inspired by the French Comité de Libération Nationale, which had been formed a few months earlier in Algiers.

6. Quoted in Roberto Battaglia, *Storia della Resistenza italiana* (Turin: Einaudi, 1964), p. 180. For an analysis of the aims of the CLN see Guido Quazza, "Che cosa furono i C.L.N." in Quazza et al., *Il governo dei C.L.N.: Atti del Convegno dei Comitati di liberazione nazionale, Torino 9-10 ottobre 1965* (Turin: Giappichelli, 1966).

7. On the Italian political parties of this period see Franco Catalano, "I partiti: Ideologie, strutture, militanti," in Enzo Piscitelli et al., *Italia 1945-48: Le origini della Repubblica* (Turin: Giappichelli, 1974), esp. pp. 293-330.

8. For an early statement of the intellectuals' views on local autonomy see Leone Ginzburg, "Il concetto di autonomia nel programma di G.L.," *Quaderni di Giustizia e Libertà*, no. 4 (Sept. 1932), 6-12, rpt. in *Scritti*, pp. 3-9.

9. Palmiro Togliatti, *La politica di Salerno, aprile-dicembre 1944* (Rome: Editori Riuniti, 1969), p. 38.

10. Togliatti's caution was powerfully reinforced by the Soviet Union's de jure recognition of the conservative Badoglio government in March 1944, and by Churchill's support of the Italian monarchy in the belief that the king would prove a more docile ally than the CLN. The effects of the Communist attitude are described in Leo Valiani's memoirs, *Tutte le strade conducono a Roma: Diario di un uomo nella guerra di un popolo* (Florence: La Nuova Italia, [1947]), pp. 217-262.

11. On the local measures taken by the CLNAI see Massimo Legnani, *Politica e amministrazione nelle repubbliche partigiane: Studio e documenti* ([Milan]: Istituto Nazionale per la Storia del Movimento di Liberazione, n.d.); and Guido Quazza, *Resistenza e storia d'Italia: Problemi e ipotesi di ricerca* (Milan: Feltrinelli, 1977), pp. 233-271.

12. Valiani, "Sul partito della democrazia," *Nuovi Quaderni di Giustizia e Libertà*, no. 5-6 (Jan. - Aug. 1945), 247.

13. Interview with Franco Venturi, Turin, 24 June 1974.

14. Quote from a pamphlet dated November 1929—the first of Rosselli's pamphlets to reach Italy. Quoted in Luigi Salvatorelli and Giovanni Mira, *Storia d'Italia nel periodo fascista* (Turin: Einaudi, 1956), p. 593. For the founding of Giustizia e Libertà see Aldo Garosci, *Vita di Carlo Rosselli*, I (Florence: Valecchi, 1973), 109-202.

15. Ferruccio Parri, "Nascita del G.L.," *Il Ponte*, 13 (June 1957), 861.

16. Carlo Rosselli, *Socialismo liberale*, ed. John Rosselli (Turin: Einaudi, 1973), pp. 433, 467, 434, 436, 456. Rosselli's treatise was first published in Italy following the Liberation in the summer of 1945. For a contemporary response

see Guido Calogero, "Il socialismo liberale di Carlo Rosselli," *L'Italia Libera*, 9 Aug. 1945, reprinted in Calogero, *Difesa del liberalsocialismo ed altri saggi*, ed. Michele Schiavone and Dino Cofrancesco (Milan: Marzorati, 1972), pp. 123-126.

17. Ferruccio Parri, "Discorso al congresso dei CLN dell'Alta Italia" (1 Sept. 1945), in *Scritti 1915/1975*, ed. Enzo Collotti et al. (Milan: Feltrinelli, 1976), p. 166; "Fiducia," *Il Ponte*, 1 (Aug. 1945), 270. For a Christian Democratic view of the negotiations leading to Parri's accession, see Giulio Andreotti, *Concerto a sei voci: Storia segreta di una crisi* (Rome: Edizioni della Bussola, 1945), pp. 61-92.

18. Agnoletti, preface to *Lettere di condannati a morte*, p. 16.

19. This sympathy was evident in Parri's speech to the First Congress of the CLNAI on 1 September 1945. "Where possible," he told the delegates, "we must govern on the spot, making use of the initiatives that arise locally." "Discorso al congresso dei CLN," in *Scritti*, p. 171.

20. "Dichiarazioni programmatiche del governo Parri" (26 June 1945), ibid., p. 146. On Parri's program and its application see Giorgio Vaccarino, "Il governo Parri e le forze politiche," in Guido Quazza et al., *L'Italia dalla liberazione alla repubblica: Atti del Convegno internzationale organnizzato a Firenze il 26-28 marzo 1976 con il concorso della Regione Toscana* (Milan: Feltrinelli, n.d.), pp. 267-314; and Enzo Piscitelli, *Da Parri a De Gasperi: Storia del dopoguerra, 1945-1948* (Milan: Feltrinelli, 1975), pp. 61-138.

21. One sign of the desire for a return to more authoritarian government was the broad support given in Rome and the South to the Uomo Qualunque ("average man") movement, whose ironic slogan was "one was better off when one was worse off." Even the Actionist paper *L'Italia Libera* admitted on 25 October that "every time a measure is taken it appears to require enormous efforts . . . as if the government were internally paralyzed because of the divergences among the various currents."

22. The traditional Italian desire to enjoy the status and pension benefits of an *impiegato*—a white-collar employee in a modest and not too demanding government post—had led the Fascist government to create an estimated 100,000 jobs for secretaries and party functionaries within the Corporate State. See Denis Mack Smith, *Italy: A Modern History*, 2nd ed. (Ann Arbor: University of Michigan Press, 1969), p. 396. The postwar purges are analyzed in Marcello Flores, "L'epurazione," in Quazza et al., *L'Italia dalla liberazione alla repubblica*, pp. 413-467. An older but still authoritative account is Achille Battaglia, "Giustizia e politica nella giurisprudenza," in Battaglia et al., *Dieci anni dopo, 1945-1955: Saggi sulla vita democratica italiana* (Bari: Laterza, 1955), pp. 319-408.

23. Muriel Grindrod, for example, remarks that Parri, "though an ardent patriot actuated by the highest motives, appears to have been too little accustomed to the arduous business of administration to keep his difficult six-party team in order and get things done." Grindrod, *The New Italy: Transition from War to Peace* (London: Royal Institute of International Affairs, 1947), p. 30.

24. *L'Italia Libera*, 25 Nov. 1945, rpt. in Parri, *Scritti*, pp. 195-201. On Parri's fall see Franco Catalano, "La crisi del governo Parri (novembre-

dicembre 1945)," *Il Ponte*, 22 (Jan. 1966), 51-71; and Parri, "La caduta del governo Parri," in *Scritti*, pp. 566-576.

25. Valiani, *L'avvento di De Gasperi: Tre anni di politica italiana* (Turin: Francesco De Silva, 1949), p. 37.

26. On the role of the CGIL during this period see Adolfo Pepe, "La CGIL dalla ricostituzione alla scissione (1944-1948)," *Storia Contemporanea*, 5 (Dec. 1974), 591-636. The postwar economic reconstruction and the question of possible alternatives are discussed in Vittorio Foa, "La ricostruzione capitalistica e la politica delle sinistre," in Enzo Piscitelli et al., *Italia 1945-48*, pp. 99-135.

27. For details of the replacement of the CLNAI committees by De Gasperi's civil servants see Valiani, *L'avvento di De Gasperi*, pp. 40-72.

28. "One wishes that the CLN groups, which have many merits and were a necessity at a certain period, might continue some of their functions in collaboration with the [political] parties," De Gasperi declared in March 1946. "But the system of responsibility is now changing." De Gasperi, "Le vie della rinascita," in *Discorsi politici*, I, ed. Tommaso Bozza (Rome: Edizioni Cinque Lune, 1956), 59. It is ironic that the DC had traditionally favored decentralization, but reversed its stand once its own ministers assumed the powers of the centralized state.

29. One of the papers that did survive the war was the Communist daily, *L'Unità*. On journalistic successes and failures during the Resistenza Armata see Frank Rosengarten, *The Italian Anti-Fascist Press, 1919-1945* (Cleveland: Case Western Reserve University Press, 1968), pp. 89-121.

30. Calamandrei had supported the short-lived Unione Nazionale delle Forze Liberali e Democratiche, founded by Giovanni Amendola in 1924. See Salvatorelli and Mira, *Storia d'Italia nel periodo fascista*, pp. 327-328.

31. "Il nostro programma," *Il Ponte*, 1 (April 1945), 1; Calamandrei, "Costituente e questione sociale," *Il Ponte*, 1 (Aug. 1945), 379.

32. "L'eredità dei bancarottieri," *Il Ponte*, 1 (Oct. 1945), 574.

33. Franco Fortini, "Che cosa è stato 'Il Politecnico,'" in *Dieci inverni, 1947-1957: Contributi ad un discorso socialista* (Bari: De Donato Editore, 1973), p. 61.

34. Benedetto Croce, *Storia del Regno di Napoli* (Bari: Laterza, 1925), p. 232; Croce, "Considerazioni sul problema morale del tempo nostro," *Quaderni della Critica*, 1 (March 1945), 1. Essay rpt. in Croce, *Pensiero politica e politica attuale* (Bari: Laterza, 1946), pp. 3-24.

35. *Rinascita*, 1 (June 1944), 10. Reprinted in Antonio Gramsci, *Lettere dal carcere*, ed. Sergio Capioglio and Elsa Furbini (Turin: Einaudi, 1968), p. 633.

36. On this point see Denis Mack Smith, "The Politics of Senator Croce," *Cambridge Journal*, 1 (Oct. 1947), 28-42, and 1 (Feb. 1948), 279-291.

37. Gramsci, *Quaderni del carcere*, ed. Valentino Gerratana (Turin: Einaudi, 1975), III, 1676.

38. Elio Vittorini, "La nuova cultura," *Il Politecnico*, no. 1 (29 Sept. 1945), 1. Portions of this article are reprinted in Vittorini, *Diario in pubblico*, 2nd ed. (Milan: Bompiani, 1970), pp. 209-213.

39. *Il Politecnico*, not surprisingly, gave special attention to American literature in other ways besides serializing Hemingway's novel. The critical

prefaces that Vittorini had written in 1940 for the anthology *Americana* were published in *Il Politecnico*, offering its readers an engaging history of American letters. For a list of the articles published in the review during its two years of existence see *Il Politecnico: Antologia critica*, ed. Marco Porti and Sergio Pautasso (Milan: Lerici, 1960), pp. 875-902.

40. *Il Politecnico*, no. 16 (12 Jan. 1946), 1; Simone de Beauvoir, *La Force des choses* (Paris: Gallimard, 1963), p. 110. The interview with Sartre and Beauvoir appeared in *Il Politecnico*, no. 31-32 (July-Aug. 1946), 33-35.

41. The review proposed, for example, that its readers aid in selecting articles for a monthly "bulletin" that would faithfully reflect their tastes. See *"Il Politecnico invita i suoi lettori a redigere une rivista,"* *Il Politecnico*, no. 2 (6 Oct. 1945), 1.

42. Among the articles that addressed themselves to the discussion surrounding a "new culture" see especially Felice Balbo, "Lettera di un cattolico," *Il Politecnico*, no. 3 (13 Oct. 1945), 1; Vittorini, "Polemica e no: Per una nuova cultura," *Il Politecnico*, no. 7 (10 Nov. 1945), 1, 4; Franco Fortini, "Chiusura di una polemica: Cultura come scelta necessaria," *Il Politecnico*, no. 17 (19 Jan. 1946), 1.

43. Cattaneo became almost a patron saint for the Italian Resistance, much like Péguy in France. Among the many articles devoted to his works in the postwar Italian press see Giansiro Ferrata, "Dal Politecnico di Carlo Cattaneo," *Il Politecnico*, no. 17 (19 Jan. 1946), 2; and Mario Furbini, "La critica letteraria di Carlo Cattaneo," *Il Ponte*, 1 (Dec. 1945), 800-806.

44. Vittorini, "Polemica e no: Per una nuova cultura," 4.

45. Vittorini, "Politica e cultura: Lettera a Togliatti," *Il Politecnico*, no. 35 (Jan.-March 1947), 2.

46. Vittorini, "Lettera a Togliatti," 2-3. On the relations between the review and the Communist party during this period see Marina Zancan, "'Il Politecnico' e il PCI tra Resistenza e dopoguerra," *Il Ponte*, 29 (July-Aug. 1973), 994-1010.

47. Article two of the 1946 party statute read as follows: "All honest workers of both sexes who have reached eighteen years of age may join the Italian Communist party, independently of race, religious faith, and philosophical convictions. Every member of the party is obliged to accept the political program and the statute of the party, to work in one of its organizations, and to pay dues regularly." Quoted in Aldo Garosci, "The Italian Communist Party," in Mario Einaudi, Jean-Marie Domenach, and Aldo Garosci, *Communism in Western Europe* (Hamden, Conn.: Archon Books, 1971), p. 202, n. 1. Vittorini could claim support for his stand from the first sentence, Togliatti from the second.

48. Vittorini had already been obliged to respond to the criticisms of the Communist Mario Alicante in the summer of 1946. See Vittorini, "Politica e cultura," *Il Politecnico*, no. 31-32 (July-Aug. 1946), 2-6.

49. Palmiro Togliatti, "Politica e cultura: Una lettera di Palmiro Togliatti," *Il Politecnico*, no. 33-34 (Sept. Dec. 1946), 4. The letter, originally published in *Rinascita*, Oct. 1946, is rpt. in Togliatti, *La politica culturale*, ed. Luciano Gruppi (Rome: Editori Riuniti, 1974), pp. 75-81.

50. Togliatti, "Una lettera," 4. On the background of the debate see Fausto

Lupetti et al., *La polemica Vittorini-Togliatti e la linea culturale del PCI nel 1945-47* (Milan: Lavoro Liberato, 1974), pp. 165-258.

51. Vittorini, "Lettera a Togliatti," 105, 4.

52. Ibid., 105, 106.

53. Ibid., 106.

54. Ibid.

55. The polemic between Vittorini and Togliatti continued even after Vittorini's departure from the PCI. See his article, "Le vie degli ex-communisti," in *La Nuova Stampa*, 6 Sept. 1951, and *Rinascita*'s reply, "Vittorini se n'è ghiuto e soli ci ha lasciato," *Rinascita*, 8 (Aug.-Sept. 1951), 393-394.

56. Vittorini, "Rivoluzione e attività morale," *Il Politecnico*, no. 38 (Nov. 1947), 4. In a postface to *The Simplon Winks at Frejus*, Vittorini wrote: "My readers are accustomed to find a 'moral' more or less suggested to them by the succession of events that I relate. This time it is different. If my story contains something similar [to a moral], it is contained in the character of the protagonists, that is, in their resoluteness, not in the actions in which they participate." Vittorini, *Il Sempione*, in *Le Opere narrative*, ed. Mario Corti (Milan: Mondadori, 1974), I, 1007.

9. THE TRIUMPH OF THE STATE

1. "Qualcosa di nuovo," *Il Ponte*, 2 (Jan. 1946), 2.

2. On the results of the referendum see Giorgio Vaccarino, "Die Wiederherstellung der Demokratie in Italien (1943-1948)," *Vierteljahrshefte für Zeitgeschichte*, 21 (July 1973), 284-324. A table of votes cast and the percentages received by the major parties can be found in Giuseppe Mammarella, *Italy after Fascism: A Political History, 1943-1965* (Notre Dame, Ind.: University of Notre Dame Press, 1966), p. 116.

3. "Qualcosa di nuovo," 2; "La desistenza," *Il Ponte*, 2 (Oct. 1946), 837-838.

4. Bertolt Brecht, "Die Lösung" (1953), in *Gedichte* (Frankfurt am Main: Suhrkamp Verlag, 1964), VII, 9; Piero Gobetti, *La rivoluzione liberale*, in *Opere complete*, I: *Scritti politici*, ed. Paolo Spriano (Turin: Einaudi, 1960), 944.

5. Interview with Carlo Levi, Rome, 4 July 1974. See also Levi, "Piero Gobetti e la 'Rivoluzione Liberale,' " *Il Ponte*, 5 (Aug.-Sept. 1949), 1009-1021, and Vittorio Foa, "Carlo Levi 'Uomo politico,' " *Galleria*, 17 (May-Dec. 1967), 203-213.

6. Levi, *L'orologio* (Turin: Einaudi, 1974), pp. 160, 167.

7. The parable appeared in the first issue of Saint-Simon's paper, *L'Organisateur*, Nov. 1819. See Frank E. Manuel, *The New World of Henri Saint-Simon* (Cambridge, Mass.: Harvard University Press, 1956), pp. 206-216. Manuel gives an English translation of the parable on p. 211.

8. Levi, *L'orologio,* pp. 167, 168.

9. Ibid., pp. 169, 148.

10. Levi has described his clandestine life in Florence in "Palazzo Pitti,"

Il Ponte, 10 (Sept. 1954) 1325-1328; and the city's liberation in "Firenze libera," *Galleria*, 17 (May-Dec. 1967), 125-128. See also Carlo Francovich, *La Resistenza a Firenze* (Florence: La Nuova Italia, 1961), pp. 205-217.

11. Levi arrived in Gagliano in August 1935 and left the following summer. *Christ Stopped at Eboli* was written between December 1943 and July 1944, and first appeared (heavily excerpted) in *Il Ponte* in 1945.

12. Levi, *Cristo si è fermato a Eboli* (Turin: Einaudi, 1969), p. 70.

13. Ibid., p. 163.

14. Ibid., p. 220.

15. Ibid., p. 222.

16. Levi had briefly served on the CLN committee in Florence as part of a subgroup charged with press matters, and had fought the central government's attempts to reduce CLN autonomy.

17. Ignazio Silone, *Pane e vino* (Lugano: Nuovi Edizioni del Capolago, 1937), p. 105; Silone in *The God That Failed*, ed. Richard Crossman (London: Hamish Hamilton, 1949), p. 88. This autobiographical essay also appeared under the title "Uscita di sicurezza" in *Comunità*, no. 5 (Sept.-Oct. 1949). I have followed Crossman's English translation.

18. Silone, *The God That Failed*, pp. 101, 98.

19. Ibid., pp. 103-104, 118.

20. So nearly destitute was Silone that the manuscript of *Fontamara* was confiscated by his Swiss landlord for a time as a pledge on his unpaid rent. See his interview with Giovanna Santostefano, "Umanismo tragico di Silone," *Fiera Letteraria*, 4 July 1948.

21. Silone, *Fontamara* (Milan: Mondadori, 1970), pp. 87, 233-234.

22. The first version of the novel, published in Switzerland in 1937, was substantially revised by Silone in 1955 prior to its first publication in Italy. As a symbol of these changes, Silone altered the title from *Pane e vino* to *Vino e pane*. Most of the changes were stylistic rather than conceptual. Though they throw an interesting light on his later intellectual and artistic evolution, I have used the first Swiss edition in preference to the later Italian edition as my principal source and for the citations in this chapter.

23. Silone, *Pane e vino*, p. 105.

24. Ibid., p. 283.

25. R. W. B. Lewis, "Ignazio Silone: The Politics of Charity," in *The Picaresque Saint* (Philadelphia: Lippencott, 1959), p. 162.

26. Silone, *Fontamara*, p. 27; Silone, *Il seme sotto la neve* (Milan: Mondadori, 1974), p. 260.

27. Silone, *Il seme sotto la neve*, pp. 158, 252.

28. Ibid., pp. 516-517.

29. On Silone's attitude toward the relations between man and nature see his essay "Fiction and the Southern 'Subsoil,'" *Italian Quarterly*, 1 (Summer 1957), 32-49.

30. Silone to Carl Seelig, 16 Nov. 1941. *Europäische Ideen*, no. 5 (1975), 46.

31. The Communist tactic seems to have been to attack Silone's writings in public while extending offers of reconciliation in private. See Luce d'Eramo, *L'opera di Ignazio Silone* (Milan: Mondadori, 1971), pp. 516-522.

32. Italian supporters of a federated Europe, such as Altiero Spinelli, played an active part in the anti-Fascist exile community in Switzerland during this period; a number of their publications appeared in the Nuovi Edizioni del Capolago, which Silone had helped to found. See Aldo Garosci, *Storia dei fuorusciti* (Bari: Laterza, 1953), pp. 212-215.

33. Silone, "Mazzini," trans. Arthur Livingstone, preface to *The Living Thoughts of Mazzini* (London: Cassell, 1946), p. 4. The essay appeared after the war with the title "Nuovo incontro con Giuseppe Mazzini (pensieri su alcune difficoltà della nostra epoca)" in *Il Ponte*, 5 (Jan. 1949), 4-18. Clement Greenberg, "An Interview with Ignazio Silone," *Partisan Review*, 6 (Fall 1939), 22, 25. One must bear in mind that the interview took place at the time of the Moscow Purge Trials.

34. Greenberg, "An Interview with Ignazio Silone," 23.

35. Quoted in Garosci, *Storia dei fuorusciti*, p. 286. Silone's cordial relations with a number of left-wing Swiss intellectuals in Zurich also nourished his belief in the possibility of international cooperation based on socialist principles. On this aspect of his exile see Peter Stahlberger, *Der Zürcher Verleger Emil Oprecht und die politische Emigration, 1933-1945* (Zurich: Europa Verlag, 1970), pp. 99-102.

36. For Silone's decision to join *Avanti!* and the frustrations that followed, see his "Esperienze socialiste," *Tempo Presente*, 12 (Jan. 1967), 2-4. *Avanti!* was printed at the same address—via IV Novembre—as the Communist daily, *L'Unità*, and the two editorial teams kept a close watch on each other.

37. Rossi to Gaetano Salvemini, 12 Feb. 1945, in Salvemini, *Lettere dall'America, 1944-1946*, ed. Alberto Merola (Bari: Laterza, 1967), p. 97; Silone, "Ideologie e politica," *Mercurio*, 2 (Feb. 1945), 9.

38. Silone, "Esperienze socialiste," 4.

39. For Silone's public reasons for resigning see his article "Autocritica," *Avanti!*, 14 July 1946.

40. Olivetti (1901-1960), heir to one of Europe's leading office machinery firms, was one of several independent-minded industrialists who played an important role in directing public awareness of social problems in postwar Italy. His movement, Comunità, gathered considerable support from former Giustizia e Libertà members in the late 1940s and early 1950s.

41. Silone, "Missione europea del socialismo," in Ferruccio Parri et al., *Europa federata* (Milan: Edizioni di Comunità, 1947), pp. 41, 41-42.

42. Silone, "On the Place of the Intellect and the Pretentions of the Intellectual," in *The Intellectuals: A Controversial Portrait*, ed. George de Huszar (Glencoe, Ill.: Free Press, 1960), pp. 261, 263. Silone's speech was also published in a French translation in *Les Temps Modernes*, no. 23-24 (Aug.-Sept. 1947).

43. Silone, "On the Place of the Intellect," pp. 264, 266.

44. Silone, in *Comunità*, 3 (July-Aug. 1949), ii.

45. Ibid., iii.

46. Cesare Pavese, "Sono finiti i tempi in cui scoprivamo l'America," in *La letteratura americana e altri saggi* (Turin: Einaudi, 1962), p. 189. The article was originally broadcast as a radio review of Richard Wright's *Black Boy* in May 1947.

47. The Italians' interest in Wright was shared by *Les Temps Modernes*, which serialized a French translation of *Black Boy*. Beauvoir's *Amérique au jour le jour* is dedicated to Richard and Ellen Wright.

48. Simone de Beauvoir, *Amérique au jour le jour: 1947* (Paris: Gallimard, 1954), p. 108. The book, composed of diary notes made during a visit to the United States in 1947, was originally published in 1948 by Editions Morihien.

49. The aesthetic presuppositions of the neorealist movement are explored in *Inchiesta sul neorealismo*, ed. Carlo Bo (Turin: Edizione Radio Italiana, [1951]). On neorealist films of the late 1940s see also Carlo Lizzani, *Il cinema italiano* (Florence: Parenti, 1954), pp. 127-172; and Patrice Hovald, *Le Néo-réalisme italien* (Paris: Editions du Cerf, 1959). Ironically, a number of film directors such as Rossellini had received their training at the Centro Sperimentale school in Rome, established by Mussolini's Fascist government in 1935. Thus one of the few Fascist cultural initiatives that bore fruit led to the film renaissance culminating after 1945.

50. This conclusion is suggested in Alberto Asor Rosa, *Scrittori e popolo: Saggio sulla letteratura populista in Italia* (Rome: Samonà & Savelli, 1965), pp. 334-348.

51. Pavese, *La casa in collina*, in *Romanzi* (Turin: Einaudi, 1961), II, 129-130.

52. Leslie Fiedler, "Introducing Cesare Pavese," *Kenyon Review*, 16 (Autumn 1954), 552. For a discussion of the reasons for Pavese's suicide see Dominique Fernandez, *L'Echec de Pavese* (Paris: Bernard Grasset, 1967), pp. 193-213

CONCLUSION: THE RESISTANCE LEGACY

1. Not until 1958 was this inward-looking mood interrupted, when the Algerian war prompted the fall of the French Fourth Republic and the return of de Gaulle to power. But conservative coalitions ruled Italy and Germany throughout the 1950s. On the domestic climate in France see Michel Winock, *La République se meurt: Chronique 1956-1958* (Paris: Editions du Seuil, 1978).

2. Walter Dirks, "Der restaurative Charakter der Epoche," *Frankfurter Hefte*, 5 (Sept. 1950), 946.

3. Michel Crozier, "Les Intellectuels et la stagnation française," *Esprit*, 21 (Dec. 1953), 775.

4. Gottfried Benn, "Probleme der Lyrik" (1951), in *Gesammelte Werke,* ed. Dieter Wellershoff (Wiesbaden: Limes Verlag, 1968), IV, 1080. "Once and for all," wrote Alain Robbe-Grillet in 1957, "we must now cease to take accusations of irresponsibility seriously, cease to fear 'art for art's sake.'" Robbe-Grillet, "Sur quelques notions périmées," in *Pour un nouveau roman* (Paris: Editions de Minuit, 1963), p. 36.

5. Georges Bidault, "Esprit de la Résistance," in *Les Idées politiques et sociales de la Résistance,* ed. Henri Michel and Boris Mirkine-Guetzévitch

(Paris: Presses Universitaires de France, 1954), p. vi.

6. Enzo Enriques Agnoletti, "Dopo dieci anni," *Il Ponte*, 10 (Sept. 1954), 1323.

7. Giaime Pintor to Luigi Pintor, 28 Nov. 1943, in *Il sangue d'Europa*, ed. Valentino Gerratana (Turin: Einaudi, 1966), p. 186.

8. Alfred Andersch, *Die Kirschen der Freiheit* (Hamburg: Claassen Verlag, 1954), p. 109.

9. Jean-Paul Sartre, "La République du silence," in *Situations*, III (Paris: Gallimard, 1949), 11. Sartre's frequent use of imprisonment as a theme in fiction is explored in Marie-Denise Boros, *Un Séquestré: L'Homme sartrien* (Paris: Nizet, 1968). See also the special edition of *Il Ponte*, 5 (March 1950) entitled "Carceri: Esperienze e documenti."

10. André Malraux, *L'Espoir* (Paris: Gallimard, 1937), p. 233.

11. For the tendency to reduce values to binary pairs in wartime see Paul Fussell, *The Great War and Modern Memory* (New York and London: Oxford University Press, 1975), esp. pp. 75-113. On this point see Michael Uhl, "Das organisierte Grauen," *Der Ruf*, no. 11 (15 Jan. 1947), 13.

12. Dolf Sternberger, "Versuch zu einem Fazit," *Die Wandlung*, 4 (1949), 700.

13. Paul Nizan, *Aden-Arabie* (Paris: François Maspero, 1967), p. 32.

14. Sartre, "Présentation des *Temps Modernes*," in *Situations*, II: *Qu'est-ce que la littérature?* (Paris: Gallimard, 1948), 15.

15. See Dietrich Bonhoeffer, *Ethik*, ed. Eberhard Bethge (Munich: Christian Kaiser Verlag, 1975), pp. 238-241. The elitist strain in Resistance thought is well represented in *Vers le style du XXe siècle*, ed. Gilbert Gadoffre (Paris: Editions du Seuil, 1945), pp. 128-204.

16. For a thoughtful discussion of the voluntaristic spirit that inspires revolutionary groups in general, see Hannah Arendt, "The Revolutionary Tradition and Its Lost Treasure," in *On Revolution* (New York: Viking, 1965).

17. The parallel with saints' lives extends to the martyrdom that awaits many of the protagonists in Resistance literature: Mathieu Delarue in Sartre's *La Mort dans l'âme* (*Iron in the Soul*) Hélène Bertrand in *The Blood of Others*, Tarrou in *The Plague*, the underground leader N-2 in *Man and Not*.

18. Andersch, "Getty oder die Umerziehung in der Retorte," *Frankfurter Hefte*, 2, (Nov. 1947), 1091.

19. On this point see Lamberto Mercuri, "La crisi del Partito d'Azione: Febbraio 1946," *Storia Contemporanea*, 7 (Sept. 1976), 547-565.

20. Leonard Krieger, "Intellectuals and European Society," *Political Science Quarterly*, 67 (June 1952), 243.

21. The intellectuals' own sense of powerlessness during the late 1940s led them on occasion to adopt just such an explanation of events.

22. See Joel Colton, *Léon Blum: Humanist in Politics* (New York: Alfred A. Knopf, 1966), pp. 453-455.

23. The end of the period of hope came in France as early as the winter of 1944-45, in Italy a year later, and in Germany in the winter of 1946-47.

24. See Alfred J. Rieber, *Stalin and the French Communist Party, 1941-1947* (New York and London: Columbia University Press, 1962), esp. chap. 13.

25. This point is emphasized in Gordon Wright, *The Ordeal of Total War, 1939-1945* (New York: Harper & Row, 1968), pp. 236-238.

26. J[ohn] P[eter] Nettl, *The Soviet Achievement* (London: Thames and Hudson, 1967), p. 178.

27. The continuity of old political forces was another factor that placed the intellectuals at a disadvantage. As Franco Venturi recalled: "We tried to make a completely new, a brand new state. But against the great resistance of the Italian state, that was absolutely impossible. Modern states are terribly conservative. You can't change them." Interview with Franco Venturi, Turin, 27 June 1974.

28. Alban Vistel, *Héritage spirituel de la Résistance* ([Lyons]: Lug, [1955]), pp. 160-161.

29. On the fortunes of the Group 47 and related associations such as the Grünwalder Circle, see Hans Werner Richter, *Briefe an einen jungen Sozialisten* (Hamburg: Hoffmann & Campe, 1974), pp. 112-128.

30. See Norberto Bobbio, "Intellettuali e vita politica in Italia" (1954), in *Politica e cultura* (Turin: Einaudi, 1974), pp. 121-138.

31. *Déclaration des droits de l'homme et du citoyen* (Marseille: J. Moissy, 1791), p. 3; Denis Diderot, *Dictionnaire philosophique* (Paris: J. L. J. Brière, 1830), VI, 218-219.

32. Emmanuel Mounier, "Faut-il refaire la Déclaration des droits?" *Esprit*, 13 (Dec. 1944), 118-120.

33. See Michel-Antoine Burnier, *Les Existentialistes et la politique* (Paris: Gallimard, 1966), for an excellent analysis of *Les Temps Modernes* and Third World issues.

34. On the new interest in sociology and the stimulus provided by the Resistance see Diana Orvieto Pinto, "Sociology as a Cultural Phenomenon in France and Italy, 1950-1972" (Ph.D. diss., Harvard University, 1977).

35. Judith N. Shklar, *After Utopia: The Decline of Political Faith* (Princeton, N.J.: Princeton University Press, 1957), p. 3; Albert Camus, "Discours du 10 décembre 1957," in *Essais*, ed. Roger Quilliot and Louis Faucon (Paris: Gallimard, 1965), p. 1073.

Selected
Bibliography

FRANCE

Newspapers and Periodicals
Combat, Lyons and Paris, 1942-1950
Confluences, Lyons, 1942-1947
Esprit, Paris, 1932-1941, 1945-1955
Le Figaro, Paris, 1944-1946
La Gauche R.D.R., Paris, 1948-1949
L'Humanité, Paris, 1941-1950
Les Lettres Françaises, Paris, 1942-1950
La Nouvelle Revue Française, Paris, 1940-1943
La Revue Internationale, Paris, 1946-1947
Les Temps Modernes, Paris, 1945-1955

Memoirs, Diaries, Recollections
D'Astier de la Vigerie, Emmanuel. *Sept Fois sept jours.* Paris: Editions de Minuit, 1947.
Audiat, Pierre. *Paris pendant la guerre, 1940-1944.* Paris: Hachette, 1946.

Beauvoir, Simone de. *L'Amérique au jour le jour, 1947.* Paris: Gallimard, 1954.

———. *La Force de l'âge.* Paris: Gallimard, 1960.

———. *La Force des choses.* Paris: Gallimard, 1963.

———. *Mémoires d'une jeune fille rangée.* Paris: Gallimard, 1958.

Benda, Julien. *Les Cahiers d'un clerc, 1936-1949.* Paris: Emile Paul, 1950.

Bloch, Marc. *L'Etrange Défaite: Témoignage écrit en 1940.* Paris: Armand Colin, 1957.

Bloch-Michel, Jean. *Journal du désordre.* Paris: Gallimard, 1955.

Bourdet, Claude. *L'Aventure incertaine: De la Résistance à la restauration.* Paris: Stock, 1975.

Brasillach, Robert. *Une Génération dans l'orage, mémoires: Notre Avant-guerre, Journal d'un homme occupé.* Paris: Plon, 1968.

Bruckberger, Raymond-Léopold. *Si grande peine: Chronique des années 1940-1948.* Paris: Grasset, 1967.

Camus, Albert. *Carnets.* 2 vols. Ed. Roger Quilliot. Paris: Gallimard, 1962.

Char, René. *Feuillets d'Hypnos.* Paris: Gallimard, 1946.

Crémieux, Francis, ed. *La Vérité sur la libération de Paris.* Paris: Pierre Belfond, 1971.

Debû-Bridel, Jacques, ed. *La Résistance intellectuelle.* Paris: Julliard, 1970.

Frenay, Henri. *La Nuit finira: Mémoires de résistance, 1940-1945.* Paris: Robert Laffont, 1973.

Gaulle, Charles de. *Mémoires de guerre.* 3 vols. Paris: Plon, 1954-1959.

Grenier, Jean. *Albert Camus: Souvenirs.* Paris: Gallimard, 1968.

Guéhenno, Jean. *La Foi difficile.* Paris: Bernard Grasset, 1957.

———. *Journal des années noires, 1940-1944.* Paris: Gallimard, 1947.

Koestler, Arthur. *The Invisible Writing: The Second Volume of an Autobiography, 1932-1942.* London: Macmillan, 1969.

Lefebvre, Henri. *La Somme et le reste.* Vol. II. Paris: La Nef de Paris, 1957.

Malraux, André. *Antimémoires.* Paris: Gallimard, 1967.

Mendès-France, Pierre. *Liberté, liberté chérie.* Paris: Arthème Fayard, 1977.

Morin, Edgar. *Autocritique.* Paris: Editions du Seuil, 1970.

Mounier-Leclercq, Paulette, ed. *Mounier et sa génération: Lettres, carnets, et inédits.* Paris: Editions du Seuil, 1956.

Nizan, Paul. *Aden-Arabie.* Paris: François Maspero, 1967.

Ophuls, Marcel. *The Sorrow and the Pity.* Trans. Mireille Johnston. New York: Outerbridge & Lazard, 1972.

Rebatet, Lucien. *Les Décombres.* Paris: Denoël, 1942.

————. *Les Mémoires d'un fasciste*, II: *1941-1947*. Paris: Jean-Jacques Pauvert, 1976.

Sartre, Jean-Paul. *Les Mots*. Paris: Gallimard, 1964.

————. *Situations*, IV: *Portraits*. Paris: Gallimard, 1964.

Segonzac, Pierre Dunoyer de. *Le Vieux Chef: Mémoires et pages choisies*. Paris: Editions du Seuil, 1971.

Vercors [Jean Bruller]. *La Bataille du silence: Souvenirs de minuit*. Paris: Presses de la Cité, 1967.

Author's Interviews

Aron, Raymond	Cambridge, Mass., 11 April 1974
Bloch-Michel, Jean	Paris, 21 June 1974
Bourdet, Claude	Paris, 21 June 1974
Domenach, Jean-Marie	Paris, 19 June 1974
Frenay, Henri	Neuilly-sur-Seine, 14 April 1977
Kriegel, Annie	Paris, 20 June 1974
Leiris, Michel	Paris, 15 February 1977
Rousset, David	Paris, 4 February 1977
Rovan, Joseph	Paris, 2 and 7 February 1977
Sartre, Jean-Paul	Paris, 22 June 1974
Vercors [Jean Bruller]	Coulommiers, 2 August 1974

Other Contemporary Materials

Alain [Emile-Auguste Chartier]. *Politique*. Ed. Michel Alexandre. Paris: Presses Universitaires de France, 1962.

Aron, Raymond. *De l'armistice à l'insurrection nationale*. Paris: Gallimard, 1945.

————. *Le Grand Schisme*. Paris: Gallimard, [1948].

————. *L'Opium des intellectuels*. Paris: Calmann-Lévy, 1955.

Audry, Colette, ed. *Pour et contre l'existentialisme*. Paris: Editions Atlas, 1948.

Beauvoir, Simone de. *Les Bouches inutiles*. Paris: Gallimard, 1945.

————. *L'Existentialisme et la sagesse des nations*. Paris: Editions Nagel, 1948.

————. *L'Invitée*. Paris: Gallimard, 1943.

————. *Les Mandarins*. Paris: Gallimard, 1954.

————. *Pour une morale de l'ambiguïté*. Paris: Gallimard, 1947.

————. *Pyrrhus et Cinéas*. Paris: Gallimard, 1944.

————. *Le Sang des autres*. Paris: Gallimard, 1945.

Benda, Julien. *La Fin de l'éternel*. 3rd ed. Paris: Gallimard, 1977.

————. *Précision, 1930-1937*. Paris: Gallimard, 1937.

———. *La Trahison des clercs.* 4th ed. Paris: Bernard Grasset, 1975.

Benoist-Méchin, Jacques. *La Moisson de quarante: Journal d'un prisonnier de guerre.* Paris: Editions Albin Michel, 1941.

Berl, Emmanuel. *Mort de la morale bourgeoise.* 2nd ed. Paris: Jean-Jacques Pauvert, 1965.

———. *Mort de la pensée bourgeoise.* Paris: Bernard Grasset, 1929.

Blum, Léon. *A l'échelle humaine.* In *L'Oeuvre,* vol. V. Paris: Editions Albin Michel, 1955.

Camus, Albert. *Essais.* Ed. Roger Quilliot and Louis Faucon. Paris: Gallimard, Bibliothèque de la Pléiade, 1965.

———. *La Mort heureuse.* Ed Jean Santocchi. Paris: Gallimard, 1971.

———. *Théâtre, récits, nouvelles.* Ed. Roger Quilliot. Paris: Gallimard, Bibliothèque de la Pléiade, 1962.

Casanova, Laurent. *Le Parti communiste, les intellectuels, et la nation.* Paris: Editions Sociales, 1949.

Cassou, Jean. *La Mémoire courte.* Paris: Editions de Minuit, 1953.

Chanson, André, André Malraux, Jean Grenier, and Henri Petit. *Ecrits.* Paris: Bernard Grasset, 1927.

Curtis, Jean-Louis. *Les Forêts de la nuit.* Paris: Julliard, 1947.

———. *Les Justes Causes.* Paris: Julliard, 1954.

Debû-Bridel, Jacques. *Les Editions de Minuit: Historique et bibliographie.* Paris: Editions de Minuit, 1945.

Drieu la Rochelle, Pierre. *L'Europe contre les patries.* Paris: Gallimard, 1931.

———. *Socialisme fasciste.* Paris: Gallimard, 1934.

Eluard, Paul. *Oeuvres complètes.* Ed. Marcelle Dumas and Lucien Scheler. Vol. I. Paris: Gallimard, Bibliothèque de la Pléiade, 1968.

Gaulle, Charles de. *Discours et messages.* Vols. I-II. Paris: Plon, 1970.

Gide, André. *Littérature engagée.* Ed. Yvonne Davet. Paris: Gallimard, 1950.

Isorni, Jacques. *Le Procès de Robert Brasillach.* 2nd ed. Paris: Flammarion, [1956].

Kanapa, Jean. *L'Existentialisme n'est pas un humanisme.* Paris: Editions Sociales, 1947.

Koestler, Arthur. *Darkness at Noon.* Trans. Daphne Hardy. New York: Macmillan, 1941.

———. *The Yogi and the Commissar.* London: Hutchison, 1963.

Malraux, André. *La Condition humaine.* Paris: Gallimard, 1933.

———. *Les Conquérants.* Paris: Bernard Grasset, 1928.

———. *L'Espoir.* Paris: Gallimard, 1937.

———. *Les Noyers de l'Altenburg.* Paris: Gallimard, 1948.

———. *Le Temps du mépris.* Paris: Gallimard, 1935.

————. *La Tentation de l'occident*. Paris: Bernard Grasset, 1926.

————. *La Voie royale*. Paris: Bernard Grasset, 1930.

Merleau-Ponty, Maurice. *Les Aventures de la dialectique*. Paris: Gallimard, 1955.

————. *Humanisme et terreur: Essai sur le problème communiste*. 2nd ed. Paris: Gallimard, 1972.

————. *Phénoménologie de la perception*. Paris: Gallimard, 1945.

————. *Sens et non-sens*. Paris: Editions Nagel, 1966.

————. *La Structure du comportement*. 6th ed. Paris: Presses Universitaires de France, 1967.

Michel, Henri, and Boris Mirkine-Guetzévitch, eds. *Les Idées politiques et sociales de la Résistance: Documents clandestins, 1940-1944*. Paris: Presses Universitaires de France, 1954.

Mauriac, François. *Oeuvres complètes*. Vol. XI. Paris: Arthème Fayard, Bibliothèque Bernard Gasset, 1952.

Mounier, Emmanuel *Oeuvres*. Vols. I-III. Ed. Paulette Mounier-Leclercq. Paris: Editions du Seuil, 1961-1962.

Nizan, Paul. *Le Cheval de Troie*. Paris: Gallimard, 1935.

————. *Les Chiens de garde*. Paris: François Maspero, 1971.

————. *La Conspiration*. Paris: Gallimard, 1968.

————. *Paul Nizan, intellectual communiste, 1926-1940*. Ed. Jean-Jacques Brochier. Paris: François Maspero, 1967.

————. *Pour une nouvelle culture*. Ed. Susan Suleiman. Paris: Bernard Grasset, 1971.

Parrot, Louis. *L'Intelligence en guerre: Panorama de la pensée française dans la clandestinité*. Paris: La Jeune Parque, 1945.

Paulhan, Jean. *Lettre aux directeurs de la Résistance (1951) suivie des répliques et des contre-répliques*. Paris: Jean-Jacques Pauvert, [1968].

————, and Dominique Aury, eds. *La Patrie se fait tous les jours: Textes français, 1939-1945*. Paris: Editions de Minuit, 1947.

————, Francis Ponge, Yvonne Desvignes, Julien Benda, Jacques Debû-Bridel, and Vercors. *Chroniques interdites*. Paris: Editions de Minuit, 1945.

Pétain, Philippe. *Paroles aux Français: Messages et écrits, 1934-1941*. Lyons: Lardanchet, 1941.

Reale, Eugenio. *Avec Jacques Duclos au banc des accusés à la réunion constitutive du Kominform*. Trans. Pierre Bonuzzi. Paris: Plon, 1958.

Rousseaux, André, ed. *Deux voix françaises: Péguy Péri*. Paris: Editions de Minuit, 1944.

Rousset, David. *Les Jours de notre mort*. Paris: Editions du Pavois, 1946.

————. *L'Univers concentrationnaire*. Paris: Editions du Pavois, 1945.

Sartre, Jean-Paul. *L'Age de raison*. Paris: Gallimard, 1945.

———. *Bariona*. Paris: Editions Elisabeth Marescot, 1967.

———. *Baudelaire*. Paris: Gallimard, 1947.

———. *Esquisse d'une théorie des émotions*. Paris: Hermann, 1939.

———. *L'Etre et le néant: Essai d'ontologie phénoménologique*. Paris: Gallimard, 1943.

———. *L'Existentialisme est un humanisme*. Paris: Editions Nagel, 1946.

———. *L'Imaginaire: Psychologie phénoménologique de l'imagination*. Paris: Gallimard, 1940.

———. *L'Imagination*. Paris: Fernand Alcan, 1936.

———. *Les Mains sales*. Paris: Gallimard, 1948.

———. *La Mort dans l'âme*. Paris: Gallimard, 1949.

———. *Le Mur*. Paris: Gallimard, 1939.

———. *La Nausée*. Paris: Gallimard, 1938.

———. *Réflections sur la question juive*. Paris: Gallimard, 1954.

———. *Situations*. Vols. I-III, VI. Paris: Gallimard, 1947-1964.

———. *Le Sursis*. Paris: Gallimard, 1945.

———. *Théâtre*, I: *Les Mouches, Huis-clos, Morts sans sépulture, La Putain respectueuse*. Paris: Gallimard, 1947.

———. *La Transcendance de l'ego: Esquisse d'une description phénoménologique*. Ed. Sylvie Le Bon. Paris: Librairie Philosophique Vrin, 1965.

———, David Rousset, and Gérard Rosenthal. *Entretiens sur la politique*. Paris: Gallimard, 1949.

Thomas, Edith. *Contes d'Auxois*. Paris: Editions de Minuit, 1944.

Vercors [Jean Bruller]. *La Marche vers l'étoile*. Paris: Editions de Minuit, 1944.

———. *Plus ou moins homme*. Paris: Albin Michel, 1950.

———. *Le Sable du temps*. Paris: Emile Paul Frères, 1946.

———. *Le Silence de la mer*. Paris: Club des Libraires de France, 1964.

Vistel, Alban. *Héritage spirituel de la Résistance*. [Lyons]: Lug, [1955].

Wahl, Jean. *Vers le concret: Etudes d'histoire de la philosophie contemporaine*. Paris: Librairie Philosophique Vrin, 1932.

Weil, Simone. *Ecrits historiques et politiques*. Paris: Gallimard, 1960.

———. *L'Enracinement: Une Prélude à une déclaration des devoirs envers l'être humain*. Paris: Gallimard, 1949.

———. *Oppression et liberté*. Paris: Gallimard, 1955.

GERMANY

Newspapers and Periodicals

Aufbau, Berlin, 1945-1950
Aufbau, Bremen, 1945-1946
Deutsche Beiträge, Munich, 1946-1947
Deutsche Rundschau, Berlin, 1933-1942, 1946-1950
Ende und Anfang, Munich, 1945-1947
Frankfurter Hefte, Frankfurt am Main, 1946-1955
Frankfurter Zeitung, Frankfurt am Main, 1933-1943
Die Gegenwart, Freiburg im Breisgau, 1946-1950
Historische Zeitschrift, Munich, 1949-1955
Horizont, Berlin, 1945-1947
Lancelot, Baden-Baden, 1946-1950
Die Neue Zeitung, Munich, 1945-1948
Ost und West, Berlin, 1947-1949
Der Ruf, Fort Kearney, R.I., 1944-1946
Der Ruf, Munich, 1946-1947
Die Tat, Jena, 1928-1934
Die Wandlung, Heidelberg, 1946-1949
Die Zeit, Hamburg, 1946-1950

Memoirs, Diaries, Recollections

Abetz, Otto. *Das offene Problem: Ein Rückblick auf zwei Jahrzehnte deutscher Frankreichspolitik.* Cologne: Greven Verlag, 1951.

Améry, Jean. *Jenseits von Schuld und Sühne: Bewältigungsversuche eines Überwältigten.* Munich: Szczesny Verlag, 1966.

Andersch, Alfred. *Die Kirschen der Freiheit: Ein Bericht.* Hamburg: Claassen Verlag, 1954.

Benn, Gottfried. *Doppelleben: Zwei Darstellungen.* In *Autobiographische Schriften.* Wiesbaden: Limes Verlag, 1950.

Bergengruen, Werner. *Schreibtischerinnerungen.* Zurich: Die Arche Verlag, 1961.

Böll, Heinrich, and Christian Linder. *Drei Tage im März: Ein Gespräch.* Cologne: Kiepenheuer & Witsch, 1975.

Brandt, Willy, and Leo Lania. *Mein Weg nach Berlin.* Munich: Kindler Verlag, 1961.

Brett-Smith, Richard. *Berlin '45: The Grey City.* London: Macmillan, 1966.

Clay, Lucius D. *Decision in Germany.* Garden City, N.J.: Doubleday, 1950.

Delp, Alfred. *Im Angesicht des Todes: Geschrieben zwischen Verhaftung und Hinrichtung, 1944-1945.* Ed. Paul Bolkovac. Frankfurt am Main: Verlag Josef Knecht, 1947.

Frisch, Max. *Tagebuch, 1946-1949.* Frankfurt am Main: S. Fischer Verlag, 1950.

Goebbels, Joseph. *Das Tagebuch von Joseph Goebbels, 1925-26.* Ed. Helmut Heiber. Stuttgart: Deutsche Verlags-Anstalt, n.d.

———. *Tagebücher 1945: Die letzten Aufzeichnungen.* Hamburg: Hoffmann & Campe Verlag, 1977.

Gollancz, Victor. *In Darkest Germany.* London: Victor Gollancz, 1947.

Habe, Hans. *Im Jahre Null: Ein Beitrag zur Geschichte der deutschen Presse.* Munich: Kurt Desch Verlag, 1966.

Hassell, Ulrich von. *Vom anderen Deutschland: Aus den nachgelassenen Tagebüchern, 1938-1944.* Zurich: Atlantis Verlag, 1946.

Jünger, Ernst. *Tagebücher.* Vols. I-III. Stuttgart: Ernst Klett Verlag, [1960].

Kästner, Erich. *Notabene 45: Ein Tagebuch.* Berlin: Cecilie Dressler Verlag, [1962].

Kardorff, Ursula von. *Berliner Aufzeichnungen, 1942-1945.* 2nd ed. Munich: Nymphenburger Verlagshandlung, 1976.

Leonhard, Wolfgang. *Die Revolution entlässt ihre Kinder.* Cologne: Kiepenheuer & Witsch, 1955.

Neunzig, Hans A., ed. *Hans Werner Richter und die Gruppe 47.* Munich: Nymphenburger Verlagshandlung. 1979.

Pechel, Rudolf. *Deutscher Widerstand.* Erlenbach-Zurich: Eugen Rentsch Verlag, 1947.

Rauschning, Hans, ed. *Das Jahr 45: Dichtung, Bericht, Protokoll deutscher Autoren.* Gütersloh: Bertelsmann Verlag, 1970.

Rauschning, Hermann. *Gespräche mit Hitler.* 2nd ed. Vienna: Europa Verlag, 1973.

Reck-Malleczewen, Friedrich Percyval von. *Tagebuch eines Verzweifelten: Zeugnis einer inneren Emigration.* Stuttgart: Harry Goverts Verlag, 1966.

Richter, Hans Werner, ed. *Almanach der Gruppe 47, 1947-1962.* Reinbek bei Hamburg: Rowohlt Verlag, 1962.

———. *Briefe an einen jungen Sozialisten.* Hamburg: Hoffmann & Campe Verlag, 1974.

Schlabrendorff, Fabian von. *Offiziere gegen Hitler: Nach einem Erlebnisbericht.* Ed. Gero von S[chulze-]Gaevernitz. Zurich: Europa Verlag, 1946.

Schneider, Reinhold. *Verhüllter Tag.* Cologne: Jakob Hegner Verlag, 1950.

Scholl, Inge. *Die weisse Rose.* Frankfurt am Main: Verlag der Frankfurter Hefte, 1952.

Schulz, Uwe, ed. *Fünfzehn Autoren suchen sich selbst: Modell und Provokation.* Munich: Paul List Verlag, 1967.

Shirer, William L. *Berlin Diary: The Journal of a Foreign Correspondent, 1934-1941.* New York: Alfred A. Knopf, 1941.

Speer, Albert. *Erinnerungen.* Berlin: Propyläen Verlag, 1969.

Wiechert, Ernst. *Jahre und Zeiten.* In *Sämtliche Werke,* vol. IX. Munich: Kurt Desch Verlag, 1957.

Zuckmayer, Carl. *Als wär's ein Stück von mir: Horen der Freundschaft.* 2nd ed. Hamburg: S. Fischer Verlag, 1972.

Author's Interviews

Andersch, Alfred	Berzona, Switzerland, 10 July 1974
Dirks, Walter	Wittnau bei Freiburg, 29 and 30 July 1974
Habicht, Hubert	Frankfurt am Main, 23 July 1974
Kardorff, Ursula von	Munich, 10 May 1977
Kogon, Eugen	Frankfurt am Main, 23 July 1974
Kolbenhoff, Walter	Munich, 22 April 1977
Neumann, Oskar	Munich, 28 March 1977
Richter, Hans Werner	Munich, 26 July 1974
Schnurre, Wolfdietrich	Berlin, 6 March 1977
Sternberger, Dolf	Darmstadt, 20 March 1977

Other Contemporary Materials

Andersch, Alfred. *Deutsche Literatur in der Entscheidung.* Munich: Nymphenburger Verlagshandlung, 1948.

———. *Sansibar, oder der letzte Grund.* Olten and Freiburg im Breisgau: Walter Verlag, 1957.

Benn, Gottfried. *Reden und Vorträge.* In *Gesammelte Werke,* vol. IV. Ed. Dieter Wellershoff. Wiesbaden: Limes Verlag, 1968.

———. *Statische Gedichte.* Zurich: Die Arche Verlag, 1948.

Bergengruen, Werner. *Dies Irae.* Zurich: Die Arche Verlag, 1946.

Böll, Heinrich. *Frankfurter Vorlesungen.* Cologne: Kiepenheuer & Witsch, 1966.

———. *Irisches Tagebuch.* Cologne: Kiepenheuer & Witsch, 1957.

———. *Und sagte kein einziges Wort.* Cologne: Kiepenheuer & Witsch, 1953.

———. *Wo warst du, Adam?, und Erzählungen.* Cologne: Friedrich Middelhauve Verlag, 1968.

Bonhoeffer, Dietrich. *Ethik.* Munich: Christian Kaiser Verlag, 1962.

———. *Widerstand und Ergebung: Briefe und Aufzeichungen aus der Haft.* Ed. Eberhard Bethge. Munich: Christian Kaiser Verlag, 1964.

Borchert, Wolfgang. *Das Gesamtwerk.* Ed Bernhard Meyer-Marwitz. Hamburg: Rowohlt Verlag, 1972.

Brill, Hermann. *Gegen den Strom.* Offenbach am Main: Bollwerk Verlag, 1946.

Dirks, Walter. *Erbe und Aufgabe: Gesammelte kulturpolitische Aufsätze.* Frankfurt am Main: Verlag der Carolus-Druckerei, 1931.

Eich, Günter. *Werke.* 4 vols. Frankfurt am Main: Suhrkamp Verlag, 1973.

Fiedeler, Hans [Alfred Döblin]. *Der Nürnberger Lehrprozess.* Baden-Baden: Neuer Bücherdienst, 1946.

Frank, Hans. *Neues deutsches Recht.* Munich: Franz Eher Nachfolger, 1936.

Goebbels, Joseph. *Goebbels-Reden.* 2 vols. Ed. Helmut Heiber. Düsseldorf: Droste Verlag, 1971.

———. *Michael: Ein deutsches Schicksal in Tagebuchblättern.* Munich: Franz Eher Nachfolger, 1931.

Groll, Gunter, ed. *De Profundis: Deutsche Lyrik in dieser Zeit.* Munich: Kurt Desch Verlag, 1946.

Haushofer, Albrecht. *Moabiter Sonnette.* Berlin: Blanvalet Verlag, 1946.

Hitler, Adolf. *Mein Kampf.* Munich: Franz Eher Nachfolger, 1932.

———. *Reden und Proklamationen.* 2 vols. Ed. Max Domarus. Würzburg: Schmidt Neustadt, 1962.

International Military Tribunal. *Trial of the Major War Criminals before the International Military Tribunal.* Vols. I-V, XXII. Nuremberg: Secretariat of the Tribunal, 1947.

Jaspers, Karl. *Die geistige Situation der Zeit (1931).* Berlin: Walter de Gruyter, 1931.

———. *Die Schuldfrage.* In *Hoffnung und Sorge: Schriften zur deutschen Politik, 1945-1965.* Munich: Piper Verlag, 1965.

———. *Philosophie*, II: *Existenzerhellung.* Berlin: Julius Springer Verlag, 1932.

Johnst, Hanns. *Schlageter.* Munich: Albert Langen / Georg Müller Verlag, 1934.

Jünger, Ernst. *Auf den Marmorklippen.* In *Werke*, vol. IX. Stuttgart: Ernst Klett Verlag, 1960.

———. *Der Arbeiter.* In *Werke*, vol. VI. Stuttgart: Ernst Klett Verlag, 1960.

Kästner, Erich. *Fabian: Die Geschichte eins Moralisten.* In *Gesammelte Schriften*, II: *Romane.* Cologne: Kiepenheuer & Witsch, 1959.

———. *Der tägliche Kram: Chansons und Prosa, 1945-1948.* In *Gesammelte Schriften*, V: *Vermischte Beiträge.* Cologne: Kiepenheuer & Witsch, 1959.

Klemperer, Victor. *LTI: Notizbuch eines Philologen*. Berlin: Aufbau Verlag, 1947.

Kogon, Eugen. *Der SS-Staat: Das System der deutschen Konzentrationslager*. Berlin: Verlag des Druckhauses Tempelhof, 1947.

Kolbenhoff, Walter. *Von unserem Fleisch und Blut*. Munich: Nymphenburger Verlagshandlung, 1947.

Kraus, Karl. *Die dritte Walpurgisnacht*. Munich: Kösel Verlag, 1952.

Lipgens, Walter, ed. *Europa-Föderationspläne der Widerstandsbewegungen, 1940-1945*. Munich: Oldenbourg Verlag, 1968.

Mann, Thomas, *Doktor Faustus: Das Leben des deutschen Tonsetzers Adrian Leverkühn erzählt von einem Freunde*. In *Gesammelte Werke*, VI: *Romane*. Frankfurt am Main: S. Fischer Verlag, 1974.

————. *Gesammelte Werke*, XI: *Reden und Aufsätze*. Frankfurt am Main: S. Fischer Verlag, 1974.

Meinecke, Friedrich. *Autobiographische Schriften*. Ed. Eberhard Kessel. Stuttgart: K. F. Koehler Verlag, 1969.

————. *Die Enstehung des Historismus*. Ed. Carl Hinrichs. Munich: R. Oldenbourg Verlag, 1965.

————. *Weltbürgertum und Nationalstaat*. Ed. Hans Herzfeld. Munich: R. Oldenbourg Verlag, 1962.

Moltke, Helmuth James von. *A German of the Resistance: The Last Letters of Count Helmuth James von Moltke*. London: Oxford University Press, 1948.

Office of the Chief of Military History. *Re-education of Enemy Prisoners of War: Projects II and III*. Declassified report 4-4.1 BB2 C1. Washington, D.C., 1946.

Pechel, Rudolf. *Deutsche Gegenwart: Aufsätze und Vorträge 1945-1952*. Darmstadt: Im Stichnote Verlag, 1953.

Richter, Hans Werner, ed. *Deine Söhne, Europa: Gedichte deutscher Kriegsgefangener*. Munich: Nymphenburger Verlagshandlung, 1947.

————. *Die Geschlagenen*. Munich: Deutscher Taschenbuch Verlag, 1969

————. *Rose weiss, Rose rot*. Hamburg: Hoffmann & Campe, 1971.

————. *Sie fielen aus Gottes Hand*. Munich: Kurt Desch Verlag, 1951.

Ritter, Gerhard. *Europa und die deutsche Frage: Betrachtungen über die geschichtliche Eigenart des deutschen Staatsdenkens*. Munich: Münchner Verlag, 1948.

Ruhm von Oppen, Beate, ed. *Documents on Germany under Occupation, 1945-1954*. London: Oxford University Press, 1955.

Schneider, Reinhold. *Apokalypse*. Baden-Baden: Hans Bühler Verlag, 1946.

————. *Die letzten Tage*. Zurich: Die Arche Verlag, 1945.

————. *Die Sonette*. Cologne: Jakob Hegner Verlag, 1954.

Schnurre, Wolfdietrich. *Man sollte dagegen sein*. Olten and Freiburg im Breisgau: Walter Verlag, 1960.

————. *Schreibtisch unter freiem Himmel: Polemik und Bekenntnis*. Olten and Freiburg im Breisgau: Walter Verlag, 1964.

Spengler, Oswald. *Preussentum und Sozialismus*. Munich: C. H. Beck Verlag, 1925.

————. *Der Untergang des Abendlandes: Umrisse einer Morphologie der Weltgeschichte*. Munich: C. H. Beck Verlag, 1969.

————. *Reden und Aufsätze*. Munich: C. H. Beck Verlag, 1951.

Sternberger, Dolf, [Gerhard] Storz, and W[ilhelm] E[manuel] Süskind. *Aus dem Wörterbuch des Unmenschen*. Hamburg: Claassen Verlag, 1957.

————. *Dreizehn politische Radio-Reden, 1946*. Heidelberg: Lambert Schneider Verlag, 1947.

Süskind, W[ilhelm] E[manuel]. *Die Mächtigen vor Gericht: Nürnberg 1945/46 an Ort und Stelle erlebt*. Munich: Paul List Verlag, 1963.

Weisenborn, Günther, ed. *Der lautlose Aufstand: Bericht über die Widerstandsbewegung des deutschen Volkes, 1933-1945*. Hamburg: Rowohlt Verlag, 1953.

Weyrauch, Wolfgang, ed. *Die Pflugschar: Sammlung neuer deutscher Dichtung*. Berlin: Aufbau Verlag, 1947.

————. *Tausend Gramm: Sammlung neuer deutscher Geschichten*. Hamburg: Rowohlt Verlag, 1949.

Wiechert, Ernst. *An die deutsche Jugend: Vier Reden*. Munich: Kurt Desch Verlag, 1951.

————. *Das einfache Leben*. In *Sämtliche Werke*, vol. IV. Munich: Kurt Desch Verlag, 1957.

————. *Der Totenwald*. In *Sämtliche Werke*, vol. IX. Munich: Kurt Desch Verlag, 1957.

Wulf, Joseph, ed. *Literatur und Dichtung im Dritten Reich: Eine Dokumentation*. Gütersloh: Sigbert Mohn Verlag, 1963.

Zeller, Bernhard, ed. *Als der Krieg zu Ende war: Literarisch-politische Publizistik, 1945-1950*. Munich: Kösel Verlag, 1974.

ITALY

Newspapers and Periodicals
Avanti!, Rome, 1945-1949
Il Bargello, Florence, 1931-1936

Comunità, Ivrea, 1947-1950
La Cultura, Turin, 1930-1933
La Critica, Bari, 1930-1944
Giustizia e Libertà, Paris, 1932-1936
L'Italia Libera, 1943-1946
Mercurio, Rome, 1944-1948
Nuovi Quaderni di Giustizia e Libertà, Milan, 1944-1946
Il Politecnico, Milan, 1945-1947
Il Ponte, Florence, 1945-1950
Quaderni della "Critica", Bari, 1945-1950
Rinascita, Rome, 1944-1950
Solaria, Florence, 1926-1934
L'Unità, Milan and Rome, 1944-1950

Memoirs, Diaries, Recollections

Alvaro, Corrado. *Quasi une vita: Giornale di uno scrittore*. Milan: Bompiani, 1951.

Amendola, Giorgio. *Lettere a Milano: Ricordi e documenti, 1939-1945*. Rome: Editori Riuniti, 1973.

Andreotti, Giulio. *Concerto a sei voci: Storia segreta di una crisi*. Rome: Edizioni della Bussola, 1945.

Benedetti, Arrigo. *Paura all'alba*. Milan: Il Saggiatore, 1965.

Bilenchi, Romano. *Amici: Vittorini, Rosai, e altri incontri*. Turin: Einaudi, 1976.

Bobbio, Norberto. *Italia civile: Ritratti e testimonianze*. Manduria and Bari: Lacaita, 1964.

Bonomi, Ivanoe. *Diario di un anno*. Milan: Garzanti, 1947.

Bottai, Giuseppe. *Vent'anni e un giorno*. Milan: Mondadori, 1949.

Brancati, Vitaliano. *Diario romano*. Ed. Sandro De Feo and G. A. Cibotto. Milan: Bompiani, 1961.

Calamandrei, Piero. *Uomini e città della Resistenza*. Bari: Laterza, 1955.

Calvino, Italo. *L'entrata in guerra*. Turin: Einaudi, 1954.

Camon, Ferdinando. *Il mestiere di poeta*. Milan: Lerici, 1965.

Ciano, Galeazzo. *Diario, 1939-43*. 5th ed. Ed. Renzo Trionfera. Milan: Rizzoli, 1971.

Ginzburg, Natalia. *Lessico famigliare*. Turin: Einaudi, 1963.

Gobetti, Ada. *Diario partigiano*. Turin: Einaudi, 1956.

Gaureschi, Giovanni. *Diario clandestino, 1943-1945*. Milan: Rizzoli, 1949.

Jemolo, Arturo Carlo. *Anni di prova*. Vicenza: Neri Pozza, 1969.

Levi, Primo. *La tregua*. Turin: Einaudi, 1967.

Livio Bianco, Dante. *Guerra partigiana.* 2nd ed. Turin: Einaudi, 1973.

Lombardo Radice, Lucio. *Fascismo e anticomunismo: Appunti e ricordi, 1935-1945.* Turin: Einaudi, 1946.

Montale, Eugenio. *Auto da fé: Cronache in due tempi.* Milan: Il Saggiatore, 1966.

Nenni, Pietro. *Taccuino 1942.* Milan and Rome: Edizioni Avanti!, 1955.

Pavese, Cesare. *Il mestiere di vivere: Diario, 1935-1950.* Turin: Einaudi, 1962.

Senise, Carmine. *Quando ero capo della polizia, 1940-1943.* Rome: Ruffolo, [1946].

Silone, Ignazio. *Uscita di sicurezza.* Florence: Valecchi, 1966.

Soffici, Ardengo, and Giuseppe Prezzolini. *Diari, 1939-1945.* Milan: Edizioni del Borghese, 1962.

Spinelli, Altiero. *Il lungo monologo.* Rome: Edizioni dell'Ateneo, 1968.

Spinetti, G[astone] Silvano. *Difesa di una generatione: Scritti e appunti. Rome: Edizioni Polilibraria, 1948.*

Ulisse [Davide Lajolo]. *Classe 1912.* Asti: Case Editrice Arethusa, 1945.

Valiani, Leo. *Tutte le strade conducono a Roma: Diario di un uomo nella guerra di un popolo.* Florence: La Nuova Italia, [1947].

Vittorini, Elio. *Diario in pubblico.* Milan: Bompiani, 1970.

Zangrandi, Ruggero. *Il lungo viaggio attraverso il fascismo: Contributo alla storia di una generazione.* Milan: Feltrinelli, 1962.

Author's Interviews

Bobbio, Norberto	Turin, 25 July 1977
Bondy, François	Zurich, 26 February 1977
Calvino, Italo	Paris, 1 February 1977
Garosci, Aldo	Rome, 3 July 1974
Levi, Carlo	Rome, 4 July 1974
Mieli, Renato	Venice, 6 July 1974
Spinelli, Altiero	Brussels, 29 June 1974
Valiani, Leo	Milan, 29 June 1974
Venturi, Franco	Turin, 27 June 1974
Volterra, Edoardo	Rome, 2 July 1974

Other Contemporary Materials

Alvaro, Corrado. *L'uomo è forte.* Milan: Bompiani, 1938.

Bo, Carlo, ed. *Inchiesta sul neorealismo.* Turin: Edizioni Radio Italiana, [1951].

Bottai, Giuseppe. *Scritti.* Ed. Roberto Bartolozzi and Riccardo Del Giudice. Bologna: Cappelli, [1965].

Calogero, Guido. *Difesa del liberalsocialismo ed altri saggi.* Ed. Michele Schiavone and Dino Cofrancesco. Milan: Marzorati, 1972.

———. *Lezioni di filosofia,* II: *Etica.* 3rd ed. Turin: Einaudi, 1960.

Calvino, Italo. *Il sentiero dei nidi di ragno.* 2nd ed. Turin: Einaudi, 1964.

———. *Ultimo viene il corvo.* 2nd ed. Turin: Einaudi, 1969.

Cecchi, Emilio. *America amara.* 5th ed. Florence: Sansoni, 1946.

Croce, Benedetto. *Discorsi parlamentari.* Rome: Bardi, 1966.

———. *Etica e politica.* 4th ed. Bari: Laterza, 1956.

———. *Pagine politiche (luglio - dicembre 1944).* Bari: Laterza, 1945.

———. *Pensiero politico e politica attuale.* Bari: Laterza, 1946.

———. *La storia come pensiero e come azione.* Bari: Laterza, 1938.

———. *Storia del Regno di Napoli.* Bari: Laterza, 1925.

———. *Storia d'Italia dal 1871 al 1915.* Bari: Laterza, 1962.

Curiel, Eugeno. *Scritti, 1935-1945.* 2 vols. Ed. Filippo Frassati. Rome: Editori Riuniti, 1973.

Einaudi, Luigi. *La guerra e l'unità europea.* Milan: Edizioni di Comunità, 1948.

Fenoglio, Beppe. *I ventitre giorni della città di Alba.* 2nd ed. Turin: Einaudi, 1963.

Gasperi, Alcide De. *Discorsi politici.* 2 vols. Ed. Tommaso Bozza. Rome: Edizioni Cinque Lune, 1956.

———. *Studi e appelli della lunga vigilia.* Rome: Magi-Spinetti, 1946.

Gentile, Giovanni. *Che cosa è il fascismo: Discorsi e polemiche.* Florence: Valecchi, 1925.

———. *Fascismo e cultura.* Milan: Treves, 1928.

———. *Origini e dottrina del fascismo.* Rome: Libreria del Littorio, 1929.

Ginzburg, Leone. *Scritti.* Ed. Domenico Zucàro and Carlo Ginzburg. Turin: Einaudi, 1962.

Ginzburg, Natalia. *Tutti i nostri ieri.* Turin: Einaudi, [1952].

Gobetti, Piero. *Opere complete.* Vols. I-II. Ed. Paolo Spriano. Turin: Einaudi, 1960-1969.

Gramsci, Antonio. *Quaderni del carcere.* 4 vols. Ed. Valentino Gerratana. Turin: Einaudi, 1975.

———. *Lettere dal carcere.* 2nd ed. Ed. Sergio Caprioglio and Elsa Fubini. Turin: Einaudi, 1968.

Levi, Carlo. *Cristo si è fermato a Eboli*. Turin: Einaudi, 1969.

―――. *L'orologio*. Turin: Einaudi, 1974.

―――. *Paura della libertà*. Turin: Einaudi, 1946.

Linati, Carlo. *Scrittori anglo-americani d'oggi*. Milan: Corticelli, 1932.

Malvezzi, Piero, and Giovanni Pirelli, eds. *Lettere di condannati a morte della Resistenza italiana (8 settembre 1943 - 25 aprile 1945)*. Turin: Einaudi, [1965].

Marinetti, Filippo Tommaso. *Teoria e invenzione futurista*. Ed. Luciano De Maria. Milan: Mondadori, 1968.

Montale, Eugenio. *Ossi di seppia*. Turin: Ribet, 1928.

Monti, Augusto. *A. XXX E. F.: Anno VIII dopo la liberazione*. Florence: Parenti, 1953.

Moravia, Alberto [Alberto Pincherle]. *Il conformista*. Milan: Bompiani, 1955.

―――. *Gli indifferenti*. Milan: Bompiani, 1954.

―――. *L'uomo come fine e altri saggi*. Milan: Bompiani, 1964.

Mussolini, Benito. *La dottrina del fascismo*. 2nd ed. Ed. G. Esposito. Milan: Ulrico Hoepli, 1939.

―――. *Opera omnia*. Vols. XXII-XXIV. Ed. Edoardo and Duilio Susmel. Florence: La Fenice, 1958.

Parri, Ferruccio. *Scritti 1915/1975*. Ed. Enzo Collotti, Giorgio Rochat, Gabriella Solaro Pelazza and Paolo Speziale. Milan: Feltrinelli, 1976.

―――. Piero Calamandrei, Ignazio Silone, Luigi Einaudi, and Gaetano Salvemni. *Europa federata*. Milan: Edizioni di Comunità, 1947.

Partito Democratico Christiano. *Orientamenti programmatici della D.C.* Rome: Segreteria Centrale S.P.E.S., 1947.

Pavese, Cesare. *Dialoghi con Leucò*. Turin: Einaudi, 1965.

―――. *La letteratura americana e altri saggi*. Turin: Einaudi, 1960.

―――. *Lettere, 1924-1944*. Ed. Lorenzo Mondo. Turin: Einaudi, 1966.

―――. *Lettere, 1945-1950*. Ed. Italo Calvino. Turin: Einaudi, 1966.

―――. *Poesie edite e inedite*. Ed. Italo Calvino. Turin: Einaudi, 1962.

―――. *Romanzi*. 2 vols. Turin: Einaudi, 1961.

Pintor, Giaime. *Il sangue d'Europa, 1939-1943*. Ed. Valentino Gerratana. Turin: Einaudi, 1950.

Pratolini, Vasco. *Cronache di poveri amanti*. Milan: Mondadori, 1970.

―――. *Il mio cuore a Ponte Milvio*. Rome: Edizioni di Cultura Sociale, 1954.

————. *Il Quartiere*. Milan: Mondadori, [1947].

Quasimodo, Salvatore. *Poesie e discorsi sulla poesia*. Milan: Mondadori, 1971.

Rosselli, Carlo. *Socialismo liberale*. Ed. John Rosselli. Turin: Einaudi, 1973.

Rossi-Doria, Manlio. *Il problema politico italiano e il Partito d'Azione*. Rome: Partito d'Azione, n.d.

Salvemini, Gaetano. *Lettere dall'America, 1944-1946*. Ed. Alberto Merola. Bari: Laterza, 1967.

————. *Opere*, VI: *Scritti sul fascismo,* 2. Ed. Nini Valeri and Alberto Merola. Milan: Feltrinelli, [1966].

Silone, Ignazio [Secondo Tranquilli]. *Der Fascismus: Seine Entstehung und seine Entwicklung*. Zurich: Europa Verlag, 1934.

————. *Fontamara*. Milan: Mondadori, 1970.

————. *Pane e vino*. Lugano: Nuovi Edizioni del Capolago, 1937.

————. *La scuola dei dittatori*. Milan: Mondadori, 1962.

————. *Il seme sotto la neve*. Milan: Mondadori, 1974.

Togliatti, Palmiro. *Discorsi alla Costituente*. Rome: Editori Riuniti, 1958.

————. *La politica culturale*. Ed. Luciano Gruppi. Rome: Editori Riuniti, 1974.

————. *La politica di Salerno: Aprile - dicembre 1944*. Rome: Editori Riuniti, 1969.

Vittorini, Elio. *Le due tensioni: Appunti per una ideologia della letteratura*. Ed. Dante Isella. Milan: Il Saggiatore, 1967.

————. *Gli anni del "Politecnico": Lettere, 1945-1951*. Ed. Carlo Minoia. Turin: Einaudi, 1977.

————. *Le opere narrative*. 2 vols. Ed. Mario Corti. Milan: Mondadori, 1974.

Index